The Guide to Ridiculously Easy Entertaining

Tips from Marfreless

By

Mike Riccetti

&

Michael Wells

Publisher's Cataloging-In-Publication Data

Riccetti, Mike.
  The guide to ridiculously easy entertaining : tips from Marfreless / by
Mike Riccetti & Michael Wells.

    p. : ill. ; cm.
  Includes bibliographical references and index.
  ISBN: 0-9714040-3-8

1. Entertaining. 2. Menus. 3. Cookery. I. Wells, Michael T., 1965- II. Title

TX731 .R53 2005
642.4   2005906359

Cover Design by Sheila Kwiatek. Illustrations by Shirl Riccetti.
All rights reserved.

Published by Tempus Fugit Press
P.O. Box 540306
Houston, Texas 77254
www.tipsfrommarfreless.com

Printed in the United States of America.

*This book is dedicated to our mothers, **Shirl Riccetti** and **Joe Ann Wells**, from whom we received the first semblances of social skills, even if those might have taken some years to become evident.*

Table of Contents

Step 6 – Hosting 107

Before the first guest arrives, you will need to finalize all the preparations, and be ready to act as host; plus, you should be cognizant of the potential adversities and how to overcome these.

Step 7 – After the Event 120

The guests have left, the drinks have stopped flowing, and all that remains for certain is a mess and memories, and possibly a headache.

Part II – Background

These are topics related to entertaining that are good to know, information on specific types of events, and food and drink recipes that you might want to employ.

Part III – Glossary

These are mostly food and drink terms that you might want to become familiar with, as these are found in many cookbooks, menus, and among the shelves of food, wine, beer and liquor stores. Or, maybe you just want to try to fit one into a conversation.

Part IV – References

This section includes more information on useful topics, plus quick reference guides.

Introduction

So, you don't have a ski chalet in Aspen, summer in East Hampton or Newport, jet off to Anguilla or Saint Tropéz (nor are confident that you can pronounce these correctly), or know any celebrities, you can still entertain in fine fashion, and have a lot of fun doing so. The information in this book will help you entertain **practically, successfully, enjoyably** and **more easily,** at home, restaurants, bars, or anywhere else.

Extravagant entertaining, the subject of many other books associated with party-planning, usually requires the help of a cadre of professionals at a considerable expense. If you can afford to entertain lavishly, the purchase of this book will be an inconsequential cost for you, and it will certainly be quite helpful, too. For the rest of us, it will help provide the knowledge, guidelines and tools that will greatly aid in the planning, provisioning, preparation and hosting. Providing these, we hope to encourage you to entertain, not just more effortlessly, but also more frequently.

This book will be beneficial to anyone interested in entertaining, from the novice to the experienced party planner. You don't have to be a natural host to entertain in fine fashion. If you feel lacking in that innate ability, this book will aid in imparting the skills and instilling the confidence for you to host more effectively. If you are in your early adulthood, we want to help you move beyond the entertaining typical of your age group. For guys, this has seemingly long consisted of getting a keg, or more than enough beer that would fit into a couple coolers, having the requisite supplies for shots, and inviting as many young women, with hopefully morally-casual attitudes, that you knew. For women, the fear of having to create attractive decorations and décor, or the feeling that your current home is not quite up to snuff, too often leads to inaction. In addition to providing the basic information necessary for planning most any social event, there is also a lot of good stuff about food, wine, liquor, beer and entertaining supplies and accessories, much of which will be helpful to even the most practiced party host. Almost anyone can use this book to improve their knowledge and skills in planning social events.

More specifically, what this book **is** useful for:

- Get-togethers **from the intimate to the not-so intimate**.
- Both purely **social and business-related** functions.
- **Finding an excuse** to plan a get-together.
- Providing tips on **types, brands** and **amounts of alcoholic beverages**.
- Providing suggestions for **supplies** to purchase.

- Providing help for stocking necessary **barware** and **kitchenware**.
- **Easy-to-use** and **tasty recipes** ideally suited for social events.
- Easy-to-follow and popular **cocktails** that **you will actually make**, not just for a single glass, but also for pitchers and blenders.
- Providing **tools, guidelines, information** and **vocabulary** to entertain more successfully.
- Providing information that you will help **decipher** restaurant **menus**, **wine labels, cookbooks**, and along the aisles of your local **liquor** store.
- Helpful **resources for planning** events.

Conversely, in the attempt at nearly full disclosure, what this book is **not** useful for:
- Huge, Gatsby-esque parties; **overly elaborate and expensive** events featuring **extravagant decorations**. If you can afford to entertain on the grand scale, you can find a party planner for these types of events. This book will help you with the events that you plan yourself.
- **Weddings**, as these are a unique and involved celebration for which there is a plethora of information already available.
- **Family-centered holiday celebrations** such as Thanksgiving and Christmas. You can find help within your family for this. There is no family counseling in this book.
- **Cookie Cutter Party Templates** – Each event is different.

This book names names and provides lists of recommended brands of accessories and supplies when helpful, and some of the stores and sites where these can be found. We also provide suggestions for the most useful types and labels of beers, wines and liquors for entertaining with an eye on value, since you will be purchasing for a group. You might notice some regional and personal biases throughout the book, as we draw on our experiences and knowledge base. Our aim is that it will enhance the value of the book by providing personal know-how. When this occurs you might want to consider your similar regional or personal preferences that might replace or complement our possibly colored suggestions.

We intend that this guide will be informative, easy-to-use, nearly comprehensive, and sometimes even humorous. Though this book is not a bar guide, a wine book, a book on beer, or a cookbook, it has a good amount of useful information about liquor and cocktails, wine, beer, food, and recipes useful for groups that will help you successfully entertain again and again.

Since this is a self-help book of sorts, it's not meant to be read as a novel from beginning to end in quick succession. Those who feel they need a lot of help or encouragement should thoroughly read the first part, The Social Event Life Cycle. For the rest, just pick out the section, chapter, or lists that can help. Hopefully, in piece-meal fashion, and with an occasional chuckle, you will eventually get through the entire book. The book is divided among four major parts, which are informative for different purposes:

Part I - The Social Event Life Cycle – These are steps that you'll need to follow when putting together most social events.

Part II - Background – These are topics related to entertaining that are good to know, information on specific types of events, and food and drink recipes that you might want to employ for your parties.

Part III - Glossary – These are mostly food and drink terms that you might want to become familiar with, as these are found in many cookbooks, menus and in articles about food, wine and entertaining, not to mention on cocktail menus or bar shelves.

Part IV - References – This section includes information on useful and fun topics, and quick reference guides.

Though we have plenty of experience planning various types of social events, both professionally and personally, we are not speaking *ex cathedra* on the subject, nor do we pretend to be the panjandrums of parties. Unlike many books on entertaining, we don't expend pages providing specific templates or detailed menus for parties, since these are seemingly never put into practice by readers. As there are many ways to skin a cat (as is said for some reason), there are also many ways to have fun in groups, and we hope that our ideas and recommendations will be helpful in getting you to **entertain more successfully, more easily, more enjoyably,** and **more often.**

THE SOCIAL EVENT LIFE CYCLE

When organizing your event, it helps to keep in mind that all social events will follow the same, very basic, life cycle. Some of these tasks are more fun attending to than others, of course. Depending on the type of event, you will have to dedicate more effort in one area or another. If the event is being held at a bar or a restaurant, the setup and cleanup will probably be less important, or not even a factor at all. The initial planning is usually the most significant, and if done properly will make the subsequent steps much easier. These major facets, or steps, we outline are generally sequential.

Step 1 - Initial Planning – Determination of Theme, Venue, Date, Time, etc.
Step 2 - Hiring Help – Deciding if you need help, and hiring it.
Step 3 - Invitations
Step 4 - Accessories & Supplies
Step 5 - Setting Up – Drinks, Food, Decorations, etc.
Step 6 - Hosting
Step 7 - After the Event

As you begin to entertain, or plan events that are new to you, it helps to think explicitly of each of these steps, and what needs to be done to accomplish these. But, as with everything else, with entertaining, the more you do it, the easier it becomes, and these will become routine. As it's a good map to guide your thoughts about organizing events, the steps outlined above make up the first, and most significant, part of the book.

PHILOSOPHY CONCERNING ENTERTAINING

Having a philosophy for entertaining is not necessary for planning and hosting a successful social event. You simply need to make an effort to ensure that you and your guests will have fun. But, it helps to be cognizant of our basic tenets concerning practical entertaining, as these are the basis of the recommendations throughout the book.

Entertaining is first and foremost about people, both your guests and you. As simple and as obvious as this sounds, it's overlooked by a great many books on entertaining and by many people who worry that their home is unsuitable for entertaining and decide to avoid the subject. Our other views include the following:

- **To entertain often is better** than infrequently – Don't worry about planning the perfect party, as that is too difficult, probably too expensive, and any attempt may possibly be discouraging. And, significantly, the more you entertain the easier it becomes.
- **Don't wait for special occasions** to entertain.
- Events should be **easily affordable** for the hosts.
- Events **should not require an inordinate amount of work** for you.
- Events should **encourage conversation** among the guests.
- **Informal is good** – Make it easy for guests to feel welcome.
- **Small gatherings can be the most fun**, and are a great way to hone your party planning skills.
- **Decorations are usually of little importance** to the success of the events.
- Having **enough alcohol** is of paramount importance.
- There is **not one right way** to throw a party. It's fun to find the types of events that are enjoyable for you and your circle of friends and guests.

WHAT IS A MARFRELESS, AND HOW WILL IT HELP ME ENTERTAIN?

Marfreless [mar-FRAY-less], a dark bar with only an unmarked blue door signifying its presence, is located in Houston, Texas, west of the skyscrapers of downtown and just east of the well-heeled River Oaks neighborhood. In its current veiled location since the late 1970s, and opened for a total of more than thirty years, long for any institution in never-look-back Houston, it has gained quite a reputation over the years. Often a destination for couples striving for a greater level of intimacy, couples that might feature one or both who are legally part of another couple, and, more recently, aficionados of a well-crafted cocktail or several, Marfreless has long had a reputation as a unique and somewhat mysterious watering hole. Since there is no real marking for the bar, the interior is shrouded in near darkness and many of the patrons seem bent on trying to combine discretion with a high blood-alcohol level, many myths surrounding Marfreless have sprung up over the years. These include: that it was once a speakeasy; a private hangout for Howard Hughes when he was back in his hometown; a bordello; or an illegal casino catering to wealthy oilmen and their visiting Saudi sheiks. None of these are true, but legends are usually more interesting than the facts. Not that any of this really matters, but we felt obligated to explain our obscure reference. The idea for this book was born at Marfreless and many of the tips were refined while catering to business meetings, happy hours, and other social events that were held or sponsored by Marfreless. And, it has a cool name, that might fit in somewhere on a book cover.

If you enjoy this book, hopefully you will enjoy yourself some more with more frequent entertaining. It can be easy, even ridiculously easy. Cheers.

Step 1 – Initial Planning

This section concerns the preliminary preparation, and the appreciation of what you'll need to do to make the event a reality. And, if you need any additional inspiration to get started, there is a chapter devoted to suggesting excuses for entertaining.

INITIAL PLANNING OF YOUR EVENT

The initial planning should include understanding what you might need to do for each facet, or significant step, of the party. Expanding upon the list shown in the Introduction, below are the questions that you should ask yourself when you begin to plan any social event. Answering these, which will follow every major step of the event (which becomes the Social Event Life Cycle) will help you to move well on the way to planning a successful party. This information is greatly expanded and elaborated upon in subsequent chapters of this section.

1) **Initial Planning** – The first things, first.

- How much **effort** do you want to make? If you want to plan a particularly large or involved event, you might want to try to get one or more co-hosts.
- What **type** of event? A particular, or special, **theme**?
- **How many** guests?
- **When** to hold your event – Date? Time? Are there any significant conflicts with that date and time?
- **Where** to hold the event, at home or elsewhere?
- What **duration**? Two hours, four hours, etc.?
- What do you hope your **budget** to be?

2) Determining Whether or Not You Need to **Hire Help**, and hiring it – Caterer, bartender, valets, entertainment, etc.?

- **Do you need help?** In which capacities?
- **Where to find** the necessary help?
- **How much** will the service(s) cost?
- What **questions** do you need to ask prospective help?

3) **Invitations**

- **Whom** to invite?
- **What information** do you need to communicate to your invitees?

- **How** will you communicate the event – Written invitations, e-mail, etc.?
- **When** to send the invitations? – If you believe that the event is formal or special enough to warrant printed invitations, you will have to start the planning process some time earlier in order to get the invitations printed, mailed, and to allow for a proper amount of time for the guests to respond. Don't forget to factor in the costs of printing, envelopes and postage into your budget, as these costs are easily overlooked, and often not insignificant.

4) Purchasing (and Renting) Supplies and Accessories

- What **supplies and accessories** will you **need for your event**?
- What **accessories** should you always have on hand? And do you?
- What types and amounts of **drinks** – What in the way of wine, beer and spirits will you need?
- What type and amount of **food**?
- **Other**, non-food, non-drink **supplies**?

5) Setup – Cleanup, decorations, drinks, food, music

- How should you **schedule your efforts** for setup?
- Do you need or want to **decorate**?
- Do you need to **setup** the drinks and food?
- Will you be responsible for **cleaning**?
- What type of **music** should you play?

6) Hosting – Do you need help in hosting your event – Friend, co-worker?

7) After the Event

- Will you be responsible for **cleaning** the venue, afterwards?
- Assessing the success of the event – **What can you learn** for the future?

These are the just the very basics to consider when beginning the event planning process. These aspects are expounded upon in greater detail in subsequent chapters.

When to Schedule your Event

You have decided to host an event, and you want it to be successful. The most significant thing to do to ensure a good event is getting your friends and other invitees to attend. You need to make sure that there are no notable conflicts with the date and time that you have chosen. For example, you might not want to hold a Christmas party on a night when you know that a number of your friends will have company holiday parties that night that they are expected to attend. And, you probably do not want to have a big party the day after Saint Patrick's Day is celebrated, as there is a good chance that many of your guests will not be in the mood for additional celebration.

It's quite easy to avoid conflicts if you plan your event several weeks before your intended date, you avoid dates where you know people will have plans, and you canvas the guests you really want to attend whether or not they have a conflict on that date. For example, you might want to send e-mails to friends announcing the event and request a response about the potential dates you are considering. Once you have secured the date, send the invitations, or at least get the word out, as soon as possible, especially to the guests you really want to attend, and to those who are the social leaders, if you are planning an event with more than just a small group of friends or family.

SOME OTHER SPECIFICS TO CONSIDER AS YOU GET STARTED

Also before you begin the serious planning, here are some other things to keep in mind when hosting an event:

- **Holidays, etc.** – You might not want to schedule an event where you could expect people to be traveling on holidays such as Mother's Day or Father's Day. A list of holidays for which you should be cognizant is included in the References section on page 327.
- **Parking** – Assuming that most guests will be driving, having nearby, adequate and safe parking is a necessity. If parking will be difficult be sure to mention that fact beforehand so that guests may carpool or take other transportation. If the parking is unexpectedly difficult, some guests might give up and miss your event.
- **Neighbors** – You have to make sure that you will not annoy your neighbors with the noise, etc., of your event. Some neighbors can be very sensitive to noise, or the fact that other people are having fun, and might call the police to complain about your shindig. If you are worried about a particular neighbor, it might be a good idea to mention it to them beforehand to try to mollify them. Or, you can even invite them.
- **Landlords, Homeowner's Association**, or **Co-op Board** – You might need approval of some such organization, or it might be wise to notify it beforehand. Or, maybe it's better to keep it in the dark, especially if there is a real chance for denial of any permission you might request.

- **Invitations** – You will need to convey all of the proper information in your invitation. See the Invitations chapter that begins on page 35.
- **Redecorating** and **Remodeling** – It's best not to attempt any major redecorating or remodeling close to when you plan to host a social event, unless you want even more aggravation. Don't do significant painting otherwise your place will reek of paint fumes.
- **Hosting** – For larger-sized parties, or parties where you feel that you might be overwhelmed, ask a friend or a couple of friends to help you host the event. You might just need help at a certain time or times during the event.
- **How much work do you want to do?** Sometimes you would like to entertain, you want to host and socialize with friends, and friends of friends, but you are busy and don't want to expend the effort to stage an elaborate soiree. Many people seem to believe that they cannot entertain without going all out, or nearly so. It's perfectly acceptable to limit the dimensions of your event in order to make it a reality. After satisfying some very basic requirements (enough alcohol and space are typically the baseline necessities), plan on having the event. A small-scale affair is nearly always better than no event at all.
- When making the choice to entertain at home, **you have committed yourself to several hours** of cleaning beforehand and afterwards.
- Try to think of **all potential costs when it comes to setting a budget**. There are more than food and alcohol costs. For example, some of the miscellaneous and often overlooked items at budget-setting time include lemons, limes, napkins, trash bags, cups, candles, flowers, plasticware, cups, cleaning services, venue costs, kitchen equipment, invitations, etc. This book can provide a lot of help in understanding what you might need to purchase. It helps to be flexible with your budget because of the difficulty in understanding everything that you might need. You certainly don't want to get into the situation where you have spent your self-imposed budget and you have yet to purchase the liquor.

WHERE TO HOLD YOUR EVENT

For most events, in terms of size, expense and scheduling, the most logical venue is the home. For those with very small apartments or who are planning business, very large or special events, an outside venue is a must. We give recommendations on setting up an event at bars and restaurants in the chapters titled, "Hosting a Dinner Event at a Restaurant" and "Hosting an Event at a Bar" on pages 138 and 148, respectively. This information is readily applicable to nearly any venue outside the home.

Below is an example event that describes the significant actions in getting it all together.

Example Event – Wine Tasting with a Wine Importer

Below are the major steps involved (excluding the necessary, but fairly obvious, ones concerning cleaning) in planning and hosting wine tasting with a decent number of guests. We were able to get a wine importer to pour and discuss some of his wines to a group at a home, in what turned out to be a very fun Friday night with 50 guests, about a dozen more than expected. The event was also beneficial for the importer, as he got to show his wines to potentially new customers. The invitation stated a start time of 8 PM, and it was slated to last for three hours.

Two weeks before –
- Talked with a wine importer who is an acquaintance about the possibility that he could bring his wines to the house for a wine tasting.
- Confirmed with a couple friends that there were no significant conflicts with the date selected.

Eight days before – Confirmed that the wine importer and his co-worker could make the event. We discussed arrangements concerning the number of wines and the format of the event.

One week before – Sent invitations via e-mail to about 60 friends and acquaintances requesting an RSVP, with the intent that there would be 30 to 40 at the event.

One week through the day before - Traded information about the event with potential guests including directions and parking, and received RSVPs.

Two days before –
- Forwarded the number of RSVPs to the importer, so that he could provision the wine accordingly.
- Tried to get at least one friend come early to help with the final preparations, and greet the guests.

Morning of event – Picked up the wine from the importer so that it could be ready to be served once they arrived that evening.

Afternoon of event –
- Picked up extra wine glasses and serving platters.
- Bought some easy-to-prepare food for appetizers plus cheese, crackers and bread for the wine tasting.
- Bought wine to have for guests before the beginning of the tasting.

Evening of the event –
- Prepared the food and set it out in three separate locations so it was within easy reach of the guests. Since it was mostly cheese, bread and crackers, the preparation time was probably no more than a half-hour.
- Got the wines and wine glasses ready for the guests and the wine importers.

The event – It was a lot of fun, informative, and fairly loud.

Monday after the event – Sent thanks to the wine importer for his time and wine.

The costs for the event were:
- **Wine**, for the time before the start of the tasting – $60 (five 1.5 liter bottles)
- **Appetizers** – $50 (cheese, crackers, bread, olives, etc.)

The costs were greatly minimized because the wine importer supplied the wine for the tasting. As is often the case with hosting an event at your home, the cleaning was the most time-consuming task, even if not included above.

SUGGESTIONS FOR SOCIAL EVENTS

In case you need any help in finding an excuse for planning a social event, this section might provide help. Some events readily present themselves for celebration, including birthdays, wedding showers, house-warmings, and the like. Then there are the popular, no-brainer, dates for holding parties such as the Super Bowl, Halloween, the Christmas season, and New Year's Eve. But, for other excuses, this chapter will provide some help. Some additional themes highlighted in this chapter are: *1)* **Food-Themed** – Dinner Parties, etc.; *2)* **Alcohol-Themed**; *3)* **Sporting Events** – On Television, of course; *4)* **Other Events on Television**; *5)* **Birthdays of Famous People**; *6)* **Costume Parties**; *7)* **Impromptu** (or short notice); *8)* **Milestone Events**; *9)* **Activity-Based Events**; and *10)* **Outdoors**; and *11)* **Miscellaneous**.

We believe that providing full examples or plans for various themed parties is a rather fruitless endeavor. Those cookie-cutter templates providing detailed instructions for parties can rarely be followed closely, as each host's situation is different, and so these are seemingly never really used. We have never been to a theme party taken from a book, nor have we even heard of one occurring. Conversely, suggestions for events can be very helpful in encouraging entertaining. The ideas listed in this chapter are not meant to be exhaustive, by any stretch of the imagination, but hopefully will provide an attractive theme, or spur some creative thinking on your part.

Regardless of the type of event, requiring formal dress or utilizing professional, if not necessarily formal service, indicates a certain amount of importance. Some level of formality is especially useful to celebrate a special occasion. That and expensive gifts.

> **You do not have to limit the size of the party** to the size of your house or apartment. Bars, restaurants, reception halls, and apartment or condo social rooms, among other venues, can also work, for additional expense, of course.

1) **Food-Themed Events** – You probably should be a decent cook to try one of these, but it's not entirely necessary, as long as you can recruit someone who is. If you want to spend the money, you can always hire a caterer to create the meal at your home. For larger food-themed parties, for some reason, crustaceans and shellfish (lobsters, crabs, clams, shrimp and crawfish) seem to make some of the best centerpieces, depending where you live.

- **Dinner Party** – These are almost by definition relatively small events where dinner is the prime attraction. Some examples are:

  - **Basic Dinner Party** – A dinner party does not have to be elaborate. It's often very enjoyable to be in the company of friends and family under any circumstance, and simply-prepared foods can do the trick. There are a wide range of ideas and themes for dinner parties, and below are a few somewhat unique ones. You might want to even consider putting together a dining group in which the various members take turns hosting and cooking. You don't have to be a good cook to participate, just have a desire to learn. See the chapter on dinner parties on page 122 for suggestions on pulling it off. Many of the recipes that we provide beginning on page 175 can also help.
  - **Progressive Dinner Party** – This can be done either at several homes or at several restaurants. Having these within walking distance makes it much easier logistically, but is not entirely necessary. A decent amount of planning is required as the idea is to have before-dinner drinks at one place, appetizers at one stop, entrées at another, and desserts at yet another.
  - **Movie Night** – An interesting take on the dinner party is inspired by the restaurant Foreign Cinema in San Francisco. During the dinner party you can project a film silently on a wall in view of the guests at the tables. It can provide an appealing distraction without being too distracting since the sound is off. The menu can follow the theme of the film.
  - **A Particular Cuisine** – Alsatian, Cajun, Venetian, Tex-Mex, Thai, Fukianese, Pacific Northwest, Provençal, etc.

- **Crawfish Boil** – Popular in Louisiana, Texas and Sweden (really).
- **Clambake** – A beach is helpful.
- **Crab Boil** – You need live crabs, for eating.
- *Shrimp boats is a comin', there's dancing tonight* – Boiled, broiled, grilled, sautéed, deep-fried, *alla scampi*, it's all good, and all good with beer. *Got to hurry, hurry, hurry home….*
- **Pig Roast** – If you do not want to tackle roasting an entire pig yourself, you probably can hire someone to do this for you.
- **Luau** – A variation of the pig roast, but with a Hawaiian theme. You can begin with a pig, a hole in the ground, and some rocks for cooking, then tropical drinks, and some leis.
- **Backyard Grilling** or **Barbecuing** – Throwing hamburgers, steaks, kabobs, or chicken breasts on the grill can be the basis for a get-together. For those outside of Texas, grilling is not barbecuing, which is slow-cooking of meat with low temperatures. Once the brisket has cooked its

requisite eighteen hours or so, barbecuing can also become a good reason to invite friends over.

- **Champagne & Desserts** – This is a fun way to help satiate the sweet tooth in a lot of your friends. It's an easy party to organize, especially if you have friends willing to bring desserts. High quality, yet more affordable sparkling wine from California, Spain or even New Mexico, might make for cost effective substitution for champagne when the guests number more than a handful.

- **Brunch** – This can be fun, and easier than a dinner party. Expectations concerning the food are generally lower, so it can be done more easily and more cheaply. Orange juice, with vodka and sparkling wine to pair with it, Bloody Marys, croissants or the like, and some main dish based on eggs are really all that are necessary. The Disco Brunch is a variation on this, or it could manifest itself later on in the day when the guests are somewhat more lubricated.

- *La Panarda* – A type of extreme feasting in the Abruzzo region of Italy celebrated on January 17 in memory of Sant'Antonio Abate, and on other special occasions. The feast is served in many stages with many dishes, sometime numbering as many as sixty over the course of many hours, and was the inspiration for some of Rabelais' tales of Gargantua and Pantagruel. It's somewhat surprising that something like this has not yet caught on in present day super-sized America.

2) Alcohol-Themed – This is where a type of booze is the theme of the party, rather than just an important part of it.

- **Cocktail Party** – The All-American classic get-together can be a lot of fun, and fairly easy to put together at home. Of course, it's even easier to convince friends to meet for an impromptu cocktail party at a fairly nice bar that can put together a decent cocktail. Liquor, rather than beer and wine are requisite for a cocktail party, but you don't need a wide range. Vodka, gin, bourbon, scotch plus a handful of mixers such as club soda, tonic water, cola and limes can usually satisfy most palates. And, you can even limit that if you want to have a signature cocktail or two such as a Gin & Tonic, or Martinis with either gin or vodka. Dress is usually better somewhat upscale, business casual can work during the week, though a suit or a coat-and-tie for men seems more appropriate, as does a cocktail dress for women, of course.

- **Wine Tastings** – There are many different ways to arrange a get-together around wine. It certainly does not have to be stuffy, nor do you have to know that much about wine. Hosting one of these is a great way to learn more about wine, have fun, and appear somewhat sophisticated. For each kind of wine tasting event, cheese and crackers make a very fitting and usually expected complement. You might want to have a cheese tray that has a diversity of cheeses; cheeses selected to match the specific wines; or just a single high quality cheese. See the section titled, "Wine Tasting Parties" beginning on page 134 for more information.

- **The Easy Way** – The easiest and often most fun event to have centered around wine is simply to choose a wine style, and ask that your guests bring a bottle in that style. Examples are Pinot Noirs under $25 or Chilean reds under $15.
- **Guided Tasting** – This is having someone, usually you as the host, leading a structured wine tasting.
- **Blind Tasting** – With this the identities of the wines are concealed, tasted anonymously and usually judged against each other. In one variation of this, you can ask your guests to guess each wine. In another, suited for more serious wine drinkers, you can pour each wine separately and try to get your tasters to name as many of the key characteristics as possible (country, region, major varietal, vintage and producer).
- **Guided Tasting with an Expert** – With this you have an expert from a wine store, a wine distributor, or a very knowledgeable friend to discuss each of the wines being tasted.

- **Beer Tastings** – This is generally the same concept as the wine tastings, though spitting is not encouraged nor allowed. Since beer is cheaper than wine and often seen as more approachable, these tastings can be easy and fun to do. One drawback is that it's necessary to have guests that are interested in beer. For many, it does not quite have the cachet that wine has. And, those who solely consume the nearly tasteless domestic light beers will often be unlikely to be terribly interested in a beer tasting unless it promises to be a lot of fun (i.e. with the fun guest list).
- **Scotch Tastings** – There are numerous, and ever-increasingly so, interesting and diverse single malt scotches. Unfortunately, many are quite expensive. Holding a scotch tasting is relatively inexpensive way to taste several different ones. To make it affordable, have each person bring a different bottle or split the cost of the bottles.
- **Martini Party** – Featuring either, or both, classic and frou-frou versions, Martinis hold a special appeal for a great many. If hosting this specialized version of the cocktail party at home you will need to have the proper number of Martini glasses plus at least a couple of shakers, depending on the size of the crowd. This might also be an occasion to hire a professional bartender to ensure appetizing drinks, and allows you, as host, to mingle in proper fashion. Important to note, given the fact that

Martinis are nearly entirely alcohol, it's a very good to provide some food for this.

- **Drink Around the World** – This works best when you can impress a few of your nearby neighbors to help you host this. Each house serves a drink that is meant to represent some part of the world, and some part of their house is usually decorated as such. Some suggestions might be **Mai Tais** for Hawaii or Tahiti (no matter if this was actually first shaken and stirred in California), **Piña Coladas** for the Caribbean, **Margaritas** for Mexico, **Saké Shooters** for Japan, **a shot-and-beer** for the industrial Midwest, etc. In lieu of willing neighbors, you can use different rooms in your house with someone acting as bartender in charge of drinks in each room.

3) Sporting Events – More than any other types of events, sports lends itself most readily and most frequently to becoming a central theme for a party of some sort. And, alcoholic beverages, usually beer, seem to go hand-in-hand with viewing those games, matches, etc. For any party centered around a televised event, it is a good idea to have more than one room with a television if you are entertaining a decent number of guests. A television-free area is also wise for those guests (women) not really interested in the particular contest.

- **Super Bowl** – One of the biggest excuses for parties in North America. Though the game is too often a blow out, and a boring affair, commercial-watching is always fun, and it's a great excuse to drink and be merry on a Sunday evening during the depths of the winter. Conducting a blind pool with a winner each quarter and for the final score will make the most casual fan interested in the game, and is almost requisite for a decent-sized gathering.
- **Men's Collegiate Basketball Championship** – The NCAA Finals usually are held on the first Monday in April.
- **Bowl Games, or the National Championship Game (or Games)** – Just after the first of the year. Football pools can also be a good idea here.
- **Your Alma Mater's Big Games** – Football and basketball, usually, though the College World Series can be a lot of fun, too.
- **A Big Fight** – With brutality inherent in the sport that interests many guys, along with the exciting prospect that either fighter has a chance of landing a punch to end the fight at any moment of the contest, a pay-per-view boxing match is a potentially fun get-together. These nearly always featuring a hyped title fight, which can also attract tepid boxing fans. Similarly, top ultimate fighting matches can also generate interest. To help make the event more interesting, especially when the contest is not expected to go the distance, you can wager on the outcome of the fight using a portion of a deck of playing cards with each person drawing a

card that signifies the round that the fight might end, and the winner (one fighter is red, the other is black).

- **Final Round of Golf's Majors** – Held on Sunday's, these four- and five-hour affairs are best suited to the golf enthusiasts. The Masters, British and US Open events seem to generate much more attention than the PGA Championships. A breakfast on the Sunday final round of the British Open can be fun. Since the final round is broadcast live from UK, it is breakfast time here in the North America. Bangers and mash, a traditional British breakfast, or your usual assortment of eggs, bacon, sausages, pastries, and fresh fruit will do.

- **Wimbledon Finals** – The Women's and Men's Finals typically begin their telecast on the first Saturday and Sunday mornings in July, respectively. This is often a great reason to invite friends over for drinks, which might be more amendable to the casual sports fan than golf's British Open. Strawberries and cream, and plenty of champagne are the traditional accompaniments to the stateside Wimbledon viewing. You might also want to serve the official drink, the Pimm's Cup garnished with a cucumber slice.

- **Your Favorite Major League Team** – An important game, especially during the playoffs is always a magnet for crowds. Though not really encouraged, a beer an inning used to be somewhat a rite of passage for beer-guzzling baseball fans. By the late 1990s, beer prices at major league ballparks had gotten out of control, so now this immature endeavor will probably cost at least $70 per person, before cab fare.

- **World Cup** – Only every four summers, though. The rest of the world will be watching, so why not join in the festivities, especially when the home country is on the pitch and the tube.

- **Indianapolis 500** – And other big races, can be lengthy excuses for beer drinking with a crowd.

Double up on your social events. When hosting a party at home, you will have done a lot of work to clean, possibly decorate and setup, so why not enjoy it twice. Your place will probably be nearly clean enough to host some more people, and more than likely you will have leftover booze and food. Follow up a big event with a smaller event, and a more formal one with a very casual get-together. This can be done impromptu, the next day, or you can schedule the second event ahead of time.

---

4) **Other Events on Television** – Does anything give as much, and ask as little as does television? It works as social vehicle for much more than just sporting events, as some other shows also lend themselves to group entertainments. Like for a sporting event seen at home, additional televisions and viewing areas are recommended with larger groups.

- **Academy Awards** – Though this is an unduly long and boring telecast, it is nevertheless watched by a great many, and can make for a fun get-together, especially when it comes time for the winners of the top categories. As with the Super Bowl, pools can make the event even more interesting.
- **Television Show Finales** – Especially the last episode of a very popular show. *Cheers, Seinfeld* and *Friends*, if not *Mr. Belvedere*, have inspired numerous watching parties throughout the land in the past.

5) Birthdays of Famous People – These recognizable historical figures led lives that were worthy of a celebration, if not a celebration of the cocktail life. The celebration can be as simple as an excuse for planning a happy hour. The short list below is weighted more toward earlier in the year, when you might be searching more so for an excuse to celebrate, and are also before the Christian Lenten season. In addition to our brief list, you might want to find another historic, or not so historic, figure to honor with a celebration.

- **Elvis – January 8** – Celebration of the music King of Rock and Roll can make for an inviting party. His music, maybe some of his food such as fried chicken, and peanut butter and banana sandwiches, Piña Coladas, but probably not Quaaludes. It is also a good excuse for at least one person to dress as Elvis.
- **Al Capone – January 17** – In case you have forgotten, Al Capone was a Neapolitan-American businessman who brought libations and entertainment to tens of thousands of Chicagoans during the 1920s and 1930s. A couple of his truisms were, "Capitalism is the legitimate racket of the ruling class," and, "You can get more with a nice word and a gun than you can with a nice word." His birthday can be an excuse for a gangster-themed costume party, a speakeasy-themed event, having a group over for *braciole* cooked in the Sunday gravy, or even one where you break out that bathtub gin recipe.
- **Federico Fellini – January 20** – The legendary Italian film director provided an array of fantastic surreal images in his films, especially in the ones after the famous *La Dolce Vita*, which itself can provide inspiration for a decadent celebration. Although finding a look-a-like for a young Anita Eckberg and having paparazzi(o) might take some effort.
- **Robert Burns – January 25** – The national poet of Scotland. His birthday is good reason to drink scotch whisky with a group; in excess, if need be. The Scots do it.
- **Rick James – February 1** – The "Super Freak," one of greatest icons of the early 1980s excess, crept back into the national conscious with the help of several very funny skits on the Dave Chapelle Show in 2003, furthered by his untimely, drug-related death in 2004. A Rick James party would

feature his rock-inflected funk music, of course, and possibly several of the illicit pleasures he used to enjoy on a very regular basis. Please respect the laws of your area, though.

- **James Joyce – February 2** – The fiction of this famous Irish author is characterized by experiments with symbolism, the use of stream of consciousness for large portions of the narrative, and that he stretched the English language to its limits (and beyond). If not on his birthday, Bloomsday, **June 16**, is possibly even a better day for celebration. This is the day that Joyce's novel *Ulysses* is set, and a cause for celebration for Joyce fanatics worldwide. Bloomsday takes its name from the protagonist, Leopold Bloom, whose odyssey during the single day of June 16, 1904 through the streets, pubs and brothels of Dublin is the story. Don't worry if you or most your guests have not read it, as hardly anyone has. It's very difficult. That Joyce was Irish, Irish stout and plenty of Irish whiskey would be requisite for any event.
- **Saint Amaund – February 6** – The Roman Catholic Church has numerous saints who serve as patrons to various alcohol-related activities. A happy hour is more than appropriate on February 6, the feast day of Saint Amaund. He is the patron saint of brewers, barkeepers, bar staff, wine makers, vintners, and vine growers. If that is not reason enough, he is also the patron saint of the Boy Scouts. Really.
- **Ernest Hemingway – July 21** – One of the greatest novelists of the twentieth century was also a romantic figure and legendary boozer. No other book regularly assigned to high school students features anywhere near the amount of alcohol consumed as by the characters in *The Sun Also Rises*. Various themes could be Hemingway in Spain, Hemingway in Cuba, Hemingway in Key West, etc.
- **Alfred Hitchcock – August 13** – The birth date of this long-popular director would make a fitting event to show a movie or two of his.
- **Winston Churchill – November 30** – Not only was this legendary British prime minister and hero of the Second World War one of the towering figures of the twentieth century, he was also a prodigious drinker and party wit. A stop at a British-themed pub for a pint or several with friends might be a fitting way to celebrate this historic personage's birthday.
- **Frank Sinatra – December 12** – Ol' Blue Eyes, with his extensive catalog of classic interpretations from the Great American Songbook, plus his image as the poster boy of post WWII cool, is a great excuse to indulge in the cocktail culture. Martinis and Sinatra's favorite libation, Jack Daniel's, would help fuel the fun.
- Though the lives of men seem to lead more naturally to events that encourage drinking, you might want to **honor an iconic woman** with a fete that might be nicer and more involved than the ones involving

almost solely alcohol that honor the men listed above. Some women and their birthdates: **Janis Joplin** (January 19), **Billie Holiday** (April 7), **Audrey Hepburn** (May 4), **Marilyn Monroe** (June 1), **Julia Child** (August 15), **Mae West** (August 17), **Dorothy Parker** (August 22), and **Edith Piaf** (December 19).

6) Costume Parties – Be aware that costume parties require a much greater effort from your guests than other types of parties. Some people do not like to dress up. It takes time, money, and some measure of planning, after all.

- **Halloween** – The weekend before is usually the best time for this.
- **Carnival**, *Carnevale*, **Mardi Gras**, *Faschting* – The famous pre-Lenten parties in Venice are often elaborate costumed affairs. Using this as a cue, you can ask your guests to wear masks and try to create a Venetian-masked soiree similar to the one in *Eyes Wide Shut*. Or, you can do it New Orleans-style and dress up as Mardi Gras Indians, or even easier just ask your guests to wear the official colors of Mardi Gras (purple, green and gold) and purchase plenty of plastic beads. Hurricanes, Dixie beer and Creole or Cajun food can help with the proper atmosphere. Your female guests may or may not be in the mood for all of the common New Orleans festivities, though.
- **Flapper** or **Roaring Twenties** – These continue to be popular, since cocktails are an integral part of the setting, and many women seem to enjoy dressing up as flappers, and men enjoy seeing women act with Roaring Twenties abandon. For this you might want to serve cocktails that were popular during that time like the Martini, Champagne Cocktail, Gimlet, French '75' and the like.
- **Toga** – You can celebrate the debauchery of ancient Rome or your fraternity or sorority days with this. And, it's easier than most costume parties, as everyone can find a sheet to use. Wait 'till Otis sees us....
- **Movies** – This is where everyone is supposed to dress up as a character from the particular, well-known movie. *Caddyshack* is a good choice, one of the favorites for seemingly every guy. *The Rocky Horror Picture Show* has created public spectacles across North America, and has also *The Big Lebowski* with its attendant White Russians, to a lesser extent.

Solicit contributions for a charity with your event. Doing this can fit in with most party themes, or it can be a reason for a party in itself. Happy hours for tsunami relief and for juvenile diabetes research are just two examples from happy hour events at Marfreless benefiting charities.

7) Impromptu (or Short Notice) – Though happening on the spur of the moment, or nearly so, these parties work much better if some or all of the prep work has been done in advance. See the chapters about provisioning the home with accessories, supplies, and booze.

- **Pre-Dinner** or **Post-Dinner** – Having friends over for a drink before or after going out to a restaurant or another social event is a very easy thing to do, and a great way to become comfortable entertaining at home. The mood of your guests will usually be casual and the expectations will be usually nothing more than for friendly conversation and a drink.
- **After Hours** – Just about the same as above, and you are probably well aware of these if you live in an area where the bars stop serving at 1:00 AM or even earlier.
- **After-work, afternoon, early evening casual** get-togethers for burgers and beer and the like is an easy and fun way to entertain friends; low stress coupled with potentially high caloric intake.

8) **Milestone Events** – Events such as big or dreaded birthdays such as the 30th or 40th, graduations and engagements readily lend themselves to organized celebrations. Any kind of party is usually welcome, though a certain level of effort is often expected. But, if not, any celebration is better than none. Also, you might want to consider a more minor event to have another excuse for friends to get together.

9) **Activity-Based Events** – Take a card game, board game or something more elaborate and invite over some willing friends or acquaintances. Willing is the key word here, so be sure to explain what the party is about and sell the notion if necessary.

- **Card Games** – Poker, especially the easy-to-learn and group-friendly Texas Hold'em, is a good excuse for a get-together.
- **Casino Night** – You will need card tables and dealers just to start. For more of a Vegas-style atmosphere, you might consider hiring staff who appear to be of southern Italian descent. If it ends up feeling all too authentic, you should probably make sure that not too much is being skimmed from the house.
- **Games** – Board games and the like can be a fun excuse for a small get-together. Though, if not planned beforehand, breaking out the old Monopoly box when conversation has lagged will just hasten the departure of most of the other guests.
- **Karaoke Parties** – These usually work best when the majority of the guests enjoy singing, and usually when it is a relatively small event. You might not know that you can rent karaoke machines, though you certainly know that singing comes easier to many after several libations.

- **Murder Mystery Parties** – This requires some planning and willing and forewarned guests, usually fairly good friends. But, it can provide a different way and excuse to have fun together.

10) Outdoors – Take advantage of expected good weather or a significant outdoor activity to plan a party outside.

- **Tailgating** – Take the party to the game, or near the game, at least.
- **Outdoors** – A nice day outside as an excuse to find a picnic spot.
- **Pool Parties** – If you have a pool, use it for entertaining. You can see more of your friends, which may or may not be a good idea. If you don't have a pool, you might have to be creative in cultivating friendships with someone that has access to one.

11) Miscellaneous – There are plenty of other types of parties, and reasons to throw them.

- **House Warming** – So that you can show off the new dwelling, which will hopefully have enough room to entertain in decent fashion.
- **Bachelor / Bachelorette Parties** – These tend to be nearly all-out affairs centered around pleasing or embarrassing one particular person.
- **Showers** – For women, please be aware that traditional showers that prominently feature a gift-opening are painful events for men to attend.
- **Happy Hour at a Bar** – Sending e-mails to friends about meeting at bar after work is about the easiest way to plan a get-together. If you are hoping for a large crowd, you might want to contact the bar beforehand to possibly arrange for drink specials, appetizers or food specials, and maybe space reserved for your group. Refer to "Hosting an Event at a Bar" on page 148.
- **Winter Holidays** (Christmas, Hanukah, Kwanzaa, Winter Solstice, etc.) – Actually before Christmas Day and Eve, but you should know that.
- **Pub Crawls** – These can be a lot of fun, though a crowd that likes to imbibe is a prerequisite. There are several ways to do this. For each of these you should scout out the sites beforehand, talk to the managers and owners to try to get drink and food specials, and publicize the event to friends and maybe friends of friends. It's practical to limit the number of stops to four or five at most. The crowd becomes less manageable later into the night. Include food at one of the stops. Try to get to the last stop by 10 or 10:30 PM, which can easily lapse. If you can find a venue with music, or even a band, for the last bar, all the better.

- **Walking** – Saturday evening is the best time to start one of these. Be sure to choose places that will not be too crowded when you are planning to arrive.
- **Bus** – Though the crowd will be limited by the size of the bus, or buses, as with the walking pub crawls, you will still need to ensure that the bar will be able to comfortably hold your crowd for the time you are scheduled to be there.

- **Formal Event** – Many women, especially, like to dress up, so make up an excuse for a group to assemble in formal attire. A room at a restaurant or a banquet hall is usually a requisite for this. Needless to say, the overall expense will be greater than most other events, but it will have more cachet than most events typically do. If you solicit contributions from your guests or sell tickets for this, giving a portion of the proceeds to a charity might not only make you feel better, but also make the event easier to pitch to potential party-goers.
- **Surprise Parties** – Make sure that the guest of honor will enjoy such a thing. Many people do not. Second, take pains to ensure that the honoree will be at the place and time of the surprise. This can often take some effort and coordination among several people who are helping.
- **House Concert** – This is where you get an individual performer or a band (if you have the room) to play at your home. This is something different, and can be easy to host, provided your neighbors' complaints are not an issue. You can either pay the performer yourself or pass the hat to pay for the entertainment. You can also have it for your friends, or open it up for anyone interested in the music. This latter event has become, if not popular, at least a small part of the local music scenes in recent years.

"Marketing" Parties – These are the bastard children of the Tupperware Party, and include jewelry, crafting, stamping gadgets and accessories, if you did not know. Just keep in mind that these can still be fun for some as long as:
- The **sales pitch is minimal**, and optional.
- There is **incentive to attend** – i.e. you get to have fun food and drink without listening to a long pitch, and you leave with free samples, or something of the like.
- **You know beforehand** what you're getting yourself into. No one likes to unexpectedly find themselves in the middle of spiel about the benefits of a product that they are suddenly and strongly encouraged to purchase.

Step 2 - Hiring Help

Sometimes, given the intended number of guests or the desire to really impress, you will feel the need to hire outside help. At other times, you are unsure whether or not it's prudent to hire help, or are unaware of some services that are available to be contracted. The types of help that are commonly hired for service at your home, or a third-party site are listed below.

- **Caterer** or **Cook**
- **Bartender**
- **Wait staff**
- **Busboy** – This can be a good idea when hiring bartenders, in addition to wait staff.
- **Valet Service**
- **Maid** or **Cleaning Service** – Before and after the event.
- **Security**
- **Musical Entertainment** – A musician, band, or a DJ.
- **Other Entertainment** – A palm reader, caricaturist, (card) dealer, etc.

There are several important items to note when you begin the process to hire help. The first thing you should answer is how comfortable are you allowing strangers in your house to do this work. If there are any concerns, determine how you can allay those. Reputable caterers and bartenders and waiters that you know will go a long way in this regard. Second, as costs can escalate quickly, be sure to keep a firm grasp on your budget, and be sure to obtain accurate and firm cost estimates from each firm or person contracted to provide help. Third, during the hiring process, be sure to spell out as clearly as possible what they are expected to do.

Though it might be difficult to plan an event on a Sunday or a weekday, keep in mind that help, especially **entertainment, is much more expensive on the weekends**, and sometimes even Thursday nights, than it is on Sundays and the rest of the week.

For each type of help you might hire for your event, shown below in the following sections are: *1) reasons* to hire that service; *2) where to find it; 3) how much* it may cost; and *4) queries* and *instructions* to pose to each vendor.

HIRING A CATERER OR COOK

1) Reasons to hire a cook or use a caterer:

- You **don't want** to cook.
- You don't have **time**.
- You don't believe that you can handle the **large number of guests**.
- You want to serve **food of a very high quality** that you might not be able to successfully create yourself.
- You want to serve **a specific cuisine** that you have little or no experience preparing.
- You want to **impress your guests** that you have spent the money for catering or a cook.
- Or simply, **you want more time** to enjoy yourself at your own party.

2) Where to find a caterer or cook:

- Call catering companies found in the **Yellow Pages** under "Caterers."
- Or, use a similar **on-line** service.
- Check your local free press or alternative publication with classifieds.
- Contact **a friend** who is a talented cook.

3) How much will a caterer or cook cost?

- Plan on paying between **$8** and **$50 per guest**. This can very widely with the type of food. Food prepared on site will certainly be more expensive.
- Be cognizant that catering companies will often **try to sell you the most** elaborate and **expensive package**.
- You might want to **bargain** with them **by suggesting deleting or adding certain items** or service that don't fit into your theme or budget. For example, you might want to forego the white truffles, or supply your own serving platters or glassware, if appropriate.

4) Questions and *instructions* for the prospective **caterer** or **cook**:

- How **long have you been in business**?
- Do you have **references** I can contact?
- Can I arrange to **sample your food**?
- Where will you cook the food? Is my **kitchen sufficient**?
- **How much of the menu can I plan**?
- Can we supply **some of our food**, if desired?
- How **large are your portions**? – This question might be useful for sit-down affairs, though certainly not when solely appetizers are needed.

- If applicable, can you **supply plates** and **utensils**?
- What happens if you cannot fulfill obligations due to **illness**, etc.?
- Will you bring any **additional staff**? **How many**?
- **Who will be in charge** of the food when it is being served? Ideally, the owner of the catering company will be there.
- Can I supply my **own alcohol**, or can I use another bartending service?
- Are there any **liability** or **insurance** issues, and are you covered for each?
- For food prepared off-site, will you **deliver** it **or** do I have to **pick it up**?
- Please detail all of the **potential costs**.
- **When** can I **cancel** without a penalty?
- **When** do you need a **final headcount**?
- Do you require a **deposit**? If so how much?
- **When** do I make final **payment**? This should be paid after service has been rendered. It's not a good idea to pay for everything up front.
- **How** do I make final **payment**? For large events, having the ability to pay by credit card can offer added flexibility for most.
- Can we **get the agreement in writing** (i.e. a contract)?

HIRING A BARTENDER

1) Reasons to hire a bartender:

- A bartender can **add some class**, especially to a more upscale affair.
- And, importantly, they should know how to **properly and efficiently make most of the drinks** that your guests might want.
- More than that, a bartender can make **specialty cocktails**.
- It also allows the **host to spend more time with guests** instead of minding the guests' drinks.
- For an expected **guest list numbering over 50**, it can be an especially good idea.
- Can also help to **slow down the consumption** and monitor the potential drunkenness of your guests.

2) Where to find a bartender:

- **Contact a bar or restaurant** that you are familiar with. You don't need to be a regular, as most bars are willing to provide extra opportunities for their staff to make money. The only problem with this is that the bartenders at most places are working on the weekends, when the bars are the busiest.
- Another option is hiring a bartender from a **bartending school**. Bartenders from these sources will likely be eager to gain experience and less expensive than those from bars, if generally not quite as polished.

- Most **caterers** can provide a bartender.
- Contact **a friend** who is a competent mixologist.

3) How much will a bartender cost? These will cost you between **$10** and **$25 per hour** with a guaranteed **minimum of probably $75 to $100**. You will pay them per hour for at least an agreed upon minimum number of hours. Or, you can pay them a flat rate, such as between $75 to $150 for the entire event.

4) Questions and *instructions* for the prospective **bartender**:

- Do you have **references** I can contact?
- Are there any **liability** or **insurance** issues I should be aware of?
- Do you need a **license**?
- If you are interviewing at a bar, ask the person to make **certain drinks** that your guests might want – Manhattan, Apple Martini, Woo Woo, etc.
- Will you **clean up**?
- Can you **stay late**, if need be?
- Can you get there sufficiently **early**, and help set up, if need be?
- Instruct about expected **attire**; usually black pants and a white shirt.
- Specify that **they should <u>not</u> solicit tips** from your guests much less put out a tip jar.
- Specify that **they should <u>not</u> smoke or drink** while on duty.
- Address when they might take **breaks**.
- **Specify the actual amount** you plan to pay them; i.e. $125 for five hours.

HIRING WAIT STAFF

1) Reasons to hire waiters:

- To handle a **large crowd**.
- To **free yourself** to mingle with guests.
- To add a sense of **class**.
- To make a **nicer, cleaner** and easier environment for your guests. They will be served instead of having to get the food themselves.
- Can help to **monitor excessive consumption by your guests,** as with bartenders, especially limiting the amount of excess imbibing, and guiding your guests to the party's specialty cocktail or drinks, if available.
- Ensure that **all of the guests get to enjoy the food** since the food will be brought to or passed by all of them.

2) Where to find waiters:

- Contact a **restaurant** that you are familiar with.
- Contact a reputable **caterer** who might have excess waitstaff available.
- Contact a **young adult** whom you can trust.

3) How much will a waiter cost? Wait staff will typically cost between **$10 and $20 per hour** with a guaranteed **minimum amount of probably at least $50**.

4) Questions and *instructions* for the prospective **wait staff**:

- Do you have **references** I can contact?
- What type of **related experience** do you have?
- Will you **clean** as well as serve?
- Instruct about expected **attire**; usually black pants and a white shirt.
- Specify that **they should <u>not</u> smoke or drink** while on duty.
- Specify that **they should <u>not</u> solicit tips** from your guests.
- Address when they might take **breaks**.
- Specify the **actual amount** you plan to pay them; i.e. $100 for five hours.

HIRING A BUSBOY

1) Reasons to hire a busboy:

- To handle a **large crowd**.
- To **free yourself** to mingle with guests.

2) Where to find a busboy:

- Contact a **restaurant** where you are familiar.
- Contact a **reputable caterer** who might have excess staff available.
- Contact a **young adult** that you can trust.

3) How much will a busboy cost? Plan on paying between **$10 to $20 per hour** with a guaranteed **minimum of probably at least $50**.

4) Questions and *instructions* for the prospective **busboy**:

- Do you have **references** I can contact?
- Instruct about expected **attire**; usually black pants and a white shirt.
- Specify that **they should <u>not</u> smoke or drink** while on duty.

- Specify that **they should not solicit tips** from your guests. Address when they might take **breaks**.
- Specify the **actual amount** you plan to pay them; i.e. $75 for five hours.

HIRING A VALET SERVICE

1) Reasons to use a valet service:

- In case **parking might be difficult** at your place.
- To add a greater sense of **class**.
- For **convenience of you guests**, especially if many might be old and decrepit or morbidly obese.
- For similar reasons, you might want to contract **a valet service for an event outside of home**.

2) Where to find a valet service:

- Check the **Yellow Pages**.
- Or, a similar service **on-line**.
- Check your local free press or alternative publication with classifieds.

3) How much can you expect to pay for valet service? This can vary considerably.

4) Questions and *instructions* for the prospective **valet service**:

- Do you have **references** I can contact?
- Are you **licensed, bonded** and **insured**? Try to obtain a certificate of insurance from them.
- **How much staff** are you planning to have? It's a good idea to have more attendants early since your guests will all arrive during a fairly small window of time, while they will leave during a longer duration. An example might be to request five attendants for the start of your event, and two after that rush.
- **Where** do you plan to **park** the cars?
- Instruct about expected **attire**; usually black pants and a white shirt.
- Specify the **actual amount** you plan to pay them; i.e. $250 for five hours.

HIRING A MAID OR CLEANING SERVICE ────────

1) Reasons to hire a maid or cleaning service:

- To ensure that your place is **properly cleaned**, both before the event and afterwards.
- **Save your time**, so that you can attend to other matters for the event.

2) Where to find a maid or cleaning service (provided you don't have one):

- References from **friends**.
- Check the **Yellow Pages**.
- A similar service **on-line**.

3) How much will a maid or cleaning service cost? This can vary. It will be more expensive if you are using a service for a one time cleaning rather than on a regular basis.

4) Questions and *instructions* for the prospective **maid** or **cleaning service**:

- What **exactly do you clean**?
- Is there **anything** that you **don't clean**?
- Do you have **references** I can contact?
- Are you **licensed** and **bonded**?
- Specify the **actual amount** you plan to pay them; i.e. $50 for an entire house.

HIRING SECURITY ────────────────────

1) Reasons to hire security:

- If it is **mandated by the venue**.
- The event needs to be **private**.
- The venue is situated in an economically depressed neighborhood, and you **would like the parking areas monitored** for the safety, or peace of mind, of your guests.
- You are planning to have a large number of members of **feuding rap communities**.

2) Where to hire security for your event:

- Check the **Yellow Pages**.
- Call your local **police**, sheriff or constable departments.

3) How much will security cost? Always more than it seems that it should. Off-duty police officers might cost **$30 to $75 an hour** with a guaranteed minimum. Some local guidelines require a minimum of two officers per the event. Non-police security guards will be less expensive.

4) Questions and *instructions* for the prospective **security detail**:

- Do you have **references** I can contact?
- Specify if you need them to help **check for invitations**, passes or ID's.
- Can you help **influence inebriated guests** not to drive?
- Can you use **unnecessary force** on a guest if I ask? Maybe not.
- Specify the **actual amount** you plan to pay them; i.e. $200 for five hours.

HIRING A BAND

1) Reasons to hire a band:

- To potentially make the **event more enjoyable**.
- The additional expense might create a **favorable impression** on your guests.
- You **don't have a stereo**.

2) Where to find a band:

- **Word-of-mouth** is usually the best resource.
- Check the **Yellow Pages** under "Musicians."
- Or, a similar service **on-line**.
- Check your local free press or alternative publication with classifieds.
- Check the **local music venues**; in metropolitan areas, there are plenty of bands looking for gigs, though they may not be interested in playing covers.
- For a solo, guitar-playing singer-songwriter type you can check **local coffeehouse-type places**, in addition to the music clubs.

3) How much you can plan to pay for a band or a musician? There is a potentially huge range here.

4) Questions and *instructions* for the prospective **band**:

- Do you have a **CD of your music**?
- **What** are you planning to play? Can I **request songs**?
- Do you have **references** I can contact?
- Address when they might take **breaks**.

- Specify the **actual amount** you plan to pay them; i.e. $500 for four hours.
- What do you need in terms of **power outlets** (or related equipment)? If you are hiring the band to play outdoors, you might need to rent a generator.

HIRING A DJ

1) Reasons to hire a DJ:

- To get the **party moving** and people moving.
- To help set the **proper tone.**
- Adds some **cachet** to the event.

2) Where to find a DJ:

- Check the **Yellow Pages.**
- Or, a similar service **on-line.**
- **Check local clubs**, especially one that play music that you like.
- Since weekend nights are when most **clubs** will want to use their best DJs, **you might want to ask for them to recommend a DJ** that they use on other nights or a newer DJ.

3) How much you can plan on spending for a DJ? **Big name DJs can be expensive.** Up-and-comers are cheaper. You can conceivably spend $500 to $2,000 or more for a top local DJ to spin records during a weekend night, though the lower end is more typical.

4) Questions and *instructions* for the prospective **DJ**:

- What is your **play-list**? Get a CD from them, if possible.
- Can I **recommend songs in advance**? If the answer is no, you probably will not want to hire them unless you are confident of their abilities to satisfy the musical needs of your event.
- Can you **bring your equipment**? How much extra is this?
- Do you have **references** I can contact?
- Address when they might take **breaks**.
- What is your **favorite band and song**? If the first answer is Quiet Riot, you might want to consider looking elsewhere.
- Specify the **actual amount** you plan to pay them.

It is common courtesy to **feed the band or DJ**. Just make sure that they don't drink so much that it impairs their abilities.

HIRING OTHER ENTERTAINMENT

1) Reasons to hire other entertainment:

- To potentially make the event **more enjoyable**.
- The additional expense might create a **favorable impression** on the guests, and provide a **diversion**.

2) Where you can find this entertainment:

- **Word-of-mouth**.
- Check the **Yellow Pages** under "Entertainment" or "Entertainers."
- Or, use a similar service **on-line**.

3) How much this might cost? Depending on the entertainment this can very widely.

4) Questions and *instructions* for the prospective **card dealer**, **palm reader**, **stripper**, and other entertainers:

- Do you have **references** I can contact?
- Specify that **they should <u>not</u> solicit tips** from your guests.
- Address when they might take **breaks**.
- Specify the **actual amount** you plan to pay them; i.e. $200 for five hours.

Tipping – Knowing whom to tip and how much can flummox all but the host who does this on a regular basis. This is tipping in addition to the guaranteed minimum amounts that were agreed upon for the service. Below are some general guidelines:
- **Caterer or cook** – The gratuity might be already included. You will need to check the bill. If not, 15% is considered standard.
- **Bartender** – As with the wait staff, if you have hired him, her or them directly, tip 10-15%. Again, the hired bartender should not be allowed to put out a tip glass, as this can be viewed as tacky. You are covering the costs of the event, after all.
- **Wait staff** – If the caterer is providing staff, the host should ask if these people expect to be tipped. If so, or if you have hired the wait staff directly, tip 10-15%.
- **Busboys** – Same as wait staff.
- **Valet staff** – You pay for the service, and the individual valet attendants are typically tipped by your guests.
- **Security** – 10-15% is standard, though you might to want to tip more if force has been employed.
- **Band or musician** – It's not common to tip a band or musician unless the performance exceeds expectations or planned duration.
- **DJ** – Same as for a band or musician.

SOME GUIDELINES FOR HOW MUCH STAFF TO HIRE

To get an idea of how much staff you might need, you will have to understand what you are trying to accomplish with the staff. The more that you expect from them, such as having bartenders clean in addition to serve drinks, the greater number of people you will need to hire.

Cocktail Parties

- **Waiters** – 1 per 20 guests
- **Bartenders** – 1 per 100 guests (beer and wine only)
- **Bartenders** – 1 per 50 guests (mixed drinks)
- **Security** – 1 per 100 guests

Dinner Parties

- **Waiters** – 1 per 10 guests
- **Cooks** – 1 per 10 guests (for a full dinner)
- **Cooks** – 1 per 50 guests (for a cocktail party, i.e. finger foods are served)

Step 3 – Invitations

You have the event scheduled and now you have to get the word out to the intended guests. In doing so, you will need to choose the medium and ensure that you are conveying all of the necessary information. The medium could be an invitation by mail, a phone call, an e-mail, or an Internet invitation service such as Evite.

WHAT INFORMATION SHOULD BE INCLUDED IN THE INVITATION?

Below is a list that includes all of the necessary information that you should include or, at least consider, for a typical invitation:

- **Date** – It's good to include both day and date; e.g. Saturday, November 6.
- **Time** – In addition to a start time, you might include an ending time, if it's necessary or useful; e.g. 5:30 to 7:30 PM.
- **Address** – This should be obvious.
- **Name of the Venue** – If not at your home.
- **Theme** – This might include an honoree; e.g. "Retirement Party for Paul Ricca," or "Birthday Celebration for Laura Petrie."
- **Type of event** – You will need to convey what your guests should bring, if anything. For example, guests are expected to bring gifts to a White Elephant Party; or, for a birthday party, no gifts, or plenty of expensive gifts are desired. This also, and especially, includes a possible monetary contribution.
- **Hosts** – Include the name of each of the hosts.
- **Contact Information** – Both a phone number and e-mail address of the hosts are good to state. If the event is held at restaurant, bar or other venue it's a very good idea to include this number, too.
- **Directions** – If your guests have not been to the site of the event before, or might need help. Including a link to Mapquest (www.mapquest.com) or Yahoo! Maps (www.maps.yahoo.com) can be very helpful for some of your guests. Some landmarks like a store (for women) or a bar or liquor store (for men) might be useful.
- **Appropriate Dress** – Especially if formal attire is requested.
- **Food** – Can your guests expect a meal?
- **Bringing Beverages** – Should the guests bring beverages (to share)?
- **RSVP** – Is one desired?
- Special instructions regarding **parking**, if necessary.
- **Whether or not it is an open party** – Most people should assume that the party is just for those invited. Wording such as "open party" will communicate that the party is open to more than the invitees. Or, "bring friends."

To include on the envelope, if mailed, or within the invitation, if electronic or conveyed verbally:

- Are **children** included? – Use the phrase, "and family," or "kid friendly."
- Is **spouse** or **date** invited? – Address the invitation to the couple as "Mr. and Mrs. O'Leary," "Catherine and Patrick O'Leary." The "and guest" should be used only for singles.

If you want your guests to bring alcohol, mention something like, "Please bring a bottle of wine," or "Bring your favorite beverage." **Try not to use the word BYOB,** as it has a less-than-positive connotation for many. Also, since "BYOB" means "bring **your own** booze (bottle)," your guests might not feel compelled to share their bottles, and it can create headaches, and space limitations in your refrigerator and coolers.

If you are looking for some additional help with the verbiage on your invitations, especially printed invitations, the web site www.verseit.com is a decent resource.

Before sending the invitations, it's a very good idea to have a friend who is literate-enough proofread your invitation to help ensure that there are no significant mistakes either in the contents of the invitations, or with the type of event that is being planned.

Start time for your event can signify to guests whether or not a meal is included. Quick and general guidelines for much of North America, unless the food service is stated explicitly on the invitation, are:
- 5:30 PM – **Appetizers**
- 6:00 to 7:30 PM – **Dinner**
- 8:00 PM and later – **No meal**, though probably **appetizers**.

DECIDING UPON THE MEDIUM FOR INVITATION

There are several ways to invite your guests:

- **E-mail messages** – If there are people whose e-mail address you do not have, you can write, "please forward to _____" to those that might have it.
- **Internet service such as Evite**
- **Physical, mailed invitation** – With the rise of the Internet and the ease in communicating via e-mail, written or printed and mailed invitations are much less common and expected than in years past.

- **Phone calls** – This should be a last resort, and typically used just for a small, casual affair. Calling an invitation list can be time-consuming, at the very least, and phone conversations are more easily forgotten than a physical or electronic invitation. However, it might be necessary to call some guests to get the contact information for others that you don't have, but you would like to invite.

Something to note in this day and age many organize their calendars at their computers. Stacks of mail at home have a tough time making it into the PDAs. E-mails are simple to respond to, and most can do it easily at work.

Even with e-mail and the Internet, physical invitations are still appropriate for momentous occasions such as showers, graduation parties, in addition to weddings, of course. Written or printed invitations are also good to employ when you want to make the honoree feel special. Note to guys, women, particularly, appreciate physical invitations. You can create these invitations with a number of different software programs, though you might want to invest more money in purchasing printed invitations from a stationary or gift store, as the end result will definitely look more polished.

Some functions where printed invitations are appropriate include:
- **Wedding Shower**
- **Baby Shower**
- **Significant Birthday**
- **Public Relations Opportunity** for a Business – A restaurant opening, a product launch, the introduction of a new business, and an art opening are some examples.
- When a **gift for the honoree is expected**.
- When **the list of invitees is meant to be exclusive**.

INTERNET INVITATIONS

Evite (found at www.evite.com) is the most common and most popular Internet-based invitation system. It's free and easy to use, and nearly ubiquitous. A couple other Internet-based services that provide electronic invitations are www.americangreetings.com and www.sendomatic.com.

DECIDING WHOM TO INVITE

What is your goal for the party? Do you want the intended venue packed with friends and friends of friends, or do you want a much more intimate gathering. In many, if not most instances, you are going to invite good friends and family, and possibly some neighbors and co-workers. The question of whom to invite becomes more of an issue with smaller gatherings, and much more pertinent with business dinners or showers.

Some guidelines for inviting guests, if you feel that you have some leeway in this regard:

- Invite an **interesting mix of people**, but not so interesting that the group will not be able to meld in some fashion. Especially in smaller gatherings, try not to invite people that you know do not get along with each other.
- Do not invite so many people that **more will show up than the venue** can hold.
- Try **not** **to invite assholes**, since they do not mix well with others. Unfortunately, this is often more difficult to practice than state, as these may be married or dating a friend, for example.
- Try not to invite **both sides of a feuding ex-couple**.
- With plenty of singles invited, **try to ensure an appropriate mix of single women and men**. Those who have been married for a while tend to forget this. Though our female friends will undoubtedly be upset by this statement, it's our experience that in a singles environment most women are disappointed if the ratio is seemingly not skewed to at least two-thirds eligible men to women.
- Be cognizant of the fact that **if you are planning to invite co-workers or business contacts to your party, you might not be able to enjoy yourself** as much as you would otherwise. You might feel the need to spend a disproportionate amount of time with them if they do not know the other guests, and you might feel somewhat inhibited by their presence. Lastly, any uninvited co-workers or contacts might feel slighted if they hear about the event.

Once you have compiled a list, as with the invitation itself, it's a good idea to review it with a friend who knows most of the invitees to ensure that you have not overlooked anyone.

> **W**hat percentage of guests should you expect to show up? This depends on a lot of things. You know your guests, and any competing event that your party might have. Parents with young children are understandably less reliable than other guests, even after responding positively. Typically, **60% is a good guess**, all things considered. However, it can range from **40% to 75% for most events**.

WHEN TO SEND THE INVITATIONS

Some guidelines for sending, usually mailing, invitations are:

- **Holiday** dinners – 2 to 4 weeks
- **Showers** – 3 to 4 weeks

- Formal or **business dinner party** – 2 to 6 weeks
- **Informal dinner** party – Several days to 3 weeks
- Small and **informal parties** – Several days to 2 weeks
- Large and **holiday parties** – 2 to 4 weeks

These are just guidelines, and you will know your guests. The greater lead time is better for those guests you don't know so well.

RSVP – **Repondez s'il vous plait**, which is French for "please respond." What it really means is that many of your guests will ignore that you want a response from each of them, whether or not they are attending.

FOLLOWING UP WHEN AN RSVP HAS BEEN REQUESTED

Without fail, a number of your friends will not have RSVP'ed as asked. It can be considered inconsiderate, but we all do it from time to time, some more so than others. Some tips, as the host:

- **Wait a couple of days** after the requested response date to contact these guests.
- **Try not to berate** them too much.
- To **tell those** who haven't replied that you've had some e-mail or phone problems and are afraid **you may have lost their RSVP**. Then they have an out, and you still get your answer without looking like an ass, or making them feel pressured or guilty.
- When using **Evite, a reminder will be sent automatically**.

HOW TO ENSURE A GOOD CROWD

There are some things that you can do to ensure a good crowd:

- First, and foremost, **plan an interesting event**; one that potential guests will want to attend. This is much easier said than done.
- **Plan the event well beforehand**.
- **Make sure that your guests don't have any significant conflicts** during the prospective date or time of your event.
- Identify and **contact the social leaders** or majordomos. These people have plenty of sway within their circle of friends or social group. It is a good idea to call or send a personalized e-mail message to try to persuade them to attend your event.
- Signal that the **event is expensively provisioned** by good food and drink.
- Send the **invitations early**.

- A **printed invitation typically carries more weight**; an attractive, printed one, even more.
- **Follow up with the guests that you really want to attend**. Hype the event to these people.
- Send a **reminder e-mail**. This can also be done with an Internet invitation service.
- Have **a proper start time** for your event. For example, setting up a happy hour from 4:00 to 6:00 PM when most invitees are still working will probably be sparsely attended.
- Have an **easy-to-comprehend invitation**.
- **Costume parties** will usually take a **more aggressive selling job** from the hosts, especially outside the Halloween or Carnival season since costumes require more effort from your guests.

WHEN HAVING A PARTY WHERE KIDS ARE ALRIGHT

Be very clear on your invitation whether or not children are welcome. If you are somewhat indifferent, but your place is not really set up for children, especially young children, you might want to include in your invitation, or communication with invitees, something like, "kids are welcome, but my house is not child-proof."

If children are welcome to your party it is wise to have some things so that they can entertain themselves in case their parents have not brought anything, or enough. The best kid care suggestion is to have a spare room with a television and a DVD player tuned to one of their favorite movies. After this, crayons and paper are a good idea. These are inexpensive to purchase; cheaper than toys. A place for them to nap is also a good idea.

Thinking of kids, it's usually **not a good idea to have your kids perform**. No one really wants to see this, as it interrupts the party and will not be entertaining to anyone but possibly another parent; rarely anyone else, though no one will dare say what they really think.

Step 4 – Accessories & Supplies

It helps to think of the various items you might need or want in terms of entertaining at home. We distinguish between accessories and supplies by defining **accessories** as being **reusable**, if not somewhat permanent, while **supplies** are **perishable**, what you purchase to be used for that event, i.e. consumables.

ACCESSORIES FOR YOUR EVENT

For the purposes of this book, accessories are the household items that you have on hand, and are replenished over time. General accessories for entertaining fall into the following categories: **cooking, serving, drinking,** and **miscellaneous**, non-food and -drink-related. This last one can be tables and chairs and the like. Then there are also those specialized items you might not have enough use or room to own, but might rent for an event.

> **Single guys**, especially, if you are planning to entertain at all, be sure to have at least the necessary, or basic, items for cooking, serving and drinkware.

COOKING EQUIPMENT

If you are an experienced cook who entertains, you will certainly have most of the items suggested below, both *1) basic cooking equipment*; and *2) additional cooking equipment* that will be helpful.

1) Basic cooking equipment to own if you are planning to cook for your guests:

- **Baking Sheet** – Also known as a cookie sheet, this can be rectangular or circular, and is useful for a great deal more than cookies.
- **Bread Knife** – This is a long, serrated knife. Bread is a necessity for most meals in some form or another.
- **Can Opener**
- **Casserole Dish** – 13″ x 9″ x 2″ – This rectangular baking dish can work for that lasagna or other baked pasta dish that feeds several or more.
- **Chef's Knife** – 8″ or 10″ – The smaller size will be easier to handle. If a friend or spouse is helping with the cooking preparation, having a second chef's knife is a good idea. These are by far the most useful cooking knives. Spend the money, and get a good one. Some excellent brands are Wüstof, J.A. Henckels and Global.

- **Coffee Maker** – Even if you are not a coffee drinker, it's a good idea to have one on hand when entertaining at home. A French Press is an inexpensive option.
- **Cutting Board** – Plastic is the most versatile, and the most inexpensive.
- **Grater** – For cheese, mostly, though it can be pressed into service to zest citrus fruits, if need be.
- **Hot Pads** (or **Trivets**)
- **Mixing Bowl** – If attractive enough, this can double as a serving bowl.
- **Peeler** – You use this for potatoes, carrots and a number of other vegetables and fruits.
- **Skillet, Large**
- **Storage Containers, Plastic** – These are for leftovers and the remnants of canned goods.
- **Turner** (or **Spatula**) – Hard plastic is usually a good idea since it can be safely used with non-stick pans.
- **12-quart stainless steel stockpot with a lid** – This can be used for boiling pasta and large stews.

2) *Additional cooking equipment* that you might want to purchase includes:

- **Blender** – A must if you plan to serve frozen drinks.
- **Crockpot**
- **Food Processor** (or small-sized **Chopper**) – A useful time-saver.
- **Juicer** – The manual small ones are much more affordable.
- **Masher**
- **Meat Thermometer** – Very useful in cooking roasts and loins.
- **Paring Knife** – This is a smaller, thinner knife than the chef's knife, and is most useful for fruits and vegetables.
- **Parmesan Cheese Knife** (or **Cheese Knife**) – There are many sizes of this fairly recognizable cheese knife, which is a fitting complement in the smaller sizes for most cheese plates. The largest versions are nearly nine inches long and are designed to open the entire large wheels of Parmesan cheese. You don't need this size, of course.
- **Soft Cheese Knife** – This strange-looking knife has holes in the blade, a forked tip, and a serrated blade. It works well for soft cheeses since these will not stick to the sides of the blade.
- **Strainer**
- **Tongs**
- **Whisk** – Necessary for complicated sauces and for baking.
- **Zester**

For the relatively inexperienced home cook, here are some tips on purchasing **cookware**:

- Try **not** to purchase pots and pans with plastic or wooden handles since you cannot use them in the oven.
- Purchase **versatile cookware** that can be used for a variety of dishes.
- **Be wary of aluminum cookware** since it reacts with acidic foods such as tomatoes, eggs and lemon juice. Try not to store anything in aluminum pans, also.
- For **flatware**, purchase easy-to-find **stainless steel**. It is dishwasher safe, and there is no need to polish it like silver. Look for **18/10 grade**, as this will last for a quite a while.

As to the where and which in purchasing these items, a professional chef we trust recommends for home use, "the **T-Fal** line at **Target** and **Pyrex** everything. **Paul Revere** (a division of Corning) still makes adequate, inexpensive pots and pans. The cooking sections of **Linens 'N Things** and **Bed, Bath & Beyond** have adequate odds and ends for the kitchen at reasonable prices." Corning, also, has reliable cooking wares.

SERVING EQUIPMENT

- **Bowl, Large for Mixing & Serving** – Be sure to purchase one that is attractive enough to be used for guests.
- **Candle Lighter** – Though not technically for serving, these extended-nose lighters will make lighting candles much easier, and potentially less painful.
- **Cloth Napkins** – Your female guests will take notice of this.
- **Cloth Tablecloth** – You can even purchase these at Sam's Club.
- **Coffee Cups** – Unless you plan on having dinner parties, you can forgo including these in your dishware collection.
- **Coffee Plates** – Paired with the coffee cups.
- **Glasses** – At the very least you will need **wine glasses** and **basic glasses** that can be used for number of things. Simple is best for both types of glasses. For the basic glasses, we recommend 16 ounce glasses of the familiar pint-size variety, which can be cheap (about $1 or so each) from your local restaurant supply store. For wine glasses, clear red wine glasses with an ample-enough bowl are the most useful and affordable option. These are similarly inexpensive.
- **Pitcher** – To use for water.
- **Placemats**
- **Plates, Dinner-Size**
- **Plates, Appetizer-Size**
- **Platters** – To have two or three, including different sizes, is a good idea.
- **Salad Bowl** and accompanying serving tongs.

- **Salt & Pepper Shakers**
- **Serving Utensils** – Serving spoons, ladles, etc. It's good to have a couple.
- **Soup Bowls** – These can usually double as salad bowls.

Purchase **dinnerware** with the notion to use your everyday dinnerware to entertain, also. This is a way to economize, especially if you have a small apartment and might not have the storage area for "entertaining dishware."

- Choose **solid, plain white** and **functional**. This might seem boring, but it provides a clean look that will complement any decorations you might have on the table, and it highlights the food on the plate.
- Make sure that it is **oven-, dishwasher-,** and **microwave-safe**. This provides the greatest versatility and the least headache for you as host.

Crate & Barrel, IKEA, and **Target** will have several affordable, quality options from which to choose. **Williams-Sonoma** has more expensive items, but this is a good place to visit especially during their periodic sales. **Pier One** is yet another choice.

DRINK-RELATED EQUIPMENT

This heading includes the items related to preparing, serving and consuming the important beverages at your event. Below are lists of barware and other drink-related equipment that is helpful for entertaining at home divided among: *1) necessary* for beer and wine, at the very least; *2)* needed for the *basic bar*; and *3) accoutrements for an even more complete home bar*.

1) Necessary Drink-Related Accoutrements – For social events at home, most people seem to serve only wine and beer, and simple cocktails. For the majority of get-togethers, the shaker does not even make an appearance.

- **Bottle Opener** – Your wine opener might contain a bottle opener. For a large party, it's good to have several of these if serving bottled beer.
- **Glassware** – Wine glasses are probably the most important. As mentioned above, clear red wine glasses are the most useful. The ubiquitous, slightly tapered 16 ounce pint glass works will also work as a shaker when coupled with another wider glass.
- **Wine Opener** (or **Corkscrew**) – We especially recommend the Rabbit, for both her and him. The air-activated types of openers allow for the least exertion.

2) Basic Bar Accoutrements

- **Coasters**
- **Cocktail Book** – It's good to have one of these on hand if you are providing a full bar.
- **Coolers** – Or ice chests, in some areas.
- **Ice Bucket** – It's better than having your guests use your freezer for ice.
- **Ice Tongs** – These might be sold with the ice bucket.
- **Jiggers** (or **Shot Glasses**) – Useful for measuring pours
- **Pitcher** – For drinks in bulk; and useful for water, too.
- **Shaker** – This is near requisite for Martinis, and several other important cocktails.
- **Strainer** – These are often built into the shakers.
- **Vacuum Sealers, Hand-pump** – These help to keep wine an extra day after opening. A preservative gas such as the Private Reserve Wine Preserver brand is another option.
- **Wine Buckets** – These look cool, and add some panache to serving white and sparkling wines at your event; and, these are very functional.

3) Accoutrements for an Even More Complete Home Bar

- **Bar Towels** – Often purloined from British or Irish-themed bars, these can add an experienced publican feel to your personal bar area.
- **Blender** – Indispensable for the frozen drinks, of course.
- **Buckets** (or **Tubs**) – These are functional and attractive enough for most events to hold beers, sodas, wine and bottled water plus ice.
- **Decanters** – See the box below.
- **Glass Rimmer** – This allows you to easily rim glasses with salt or sugar. It's certainly worth purchasing if you make Margaritas at home on a regular basis.
- **Martini Pitcher** – This is a near necessity if you believe that Martinis should be stirred not shaken. It's also a great party accoutrement, as it allows you to make a number of drinks at once.
- **Muddler** – This long, thin pestle-like device is used to mash and stir ingredients for cocktails such as the mint leaves in Mint Juleps.
- **Pour Spouts** – These are good to have if you are hiring a professional bartender, as these allow a faster and more accurate pour when used properly. Don't expect your guests to use these correctly since most people will create a mess when pouring drinks with these affixed to the liquor bottles.
- **Plastic Straws** – These are great for parties, especially when frozen drinks are served. Those labeled "short milk straws" work very well for this.

- **Stirrer** – These long stirrers are necessary when using a Martini pitcher, and useful for making any drinks in bulk.
- **Umbrellas** – Can actually make certain drinks taste better....
- **Wine Coasters** – Or something that do the same function such as a hot plate, which is typically not as attractive, though.
- **Wine Charms** – These are quite inexpensive, and worth picking up for the occasions when several folks will be drinking wine at your place.

In practical terms, **a decanter** can be nearly any glass pitcher or carafe that holds wine. Typically, it's made of clear glass and features a narrow neck. In addition to holding wine from another vessel, be it a large format bottle or a box that might be unyielding and unattractive for your guests (or they could get the incorrect or proper impression that you are cheapskate), a decanter allows wine to aerate, which usually enhances its flavors. Many red wines, **especially tannic, young, red wines, can benefit from resting in a decanter for a half-hour or so** before guests arrive. With the exception of the pricey white burgundies, most white wines will not improve in a decanter.

DRINKWARE

Most drinks feature a type of glassware that is most conducive for its enjoyment. For beer, there are mugs, pilsner glasses and pint glasses just to start. For wine, there are the basic, stemmed glasses with bulbs of slightly different shapes for reds and whites, not to mention a separate glass for each important varietal or style. Specially-crafted wine glasses, like those from the Austrian stemware maker **Riedel**, can greatly enhance the appreciation of quality wine (though we have to laugh at those who carry around their own Riedel-style glasses to restaurants and others' homes whose pretensions usually greatly outweigh their wine knowledge). For most simple mixed drinks, lowball and highball glasses will do the trick. Martini glasses are designed specifically for Martinis, and now their many descendants. There are also many specialty glasses for the range of cocktails. When at a bar or restaurant, especially at a nicer establishment, you expect the glassware to match the drink. But, as a host in your own home, you don't need to bother with all this. Your guests will not be expecting a high-class restaurant or bar experience at your place.

For larger gatherings, we recommend plastic cups; small, clear plastic ones for cocktails, and larger and sturdier ones for beer. The amount of glassware necessary can be difficult to store, clean and manage during an event. Plastic cups for drinks are acceptable and expected for the majority of events. But, for dinner and cocktail parties glassware can be nice and is more readily expected. Below are some suggestions for purchasing glassware. For a typical household you might consider stocking the following types of glassware (in generally small quantities) to use for events at home when the size of the party is fairly small.

- **Beer Glasses** – In addition to mugs, there are pilsner glasses, which are especially good for quality pilsner and pilsner-style beers. Useful for entertaining, these are often sleek and more than attractive enough for presentation. There are also a great many other glasses dedicated to a wide range of beer styles or individual beers.
- **Champagne Flutes** – Champagne is better in a champagne flute, though these usually fragile glasses seem to break regularly.
- **Highball Glasses** – Not as necessary as the lowball glasses, though the larger 12 ounce size will be convenient for large Gin & Tonics and Bourbon & Waters. Collins glasses are the same as these 12 ounce highball glasses except that the Collins glasses are partially frosted.
- **Lowball Glasses** – Commonly referred to as **Rocks** glasses or **Old Fashioned** glasses (though there is actually a very subtle difference between true lowball and old fashioned tumblers). It's a good idea to own some of these if you ever plan to entertain liquor drinkers.
- **Martini Glasses** – Martinis seem to taste better in Martini glasses.
- **Pint Glasses** – These are typically 16 ounces and very versatile, which work equally well for water, juice, ice tea, soft drinks, beer and plus-size cocktails.
- **Wine Glasses** – For entertaining purposes, the standard red wine glass with a good-sized bowl is probably the best all-around wine glass.

If interested, more types of glassware are shown in a References chapter beginning on page 366.

MISCELLANEOUS, BUT NEARLY INDISPENSABLE ACCESSORIES

In addition to having items so that you can provide food and drink, you will need a few other things to entertain, which should be apparent. But, the proper quantity can easily be overlooked for the following:

- **Chairs** – Though you might not need or want to sit everyone, having some seating will be necessary, and you might need to remember to borrow chairs for your event.
- **Towels for the bathroom** – It's a good idea to have some extra ones on hand, as the ones initially on the towel rack might soon become soggy.
- **Towels for the kitchen** and **cleaning** – White towels, without dyes that can run, are the best for removing stains.
- **Tables** – See below.

Some thoughts about the exciting topic of tables, and their relationship to entertaining at home:

- Chances are that you will not be interested in purchasing a new dinner table, but if you are in the market for one, be aware that **round tables can be more conducive for entertaining** since it's easy for each guest to talk to every other guest at the table. This is more difficult with traditional, rectangular tables. You should keep this in mind when requesting tables at private rooms in restaurants or when renting tables for large dinner parties or receptions.
- **A card table is great to have on hand when entertaining**. A card table, especially when fitted with a tablecloth to enhance its appearance, can work for additional seating at a dinner party, a setting for your drinks, food presentation, and a place for gifts at a shower.
- Having a **flat plywood extension** available for your dining room table is a useful and inexpensive way to expand seating capacity, especially for dinner parties. It is easy to cut, or get cut, to a size that fits exactly with your table's dimensions. Tablecloths can effectively cover nearly everything.

ENTERTAINING OUTSIDE – MOSTLY ACCESSORIES

Listed below are additional items that are necessary or usually helpful for outdoor entertaining:

- **Coolers**
- **Extension Cords**
- **Grill**
- **Lights**
- **Outdoor Tables** – Or, tables that can be used or moved outside.
- **Portable Chairs**
- **Portable Stereo** – Also known as the boombox.
- **Tent**
- **Tiki Torches**
- **Trash Cans** – The large variety are acceptable outdoors.

Specifically for the **warmer** temperatures:

- **Fans**
- **Games** – Badminton, bocce, croquet, horseshoes, Frisbee and lawn darts are a few of the options here.
- **Insect Repellant Candles** or **Sprays**
- **Sunglasses**

- Sunscreen

Specifically for **cooler** temperatures:

- **Blankets**
- **Coats**
- **Heaters** – A *chiminea* can do the trick, too.

RENTING STUFF

There are times, especially with large events, when you should consider renting items. You can rent a wide variety of items, some of which might not be expected. Below is a partial list of items plus some of their prices, which can vary depending where you live. The prices are often good for the entire weekend, but you will certainly need to check with the rental company.

- **Banners**
- **Candelabras**
- **Carving Stations**
- **Chafing Dishes**
- **Chairs** – From $1 to more than $10 each.
- **Champagne Fountains**
- **Coat Racks**
- **Coffee Maker & Cups**
- **Costumes**
- **Dance Floors**
- **Decorations** – There is a wide variety of things here.
- **Fans** – In an array of sizes.
- **Film Screens & Projectors**
- **Flatware** – Roughly 50¢ a piece.
- **Fog Machines**
- **Frozen Drink Machines** – Typically around $100 or less.
- **Glasses** – Around 40¢ per glass.
- **Heaters**
- **Karaoke Machines**
- **Keg Accessories**
- **Linens** – For a table for eight will run around $10.
- **Moonwalks** – Just for kids, though.
- **Multi-Tier Serving Trays**
- **Napkins** – About 50¢ each.
- **Plates**
- **Plants**

- **Portable Propane Grill** – At least $100 for this.
- **Portable Toilets** – If you are hosting an event at home, and you are planning for a large crowd, you might want to invest in one of these. We have been to parties where that one toilet has broken. Look under "Toilets" in the Yellow Pages. Plan on paying around for $100 for a unit per day or often for the weekend. Don't worry; you won't be responsible for cleaning it.
- **Punch Bowls** – About $10 for a large one.
- **Raffle Drums**
- **Serving Utensils**
- **Sound Systems** – For entertaining on a large-scale outside, an at-home disco, or if entertaining at a venue without a sound system.
- **Tables** – We believe that round tables are the most conducive for entertaining; 60" in diameter seats ten comfortably, 52" seats eight, and 42" seats six. A round table 52" in diameter to seat eight will cost around $12 or so.
- **Tents**
- **Tiki Torches**
- **Video Arcade Games**
- **Volleyball Nets**

Look under "Party Rentals," "Party Supplies" or something similar, in the Yellow Pages for companies that rent these items. Another resource to find these items in your area is www.specialeventsite.com.

It's good to note that local health codes require companies that rent you plates, glasses, flatware and other food-related equipment to thoroughly wash these items. So, when returning these, you will not need to wash these before returning. Be sure to check the contract.

When hosting a large cocktail party at a residence that you want to be very nice, and insist upon using glassware instead of plasticware, you should **provision at least three glasses per guest**. This is because, unlike a restaurant, bar or reception hall, a private residence won't have an industrial dishwasher. Guests will reuse their glassware sometimes during the party, but not every time.

SUPPLIES FOR YOUR EVENT

This section provides the lists of perishable items that you might need for your event. These are basic, but are easily overlooked. It's easy to do so, even if you have entertained numerous times.

NECESSARY FOR MOST EVENTS AT HOME

First and foremost, when it comes to entertaining, you need to think about drinks. For serving drinks when you don't want to use glassware, and for larger events, plasticware is certainly recommended.

- **Buy 8 or 10 ounce clear plastic cups for drinks** – Plastic is cheap, and you don't have to worry about cleaning these cups. 10 ounces is a perfect size to minimize waste and discourage drunkenness. These are good for both cocktails and wine. It's our experience with larger cups, especially the 16 and 20 ounce sizes, that the result will be many barely consumed drinks, and often some quickly inebriated guests.
- **For beer from a keg** and soft drinks **12 ounce, sturdy plastic cups are recommended** – You can use 16 or 20 ounce cups, but much more beer will be wasted with these larger cups. The exception is when you are hosting mostly serious beer drinkers such as rugby players or a great many people with Irish, German or Slavic surnames.

These plastic cups provide a suitable vessel for most drinks, and don't impart an off-taste that Styrofoam cups can. In addition to the versatility, these are inexpensive, and easy to clean up.

A list of supplies to have for most at-home social events (there will be more for dinner parties) should include:

- **Beer Bottle Opener** – Depending on whether or not the corkscrew can double as one, and if you have purchased any beer that needs a bottle opener.
- **Candles** – Especially ones for the bathroom.
- **Club Soda** – For removing stains.
- **Corkscrew** – May also contain a beer bottle opener. If not, you need one.
- **Duct Tape** – You shouldn't need to ask about this.
- **Napkins** – Beverage-sized napkins usually do the trick.
- **Paper Towels**
- **Plastic Straws** – These are useful for most cocktails, and are a near necessity when serving frozen drinks.
- **Plastic Wrap** – Necessary if you have food; you will have leftovers.

- **Soap for the Bathrooms**
- **Toilet Paper** – It's always a problem if you run out.
- **Trash Bags** – Be sure to have the trash cans that these are made for. If not, purchase another trash can, as it will probably come in handy.
- **Water** (bottled) – Your guests will often want a change from alcohol, and it can help decrease the chance for rampant drunkenness. Bottled water is often a good idea since it is convenient, easier than having to supply glassware for it, and it's very inexpensive.

Some stores with a national presence to purchase supplies for your event include:

- **Costco**
- **IKEA**
- **Party City**
- **Pier One**
- **Sam's Club**
- **Target**

When stocking your pantry for future guests or events, be aware that **diet soft drinks usually remain in good shape no more than three months after purchase,** less time than most similar products.

Step 5 – Setting Up

Once you have outlined what you are going to do, you'll have to put it all together. This will include decisions and actions concerning decorating, general setup, music, wine, beer, liquor, non-alcoholic beverages, and food. There are additional requirements for the more involved or unique events, such as the dinner party and the wine tasting (see pages 122 to 137 for these).

DECORATING FOR YOUR EVENT

Decorations can be fun for your event, but oftentimes these adornments are overlooked by most of your guests, or otherwise contribute very little to their overall enjoyment. When not done properly, decorations can often look cheesy or cheap, and can send an unintended signal to your guests. Decorating successfully can often be difficult artistically, physically, time-consuming or expensive. For these reasons, when planning an event, we recommend that you don't really decorate that much. Not decorating has the added benefit of reducing the cleanup effort. But, if you do decide to decorate, plan to do it right, which invariably means spending more money and taking more time to prepare for your event.

> **Making sure your place is clean** is certainly the first to-do related to decorating.

A little effort can go a long way in terms of decorations. This is what we recommend for most entertaining at home. Don't spend too much time decorating, but what you do create, make it worthwhile and noticeable without being obnoxious.

Some easy decorations that do go a long way:

- **Candles**
- **Centerpiece for the Dining Room Table**
- **Flowers** – Your guests will find the fragrance of fresh flowers pleasing.
- **Fresh Fruit in Bowls** – These can work as table centerpieces or displayed elsewhere, and can be functional, too.

> **Candles** are great for events at home. A couple tips are:
> - **Use unscented candles for most of the house**. Scented candles will often be too pungent for most rooms, and for most people who will gather in these rooms for any length of time.
> - **Use scented candles for bathrooms**. Strong, but pleasant scents are good here.
> You might want to invest in long-stemmed matches or a lighter designed for candles.

If you know nothing about flowers, simply tell the florist what you are trying to accomplish (a centerpiece, a bunch of flowers on a counter, etc.) and how much you want to spend. Most florists should be able to quickly and easily provide insight and the accompanying flowers.

Some tips for **fresh flowers**:
- **Cut the stems** at an angle, so that the flowers will absorb more water.
- Put the flowers in a vase (or pitcher) with **warm water** and the flower preservative that usually comes with the flowers.

Some other decoration-related suggestions:

- **Hide unsightly items** as well as you can.
- **Keep centerpieces low** for dinner parties, so guests can see each other across the table.
- **Halloween** and **Christmas** parties carry with them a certain level of expectations in terms of decorations, i.e. more decorations and season-specific ones.
- **Birthday** parties also have some specific decorative items that are usually anticipated, at least from the honoree, such as a banner announcing "Happy Birthday," plus a cake.
- Be sure to **remove your self-help books** from easy view.

Some other fairly simple decorations you might want to consider:

- **Coasters that are Customized** – Keep in mind that these are surprisingly expensive if you do not make them yourself.
- **Ice Sculptures** – It's easy labor-wise if you purchase these. But, these are also not inexpensive.
- **Licorice Sticks as Stirrers** for your cocktails.
- **Logo Cups** – Especially good for theme parties. These are inexpensive.
- **Wine Bottles that are Personalized** – More accurately, this is wine that has a personalized label such as "Carrie & John's 10th Anniversary Zinfandel."

Though we believe that decorations are a minor matter of concern for most social events, you might want to decorate lavishly for your party. It's your party, after all. In the References section on page 359 we list several other books that might be helpful in this regard.

In regard to party props, we recommend that you use your discretion. Do what you've got to do, though you don't necessarily have to.

GETTING YOUR HOME READY FOR YOUR EVENT

When readying your home for an event, you need to consider what must be purchased, set out, set up, and, how you might need to rearrange your furniture so that your guests will have an adequate space, and that there will be proper flow of foot traffic during the party.

CREATING THE PROPER SPACE

Some thoughts about creating space for your event:

- Take some time to walk around your place to **try to visualize where your guests might gather**, and where it might become too crowded. Move furniture accordingly to create better spaces and better flow of traffic.
- One thing is to **minimize the bottlenecks** in the areas where guests will congregate during your party. A narrow hallway or small amount space between a sofa and wall are a couple of examples. One tactic is to move chairs and tables to create walkways where people will move.
- **People tend to congregate in the kitchen**. This is due, in large part, to the fact that the beer and white wine are usually in the refrigerator along with other drinks, especially if a blender is involved. And, food might also be served from the kitchen. To help keep the kitchen from becoming too crowded, place at least some of the drinks and food in other areas of your home.
- **Move your large or bulky furniture**, if it makes sense to create more room, or a better flow of guests.
- With the exception of dinner parties, **you will not want to provide seating for each guest**. You want them to move around and mingle.
- Be aware of the fact that if you have a large sofa in the middle of where you hope guests will congregate, **they will sit on the sofa, which might slow down the party**.
- **Close doors to the rooms that you don't want visited** during your event.
- If possible, try to **create spaces where guests can lean**, if not sit, and place their drink. Spaces where this is possible will create areas where guests can be somewhat more comfortable and will assemble.
- Keep in mind that communal or **shared seating can help induce conversation**. You might want to create areas where disparate guests sit together. Think about all the fun you had at Oktoberfest at those long picnic tables with those fellow drunks from other countries who became your great friends by the end of the day even though neither of you spoke the same language.

We hope you are not like this, but it bears mention. Maybe you have been to the party where the hosts, to the detriment of the mood of the event, declare large parts of their home off-limits, or make it a point that much of their furniture is expensive or antique, and so, that it is really only for decoration, not for use, much less enjoyment. Many guests might end up treading too cautiously to enjoy the party. In these cases, the event should not have been held at their home.

SOME TASKS TO DO BEFORE THE GUESTS ARRIVE

Some important tips to consider before an event at your home are described below. Some can be done *1) a day or days before the event*; others *2) several hours beforehand*; and those that must wait until *3) immediately before your guests are due* to arrive.

1) Some things to do a day or days before the event:

- **Purchase enough liquor, as you can always use it in the future**. Liquor does not have an expiration date, so do not worry if you have provisioned too much. Of course, if you want to limit the chance for overexposure to liquor-induced buffoonery, you might want to purchase just a few bottles with the expectation that it will run out before major idiocy ensues.
- Make sure that you have an **extra cooler**, or several for beer, soft drinks, bottled water, and extra ice, as the refrigerator will not be large enough if you have more than a dozen guests. A **sink**, most likely in the kitchen, can be pressed into service. A bathroom sink is usually not a good idea unless you have a couple sinks in the bathroom. Reserve the bathtub for a very last resort.
- If you have a lawn that needs **mowing**, and part of the event is outside, be sure to do that **a day or two beforehand**, so those afflicted with allergies will be much less affected. The same goes for the large-scale **insect spraying**.
- Where appropriate, remember to **marinate, thaw, and make desserts**.
- If serving these, make the **Jell-O Shots** the night before. See page 264 for a recipe.
- The same goes for the **Vodka Infusions**, which are pineapples or other fruit immersed in vodka. See the recipes beginning on page 228. These are easy to make and help enliven a party.
- If hosting a party outside, or if some of the crowd will spill outside during those warmer months, be sure to have **insect repellant** handy, be it sprays, candles, etc.
- Do any **touch-up painting** that you might feel is needed.

2) Some things to do <u>several hours before</u> the event:

- **Start setting up early.**
- **Clean the bathrooms** and stock with enough soap, toilet paper and clean towels.
- Place **candles in each bathroom.**
- **Have plenty of ice.** Always buy more ice than you believe you will use. You won't be disappointed. And, ice is relatively inexpensive, and if you don't use it, it will simply melt.

Some Guidelines for **Ice** and **Cooler Capacity** for Various Purposes:
- **Standard size bag of ice = 7, 8 or 10 pounds**
- **Pound of ice ≈ Quart of ice**
- **Cooler Sizes:**

16-quart ⇨	13 bottles ⇨	6 pounds of ice ⇨	**1 bag**
24-quart ⇨	20 bottles ⇨	9 pounds of ice ⇨	**1+ bags**
54-quart ⇨	40 bottles ⇨	15 pounds of ice ⇨	**2 bags**
120-quart ⇨	65 bottles ⇨	30 pounds of ice ⇨	**4 bags**
152 quart ⇨	90 bottles ⇨	40 pounds of ice ⇨	**5 bags**
Keg of Beer (cold) ⇨		40 pounds of ice ⇨	**5 bags**

Putting salt on the ice around the keg will help slow its melting, but this can freeze the lines. You will need more ice with warmer temperatures, if the keg is outside.
- **For cocktails and soft drinks** – 7 pounds for every **20 people** ⇨ **1 bag**

- **Be prepared to make coffee.** Although coffee will not sober up your guests, the caffeine can help them stay awake, which is especially helpful for the designated drivers. It's a good idea to have coffee, filters and a device to make coffee all readily handy before the party starts. Plan to have sugar and milk (or cream or a powdered creamer) available, too.
- **Have a place for smokers and an ashtray outside**, if you don't want people smoking in your place. Most likely some of your guests will want to smoke. Alcohol seems to encourage the want for nicotine at night. Plan for an ashtray or two in front of your door, or on a balcony or patio. In case you do not have an ashtray on hand, you can use a bucket filled with sand; smokers will recognize this as a place for cigarette butts.
- **Be sure your glassware is clean.** Some long unused stemware could have collected dust.
- **Plan to serve at least some food.** Guests will not get as drunk as quickly, and for guys when hosting, it shows at least a small amount of maturity.
- **Chill the white wine.** Placing it in the refrigerator is the easiest way to do this, of course. If pressed for time, you can chill the wine in a bucket with ice and water, which will work quite quickly.
- If you want to have a few frozen glasses or mugs for beer, **put the glasses and mugs in the freezer at least an hour beforehand.**

- **Cool or heat your place before guests are due to arrive** – It takes a while for temperature to change, especially with many people.

- If you are using your **oven** be prepared **to run the air conditioning** earlier and at a colder temperature.

- If cooking, **plan your oven** resources in advance. If not, you could be trying to cook several dishes at once, and there might not be room or it might lengthen the recipes cooking times.

- If there is a chance that your guests will quickly go through all of the glassware you have put out, or will overlook the prominently displayed plastic cups, **it is a good idea to put signs with a Post-It Note or the like on the cabinets identifying the location of the different types of glasses** (wine glasses, glasses for water, etc.). Doing this will reduce the time you spend as host getting glasses for guests or directing them to the proper cabinet, and will lessen the chance that your guests will go through the entirety of your kitchen storage facilities.

- If you have a **frozen drink machine** be sure to **get it started** a couple of hours before your guests are due to arrive, which will allow for the drinks to be properly frozen and ready to be consumed when the party starts. Be aware that you will need to attend to this periodically throughout the party.

If your event is at home, it's not a bad idea to have a **frozen pizza** or two in the freezer. Frozen pizzas, which are cheap, easy to prepare and served hot, can make for a welcome treat during the latter stages of a non-dinner party. Though frozen pizzas are certainly not the tastiest of foods, these usually hit the spot when your guests are hungry and their taste buds are somewhat dulled from drinking.

---

3) Some things to do <u>immediately</u> before the event:

- **Turn down the lighting.** Have enough light, but harsh lights usually are unwelcome for the mood of the event, nearly any event, outside of an interrogation. And, importantly, you and your guests will look better with low lights. They will look even more attractive and younger when candlelight is the predominant light source.

- **Light any candles.**

- **Wipe off the outdoor furniture.**

- **Put out coasters.** If you don't, your furniture will feature not-so-attractive rings from the condensation.

- **Remove decorative pillows from your sofas.** These tend to get in the way of people actually sitting on the sofas. Otherwise, these could end up on the floor.

- When laying out food for a large group, **place the food in at least a couple locations**, otherwise, long lines might form to get to the food.

- Make sure that there are **proper utensils for all of the food.**
- Be sure your guests have **ready access to trash cans.** More than one trash can is usually a good idea when there are more than twenty-five or so guests. Additional trash cans make it easier for guests to find one, plus your place will be cleaner. The ensuing cleanup will also be easier.
- Ensure **easy access to drinks**.
- **Hide the expensive liquor and wine,** or that you don't want to share at this event.
- **Hide the porn**.
- **Hide the toys**, or at least make sure that these are clean.
- **Remove the incriminating drugs,** legal and otherwise, **from your bathroom cabinet.**
- For the single guy, **be sure to hide those prominent photos of the most recent ex-girlfriend**. You might be perceived as "having issues."

Some suggestions concerning **lighting**:
- Though it's a good idea to dim the lights for the areas where the guests are expected to congregate, **the entrance should be well lit.**
- **If using candles, one or two candles per each 100 square feet** (that is just ten feet by ten), is a decent rule of thumb, though you will want to determine beforehand what will work for your spaces. Have extra candles on hand.
- **Too many candles can make your space seem creepy**.

COST-SAVING IDEAS

Sometimes you need to stretch the dollar when planning your party. Below are helpful hints for ease of effort and ease on the wallet:

- **Provide just beer and wine, <u>not</u> liquor** – You can save money by excluding liquor, which costs far more than beer and most wine. It is also simpler for which to plan, and has the added benefit that guests will not get as drunk.
- **Wines from boxes poured into decanters as an option** – There are actually some decent wines, especially from Australia, that are packaged in boxes. These have the benefit of being cheaper per ounce than bottles. The quality of a Shiraz, Cabernet Sauvignon / Shiraz blend, or Chardonnay will be of sufficient quality for quaffing during most parties. The nearly ubiquitous Hardy's is a label worth recommending. These are often the same wines that are also packaged in a bottle. The vast majority of wine snobs will not be able to tell that it's not from a $10 - $20 bottle of wine, especially after a glass or two. Serving it in a decanter will not only obscure the origin of the wine, but it will let the red wines aerate, and generally taste better, but guests might give you kudos for using a more

sophisticated serving vessel. Just don't let most guests know about the boxes.

- **1.5 liter bottles of wine are quite cost effective** – There are a much greater number of wines available in the 1.5 liter format than in boxes. The 1.5 liter format (or magnum-size) is more cost-effective than the standard 750 ml size. These also may be decanted for effect.

- With a large group that is inclined to drink beer, **kegs can be a cost-saver.** Full kegs (that typically hold 15.5 gallons) begin to make sense with at least 25 people; half-kegs (usually 7.9 gallons) with 15 people.

- If serving liquor for **large parties**, especially when a bartender can control the pouring, purchase **large format bottles (1.75 liter)**.

- **Punch** is good for two significant reasons. It's a good way to make inexpensive liquor tasty, and, if made properly, the punch can go a long way towards making the party more festive.

- During daytime parties, especially brunches, **Mimosas** can give the impression of elegance while, in fact, being very cheap to make. For most parties, and certainly large ones, Mimosas can be made with a very inexpensive sparkling wine whose lack of pedigree is completely masked when mixed with orange juice.

- **Host a wine- or beer-tasting party where guests are encouraged to bring beer or wine.** This will lessen your burden, while ensuring that there is enough in the way of beverages for a fun event. See suggestions on how to conduct a wine tasting event in the chapter that begins on page 134.

Decanting is properly separating the sediment, which builds up in older wines and vintage port, from the wine by pouring the contents of the original bottle into another container. Decanting also allows the wine to interact with air for a time before consuming. This interaction will often let wines "open up" or "breathe," and become more flavorful and easier to drink. Decanting is usually more beneficial for red wines rather than white, and an hour is usually plenty of time for most wines that you will be serving. A decanter is typically a glass container with a narrow neck.

MUSIC FOR YOUR EVENT (PORQUE NO HAY BANDA)

Music is a nearly necessary accompaniment to most social events. It can help to give some life to the party, cover up those awkward silences and get people on their feet. The first and most important thing to do is to understand the type of event and determine the appropriate purpose of music, which can change during the course of the evening (or afternoon). Music for entertaining can be divided into roughly three purposes:

- **Background** – It fills the space, and is not continuously listened to by most guests. When selected properly it can contribute to an appropriate and enjoyable atmosphere.
- **Filler** – The music is listened to, and hopefully enjoyed by most. These will be selections that might include your favorites, and can include almost anything depending upon your tastes and that of your guests.
- **Dancing** – Music that will encourage your guests to dance. This is easier said than done.

After understanding the purpose for the music, you can pick the specific CDs according to your tastes. Musical tastes are very personal, and individualistic. Be sure to understand what mood you want to set, and the general tastes of your guests, or what they might accept. Most music can work, depending on your crowd. The music, at the very least, should be inoffensive. Well, better than inoffensive. Music that your guests enjoy when used as a filler, and even more so when used for dancing, can make your party much better. Very bad choices in this regard, especially when played loudly, can cause guests to curtail their evenings.

Background music is supposed to be played in the background, so it should be played at a low volume. Filler music is played at a level somewhat louder, but not to interrupt conversation. When dancing is not (yet) encouraged, no matter what type of music you choose, it should be played at a low enough volume so it does not make it difficult to speak over for all of the guests.

Unless dancing to it, **people tend to move away from the source of music**.

BACKGROUND MUSIC

Background music should be pleasant. But, make sure it is music rather than Muzak. Acoustic Jazz can work well for this. And, non-Jazz partisans might believe that Jazz is only good as background music. Acoustic Jazz's suitability in this role, primarily in its instrumental form, is why you will often see Jazz combos playing at the more expensive social gatherings. Since most of us will not have the suitably-sized event, venue or discretionary money, Jazz recordings will have to do the trick. Though much of the early Jazz is great, many recordings made prior to the early 1950s had relatively primitive production values, which can make the music feel antiquated to many ears.

If chosen properly, Classical music also can work well as background music for your event. The benefits of acoustic Jazz over Classical music are that it is hipper and more associated with the cocktail culture, it does not have as many dramatic swings in volume, and it's often more melodic. The problems with much Classical music when used for background are the often great range in sound levels within a piece, and the possible change in style from movement to movement, from upbeat and dramatic, to slow and subtle, for example. Thinking of individual selections, though undeniably a great piece, you might want to avoid Vivaldi's "The Four Seasons," as it has been played nearly to death at "fine dining" restaurants and department stores from coast to coast, and your guests might believe that you are lacking in imagination with this selection.

> **T**hough it should be obvious, don't forget that **Christmas music is a near must** for a party near the Christmas season.

FILLER MUSIC

Distinction between music for this purpose and background music can be slight, but a change from background music might be needed after the first guest asks if the music can be played louder. This is when the music plays a more noticeable role in the festivities. Filler music should be music that is familiar and hopefully enjoyed by the majority of guests. Music in this vein is generally used for outdoor events.

MUSIC FOR DANCING

For dancing, the choices are innumerable depending on your tastes. Just try to make sure that your guests will like to dance to it, especially the women who are always the first ones on the dance floor. Unlike background music or music for casual listening at events, which can be, and usually are in album format, dance music is usually on a song-by-song basis. It's unusual that an entire album by an artist, even a compilation, is all dance or danceable music. There are often ballads, or slower songs in the mix. For this reason, selecting music for dancing might take some pre-event planning, more so than music for the other purposes.

What characteristics work for music for dancing, i.e. the freestyle movement likely that passes for dancing at parties (not swing, ballroom, tango, etc.)?

- It has to have a **beat**.
- It is generally **upbeat**.
- Music that will be **recognizable** by your guests is usually better.
- A **mix** is good, as one artist, or one style can eventually prove boring. And, having a mix of styles **can encourage a greater range of people** to dance. Someone who won't be bopping to the big beats of Fatboy Slim, much less current hip-hop, might race to the dance floor at the first strains of a Tom Jones tune.

SUGGESTIONS FOR ASSEMBLING THE MUSIC FOR YOUR EVENT

You might want to create CDs for the different purposes to play during the event, a couple to be used in the background, a couple for filler music and a couple for dancing. Some tips on finding the appropriate music:

- Utilize the **Internet** as a very valuable source of what's hip and what's not. For instance, www.amazon.com has an enormous amount of feedback from music aficionados who have created best-of play-lists for everything from Classical to Jazz to Alternative to House. A few minutes surfing these suggested play-lists will provide you with ample suggestions for your own party. Look under "Essentials by Style" for the Amazon-generated recommendations.
- Consider **mixing your own** play-list from various CD's. No single CD is perfect, but by mixing your own play-list you can take the best of the best and create a superb play-list that complements your social event perfectly. You can burn your own CD using a computer. iTunes (www.itunes.com) or Real Music are two notable music software packages that make it easy to manage and burn songs to CD's. Or, you can use some of the more current MP3 devices out on the market, such as the iPod or an equivalent, from which to play your selected play-lists.
- **Satellite radio** or **cable radio** is another option. These have a large variety of channels and formats that will work for any party type. And, you can easily change the station during the course of the event.
- Consider carefully **your core audience** when selecting your music. If your guest-list consists mostly of metal-heads, or those who enjoy bluegrass, plan accordingly. Always keep your guest list in mind, as the party is for their enjoyment as well as yours.

- If you do decide to create your own play-list, **consider staging your music**. By this, we mean starting off with something light and non-intrusive or ambient, then move into something with more beat and lyrics like Trip Hop (from the clubs, but more appropriate for head-nodding then body-moving) or Acid Jazz and, if you really want to wind up the evening with a free-for-all dance-fest, wrap up the last two hours with catchy dance mixes. This is a great way to build the party up from the beginning and end it with a great climax (obvious, bad sexual pun fully intended).

See the chapter beginning on page 361 in the References section for specific music suggestions.

WINE FOR YOUR EVENT

We do not intend for this book to be a wine primer, as there are many excellent books for that, but we believe that a contemporary book about entertaining needs some information on the subject. Wine is a necessity at most events, and it seems to be the socializing beverage of choice for many. You should plan on purchasing at least one type of red wine and one type of white wine for most of your events, so it's a good subject to have at least cursory knowledge.

There is a lot to learn about wine, and it's a subject that some find intimidating. The wine world continues to evolve and expand, as has the amount to possibly understand. Winemaking technology and expertise has improved greatly since the 1970s. Wine guru Robert Parker stated that the quality and diversity of wines has grown at least ten-fold in the twenty-five years since 1980. There are many more wines, brands and wine regions that are worthy of exploration. Not just in the famous regions of France, Italy, Germany and California, but there are now excellent wines made in Australia, New Zealand, Chile, Argentina, South Africa, Austria, Washington, Oregon, plus other areas of California.

The wine marketplace is always changing. For example, in the late 1970s and early 1980s, white wines generally outsold red wines two-to-one. Since the *60 Minutes* broadcast of the "French Paradox," which touted the health benefits of red wine, the market changed rapidly, and red wines began to regain popularity vis-à-vis white wines, so that the proportion of sales eventually reversed. Different types of wines have come in and out of fashion as the consumer base in North America continues to expand and become more sophisticated.

To enjoy wine you certainly don't need to understand it all. You don't need to be able to be explain the nuances of the first growth Bordeaux in the great vintages of 1961, 1945, etc., nor be familiar with Chateau d'Yquem, the top Burgundies, top vintage champagne, and the cult Napa Cabernets in order to be able to enjoy and appreciate wines. In fact, it's just a very small percentage of wine aficionados, usually just the most prominent folks in the wine trade and wine writers who can claim to be familiar with these types of wines. For the rest of us, we can still enjoy wine as much as anyone.

BASICS ABOUT VARIETALS AND REGIONS

Below is some very basic information concerning the most popular wine styles, regions, and varietals. As with any subject, it helps to have a certain vocabulary to be able to understand it. With wine, that vocabulary might be somewhat more important and lengthy, and at the same time seemingly more imposing for the beginner. This is due, in part, to the fact that many of the terms are in a foreign language, and peculiar to the wine industry.

> "**Varietals**? I don't believe in varietals...." – A supposed wine lover

Varietal simply means a wine that is produced predominantly of one grape, usually at least 75% by law (in most American states), from which it takes its name. Cabernet Sauvignon, Merlot, Zinfandel, Chardonnay, Sauvignon Blanc are some of the popular grapes among the many varietals. In the traditional wine-producing countries in Europe, the wines usually took their name from a place, either a village or a region, such as Bordeaux, Côte de Nuits, Pommard, Hermitage, Vouvray, Champagne, Barolo, Chianti, and Rioja. With no similar regional tradition, winemakers in California began to list the primary grape on the label.

RECOMMENDED FOR ENTERTAINING — BASIC WINES

For entertaining with wine, the easiest thing to do is to provide a single type of red and white. Below are several varietals that we believe work best when entertaining, especially when a number of people and bottles are involved. Though varietals are a New World invention, many well-made European wines are also labeled as varietals, especially at the lower end of the price spectrum.

Red – These are the most popular or useful red varietals at events.

- **Shiraz / Syrah** – This fruity varietal is very easy to drink. Even better, there are many high quality and low price wines, mostly from Australia that are very easy to find. The wines labeled Shiraz are usually made in the style that is better suited to drinking alone, without food.
- **Merlot** – This varietal is very popular, and liked by most casual wine drinkers. Some self-styled wine snobs might not care for wines that feature this grape outside of Chateau Petrus, but it's easy to find a well-made bottle that will satiate most red wine drinkers.

White – These are the most popular or user-friendly at parties.

- **Chardonnay** – This is most recognizable and most popular white wine grape. Even on the lower end of the price scale, which can be found everywhere, these wines are made in a fruity, slightly oaky style that are enjoyable to drink by itself, without a food accompaniment.

- **Pinot Grigio / Pinot Gris** – This is a light-bodied, dry and mellow white wine that most white wine drinkers find palatable when drinking as an aperitif.
- **Sauvignon Blanc** – This is often herbaceous and dry, but with enough fruit to be enjoyed without food. Also, there are many well-made versions that are value-priced.

The vast majority of wines are meant to be drunk soon after bottling. Only a few are meant for aging. These are typically on the higher end of the price scale, are full-bodied and, generally, have an alcoholic content that is at least 13%. Alcohol acts as a preservative. So, be careful at the bargain bin at your wine store when you find a very cheap wine from a good winery that is four or five years old. **It is our experience that <u>inexpensive</u> red wines under 13% alcohol are generally only reliably good about two-and-a-half years after the vintage date**. White wines, even less so. There are exceptions, of course, especially with Old World wines. Check with your wine merchant. Wines from the Northern Hemisphere have a vintage date from late in the year when the grapes are harvested. Those from the Southern Hemisphere have a vintage date that corresponds to early in the year when the grapes are harvested there. So, an inexpensive red wine from Italy that is 12.5% alcohol with a 2005 vintage may be good through mid-2008. From Australia, a similar wine with a 2005 vintage might only be good until late 2007.

SOME GOOD THINGS TO KNOW ABOUT WINE – AT THE STORE

Below are basic things that are good to know when looking for wines:

- Generally, **New World wines are better when drunk alone, without food, than the Old World wines. This is a great generalization**, but we find that it's true, especially at the lower price levels. Old World wines are made to be a part of the meal, and in the wine-producing countries of Italy and much of Spain and France, wine is primarily consumed with food. New World wines tend to have generally low acidity for many of the popularly priced wines, and exhibit a fruitiness that engenders drinking alone. For the similar prominent varietals, Old World wines have higher acidity, which calls for food.
- **Nearly all white wines are meant to be drunk within a year to two from the vintage date.** Almost all of the whites that do last for several years have been aged in oak prior to release. This is important to stress to those who don't drink wine and plan to open a few gift bottles they received several years ago, and their guests find these wines well on the way to becoming vinegar.
- **Screwtops are good for wine.** More and more wines are being bottled with screwtops, which have proven to be more effective than the

traditional corks in keeping wines. Though not perfect, screwtops will continue to become more common, as consumers get accustomed to these on quality wines.

- As a social beverage, instead of an accompaniment for a meal, **red wines are generally consumed at a roughly two-to-one clip over white wines at social events** in North America.

Wine sales (by volume) at supermarkets, according to data from The Wine Institute:

1991	–	**Reds - 17.0%**	**Whites - 49.0%**	Blush, etc. - 34.0%
2004	–	**Reds - 40.5%**	**Whites - 40.4%**	Blush, etc. - 19.1%

- **Men and women have fairly similar wine consumption patterns**, in terms of red versus whites, and types of varietals. Women might drink white wines at a greater pace when they don't want the red wine to stain their teeth. Men typically don't seem to regard this as a problem.
- Though **white wines are drunk more frequently during warmer months and in warmer climates, this pattern is <u>not</u> pronounced**. Based on our experience, this holds true in the often-hot Sun Belt. Nearly every venue where wine will be consumed is air conditioned, after all.

SOME GOOD THINGS TO KNOW ABOUT WINE — AT HOME

Below are basic things to know about storing, serving and consuming wine:

- **When wines are very cold, the aromas and tastes are muted.** When wines are served too warm, the alcohol, acidity, and with red wines, tannins all become more pronounced. So, the cheaper the white wine you are serving, the colder you want it before serving.
- **Wines should be served at different temperatures depending on the style.** Ideally. This is often very difficult to do at home, and especially when hosting a party. If you can do so, here are some guidelines: Big reds such as Cabernet Sauvignon, red Bordeaux, Barolo, Barberesco, red Zinfandel, and red Rhône wines should be served at 64° to 68° F (18° to 20° C). Generally, medium-bodied reds such as Merlot, Pinot Noir should be served at 60° to 64° F (15.5° to 18° C). Light-bodied reds such as Beaujolais, Bardolino, and many Valpolicella should be served even colder at 55° to 60° F (13° to 15.5° C). Most all white wines including Chardonnay, Chablis and the other white burgundies, Sauvignon Blanc, Pinot Grigio, Riesling, etc. should be served at 45° to 50° F (7° to 10° C). Sparkling wines and rosés should be served at 42° to 45° F (5.5° to 7° C). Lower quality, usually very cheap, white wines and sparkling wines taste better colder 40° to 42° F (4° to 5.5° C). This helps to make the off-tastes more palatable.

- **Wine bottles stopped with cork should be stored on their sides in relatively cool temperatures.** Storing a bottle on its side keeps the cork moist and in proper condition to keep the air away from the wine, and thus not damage the wine.
- **Wines with screwtops** should be stored **vertically**, as there is no need to keep the screwtop moist to be effective.
- **Most red wines should be opened at least thirty minutes or so prior to drinking.** Red wines contain tannins that come from the grape skins and other excess. These tannins can give wine a "tinny" taste when first opened. This taste eventually will dissipate when the wine has been given proper time to breathe, or aerate. Opening the bottle will accomplish this though pouring the wine in a decanter is more effective, as is pouring wine into a glass or glasses. Both allow air to interact with much more of the wine's surface. During an event, you certainly should not wait on the wine to aerate if you have run out of red wine. Slightly less-than-ideal wine is better than no wine at all.
- **The most versatile wine glass is the basic red wine glass.** These are typically 10 ounce, clear glasses with a nice, full bowl. It works well enough for all types of wine, excepting sparkling wine, and certainly for entertaining purposes. Decent quality glasses can be purchased at IKEA, Target and your local restaurant supply store for $1 or less each. There are dozens of shapes and styles of wine glasses. Overly-serious wine enthusiasts have specially crafted glasses in different shapes and sizes for the specific wines for the major varietals and wine regions. You might even notice some people who might bring expensive crystal glasses with their own carrying case with them when they are drinking wines outside of the house. These are often those whose wine knowledge is far less than their pretensions. Though these type of wine glasses actually do help to taste the wines more effectively, this type of obnoxious behavior is best avoided unless you have your Master of Wine certification.
- **Wine glasses should be filled to about one-third to halfway.** Wine should be poured to the widest part of the wine glass, and not more than halfway. This is done to allow the wine to be swirled in the glass and for the aromas to collect in it, which enhances the taste of the wine. Champagne flutes can be filled higher, as can the specially designed glasses for dessert wines. But, excepting the early moments at the dinner party when appropriateness is more important, wine glasses can be filled as high as you and the guests want or need.
- **Champagne and other sparkling wines should be served in flutes.** The thin bowl of the flutes helps to reduce the exposed surface of the wine, and so slow down the loss of carbonation.
- **Wines do not last very long after opening.** Wines are meant to be consumed within a few hours after opening, and will not last a second

day unless you have a device like a hand-pump vacuum sealer that helps to remove the air from the bottle, and then stops it with a sealant. Another option is a neutral preservative gas such as the Private Reserve Wine Preserver brand that helps keeps wine usable for a while longer with its original cork or cap. Though not nearly as effective as these, the easiest and most convenient way to keep your wine in decent shape for another day or two (three is a stretch), is to simply put the cork back onto the bottle and put it in the refrigerator. Prior to drinking the stored red wine, if possible, pull it from the refrigerator an hour or so beforehand so to allow it to warm to near room temperature.

- **Once a bottle is opened, you should enjoy it until the last drop**. If you have had your fill and there is still is some wine, do not throw it away. To paraphrase a character in a later Graham Greene novel, "no wine can be regarded as unimportant since the wedding at Canae."

RECOMMENDED FOR ENTERTAINING — WINERIES AND LABELS

Expensive wines are usually not a good idea for parties because these serious wines won't receive the proper attention at a lively party, and more so, providing these will make it much costlier for the host. Some recommended wineries for **high quality, value-priced wines with large productions**, which are great for parties are:

- **Chateau St. Jean** – *Sonoma, California* – Cabernet Sauvignon, Merlot, Chardonnay – This winery has a well-earned reputation for producing excellent wines at moderate prices.
- **Chateau Ste. Michelle** – *Washington* – Merlot, Chardonnay, Cabernet Sauvignon
- **Columbia Crest** – *Washington* – Chardonnay, Shiraz, Syrah – Many of their wines are available in the larger 1.5 liter bottles.
- **Concha y Toro** – *Chile* – Cabernet Sauvignon, Merlot, Chardonnay – Many of their wines, under the Frontera and Sunrise labels, are available in the larger 1.5 liter bottles. The Xplorador labeled wines are often cited as being very good values.
- **Hardy's** – *Australia* – Shriaz, Merlot, Cabernet Sauvignon – Several of their wines are available in the larger 1.5 liter bottles, and in 3 liter boxes.
- **Hogue** – *Washington* – Chardonnay, Merlot, table reds – Several of their wines are available in the larger 1.5 liter bottles.
- **Louis Bernand** – *Rhône Valley, France* – In good vintages, this label produces very well made, food-friendly and value-priced wines from the Côtes du Rhône, Côtes du Rhône Villages and Côtes du Lubéron. Their wines from the smaller and more expensive appellations such as Gigondas and Vacqueras, are also usually good values.

- **Meridian** – *California* – Cabernet Sauvignon, Merlot, Chardonnay – Many of their wines are available in the larger 1.5 liter bottles.

To generalize, **vintages are much more important for European wines than for New World wines**. A region that provides very good wines one year, can struggle the next. This is even more important for inexpensive wines.

On other occasions you don't need to purchase in bulk for a party, but just need a bottle or two to impress the boss for a dinner at home, or are choosing a wine at a restaurant that will show your customer the proper respect. Below is a list of **well-regarded wineries** that will be **recognizable** by many casual wine drinkers in North America as being of **good quality and somewhat pricey**. Top quality Bordeaux, Burgundy, Rhône, Barolo, Brunello and Super Tuscans are less known to most and pricier.

- **Cakebread** – *Napa, California* – Cabernet Sauvignon, Chardonnay
- **Clos du Val** – *Napa, California* – Cabernet Sauvignon, Chardonnay
- **Dehlinger** – *Sonoma, California* – Pinot Noir, Syrah, Cabernet Sauvignon
- **Ferrari-Carano** – *Sonoma, California* – Chardonnay, Fumé Blanc, Siena (Cabernet-Sangiovese blend)
- **Far Niente** – *Napa, California* – Cabernet Sauvignon, Chardonnay
- **Jordan** – *Napa, California* – Cabernet Sauvignon, Chardonnay
- **Joseph Phelps** – *Napa, California* – Insignia (a red Bordeaux blend), Cabernet Sauvignon
- **Kistler** – *Sonoma, California* – Chardonnay, Pinot Noir
- **Ponzi** – *Oregon* – Pinot Noir, Pinot Gris, Chardonnay
- **Stag's Leap Winery** – *Napa, California* – Cabernet Sauvignon
- **Williams-Selyem** – *Sonoma, California* – Pinot Noir, Chardonnay

DON'T IGNORE SPARKLING WINES

Though sparkling wines are often reserved for special occasions, these can be a good addition to many events for many good reasons:

- **Complementary to food** – Sparkling wine that is dry complements a wide variety of food, probably more than any other type of wine.
- **Denotes celebration** – Sparkling wine, with the pop of the cork, the overflowing bubbles, and its presence at many special occasions, is strongly associated with celebration.
- **Impression of expense** – This can impress your guests.
- **Women**, particularly, **seem to enjoy sparkling wine**.
- **It can be affordable** – There is very good, affordable sparkling wine, from the *méthode champenoise* wines made in California for roughly $20, and

similar, if slightly lesser, but very good valued ones from Spain, Oregon and even New Mexico. Prosecco, the lighter-bodied, but still dry sparkling wine from northeastern Italy, is even more inexpensive.

- **Takes effect quickly** – Sparkling wines can help make your event more festive quickly, as the carbonation in it helps the body incorporate the alcohol more rapidly than still beverages.

We are referring to bubbly wines that are made by the champagne method (*méthode champenoise*, where secondary fermentation is occurs in each bottle), or the more inexpensive bulk *charmat* method. The wines made by the champagne method are generally more complex, and expensive. To officially be called champagne, the sparkling wine must be made in the designated Champagne region of France from some combination of the Pinot Noir, Chardonnay and Pinot Meunier grapes, and employing the *méthode champenoise* to induce carbonation. Even for true champagnes, there are differences in style. Champagnes can be relatively light- or medium-bodied, but the biggest indicator of style is the level of residual, or left over, sugar in the bottle. Most champagne sold is Brut. This is a dry style that has a maximum of 1.5% residual sugar. Extra Brut or Natural are even drier. Another dry style is Blanc de Blanc. Its name denotes that the champagne is made solely from Chardonnay grapes in France, though in the US, another white grape might also be used. These are typically light-bodied. Blanc de Noirs champagne, which is still pale colored, is made from one or both of the allowable red wine grapes, Pinot Noir and Pinot Meunier. These are generally fuller bodied than either Brut or Blanc de Blancs. If you might prefer sweeter styles, there are Extra Sec, Demi-Sec and Doux, all of which contain more than 5% residual sugar. The Demi-Sec and Doux, especially, work well as accompaniments for dessert.

> **Prosecco** is a dry sparkling wine from northeastern Italy that makes for a great party beverage, especially for your female guests. Made by the bulk charmat method rather than the more costly *méthode champenoise*, prosecco is much cheaper than champagne and the similar sparkling wine from America. Though lacking the complexity of these other sparkling wines, prosecco is flavorful and dry enough to impress most of your guests. Popular in Venice and the surrounding region, prosecco makes for a welcome addition for almost any event where a sparkler might seem appropriate. It's very affordable, too, with well regarded brands selling at $10 to $15. Tell your guests you picked up a taste for it when you were in Venice if your friends are not suitably impressed with your inexpensive, but tasty bubbly.

HOW TO OPEN A BOTTLE OF SPARKLING WINE

Since the contents are under pressure, opening a bottle of sparkling wine can be dangerous. Really. Some people actually do lose an eye each year because of this. The two most important things to remember begin with that you **do not point the bottle at anyone**, especially anyone's face when opening. If you want to injure them, it's fine, of course. Second, **do not shake the bottle before opening**. This will cause the pressure to build and the cork release at a greater velocity. Also, you are sure to waste the wine as it will gush out. Other than that it's easy:

1. **Point the bottle away from everyone** and anything that might be damaged by a flying cork.
2. **Undo the foil** around the opening, and undo the wire cage that surrounds the cork.
3. **Tilt the bottle** to a slight upwards angle.
4. With a towel around the neck and the cork to catch any wine, slowly, **turn the cork, and ease it out of the bottle**.

For single guys, it's a good idea to keep **a bottle of sparkling wine** (be sure to call it "champagne," regardless of origin) chilled **in the refrigerator**, just in case.

RECOMMENDED FOR ENTERTAINING — SOME MORE SPECIFIC WINES

The wines recommended in this chapter have fairly large productions and should be available throughout much of North America. This listing provides a number of worthwhile choices, but is not meant to be comprehensive. Brands and marketing efforts change, so the wines shown below might not be available in the future.

The retail price ranges for standard-sized bottles (750 ml) of **wine** and spirits are: $ ($0-$10), $$ ($10-$20), $$$ ($20-$30), $$$$ ($30-$40), and $$$$$ ($40-$50). You should probably save bottles over $50 for your own consumption.

Sparkling Wines

- **California** – Gloria Ferrer Carneros Blanc de Blanc ($$), Gloria Ferrer Carneros Brut ($$), Roederer Estate Anderson Valley Brut ($$), Domaine Carneros Brut ($$$)
- **Champagne** – Montaudon Brut NV ($$$$), Piper-Heidsieck Brut NV ($$$$), Laurent-Perrier Brut NV ($$$$), Mumm Cordon Rouge Brut NV ($$$$), Moët Brut Imperial ($$$$), Roederer Brut NV ($$$$)
- **Italy** – *Prosecco* – Villa Sanda ($), Nino Franco ($$), Zardetto ($$); *Spumante* – Rotari Brut ($$)
- **New Mexico** – Gruet Brut ($$), Gruet Blanc de Noir ($$)
- **Oregon** – Domaine Ste. Michelle Brut ($$)

- **Spain** (Cava) – Cristalino ($), Segura Viudas Brut Reserva ($$), Freixenet Estate Brut Cava ($$)

Red Wines

- **Beaujolais** (Gamay) – Georges Duboeuf Beaujolais-Villages ($$)
- **Blends** – Cline Big Truck (California - $), Hogue Harvest Red (Washington - $ for 1.5 liters), Beringer Stone Cellars Shiraz-Cabernet Sauvignon (California - $$ for 1.5 liters), Penfolds Shiraz-Mourvèdre Bin 2 (Australia - $$)
- **Cabernet Sauvignon** – Concha y Toro Xplorador (Chile - $), Black Swan (Australia - $), Lindemans Bin 45 (Australia - $), Rex Goliath (California - $), Bodega Norton (Argentina - $$), Chateau St. Jean (California - $$), Estancia (California - $$), Peter Lehmann (Australia - $$)
- **Chianti** (Sangiovese) – Gabbiano Chianti ($$), Querceto Chianti ($$)
- **Malbec** – Alamos (Argentina - $), Trapiche Oak Cask (Argentina - $), Bodegas Nieto Senetiner (Argentina - $$)
- **Merlot** – Columbia Crest (Washington - $), Rex Goliath (California - $), Meridian (California - $), Hogue (Washington $$), Covey Run (Washington - $$), Marcato (Italy - $$), Chateau Ste. Michelle (Washington - $$)
- **Petite Sirah** – Bogle (California - $), De Bortoli (Australia - $)
- **Pinot Noir** – Rex Goliath (California - $), Smoking Loon (California - $), Estancia (California - $$), Alexander Valley Vineyards (California - $$), Erath (Oregon - $$)
- **Rhône** (Mourvèdre, Grenache, Cinsault, Syrah) – La Vieille Ferme ($), Louis Bernard Côtes du Rhône ($$), Louis Bernard Côtes du Rhône-Villages ($$), Louis Bernard Côtes du Lubéron ($$), St. Cosme Côtes du Rhône ($$)
- **Shiraz / Syrah** – Banrock Station (Australia - $), Stonehaven (Australia - $), Black Swan (Australia - $), Oxford Landing (Australia - $), Smoking Loon (California - $), Columbia Crest Shiraz (Washington - $), Covey Run (Washington - $$), Peter Lehmann (Australia - $$), Columbia Crest Syrah (Washington - $$)
- **Tempranillo** (Rioja, Penedés, Ribera del Duero regions) – Torres Sangre de Toro ($), Borsao ($), Penascal Tinto Tudela del Duero ($), Viña Mayor Tinto Roble Cosecha ($), Bodegas Palacio Rioja ($$)
- **Valpolicella** – Allegrini Classico ($$), Zenato ($$)
- **Zinfandel** – Ravenswood Vintner's Blend (California - $), Cline (California - $$), Foppiano (California - $$), Pedroncelli Mother Clone (California - $$), Seghesio (California - $$)

White Wines

- **Blends** – Hogue Harvest White (Washington - $ for 1.5 liters), La Vieille Ferme Blanc De Blanc (France - $)
- **Chardonnay** – Concha y Toro Xplorador (Chile - $), Beringer Stone Cellars (California - $), Lindemans (Australia - $), Mezzacorona (Italy - $), Columbia Crest (Washington - $), Yellow Tail (Australia - $), Ruffino Libaio (Italy - $$), Hogue (Washington - $$), Meridian (California - $$), Columbia Crest Two Vines (Washington - $$), Chateau Souverain Sonoma (California - $$), Chateau St. Jean Sonoma (California - $$), Sebastiani (California - $$)
- **Chenin Blanc** – Beringer (California - $), Dry Creek Vineyards (California - $), Backsberg (South Africa - $), Ken Forrestor (South Africa - $)
- **Gewürztraminer** – Hogue Cellars (Washington - $), Pierre Sparr Selection (France, Alsace - $$), Trimbach (France, Alsace - $$)
- **Grüner Veltliner** – Glatzer Kabinett ($$), Heidler "Loss" ($$)
- **Pinot Grigio / Pinot Gris** – Bogedas Lurton Pinot Gris (Argentina - $$), Bollini Pinot Grigio (Italy - $$), Marcato Pinot Grigio (Italy - $$), Alois Lageder Pinot Grigio (Italy - $$), Erath Pinot Gris (Oregon - $$)
- **Riesling** – Covey Run (Washington - $), Hogue (Washington - $), Snoqualmie (Washington - $), Pierre Sparr (France, Alsace – $$), Saint M (Germany - $$), Dr. Loosen QbA (Germany - $$)
- **Sauvignon Blanc / Fumé Blanc** – Robert Pepi (California - $), Snoqualmie (Washington - $), Tin Roof (California - $$), Miguel Torres (Chile - $$), Casa Lapostolle (Chile - $$), Nobilio (New Zealand - $$), Kim Crawford (New Zealand - $$)
- **Viognier** – Cline (California - $$), Jewel (California - $$)

> **R**efer to the *Wine Spectator*, the *Wine Enthusiast*, and *The Wine Advocate* for more wine recommendations. **These publications do a fine job in recommending wines**.

Rosés – Last, and least; we have to confess that we are not big fans of most rosés, as we find these too often simple and overly sweet. Your tastes might differ, and these are enjoyed in much of southern France, Alsace, in Spain and Italy, often as easy-to-drink summer wines. Look for these when shopping for rosés:

- **Provence** – Look for wines from the following appellations: Bandol, Coteaux des Baux, and Côtes de Provence.
- **Tavel** – This appellation in the Rhône valley produces well-regarded versions that are typically pricey for rosés.
- **Vin Gris** refers to rosés made from Pinot Noir.

What about White Zinfandel? This is an inexpensive, simple and easy-to-drink, usually off-dry rosé that is popular among neophyte wine drinkers and thoroughly derided by most wine drinkers who consider themselves somewhat sophisticated. Our belief is that a bad wine is better than no wine at all, especially if people are going to drink it. But, **for most gatherings do not purchase White Zinfandels**, as there are higher quality white wines for about the same price that will satisfy the usual White Zinfandel drinker. And, the other guests might begin to doubt your tastes if you are serving White Zinfandel. But, if you believe a number of guests will be drinking White Zinfandel, and you don't care about what anyone might think, stock some.

ENGAGING THOSE ANNOYING WINE SNOBS

Though you may get tired of reading directly and between the lines that wine is to be enjoyed rather than fussed about, we feel the need to reiterate this point. It is our experience that many people don't seem to enjoy wine as they should because of the supposed mysteriousness of it, the long list of rules concerning wine and food pairings, and the pretentiousness that many can attach to wine. This is a shame.

Questions for those annoying wine snobs (from easily known to more obscure):
- **Do you like white Barolos?** There is no such thing, just the red ones.
- **Which do you prefer Pinot Noirs or Burgundies?** From Wine 101, red burgundy is made from Pinot Noir, and so these are really the same thing.
- **Which do you find more tannic when young, a top Burgundy like Montrachet** [mohn-truh-SHAY] **or a Carneros** [kar-nehr-ROS] **Chardonnay like Kistler** [kiss-LER]? This is a trick question, as these are both white wines, which do not have tannins.
- **Which do you like better, Pinot Gris or Pinot Grigio?** These are technically the same grape, though wines labeled Pinot Gris are usually made in the style popular in Alsace, which are generally more flavorful than the Pinot Grigio's made in the style that has become lucrative for wine concerns in northeastern Italy. Pinot Gris is somewhat of the correct answer here.
- **What is your favorite vintage?** Vintage of which region and which wines? They will most likely make up some bullshit.
- **How do you believe that Grange stacks up versus the best Hermitages? Why?** Grange is the Syrah- (Shiraz) based red wine from Australia that is regarded as not only the best wine from Australia, but one of the world's best. Hermitage is traditionally the most expensive wine from the Rhône valley in France, and is also based on the Syrah grape. These are typically quite expensive and off-the-beaten track for most annoying wine snobs.
- **Which do you prefer, the 1945 or the 1961 vintage?** This refers to the two best vintages of the red Bordeaux in the past century. These wines are very rare and very expensive, and it's very doubtful that the person has tasted any wines from these two vintages.
- **Do you prefer Richebourg** [reesh-BORG] **or Gevrey-Chambertin** [zhev-REE sham-behr-TAN]**? Why?** These are two very expensive red burgundies that these folks doubtfully have tasted. If they have, ask which vineyard and which year. Just nod at any response.

Then there are those usually obnoxious wine snobs. These are the people who feel the need to show off some portion of their often limited knowledge about wine. At some event where wine was served, you are sure to have come across one or two people pontificating about this or that aspect of a wine. Maybe you have a friend or acquaintance that slips into this kind of behavior. These people can be a hindrance to the enjoyment of wine at a party, as the other guests might either be intimidated by their own comparative lack of knowledge, or just annoyed by these pretentious boors. So, on the preceding page is a list of several simple questions you might want to ask your annoying wine snob guests. It is enjoyable to put a cork in these types when they begin to try to show off.

A NOTE ABOUT MODERN WINES — "I GET A KICK OUT OF YOU...."

Something to note, since the early 1990s, New World wine, especially Californian wine has become increasingly more alcoholic. It's easy to find Californian wine that nears and exceeds 14% alcohol. Many now hit 15% or 16%. The difference between this and wine labeled a few percentages lower may seem insignificant. But, a 15% bottle contains 25% more alcohol than one labeled 12%. It's wise to be cognizant of what you are serving, as someone who usually does fine with two or three glasses of wine under their belt might not do so when drinking a more highly alcoholic wine.

BEER FOR YOUR EVENT

The trend in recent years is that people are drinking less, be it spirits, wine, or beer, but are generally drinking higher quality products. Related to this is the inclination by a high percentage of those of recent generations to imbibe wine or beer when going out rather than liquor. We are a generation or two removed from the joys of three-Martini lunches. And practically, in sprawling and auto-centric modern cities, the cocktail culture is more difficult to enjoy to its full extent.

Given this, too many people still ignore the wonderful array of beer styles that is readily available. It's ironic to note the wine snob who might look askance at an inexpensive wine, but when it comes time to enjoy a beer will nonetheless reach for a light-bodied and nearly tasteless, popular national brand of beer that is justifiably derided throughout the rest of the world. Beer, or rather good beer, is still underappreciated for the quality food product that it is. Some of the diverse range of high quality beers include the slightly sweet Bavarian wheat beers that are perfectly suited as refreshers during the warm summer months; the hoppy, medium-bodied ales from the West Coast, Colorado, and England; the crisp, clean-tasting, yet flavorful German lagers; the deep, rich dry stouts brewed in Ireland; the strong, complex barley wines; and the idiosyncratic lambics made from wild yeasts only in a small region near Brussels.

Like most food products, one of the most important factors in the quality of beers is freshness. This fact cannot be overstated. Englishman Michael Jackson, the world's leading writer on beer (not Wacko Jacko), writes, **"beers are...at risk of general deterioration from the moment they leave the brewery. They are intended for immediate drinking, and not for keeping."** Unlike its relatively masculine and macho image, **beer is actually a very delicate product**. This fact should keep you from choosing a beer that might be stale from being too old or not stored properly. There are many wonderful beers made in small breweries around North America, but often the distribution networks are not very extensive and the beers, once reaching your store shelves, might be past prime and not worth purchasing. Another reason to be cautious about purchasing what might seem to be exotic beer, either national or imported, is that the customer base at your local store might be unfamiliar with it, causing it languish and become too old to enjoy.

Some very general tips on purchasing good and hopefully fresh beer from your local grocery, beer, liquor, packaged goods, or convenience store include:

- Avoid bottles that are notably **dusty**, which is a sure sign of age.
- Check the **expiration date** that exists on some brands of beer.
- **Be careful of very exotic** (for your area) beer unless you are sure that is fairly new and mostly fresh.
- Higher alcohol and more highly hopped beers last longer – Pale Ales, IPAs (India Pale Ales), etc. **Alcohol and hops both act as preservatives**.
- Some excellent brands that do seem to travel well throughout the continent are: **Sierra Nevada** (Pale Ale and Celebration Ale), **Sam Adams** (Lager and Boston Ale), **Spaten** (Premium, Oktoberfest and Franzikaner Hefe-Weizen), **Guinness** (Pub Draft and Extra Stout), and **Pyramid** (India Pale Ale).
- Chalk it up to their trademark efficiency, certainly when it comes to distribution, **nearly all German beers seem to arrive at local stores in very good shape**, much more so than other European beers.

BEERS – A NECESSITY FOR MOST SOCIAL EVENTS

What types of beer to recommend? People have preferences for very light-tasting beers, for the most part. The one benefit of this is that it's cheaper for the host. Most of the beers produced in the U.S. are these light-bodied lagers (made from bottom-feeding yeast, etc.) that are made with comparatively inexpensive rice and corn in addition to the traditional barley malt. The use of rice and corn (which are called adjuncts) gives these American lagers a generally smooth taste, a lighter color, and also less body and character than higher quality lagers made without these adjuncts produced in U.S. and in other countries, especially Germany and the Czech Republic.

Do not worry about getting a wide range of beers – Depending upon the party, three types of beer is usually sufficient. If you know that certain guests have a preference, certainly buy those brands if it fits into the overall event scheme. Certainly, **if you know that everyone drinks Bud Light, buy just Bud Light** or the like.

- An **American light lager beer** (Lite, Coors Light, Bud Light) that has very little taste, but is very popular, especially among female and quantity beer drinkers. When chilled ice cold, these are nearly indistinguishable from each other. You might want to get something that is locally or regionally popular. If you are a beer drinker, you will know these.
- A **good lager beer, which is clean-tasting but flavorful** that can be an American pilsner, a Czech or German pilsner or lighter lager, or an Oktoberfest (or Marzen). Other suggestions that are available throughout much of the country are Paulaner 1634, Spaten Lager, Pilsner Urquell,

Brooklyn Lager and Spaten Oktoberfest. These are recognized as excellent beers that usually arrive at your local retailer in pretty good shape. There are some top-notch regional examples like Summer Pils from the Saint Arnold Brewery and Baltimore Brewing Company's DeGroen's Helles. A beer like Heineken might be a satisfactory substitute for many guests.

> If you are unlucky enough to end up with a beer that emits an odor usually described as **skunky**, which seems to happen quite often with imported lager beers that are packaged in green bottles, **serving that beer in an open-mouthed glass may reduce or eliminate that problem**. A typical pint glass will do.

- A **Hoppy Ale** will usually satisfy most self-styled beer geeks. The very hoppy, medium-bodied and well-regarded Sierra Nevada Pale Ale is a very good choice, and is widely available. The hybrid and unique Anchor Steam Beer or its hoppier stablemate, Liberty Ale, are also good choices. If none of these appeal to you, a pale or India Pale Ale will fill the bill.

Some extra styles of beer for your party:

- A **Bavarian wheat beer** – These beers that substitute a portion of the traditional barley malt for wheat are sweeter than most beer styles and can be very refreshing during the summer months, or in hot climates year-round. These beers come in the filtered (*kristal*, which is "crystal") and unfiltered (*hefe-weizen* meaning with "with yeast" that refers to the yeast suspended in the beer) versions. The *kristal* versions are generally cleaner tasting, while the more popular *hefe-weizens* are usually a bit more flavorful. Slices of lemon are a traditional and fitting complement to these beers. The mostly similar Belgian white (*wit*) beers fulfill a similar purpose.
- **Dry stout** – The ubiquitous Guinness is popular worldwide. Served in specially designed cans and bottles that do a great job in simulating a freshly poured draft stout, these need at least a 16 ounce glass or plastic cup, as the contents are activated in the can when opened and need to be poured immediately. The slightly sweeter Murphy's Irish Stout is also available in similar cans, and is preferred by some stout aficionados. Be sure to note that Guinness Extra Stout, which is available solely in bottles, is a different product than the Guinness in cans or on draft. It is good, but heavier and more alcoholic, and so will be enjoyed less readily by your guests.
- A **lighter, clean-tasting lager beer** – Since most Americans prefer this style of beer, a good suggestion for an all-purpose use is the Bavaria brand from Holland, if you can find it. This beer is light in body, though

slightly heavier than the national lager beers like Budweiser and Coors. It's also more flavorful while having a clean, crisp taste, and so is probably acceptable to a wider range of beer drinkers. It is also priced at around $5.00 per six-pack, a very good value. In addition to being cheaper, it's better than its more popular and often skunky-tasting Dutch neighbor, Heineken.

- **Fruit-flavored beers** such as lambics from Belgium, or from American microbreweries can offer a unique touch at an event. Women, especially, enjoy these unusual beers. The lambics that are brewed with fruit are usually labeled as *framboise* (raspberry) or *kriek* (cherry), the two most popular flavors. These are viscous, effervescent and teaming with ripe fruit flavors. These might be difficult to find, and are not cheap. Though not in the same category quality-wise, fruit-flavored beers from brewers such as Sam Adams with their seasonal Cherry Wheat and Raspberry beers can provide enjoyable and diversity in the refrigerator.

- **Cider** is not beer, but is bottled in the same fashion. Ciders are fermented fruit juices, typically apple, though pear is also common. These are more alcoholic than most beers, slightly sweet, and work well as a thirst quencher. So, these might be an appropriate addition to the pool party. Cider and dry stout, typically Guinness, work well together in the easy-to-drink Snakebite. Be careful, as some of your guests might find these too easy to drink.

- **Non-traditional malted beverages** can provide another option for your guests. Smirnoff Ice, Mike's Hard Lemonade and Bacardi Silver are a few of the more widely distributed examples. Commercial beverages like these are surprisingly popular, especially during the warmer months. Stocking these for a party might be a good idea if you know that your guests will include those who are not fond of beer.

LIQUOR FOR YOUR EVENT

If you are intent on providing liquor, this chapter will provide some tips on provisioning a bar at your home in several ways. Again, you should know your crowd. If there are mostly bourbon drinkers, get plenty of bourbon, and the label that they like.

SUGGESTIONS FOR PROVISIONING LIQUOR FOR YOUR EVENT

Our suggestions for liquor for your event are presented as three groups: *1)* a *basic* bar; *2)* a *fairly generous* offering; and *3)* a *generous* array. The recommended spirits are listed in order of popularity or usefulness for an event.

> In regards to booze, keep in mind: **Liquor = Spirits** and **Liqueur = Cordial**.

1) Basic Bar – This suggested lineup is cost effective.

- **Vodka** – This is the most popular liquor by a wide margin. Sporting a fairly neutral flavor, it makes for the most versatile mixing spirit. Popular drinks from these are the Martini, Cosmopolitan, Vodka & Tonic, Vodka-Soda, and several others featuring fruit juices.
- **Bourbon** – This is popularly mixed with cola, soda or water.
- **Gin** – This is used in the original Martini, and also commonly mixed with tonic, especially during the warmer months.
- **Light Rum** – "Drinking rum and Coca-Cola..." was a popular refrain some time ago, but still relevant. It's often one of the first cocktails in most drinkers' repertoire. For more sophistication you can also make *Cuba Librés*, which are rum-and-colas with a slice of lime, and a Spanish accent. Light rum, which has a relatively mild flavor, is the most versatile. Rum is a near necessity at beach parties, and is the liquor in many popular frozen concoctions such as the Frozen Daiquiri and the Piña Colada.
- **Dry Vermouth** – Necessary for Martinis, if you are planning these.

2) Fairly Generous Bar – This is when you want to provide more than just the minimum.

- Vodka
- Bourbon
- Gin
- Light Rum

- **Dry Vermouth**

- **Tequila** – Now you can make Margaritas. A *blanco* or *reposado* that is 100% agave will do the trick.
- **Triple Sec** – Along with the tequila, you will need this to make Margaritas.
- **Canadian Whisky** – These are popular, especially with cola, and inexpensive.
- **Scotch Whisky** – Just purchase an inexpensive, but satisfactory, blend like Dewar's or Johnnie Walker.
- **Peach Schnapps** – This is cheap, and it expands the drink repertoire to Bellini's, Fuzzy and Hairy Navel's and Sex on the Beach.
- **Shooter liqueur** – If you believe that your guests might want to do shots, or you want to encourage shots, especially later in the party, you should stock a popular liqueur commonly used for this. **Jägermeister**, **Goldschlager** (cinnamon schnapps), or **Rumple Minze** (peppermint schnapps) are good choices for this purpose.

3) *Generous Bar* – You want to impress your guests with your largesse, especially if there are expected to be many spirits drinkers.

- **Vodka**
- **Bourbon**
- **Gin**
- **Light Rum**
- **Dry Vermouth**
- **Tequila**
- **Triple Sec**
- **Canadian Whisky**
- **Scotch Whisky**
- **Peach Schnapps**
- **Shooter liqueur**

- **Irish Whiskey** – Irish whiskey has a few aficionados, and now you can serve Irish Coffees.
- **Brandy** – Though brandy is an excellent drink, especially when served as a *digestif*, or after-dinner drink, neat in a snifter, it's not really a drink for most parties. This changes, of course, if it's a hip-hop crowd.
- A Second **Liqueur** – **Bailey's**, **Kahlúa** and **amaretto** are good options.
- **Flavored Vodka** – These are popular, especially the orange, lemon and vanilla flavors.
- **Dark Rum** – The more intensely flavored dark rum has its fans, and is good in the traditional Rum Punch.

- **Flavored Rum** – Depending on your crowd, coconut- or lemon-flavored rum can be a hit.

You might want to get several liqueurs if you know that your crowd will drink it.

So what exactly is the juice in **Gin 'N Juice**? Five out of six rappers will tell you that it is orange juice. Pineapple juice is the second choice as the mixer for this.

TIPS FOR PURCHASING LIQUOR

The first and most important step in creating cocktails is purchasing suitable liquor. Here are some tips:

- Typically, **the better the liquor, the better the drink**. The more the liquor is diluted in the drink, the greater the chance that the quality of a cheaper liquor can be obscured in the drink.
- When selecting **tequila for your drinks**, choose **a *blanco* or a *reposado***, which are crisper and have more of an agave flavor that works better in cocktails than the wood-aged *añejo*. Use tequila that is labeled, "100% Agave," of course.
- **Scotch is distinctive** and there is no good replacement for it.
- If you are not a fan of **gin**, which has quite an idiosyncratic taste, for cocktails you can **substitute vodka**, which has a fairly neutral flavor.
- **Tequila is similarly unique, but in cocktail recipes, rum** can be used in its stead. And, tequila can work in rum drinks. The tastes will be different, but the results will usually be palatable.
- Blended American whiskey and Canadian whisky are fairly similar and easily substituted for each other in cocktail recipes.
- **Rye whiskey** can work in a pinch as a substitute **for bourbon**.

Chocolate shells, which are hollowed to allow room for liqueurs, make a great addition to parties, especially during the cooler months. These chocolate shells are widely available at candy stores and other large retailers. Amaretto, Bailey's Irish Cream, Cointreau, crème de cacao and Kahlúa are some of the **liqueurs** that work very well for this task.

Provisioning liquor at a restaurant, bar, or reception hall will be similar to what you might want to stock at home. The big difference is that it will be much more expensive.

You might want to have **a special cocktail for your party**, maybe related to a theme, if one exists. Good examples are a Mardi Gras Hurricane and a Mint Julep for the Kentucky Derby-watching party.

CALCULATING THE PROPER AMOUNT OF BOOZE FOR YOUR EVENT

This is a difficult task for many except the most experienced event planners. Not only do you have to know which types of alcoholic beverages, but you will have to estimate how much of each to purchase. Once you have a basic idea of what the various spirits are, and a notion about choosing the appropriate brands, you need to determine how much of each to buy. If you have done this before, you will probably agree that this can be a relatively complicated procedure. Unless you are in good with a reliable and reputable psychic, you are going to need to use some rules-of-thumb that are very general indeed. Additionally, you will need to know your guests. **On average, guests will drink two drinks during the first hour, and one drink each extra hour.**

If you are planning on hosting <u>**40 people**</u> from roughly **8:00 to 12:00 PM**, for example, the calculations to determine alcoholic beverages would go as follows:
[(40 people) x (2 drinks for the first hour)] +
[(40 people) x (1 drink for each additional hour) x 3] = <u>**200 drinks total**</u>

So, you should plan on 200 drinks for a typical four hour event. Of course, some guests will have seven or eight drinks, some two or three, some will have none, etc. But, this calculation has served us well for years. You have determined that you will need to provide your guests with 200 drinks, but how do you go about determining how much liquor, wine and beer to purchase. Beer is easy, one bottle or one can is one drink. It's less straightforward for wine and liquor, but still easy to calculate.

Approximate capacities for wine and liquor bottles:

Wine (750 ml bottle)	≈	25 ounces	⇨	4 six ounce glasses	⇨ <u>**4 drinks**</u>
Wine (1.5 liter bottle)	≈	50 ounces	⇨	8 six ounce glasses	⇨ <u>**8 drinks**</u>
Champagne (750 ml btl.)	≈	25 ounces	⇨	6 four ounce glasses	⇨ <u>**6 drinks**</u>
Liquor (750 ml bottle)	≈	25 ounces	⇨	12 two ounce pours	⇨ <u>**12 drinks**</u>
Liquor (1 liter bottle)	≈	34 ounces	⇨	17 two ounce pours	⇨ <u>**17 drinks**</u>
Liquor (1.75 liter bottle)	≈	59 ounces	⇨	29 two ounce pours	⇨ <u>**29 drinks**</u>

With the capacities for cocktails above we have assumed two ounce pours of liquor. Though most bars will make cocktails with 1 ounce or 1½ ounces of liquor, it's our experience that people will make larger or stiffer drinks for themselves at a self-service bar. In general, plan on 2 ounces per average size cocktail.

Among beer, wine and the types of liquor, what can you expect your guests to drink? Again, you know your guests. You can plan on the fact that the guests coming to your event will drink what you provide. On the other hand, you would like to give the people what they want. Some handy rules-of-thumb when a full bar is provided are that:

- About **30%** will drink **beer**.
- **20%** will drink **wine**.
- **50%** will drink cocktails (**liquor**).
- For **liquor**, expect that **vodka** will make up **75%** of the liquor consumption.
- Generally, red wines will be consumed at a roughly two-to-one clip over white wine, i.e. for the wine drank, ⅔ **will be red** and ⅓ **will be white**. This ratio is used in the table below.

> **Single and unattached women will often drink white wine** over red since white wine will not discolor teeth, an important consideration if it is an event where they might meet someone. You might want to provision wine with this in mind.

So, for our typical party with 40 guests that is expected to last about four hours, this will result in about 200 drinks. Given our experience, we suggest purchasing the following for a self-service bar for a typically-sized event:

---

40 people for a party between **8:00 and 12:00 PM**, or so:

[(40 people) x (2 drinks for the first hour)] +
[(40 people x 1 drink for each additional hour) x 3] = **200 drinks**   *Same as above.*

30% will drink beer ⇨ (200 drinks) x (30%) = **60** beers
⇨ 60 / (6 beers in a 6-pack) = **10 six-packs of beer**

20% will drink wine ⇨ (200 drinks) x (20%) = **40** glasses of wine
⇨ (40 glasses) x (⅔) ≈ **27** glasses of red ⇨ [27 / (4 glasses each)]   ≈ **7 bottles red**
⇨ (40 glasses) x (⅓) ≈ **13** glasses of white ⇨ [13 / (4 glasses each)] ≈ **3 bottles white**

50% will drink liquor ⇨ (200 drinks) x (50%) = 100 pours of liquor
⇨ (100 drinks) x (75%) = **75** vodka drinks ⇨ [75 / (12 drinks each)] ≈ **7 btls. vodka**
⇨ (100 drinks) x (15%) = **15** whisky drinks ⇨ [15 / (12 drinks each)] ≈ **2 btls. whisky**
⇨ (100 drinks) x (10%) = **10** rum drinks   ⇨ [10 / (12 drinks each)] ≈ **1 btls. rum**

These are guidelines, and you will know your crowd. If you are confident that no one on your guest list drinks whiskey, don't purchase any whiskey. If no one, or everyone, drinks red wine, stock accordingly.

Vodka is more popular than all whiskies combined. – According to the Distilled Spirits Council of America, in 2002, U.S. consumers spent about $9.5 billion on vodka, which is more than sales of bourbon, blended whiskey, Canadian whisky, blended and single-malt scotch and Irish whiskey combined. The trend toward vodka has become more apparent since then.

Also, **it usually makes sense to overstock.** What is not used for your party can always be used in the future. Beer will last for a few weeks, usually longer. Wine will last for months, at the very least, most likely a year or several. The shelf life for liquor is nearly indefinite.

Conversely, there can be a big benefit to running out of alcohol. If you don't want the party to last too long, and you suspect that you might have trouble persuading some guests to leave at a decent hour, you might plan to run out of alcoholic beverages a few hours into the event. No alcohol is one sure way to end a party.

Amounts and types of alcohol will also depend on whether or not the bar is self-service or manned by a professional bartender. Most self-service bars will end up pouring drinks like Bourbon & Cola, Vodka & Tonic, and the like; liquor and one mixer and done. Professionally-manned bars, if properly stocked, will pour Martinis, Apple Martinis, Cosmopolitan, Margaritas, Manhattans, etc.

People will drink a greater percentage of cocktails versus other alcoholic beverages if the bar is manned by a competent bartender. If the bar is stocked with a top shelf vodka or gin, and bartender is known to make a good Martini, a guest may order one instead of their usual beer or wine.

DRINKING HABITS CHANGE DURING THE SEASONS

In the aggregate, drinking habits change during the seasons, and even during the time of the day. Here are some things that we have noticed over the years related to consumption patterns at parties:

- During the **daytime**, more beer and non-alcoholic drinks are consumed, as many people try to show more restraint before nightfall.
- During the **warmer months** – Gin, fruity drinks, frozen drinks and, to a lesser extent, white wines are more popular.

- During the **cooler months** – Martinis, scotch, Irish Coffees, toddies, and, somewhat less so, red wines are more popular.
- The **Christmas** season calls for **eggnog** for some reason.
- During the **Christmas** and **New Year's Eve** celebrations – Sparkling wine is the celebratory beverage for most.

FROZEN DRINKS

Frozen drinks can be a lot of fun, but require some more consideration and planning. Frozen drinks can be very **messy**, **time-consuming** to make, and **difficult to make well on a consistent basis**. Your guests who insist on making these at your party will often screw these up, in part because they probably already have had several drinks in them.

Some recommendations concerning frozen drinks:

- For a group of up to eight, a good blender will be sufficient, though **having an extra blender** or two is a good idea.
- Have **an area dedicated and ready** for making frozen drinks that includes in close proximity: an electrical outlet, a sink, and plenty of towels.
- One of the biggest problems with the taste of frozen drinks is that they end up **watered down**. For example, if you make a good Margarita on the rocks and use a similar recipe for a blender, the need for the additional ice will cause the mixture to taste comparatively weak and unbalanced. To rectify this problem, **use frozen concentrated juices or mixes**. For example, for Frozen Screwdrivers, use frozen orange juice and vodka and ice.
- **Test your recipes before your party**. The practice can be fun. We have also provided several good recipes beginning on page 217.
- For larger groups, think about **renting a frozen drink machine**. If you do rent a machine, be sure to get it going a **couple of hours before the party** is scheduled to start so that the frozen drinks will be ready. Remember that you will have to **attend to the machine during the course** of the party.

Be sure to note, if you are not planning on serving frozen drinks, hide your blender because your guests might be tempted to make frozen drinks with it, and, in most cases, screw up the drinks, and make a mess on top of it.

PROVISIONING THE HOME BAR (AKA THE LIQUOR CABINET)

Our suggestions for liquor for your home bar are similar to that of the **basic** bar for an event with some additions in terms of selection and expense.

With the home bar, you will want to be able to satisfy the alcoholic cravings (to some extent) of friends who happen to drop in, but most of all you will need to satisfy your own tastes. Since you are mostly provisioning for you (and possibly your spouse) you should spend more money on better quality liquor. A bottle of each type should work for most small, casual and unexpected gatherings.

> **T**hose **small liquor bottles** that you have collected from flights over the years are 50 milliliters. This is about 1.7 ounces, **about the size of a stiff-enough drink**.

Certainly stock more of what you (and if you are generous, your friends) are going to drink. See our recommendations for specific brands in the "Some More about Spirits" chapter in the Background section beginning on page 154.

- **Bitters** – Angostura or Peychaud's
- **Bourbon**
- **Cointreau** or **Triple Sec**
- **Dry Vermouth** – Almost any label will do.
- **Gin**
- **Light Rum**
- **Scotch** – If your friends are scotch drinkers, it might be a good idea.
- **Tequila**
- **Vodka**

> **O**ther **alcoholic beverages**, in addition to the list above, that are good to have on hand **for those impromptu get-togethers** are shown below. You know your friends, of course.
> - **Beer** – A couple six-packs to be on the safe side, chilled.
> - **Red Wine** – A couple bottles, at the very least, that you are willing to share. With any wine it is advisable to have inexpensive bottles an hand that you can easily share, rather than having to delve into that wine cellar in case friends drop by.
> - **White Wine** – A couple of bottles in the refrigerator is a good idea.
> - **Sparkling Wine** – Have a bottle chilled in the refrigerator, or a couple half-bottles (375 ml) or splits (187 ml).

ACCOMPANIMENTS FOR COCKTAILS

If you are providing liquor, unless you happen to be entertaining a group of Scotsmen who are just drinking their whisky neat, you will need to purchase mixers and the like. And, certainly, it is wise and necessary to have non-alcoholic beverages on hand for any occasion.

MIXERS, GARNISHES, ETC. THAT YOU MIGHT WANT FOR YOUR EVENT

Here are some things that you might need, which include: *1) sodas*; *2) carbonated mixers*; *3) non-carbonated beverages*; *4) fresh produce* for cocktails and garnishes; *5) condiments and garnishes*; and *6) packaged cocktail mixes*. The suggested provisions are listed with the most popular or familiar cocktails in which these belong.

1) Sodas

- **Cola** – For those guests whose caffeinated beverage of choice is cola, there might be a great deal of concern if only one or the other of the two major brands, Coca-Cola or Pepsi, is served.
- **Diet Cola** – Same as above, except, these are more often drunk as an alternative to alcohol during events rather than used as a mixer.
- **Ginger Ale** – This mixes well with whiskey and vodka.
- **Sprite / Seven-Up** – Used in 7 & 7's, among others.

2) Carbonated Mixers

- **Club Soda** – Scotch & Soda, etc. Purchase these in small bottles, which are typically 10 ounces.
- **Energy Drinks** – Keep in mind these are usually over $2 for 6 ounces. Red Bull is the most popular brand that is used to mix with liquor, vodka, mostly. The various brands of energy drinks have a wide range of flavors, so be careful when substituting.
- **Tonic Water** – Gin & Tonic, Vodka & Tonic, etc. Buy these in the 10 ounce size bottles, too.

Some terms that you might find in older editions of bartender's guides:
- **Quinine = tonic water**
- **Carbonated water = soda water = club soda = seltzer**

---

3) Non-carbonated Beverages

- **Bitters** – Angostura Bitters is the most widely used and needed for the Manhattan, Old Fashioned and the Champagne Cocktail among others. Purchase Peychaud's Bitters for a more authentic New Orleans feel, and for cocktails from there like the Ramos Gin Fizz and the Sazerac.
- **Coconut Milk** or **Cream of Coconut** – Piña Colada
- **Coffee** – Irish Coffee; and good to have after dinner and later at night.
- **Cranberry Juice** – Cape Cod, Cosmo, Madras, Sea Breeze, etc.
- **Cream** or **Half-and-Half** – White Russian
- **Grapefruit Juice** – Grapefruit juice might be a more suitable match for vodka than orange juice, even if it's less common. Purchase in small-can format, as it's used sparingly at most events.
- **Grenadine** – Mai Tai, Tequila Sunrise, Kentucky Cooler
- **Milk** – White Russian
- **Orange Juice** – Screwdriver, Cosmo, Madras, Fuzzy Navel, etc.
- **Peach Nectar** – Bellini
- **Pineapple Juice** – Typically this is used as a splash here and there, so purchase in small can format, also.
- **Tomato Juice** – Mostly used for Bloody Marys. Some assembly is required for these when using tomato juice. A Bloody Mary mix is typically much easier to use, especially for parties.
- **Water** – Bottled water can be a good idea, as it's easy to set up for parties, as you just stock in coolers or the refrigerator, and it's inexpensive.

4) Fresh Produce for Cocktails and Garnishes

- **Cucumber** – Pimm's Cup; one will usually suffice for all of the Pimm's Cups that you might need to make.
- **Green Apples** – Apple Martini
- **Limes** – Gin & Tonic, Vodka & Tonic, Margarita, etc. Indispensable.
- **Lemons** – Lemon peels are used as garnish for a number of drinks, and lemon juice also makes its way into a number of others.
- **Oranges** – Sangria, otherwise, for a garnish.
- **Raspberries** – Used as a miscellaneous garnish.
- **Strawberries** – These are a great match for sparkling wine.

5) Condiments and Garnishes

- **Cinnamon** – Irish Coffee
- **Coarse Salt** – For lining glasses for Margaritas. There are containers designed specifically for salting rims that can make this task much easier.

- **Maraschino Cherries** – Use mostly for garnish, though the juice in the jar can be used instead of Grenadine.
- **Mint Leaves** – Mint Julep, *Mojito*
- **Nutmeg** – White Russian
- **Olives** – Martini; the juice in the bottle is used for dirty Martinis.
- **Olive Juice** – Dirty Martini; this is an especially good idea when a lot of Martinis are expected to be poured.
- **Orgeat Syrup** – Just used in the Mai Tai
- **Pickled Onions** – Gibson
- **Sugar** – The finely granulated sugar designed to dissolve more quickly in cocktails might be worth the extra few cents.
- **Whipped Cream** – Irish Coffee

Bloody Marys from scratch – A good Bloody Mary requires ingredients that are used solely for Bloody Marys. These are:
- **Beef Bouillon Cubes** – For a variation on the Bloody Mary, the Bloody Bull.
- **Black Pepper**
- **Celery**
- **Clamato Juice** – A mixture of tomato juice and the juice from clams, this can be used as an interesting substitute for regular tomato juice. Made with Clamato Juice instead of tomato juice creates a Bloody Caesar.
- **Cumin** – Ground, not the whole seeds.
- **Dill** – Dried, not fresh.
- **Horseradish**
- **Limes** or **Lemons**
- **Tabasco Sauce** – Can also use for *Micheladas*.
- **Worcestershire Sauce**

---

6) Packaged Cocktail Mixes – Making the drinks from the component parts, especially when citrus juices are involved, is preferred, but oftentimes convenience is warranted, especially with a large or thirsty crowd. For around $20, you can cover a great array of drinks, and these mixes will usually last for a while. Some of the most useful and popular mixes include:

- **Bloody Mary Mix**
- **Daiquiri Mix**
- **Margarita Mix**
- **Piña Colada Mix**
- **Sour Mix** or **Packaged Sour** – Used in a variety of cocktails; some brands are not labeled as such, and you might have to look for something like "Lemon Cocktail Mix," "Bar Mix" or "Sweet-and-Sour Mix." Lasco is a popular brand of sour mix.

The following tables provide guidelines for accompaniments for several levels of the bar. To be able to provide **the necessities** for a cocktail party:

Essential for most events with cocktails:
- Sodas – **Cola, Diet Cola, Sprite** or **Seven-Up**
- Carbonated Mixers – **Club Soda, Tonic Water**
- Non-Carbonated Beverages – **Water, Orange Juice, Cranberry Juice**
- Fresh Fruits – **Limes, Lemons**
- Condiments & Garnishes – **Olives, Maraschino Cherries**
- Drink Mixes – **Sour Mix**

For **a more generous bar**, to make a greater variety of cocktails:

When you have a **professional bartender** at your event you might want to have this:
- Sodas – *Cola, Diet Cola, Sprite or Seven-Up*, **Ginger Ale**
- Carbonated Mixers – *Club Soda, Tonic Water*
- Non-Carbonated Beverages – *Water, Orange Juice, Cranberry Juice,* **Grapefruit Juice, Lime Juice, Pineapple Juice, Tomato Juice, Grenadine, Bitters, Milk, Coffee, Cream** or **Half-and-Half**
- Fresh Fruits – *Limes, Lemons,* **Oranges, Green Apples**
- Condiments & Garnishes – *Olives, Maraschino Cherries,* **Pickled Onions, Coarse Salt, Nutmeg, Cinnamon**
- Drink Mixes – *Sour Mix,* **Bloody Mary Mix, Margarita Mix**

To make almost every cocktail you might want to serve:

If you want to be able to make **nearly every type of cocktail,** use this list:
- Sodas – *Cola, Diet Cola, Sprite or Seven-Up, Ginger Ale*
- Carbonated Mixers – *Club Soda, Tonic Water,* **Energy drinks**
- Non-Carbonated Beverages – *Water, Orange Juice, Cranberry Juice, Grapefruit Juice, Lime Juice, Pineapple Juice, Tomato Juice, Grenadine, Bitters, Milk, Coffee, Cream or Half-and-Half*
- Fresh Fruits – *Limes, Lemons, Oranges, Green Apples,* **Strawberries, Raspberries, Cucumber**
- Condiments & Garnishes – *Olives, Maraschino Cherries, Pickled Onions, Coarse Salt, Nutmeg, Cinnamon,* **Mint Leaves, Coconut Milk, Peach Nectar, Whipped Cream, Orgeat Syrup**
- Drink Mixes – *Sour Mix, Bloody Mary Mix, Margarita Mix,* **Daiquiri Mix**

TIPS FOR PURCHASING COCKTAIL INGREDIENTS

- During the party **have ice dedicated for mixing cocktails and drinks,** not for chilling beer, soft drinks, etc. This should be a no-brainer.
- **Freshly-squeezed fruit juices are preferable.** This is especially important with simple combinations such as a Screwdriver, Mimosa, or Greyhound where **freshly-squeezed orange or grapefruit juice can make a very satisfying cocktail even when paired with the cheapest vodka.** Pre-packaged juices labeled "Not from Concentrate" can be a fine substitute. Other bottled juices are quite adequate, but avoid artificially-flavored fruit drinks.

- Champagne and most other **sparkling wines and strawberries,** sliced or whole, match well.
- **Use freshly ground spices**, if possible. The most commonly used ones are nutmeg, cinnamon and black pepper. These are easy to find, and can be quickly grated when necessary.
- **Purchase small bottles** of the following, as they keep much longer unopened, unless you believe that you will use a lot during your event: **tonic water, soda water, grapefruit juice, pineapple juice, olives,** and **pickled onions**.

What makes for a great cocktail? High quality liquor, fresh ingredients, and freshly ground spices (if used) coupled with competent mixing, which is done in a timely fashion. This sounds simple enough, though can be easier said than done. Remember, you will never have a superior cocktail with inferior ingredients.

THE BEGINNER'S GUIDE TO ASSEMBLING A COCKTAIL

Making a cocktail is as simple as putting ice in a glass and adding in all of the proper ingredients. Stating that, there are a couple of basic ways to make it, and there are still ways to screw it up. An inexperienced bartender will sometimes put the alcohol and mixers in the glass and then add the ice. While doing this won't result in a horrible concoction and ruin your event, the chance for creating a very satisfying cocktail is slim. The reason for putting the ice in first is that there will be balance among the ice, the water from the ice as it melts, and the other components of the drink. Below are some guidelines:

Basic Cocktail Assembly – **1)** Select the glass; **2)** Fill the glass with ice; **3)** Pour in the liquor(s); **4)** Pour in the mixers; **5)** Place a straw, stir stick or a spoon and give the drink a quick stir.

Some cocktails are not served over ice but still need to be chilled. Some popular examples are Martinis, Cosmopolitans and Kamikazes. Other cocktails are better when the ingredients are shaken together like Margaritas on the rocks and most Sour concoctions.

Shaken not Stirred – Martinis and the like – **1)** Chill the glass (preferably a Martini glass); **2)** Fill the shaker with ice; **3)** Pour the liquor(s) into the shaker; **4)** Add the mixer; **5)** Enclose the shaker; **6)** Shake baby, shake (the longer you shake, the colder the drink will be); **7a)** If the drink is to be served straight up, strain into the glass (if the drink is very cold, ice crystals will form on the top of the tip), otherwise, **7b)** pour all the contents of the shaker into a large enough glass.

OTHER TIPS FOR MAKING DRINKS

Though you might not be a novice when it comes to employing the cocktail shaker, below are some tips that are good to keep in mind:

- For drinks calling for sugar, **place the sugar in the glass before adding the liquor**. Think about using powdered sugar when sugar is called for, as it dissolves more quickly than granulated sugar at cool drink temperatures.

- **Don't shake, or stir vigorously, drinks featuring carbonated beverages** (tonic water, club soda, cola, champagne, etc.), as this will dissipate the bubbles. A possibly even more pressing concern is the resulting mess from the carbonated beverages overflowing the shaker.

- For all drinks, **too much stirring will overly dilute the result** since it melts the ice.

- **Shake drinks containing fruit juices** or **cream**, or any ingredient that might be difficult to mix, if possible. A blender will also do the trick, and a blender or mixer is an easy way to get a drink frothy if that is desired.

- Most guests will agree that a **stiff drink** is a good drink. Don't go overboard, though.

- **A dash or two of bitters is sufficient** as a small amount of bitters goes a long way.

- If you prefer **a cocktail on the rocks,** and the recipe calls for it straight up, simply make it as directed then pour it over ice.

- **To salt or sugar the rim of a glass**, run a slice of lime (for Margaritas, especially), lemon or even water, around the rim and dip into a plate spread with coarse salt or granulated sugar. Another way, and better when only one glass needs to be rimmed with salt or sugar, is to wet a paper napkin than dab it with the salt or sugar and run it around the rim of the glass.

- **There are two ways to frost a glass**: place it in a freezer for at least a half an hour; fill it with ice and a little cool water for at least a minute before emptying and using.

- **A quick shake when making a cocktail that contains citrus juices** will give the final product an attractive froth.

- For **Margaritas on the rocks or straight up**, a splash of orange juice cuts the tartness to round out the flavor and adds a nice sheen to the color.

- If you want to use **crushed ice**, simply place ice cubes in a clean plastic bag or wrap them inside a cloth on a counter and give it a few whacks with a rolling pin or a meat tenderizer.

When **mixing cocktails**, the following **substitutes can be made, if necessary** (though strong brand loyalists may disagree):

- Bailey's = Carolan's = Brendan's = Emmett's ≈ Amarula ≈ any other cream liqueur
- Blended Canadian whisky ≈ Blended American whiskey
- Canadian Club ≈ Seagram's VO ≈ Crown Royal
- Champagne > *Méthode Champeniose* sparkling wine
- Grand Marnier ≈ Cointreau ≈ curaçao ≈ triple sec
- Hypnotiq ≈ Blue Alizé
- **Irish Coffee**, Canadian Club or Seagram's VO ≈ Irish whiskey
- Juice from a jar maraschino cherries ≈ grenadine
- Kahlúa ≈ Kamora ≈ most other coffee liqueurs
- Rye whiskey ≈ bourbon
- Seagram's VO and Sprite ≈ **7 & 7**
- Sour Mix ≈ Lemon Cocktail Mix ≈ lemonade ≈ (Water + Lemon Juice + Sugar)
- Sprite or 7-UP with a splash of cola ≈ ginger ale (Though the faint flavor of ginger is absent, the color and sweetness is the same; and this rarely elicits a complaint.)

Practicing making the drinks before your event will help you impress your guests with new skill. Also, even the mistakes during the practice sessions can be enjoyable.

A part is the base measurement, which can be ½ ounce, an ounce, two ounces, and the like. For example, if a cocktail recipe states 1 part lime juice, 2 parts triple sec, and 3 parts tequila, the part can be whatever the size and strength you desire for your cocktail. Most cocktails at home have about 2 ounces of the primary liquor. For the example above, this could translate to ½ ounce lime juice, 1 ounce triple sec, and 1½ ounces tequila.

TIPS FOR EXPANDING THE DRINK RECIPES FROM ONE TO MANY

Don't you hate when you expand the drink recipe found in some bartender's guide from its stated single serving size to multi-person size, either for you or you and other guests, and often it does not taste as good as it should? Though we have included several very good and easy pitcher-sized drinks, you might want to expand other interesting cocktails into sizes suitable for sharing. Below are some hints to inflate those individual cocktail recipes into the standard 64 ounce pitcher size and beyond. The most important notion is that **you can always add more, but it is difficult to take away**. When multiplying the recipe, do the following:

- If the recipe calls for **sugar** or sweet liqueur like triple sec or Grenadine, **cut the amount by a quarter**. In large quantities, the sweetness is intensified. You can always put in more if it's not sweet enough.
- If the recipe calls for **water, cut back volume by a third**. Ice melts, and, like sugar, you can always add more.

- If you are using fresh **lemon or lime juice, add an extra ounce or so per pitcher**. Juice is easily diluted when the ice melts.
- For drinks with herb-based liqueurs such as **vermouth, halve** the measurement then adjust the final product.

After seemingly following the recipe exactly, sometimes the final result is less than desired. **Pineapple juice works wonders in fixing a cocktail made with citrus juices** (orange, lime, etc.), especially pitcher-sized drinks. It seems to mask the taste of alcohol, and complements the flavors of most spirits.

ENTERTAINING NON-DRINKERS AT YOUR EVENT

There will certainly be guests at your event that will not drink alcohol for one of a variety of reasons. Even if you enjoy a tipple or several, as a host you should certainly make these people as welcome as the other guests. Here are several tips for hosts regarding this matter that we have garnered from a long-standing addiction treatment center:

- **Don't make a big deal** about any guest not drinking. If a guest declines an offer of a drink, you don't need to press the issue.
- **Do serve alcoholic drinks at your event**. If there are recovering alcoholics at your event, they won't suddenly relapse because alcohol is available.
- **Be sure to serve non-alcoholic drinks**. Even drinkers might want the option for something without alcohol during the course of the evening.
- If serving wine at a dinner party, make sure to **offer guests an alternative.** Water is always easy.
- **Dishes cooked with an alcoholic beverage are technically okay** for recovering alcoholics. This is assuming that the alcohol has been cooked sufficiently long enough, as most if not all of the alcohol in the dish will have evaporated during the cooking process.
- **Dishes with uncooked alcohol** in it like rum balls **will contain alcohol**. You should certainly warn those guests who are avoiding alcohol about these dishes.
- **Punches should be labeled** as containing alcohol if these do.

BEVERAGES YOU MIGHT HAVE ON HAND FOR NON-DRINKERS

It's a good idea to have at least a couple types of non-alcoholic beverages available as an alternative to alcohol. Here are some suggestions:

- **Coffee**
- **Cola**
- **Diet Cola**
- **Fruit Juices**
- **Ginger Ale**
- **Iced Tea**
- **Lemon-Lime Soda**
- **Non-alcoholic Beer** – Some brands of these such as Kaliber are actually quite palatable.
- **Non-alcoholic Punch** – If you know that there will be a number of non-drinkers, or children, this can be much appreciated gesture.
- **Sparkling Water**

FOOD FOR YOUR EVENT

It's generally a good idea to serve at least some food at your event. Even if food is not the primary focus, it's a good complement to drinks, satiating the inevitable hunger pangs of your guests and keeping them somewhat more sober. Plus it adds another dimension to your event. Some of the most useful suggestions for food for social events are the *antipasti* selection, vegetable, and cheese plates. A big benefit for these is that much of it can be prepared well before your guests are due to arrive.

> **Finger foods are great for most parties**, excepting dinner parties, of course. These are easy to eat, which is especially important since there are usually more guests than seats at tables and counters. Easy to consume foods encourage guests to be mobile, and makes the chance to mingle greater.

Unless you are throwing a dinner or birthday party, desserts are usually unnecessary. Something to keep in mind, however, is that people who don't drink usually look forward to desserts, even if it might be just a plate of cookies, as it is one indulgence they might allow themselves.

> **What about vegetarian or vegan guests**? Unless you are a vegetarian or a vegan yourself, you are likely to overlook the desires of guests who ascribe to these lifestyles. You should not plan the party around one guest, so unless it's the guest of honor or a significant number of guests, don't worry about it.

APPETIZERS AS ANTIPASTI

An easy appetizer or *antipasti* spread will certainly impress your guests. This has a definite Italian temperament to it, but most everyone seems to enjoy these items. It's best when it consists of a variety of *1) meats; 2) vegetables*; and *3) cheeses*.

> **K**eep in mind that **people tend to eat more during colder weather**.

1) Meats – Italian and Italian-style cold cuts (or properly *salame* in Italian) are perfectly suited for this, but you don't have to limit yourself to just those choices.

- *Capicollo* [cahp-ih-KAHL-oh] – This is a tasty type of salami; commonly called "cob-ih-call" in the Calabrese dialect of many Italian-Americans. It might also be found as, *capocollo*, its singular form; *capicollo* is the plural.

- *Mortadella* – High quality imported *Mortadella di Bologna,* the real stuff, is now available at some high-end supermarkets and Italian food stores. Make sure you get the good stuff otherwise guests might just assume it is just baloney.
- **Pâté** – Depending on your budget and its availability in your area or your desire to make it yourself, any one of a variety of pâtés can work well at your event when served with crackers or toast points.
- **Pepperoni** – This is also found more expensively and flavorfully in gourmet food stores as *Salame Calabrese.*
- *Prosciutto crudo* – This will certainly be the most popular, though also the most expensive of the meats that you might put out.
- **Salami** – Thinly sliced, good quality salami is a staple for *antipasti* trays.
- **Smoked Salmon** – Though not Italian, and not inexpensive, this always seems to go very quickly at most events.

Prosciutto – High quality, cured ham sliced paper-thin **makes for a classic appetizer** solo, or as a component in an array of cold appetizers such as *prosciutto* and melon, *prosciutto* and fig, etc. Excepting its cost, often more than $20 a pound, it works especially well for parties because it is ready to serve when purchased, and nearly everyone seems to really like it. *Prosciutto* is now the default name in North America for several types of cured hams including the Spanish *jamon serrano* and the German Westphalian ham. *Prosciutto* and its European and North American cousins are air-cured with a minimum of salt for nearly a year or more. When buying *prosciutto,* first make sure that it is **prosciutto crudo,** which is not cooked. This is marketed in what looks like a ham bone. The less common *prosciutto cotto* is cooked, and is basically very similar to most supermarket lunch meat ham, although it is of generally higher quality than that, but still not terribly interesting as a cold appetizer. The best *prosciutto* (*crudo*) is from Italy. The best types of *prosciutto* from Italy are labeled *Prosciutto di Parma, Prosciutto di San Daniele,* or the rare *Prosciutto di Carpegna,* designating their origin. Each has a slightly different, but very good taste. Though the **American and Canadian prosciutto** are of lesser quality, at half the cost of the Italian product, these versions **are usually more than sufficient,** and your guests will readily gobble it up. The Spanish *jamon serrano* is also excellent. It is a fine substitute for the Italian *prosciutto,* though generally at least as pricey. If you serve *jamon serrano* to guests from Italy, just tell them it is *prosciutto* otherwise you might offend their tender sensibilities.

---

2) Vegetables – These can provide a useful diversity of choices and contrast in flavors with the meats; and olives have been an accompaniment to wine since ancient times.

- **Artichoke Hearts** – The packaged ones are easy and tasty.
- **Baby Corn** – As with the salmon and pâté, it doesn't all have to be Italian.
- **Cherry Peppers** – Can be purchased ready-to-eat as well.
- **Grape** or **Cherry Tomatoes** – Technically a fruit, but still good.
- **Olives** – Almost any type of cured olive will work, though the best to choose for this might be Picholine, Kalamata and Niçoise.

- *Pepperoncini* – Jarred are good.
- **Roasted Red Peppers** – Those from a jar work well, too.

3) Cheeses – Easy and tasty. Below are some recommendations, though nearly any cheese that you enjoy will probably work.

- **Hard Cheeses** – These might include Parmigiano-Reggiano or the slightly cheaper Grana Padano, or Dry Jack.
- **Mozzarella** – Even better when marinated for a couple of hours in olive oil and black pepper. See the recipe for this on page 184.
- **Swiss-style Cheeses** – Gruyère, Fontina or Emmentaler.

Some assembly is required for an *antipasti* plate, which can and should be done ahead of time:

1. Select between five to eight items from the above list. A variety works best when mixing the cured meats, vegetables and cheese.
2. On a platter or a large plate, neatly arrange the food items in a way that takes into account their varying colors and shapes. When possible include something red (roasted red peppers), something green (olives, *pepperoncini*), a meat, and cheese. If you have more than one item that is similar like black olives and Kalamata olives, Genoa salami and pepperoni, or cherry peppers and *pepperoncini*, separate them for effect.

Caviar – This is fish eggs from various species of the sturgeon that can be, maybe surprisingly, part of your entertaining plan. It certainly adds a degree of elegance and *savoir faire*. The most famous caviar is from the Caspian Sea, and the species that give their names are **beluga**, **osetra**, and **sevruga**. Caspian beluga might cost $200 an ounce. By the mid-2000s, the quality of the expensive Caspian caviar has diminished appreciatively since the collapse of the Soviet Union. Though Iran has maintained very high standards for caviar production in the Caspian, Russia and the other former Soviet countries have not, and illegal fishing has flourished. So much so that the prized beluga sturgeon population has diminished to about 10% of what it was in 1985. **Caviar from California and Uruguay has been touted as being good alternatives** to that from the Caspian, and ranges from about $35 to $50 an ounce. There are also other more inexpensive, if not sublime alternatives such as that from paddlefish and the bowfin from $5 to $20 an ounce. If you decide to indulge in caviar, serve it about 60° F (15.5° C), if possible, not too cold. Once the container is opened, it will last just a couple of days. **Consume it unadorned on toast points or directly with non-silver spoons** (silver reacts with the caviar), or the traditional mother of pearl caviar spoons, if you have them. Stainless steel is actually fine with caviar, as are plastic utensils. Champagne and vodka are classic pairings for caviar, but a crisp white wine will work well, too.

VEGETABLE PLATTER

Like the *antipasti* spread, vegetable platters can be an easy and inexpensive addition to your event. Most grocery stores sell pre-cut celery, carrots, broccoli, etc. You can purchase these pre-cut vegetables or cut them yourself, which is not very time-consuming and even cheaper. It depends on your time and budget. For a good spread, choose four or five of the following:

- **Bell Peppers** – Green, red, and yellow bell peppers will add a great deal of color to your vegetable platter, especially together. Remove the stems, seeds and ribs then slice into ½" wide strips. Even better, first char the peppers in the oven (or on a grill) and enclose in a paper bag for about twenty minutes. This will help you easily remove the skins for an easier tastier treat. This can be done hours before your guests arrive.
- **Broccoli** – Separate into bite-sized crowns and stems.
- **Carrots** – Peel, then cut into pieces that are 2" long and ¼" wide.
- **Cauliflower** – Separate into bite-sized crowns and stems.
- **Celery** – Cut into pieces that are 2" long and ¼" wide.
- **Cherry** or **Grape Tomatoes** – Remove stems and leaves.
- **Cucumbers** – Cut off the ends and peel. Then, cut into four equal pieces length-wise. Cut each of these pieces into ¼" thick rounds.
- **Mushrooms** – For this purpose only fresh mushrooms will do. Wash thoroughly, as these are often flecked with dirt. Cut into ½" pieces.

You can use the extra bell pepper to hold your dip. To do this cut off the top of the pepper, then clean out the seeds, and fill with either ranch or blue cheese dressing. It makes for an attractive centerpiece.

To assemble, on a platter or large plate, place the bell-pepper-dressing-holder in the center, then group the vegetables around it, separating colors. For example, celery (green), then mushrooms (mostly white), carrots (orange), broccoli (green), and cherry tomatoes (red).

ASSEMBLING THE BASIC CHEESE PLATE

Below are suggestions for what to include in the basic cheese plate that will work with most wines and beers, and certainly for your event. The list of cheese types below provides nice contrasts in terms of flavors and textures that should be complementary to at least some of the beverages while providing some diversity for your guests.

Amounts will obviously depend on the number of people. First you need a plate, cutting board, or serving tray. It's nice to get a variety of cheeses for the sake of diversity, and to complement the different range of tastes, and beverages that your guests might have. Since people begin to eat with their eyes, go for varying shapes and colors. A suggestion to start with might begin with a nice **Gouda** wedge, a small piece of creamy **Brie** or **Camembert** wheel, a block of **Sharp Cheddar**, and maybe a flavored cheese like **Pepper Jack** (Monterey Jack spiked with chile peppers) or **Havarti flavored with Dill**. If it's a bigger group and you want to add more, a small wedge of **Gorgonzola** or another high quality blue cheese, is good as you can crumble it beforehand for effect. **Swiss** is always good, especially **Gruyère**. **Sharp Cheddar** or an **Applewood-flavored Cheddar** are each very tasty and have attractive and complementary colors. **Manchego** and **Pepper Jack** also make for fine choices for a cheese plate. There are so many fantastic cheeses from which to choose. Spread them out nicely and then lay **grapes** (still on the stem, but seedless) in between, and all over. Other fruit can work such as raspberries and strawberries. Don't forget to have some cheese cutters, slicers, knives, and crackers (**Carr's Water Crackers** are a good choice). A log of **salami** or a **summer sausage** goes with nicely these. All in all, cheese trays take very little effort to put together.

EXAMPLE CHEESE PLATE

The image above shows the contrast in shapes and items that can help make for a more inviting presentation.

Some other related suggestions:

- About **two ounces of cheese per person** is a good rule-of-thumb to estimate when determining the quantity to purchase.
- **Four cheeses is a good number for a cheese plate.** But, it is also advisable to serve one excellent cheese rather than several bland ones.
- **Take the cheeses out of the refrigerator about an hour or two in advance**, so that these can reach room temperature.

- **A very strong-smelling cheese should <u>not</u> be placed next to a mild cheese**, as the mild cheese will pick up the odor.
- **Have the cheese cut into small, bite-sized pieces**, usually cubes. Or, make sure that you have the **proper utensils**: a knife, or knives, a cheese slicer, toothpicks, etc.
- **Don't worry that some cheeses won't be a perfect match** for the wines being served. A less-than-ideal match will complement each other well enough, and good-quality cheeses will be enjoyed by your guests.

SOME MORE FOODS WITHOUT COOKING OR MUCH MORE WORK

In addition to an *antipasti* plate, vegetable plate and a cheese plate with crackers, there are a few other things that you can do before resorting to cooking. These are time-saving tips and also very affordable.

- **For appetizers, cold appetizers are the way to go** – Cold appetizers are easier, as you do not have to worry about preparing food after the event has started. You simply have to remove them from the refrigerator and place them on the table or counter-side.
- **Purchase some of the foods** – Most supermarkets and delis will have platters of party-appropriate foods such as cheese and sandwich platters. Cutting cheese really is not much fun. Really.

Some specific food suggestions:

- **Shrimp that are pre-boiled** and sold frozen are available in most supermarkets. Simply thaw and serve with cocktail sauce and lemon wedges.
- **Nancy's brand food appetizers** such as tartlets, small quiches, crabcakes, spinach puffs, and deli spirals that are found in the frozen food section at most grocery stores work surprisingly well for most events.
- A **small block of cream cheese topped with one of a variety of toppings and served with crackers** is a very simple and popular appetizer that has been around for a while. Some toppings that work well are:

  - **Chipotle-Raspberry Salsa** – This seemingly unusual salsa combination works especially well with cream cheese.
  - **Jelly** or **Jam** or other preserves – Simple grape or black currant preserves seem to pair the best.
  - **Pickapeppa Brand Sauce** – This product of Jamaica is a New Orleans favorite when coupled with cream cheese
  - **Tomato-based Salsa** – Your basic salsa.

STUFF YOU CAN PURCHASE READY-TO-GO – EASIEST OF ALL

All decent-sized metropolitan areas have stores, supermarkets or specialty food stores, where you can purchase pre-made foods that are designed for large events. Some of these include:

- **Sandwiches** – Purchasing a platter of small sandwiches can be a great idea, as these can be a dinner substitute for the light eaters among your guests and heavy appetizers for the others. Just make sure that sandwiches will be enjoyed. Those old-fashioned cucumber sandwiches will not usually cut it with a group of guys.
- **Cheese Platters** – This is definitely time-saving.
- **Mixed Deli Platters** – These might consist of cold cuts, cheeses, sandwiches and dips. Purchase one or two and you might be ready for a group of a dozen or two in support of their drinks.
- **Snacks** – Such as Chex Mix brand party mixes.
- Bottled **tapenades** can make for quick and tasty appetizers. The tapenades simply can be placed in small bowls for self-service with bread or crackers, or broiled with cheese for easy-to-make *crostini*.
- **Mixed Nuts** such as cashews, pistachios and shelled peanuts.
- **Chips** should be a no-brainer, especially for the most casual of social event.
- **Dips** – These make for easy-to-assemble appetizers. Simply put the dips into more attractive bowls (if you want to obscure its source) and serve with crackers, chips, slices of bread or toast. Some dips that work well for parties are:

  - **Baba Ganoush** – Best served with pita chips or pita bread.
  - **Bean Dip** – Tortilla or potato chips are usually a good accompaniment.
  - **Guacamole** – Best served with tortilla chips.
  - **Hummus** – As with the baba ganoush, pita chips and pita bread.
  - **Queso** – Tortilla chips or tortillas are necessary accompaniments. See the recipe on page 183 (where it is properly called *chile con queso*).
  - **Spinach-Artichoke Dip** – The staple of every fern bar that serves food from coast-to-coast, this is nonetheless quite enjoyable with bread or crackers.

Moving these from the standard plastic container onto your (nicer) serving plates will make these even more presentable.

Food that is good to have on hand **for those impromptu get-togethers** usually consists of munchies with a decently long shelf-life that go well with drinks. Some fairly obvious suggestions are:

- **Chips** – In addition to potato and tortilla chips, you might also consider plantain.
- **Crackers**
- **Cream Cheese** – As mentioned above, this is an easy and versatile appetizer.
- **Dips**
- **Frozen munchies** – Egg rolls, pizza, etc.
- **Hot Sauce**
- **Lemons**
- **Limes**
- **Nuts**
- **Red Peppers**, jarred
- **Salsa** – Different than hot sauce, of course.
- **Tapenades**

FOOD SAFETY

Being a good host includes serving food that is safe to eat. Chicken, eggs, and shellfish require more attention than do other foods.

- For **outdoor events**, avoid serving dishes with **eggs, mayonnaise, milk** and **cream** that could become a hazard if left in the sun for a while.
- **Rinse poultry thoroughly under cold water** before cooking to remove bacteria.
- **Rinse fruits and vegetables well** before cooking or serving to wash off any pesticides or contamination that occurred in the field.
- When preparing **chicken** and **seafood** for cooking, be especially careful to **wash** the cutting board, utensils and your hands well before using it for other ingredients due to the danger of salmonella. Hot water and soap will suffice for the cleaning.
- Also because of the risk of salmonella, **raw eggs should <u>not</u> be used in food that might be consumed by pregnant women, children** and anyone with a compromised immune system.

Step 6 – Hosting

There are a number of tasks that you can do to prepare to host an event, which will make it more manageable and enjoyable for you. It bears mention that the host sets the tone for the party, and if you are too uptight, frantic or are not in a good mood, this can make the evening forgettable, both for you and your guests. Some people (and you probably know who you are) should really take time to emotionally prepare themselves for being a good host prior to their event, especially when it is at home.

PERSONAL READINESS FOR YOUR EVENT

There are certain things that you should try to do as a host before your event that will make the event run more smoothly, and help to ease any potential pre-event anxiety.

FOR AN EVENT OUTSIDE OF HOME

Some very general things to do before your event:

- If it is a restaurant or bar event, first and foremost, **call several hours before the event to re-confirm** with the manager or your contact. Be sure to confirm room availability, wait staff availability, and parking, if important.
- **Arrive early** to the restaurant or bar to ensure the establishment has made the proper preparations, and for you to set up anything that needs set up.
- **Try not to gorge** on the appetizers provided. Save some for your guests.

When hosting an event at a restaurant or bar, it's good to be aware of the unique tasks that should be considered for these types of venues. There is much more on this in the chapters "Hosting a Dinner Event at a Restaurant" and "Hosting an Event at a Bar" that begin on pages 138 and 148, respectively.

FOR AN EVENT AT HOME

For home-based events, there are certain things that you should try to do prior to your event: *1)* some **days beforehand**; *2)* some **a few hours beforehand**; and, others which have to wait until *3)* **immediately before** you begin the hosting duties.

1) Some things **to do a day or more before** the event:

- If hosting the event at your place, you might want to schedule a special visit from **a maid** to aid in cleanup.
- You will know your guests, or should know most of them, so you can **prepare for any potential unpleasantries** beforehand.
- **Call a friend or two to aid in the final preparations**, or at least show up early to help you greet the early-arriving guests, and with other minor hosting duties.

Being able to pronounce dishes, wines and other entertainment-associated items correctly, which are mostly French and Italian words and names, **will give you an air of legitimacy**, authority and suaveness, even if these attributes are fairly ill-begotten. For example, appetizers sound better when presented to your guests as *hors d'oeuvre* or *antipasti*. It might be a good idea to practice before the event some of these that you might be serving or planning to insert into a conversation.

---

2) Some things to try **to do several hours before** the event:

- **Shower early** so you are not rushing. You want to try to avoid greeting your guests with wet hair.
- For men, **shave early**. Your blood is thinner when you are excited and more apt to bleed freely when nicked.
- **Make sure that the oven is clean**, and so, will not produce smoke when it is turned on. This can happen with long-neglected ovens.
- **Do as much of the cooking as you can**, well before your guests arrive.
- Run the dishwasher to **clean the glasses** for dust, water spots, etc.
- If you don't have a dishwasher or time for running a load, be sure to **check, and rinse if necessary, the glasses to be used for dust and water spots**. Wine glasses seem to readily attract these.
- **Check bathrooms** for toilet paper, soap, etc.
- Try to have a **plunger** in each bathroom.
- If you have appetizers that utilize toothpicks, **have a trashcan or a tabletop receptacle for the toothpicks within eyesight**. If not, toothpicks might end up anywhere. At the very least, a saucer or a coffee cup will suffice. Putting a toothpick or two in beforehand will give your guests the clue this is to be used for the discarded toothpicks.
- **Purchase ice**, if you need to.
- Make sure that **beverages are**, or are on their way to becoming, **cold**.
- If you are planning to use a **fireplace, be sure to open the flue.**

3) Some things **to do immediately before** the event:

- Put out the **ice bucket**.
- Put out the **appetizers**.
- **Slice lemons and limes**.
- Make sure that the **bar is self-sufficient**, or, very nearly so.
- Have **a place for guests' coats and purses**.
- **Light any candles**.

If Bellinis or **Mimosas** are an integral part of the event, let's say for a brunch or another late morning event, and the number of guests is more than a handful, **a time-saving tip is to fill a of number of the champagne flutes with the peach puree or orange juice**, respectively, before the guests arrive. These drinks can then very quickly be completed with addition of the sparkling wine just before serving.

DURING YOUR EVENT AT HOME

There are a number of things that you can do to be a good host at home. Several of the most important, and easiest, are listed below.

- **Have a friend or two arrive early to help** – You should have contacted them beforehand, but, otherwise, you might be able to conscript a friend once they have arrived. These friends can be especially useful if you will be handling a large group, might not know all of the guests very well, or if there will be a lot of demands on you as a host, as during a dinner party when you are cooking. If possible, call these friends before they are expected to leave in case you need them to pick up any items that you have missed. If these are useful friends, their presence can help you relax. And, having a couple people arrive early will get the party started before the other guests make it.

- **Try to greet each guest as they arrive** – This is helpful, but as a host don't feel that you need to be tied to the front door, if that will take away from you insuring that guests are enjoying themselves.

- **Offer drink and food soon upon the arrival of each guest**, if possible. A big reason that they came to your home is to drink your alcohol, after all.

- **Talk to each guest at some point during the event** – Take a minute or two with as many of your guests as possible to welcome them, point out the location of the drinks, food and bathrooms, and encourage them to "help themselves" and "make themselves at home." These greetings, especially to those that don't know you very well, goes a long way helping these guests enjoy themselves.

- **Introduce guests to each other** – This might be the most significant thing that you can do as host, especially during a relatively small gathering when guests might not know each other. Even if you do not feel comfortable as a host, or maybe are somewhat shy, once you introduce guests to each other, they will feel more at ease at your event, and there is a greater chance they will interact with each other. People tend to mingle with people that they know. For example, you might have your work friends in the kitchen, the friends from college in the living room, and the friends from the neighborhood, golf course, or book club in the middle, and those from the swingers' bar already in the hot tub. A great way to introduce people is by finding something that each has in common, or by sharing a story: "Bob, this is Steve. He is my buddy that I told you about who has a collection of doodlebugs," or "Tyrone, this is Sue. Sue just got back from Cambridge. And, Tyrone, didn't you used to live in London, Clapham, I believe?"

- **Be patient with your guests** – As they are probably not as cool as you.

If someone arrives at your event with a **bottle of wine**, ask them whether or not they would like you to open it. Unless you ask, it might be difficult to know if it's intended as a gift or for immediate consumption. **You shouldn't feel obligated to serve it**.

The state of mind for a successful host calls for the following:

- **Relax** – If you are tense or stressed out, you are much more likely to make your guests, especially the first few arrivals, feel uneasy and maybe not terribly welcome. This could get the party off to a shaky start, and set the tone for the rest of the event. If it helps you, have a drink or two to settle your nerves. Don't overdo it at the start, though.
- **Try to maintain a relaxed attitude throughout** – Having another drink or two can help this feeling, though don't overdo it, of course.
- **Have fun** – After all, this is the purpose of hosting a social event in the first place. Just remember that the hardest work, the preparation, is done, and make an effort to enjoy yourself. Have yet another drink or two, or more, again. Just don't overdo it, of course, but it's your party.
- **Embrace spontaneity** – Not everything will go according to your pre-conceived mental plan. Be aware that things will change, and be prepared for it, at least with your positive state of mind.

Typically, **the more diverse a group of guests, the more you will need to work** as a host to ensure that everyone is mingling and enjoying themselves.

Some more specific tips for being a good host:

- **The host should be in charge of the party** in the sense that you need to make sure that the mood of the event moves appropriately and as naturally as possible through the different phases, such as mingling, dining, gift-opening, dancing, etc.
- If you can **identify difficult guests beforehand**, try to deal with them prior to them ruining at least part of the party. This is easier to say than do, of course.
- **A computer can be a big distraction** during a party. An exception might be to show digital photographs. Use your discretion. There are certainly some images on your computer that aren't meant to be shared with others.
- **Don't drink so much** that you become impaired.
- As host, **you don't have to be the center of attention**.
- If you notice that **a guest is imbibing at a far too rapid rate for them, try to slow them down** by engaging them in conversation and try to get them to slow their consumption. Or, warn the wait staff or bartender so that

they should be slower in returning their drink requests, or have them reduce the strength of those drinks.

- **Keep the areas** where guests are congregating at least somewhat **clean**. Overflowing trash cans are a nuisance.
- If you have a **frozen drink machine**, you will need to keep on eye on it, and **replenish** it when necessary.

To be a good host, or a good guest, **avoid talking about religion or politics**. Unfortunately, most people seem to have undeveloped and inarticulate notions and opinions that become even more pronounced with the addition of alcohol. Some good topics can be food, restaurants, cooking, travel and movies. Weather is always a safe, if possibly boring fallback unless some interesting weather has hit recently, then it becomes much more engaging: "Wow, that hurricane in Florida was horrible."

If you receive fresh flowers, put these in a container, preferably a vase with water. If no vase is available, then a pitcher will do. Cut the stems diagonally and put an aspirin tablet into the vase before putting in the flowers. Not attending to the flowers might offend the giver, as you are both not displaying the flowers (even in an out-of-the-way area), and you are vastly shortening the useful life...of the flowers.

If you are hosting and a **White Elephant gift exchange** is involved, **it's a good idea to have a few extra gifts** ready to go for those who have forgotten to bring one, or who never got word of the exchange.

CONVERSATION IS KEY

It has been largely assumed that you know that the primary entertainment at most events, and certainly the events we have in mind, is conversation. As a host it's your duty to properly get guests engaged in lively talk, but not too lively that it becomes contentious. Thankfully, having spent at least several years in normal society, you, as most adults, are readily equipped with the basic understanding of how to conduct good conversation.

Esquire's Handbook for Hosts, published a few years after the end of the Second World War, gives some hints on conducting successful conversations that are still valid today. The spirit of much of this wisdom is combined with our experiences to produce the following more useful and current group of suggestions:

- **Try <u>not</u> to use too many obscure words**. This can be seen as pretentious, and snotty.

- Try **not** to use **too many foreign words** or expressions. You will retain the group's attention longer if they can understand nearly all of what you are saying.
- Try **not** to provide **lengthy dialogue** from someone else, television or a movie. This can be tough for others to follow. And, unless you are known for having a very good memory, your veracity might be doubted, as you recite at great length what you heard just once.
- When telling a story **introduce and identify the major characters**, even under *a nome de guerre* rather than "he," "she," "this person." This makes it much easier for your listeners to follow.
- Try to **avoid asking your listener, "Do you understand?"** This can be interpreted as being condescending. Try to avoid doing this when you are discussing something complicated with some assembled dullards.
- Try **not** to name-drop too much, which should be obvious.
- You might **not** need to follow each story with one of your own, or make it a point to interject yourself into a conversation with a story of your own. It could very well be that your guest, or guests, have much more interesting stories, and lives, than you do. Possibly.

Sometimes you may become too emotional during a discussion, which is especially unwelcome when you are hosting an event. This is when the discussion has likely turned, or is turning, into an argument, and you find yourself doing some of the following:

- Raising your voice to try to **shout down** the other person
- Making **irrelevant references** to the other's nationality, family, physical stature, or occupation.
- Becoming overly sarcastic or **snide**
- **Avoid discussing points that are true** but weaken your argument.
- **Not admitting** when you are obviously wrong. This assumes that you can still follow logic at this point.

When you notice yourself employing one or more of these tactics it might be a good idea to try to end the discussion. Civility is one important trademark of a good host.

WHAT ABOUT THOSE ANNOYING EARLY BIRDS?

Greet them, give them a drink, and ask them to let you finish setting up. Be polite, but be sure to communicate that you are not quite ready to entertain them just yet. Or, even better, have these people help you with anything left you might need to finish before the event really starts.

> **"We're goin' to a bad party. It's the worst party that's ever been...."**
> *– The Dead Milkman*
>
> We have all been to bad parties. Ones where you are not having fun, or worse, never feel comfortable. Some things that make for a bad party, and things to try to avoid or mitigate for your event:
> - An overly cute **invitation which provides unclear information** – This is where you or other guests are unsure of dress, style, or the notion of gifts, and have not really come prepared for what entails.
> - **Unfriendly** people
> - **Obnoxious** people
> - For singles, **too few of the eligible opposite sex**
> - Guests segregated into **cliques**
> - **Tense** or **unprepared hosts**
> - **Extended gift-opening** and associated guffawing; gift-opening has its place at showers and some fawning there is fine, as long as it does not last overly long.
> - **Poor access to drinks**
> - **Not enough alcohol**
> - Annoying **"party coaches"** who try to get guests to play games, or direct the aggregate to do something or another that no one really wants to do, and which usually disrupts conversations and the overall level of enjoyment.

ASKING FOR (AND ACCEPTING) CASH AT YOUR EVENT

It can often be difficult to ask your guests for money, even when they are good friends. Some rules of thumb for when it is acceptable and in good taste to ask your guests for money:

- **You have told them beforehand** that you are expecting a payment from them for the party's centerpiece, which could be a big fight on pay-per-view, a meal at a restaurant, adult entertainment, etc.
- There is **a reasonable expense, most often exceptional, that you are incurring for the event**, for which you are charging them. For example, a pay-per-view boxing match will usually cost at least $50.
- You have ordered **food delivery**, usually after the event was expected to be finished.

> **T**ry **not** to ask guests to help clean up, unless they are lingering well past the expected departure time and don't seem to take a hint. Of course, if they are very good friends and you need help, it can't hurt to ask, especially if you don't want them to enjoy themselves that much anymore.

GETTING GUESTS TO LEAVE

You might consider playing the dirge-like "Wreck of the Edmund Fitzgerald" or something else as annoying if the more subtle hints do not work. Actually, turning up the lights, as is done in performance arenas, is polite, but a nearly unmistakable signal that the festivities are over.

A NOTE ON HOSTING AN EVENT AND ALCOHOL

When hosting an event where your guests may consume alcohol, you need to be aware of the dangers. Some of your guests, when alcoholic beverages are available and free of charge, will over-indulge and get drunk. You should always look out for guests who may be impaired and should not get behind a wheel. You definitely don't want them to hurt themselves or others, and certainly don't want them sideswiping your car and maybe someone else's car when leaving the party. Also, most states have now either codified or recognized "social host laws" that impose liability on a purely social host if a guest becomes inebriated and as a result causes damage to someone after departing the event.

If you see someone at your event who starts to exhibit signs that they are over the limit, so to speak, try to arrange a ride for them, insist on calling them a cab, or even take them home yourself. Be aware that a cup or two of coffee when they are drunk will just help to keep them awake, but will not sober them up. Only time, other fluids and rest will do that.

Disaster Relief at Your Event

For all of the planning that you might do prior to your event, some things are just out of your control. What should you do when the toilet backs up? When a guest is choking? Etc.

Toilet Problems

It is a good idea to have a plunger in at least one of the bathrooms, something like Drain-O, and a number handy for a plumber that you might need to call. The most common problem is too much toilet paper or a tampon that cannot be flushed. For those inexperienced with a plunger, simply get the suction part completely over the drainage hole of the toilet. Then give the plunger a hard push or several to create a good suction and pull to release the obstruction. You might have to repeat this several times. Flush once after the obstruction is cleared. It this doesn't work, you might have to call a plumber.

Another common problem you can fix is when the lever does not seem to work and the toilet does not flush. This occurs when the chain connecting the lever to the valve that releases that water to flush becomes unattached. To fix this, just lift the lid from the back of the toilet bowl to access the tank. Be careful to set the lid where it won't fall and break, as it is porcelain. It should be easy to find where the chain should be re-attached. This chain goes from the end of the lever, which is attached to the handle on the outside, and the rubber stopper at the bottom of the tank. Don't worry about getting your hands wet; the water in the tank is not the funky toilet water. The chain should clip back on, but if it is broken, a paper clip can help fix it quite easily.

Another fixable problem is when the toilet keeps running. This is usually caused when the rubber stopper at the bottom of the tank is not fully closing. This can be due to a kink in the chain or when something is obstructing the stopper. To remedy this problem simply fix the chain or remove the debris from near the stopper.

For other more serious problems you might consider turning off the water to the toilet. This valve is usually found close to the floor near the wall in the vicinity of the toilet, or on the bottom of the water tank.

CLEANING SPILLS

For spills use a white cloth rag or a white paper towel, if at all possible. Some of the stuff that might be spilled could possibly cause whatever colored dye is on the rag to be transferred to the just stained carpet, furniture or article of clothing to make the stain more colorful and more permanent. For a wide range of stains caused by spilled drinks, soda water works very well when applied soon after the spill.

SOMETHING GETS BROKEN

You should have hidden the most valuable and most fragile items before the party. If something else gets broken, don't worry about it too much, as it's bound to happen eventually if you entertain frequently. In most cases the person that has broken it will feel as bad, or worse, than you do.

BURNT OR RUINED FOOD

Have a sense of humor about this. Throw it away and order take-out or delivery.

AN INSISTENT DRUNK

If you cannot pry the keys away from a drunk after repeated efforts or cannot get others to take care of this person, you might want to try to render their car inoperable. Deflating the tires is one way.

AN ARGUMENT BECOMES TOO HEATED

Even if there is no chance of fisticuffs, a loud and heated argument can ruin the mood at the party, at least for the group of guests within earshot of it. As a host you should do your best to diffuse the situation. Ask them to cool down, and it's often a good idea to separate the parties involved. Enlist a friend or another guest to help, if need be.

THE POWER GOES OUT

First, check if your neighbors' power is also out. If so, you'll have to wait until the power company can restore it. If not, check your circuit breaker. During a party, chances are good that there are too many devices connected to a single circuit, and it becomes overloaded. Simply move the popped circuit (it will be the one in a different position from the others) back into place and reduce the number of devices on that circuit. If you don't know exactly where the circuit connects, just reduce the total number of items plugged in. It is a good idea to know where your circuit box is before the party starts.

A GUEST IS CHOKING

To help a guest that is choking, follow the Heimlich Maneuver for choking (from the Heimlich Institute):

A choking victim can't speak or breathe and needs your help immediately. Follow these steps to help a choking victim:

1. From behind, **wrap your arms around the victim's waist**.
2. Make a fist and **place the thumb side of your fist against the victim's upper abdomen**, below the ribcage and above the navel.
3. Grasp your fist with your other hand **and press into their upper abdomen with a quick upward thrust**. Do not squeeze the ribcage; confine the force of the thrust to your hands.
4. **Repeat** until object is expelled.

In case you might forget, the number for 9-1-1 is 911.

A GUEST IS HAVING A HEART ATTACK

From the American Heart Association, these are signs that can mean a heart attack is happening:

1. **Chest discomfort**. Most heart attacks involve discomfort in the center of the chest that lasts more than a few minutes, or that goes away and comes back. It can feel like uncomfortable pressure, squeezing, fullness or pain.
2. **Discomfort in other areas of the upper body**. Symptoms can include pain or discomfort in one or both arms, the back, neck, jaw or stomach.
3. **Shortness of breath**. May occur with or without chest discomfort.
4. Other signs: these may include breaking out in a **cold sweat**, **nausea** or **lightheadedness**.

If you or someone with you has chest discomfort, especially with one or more of the other signs, don't wait longer than a few minutes (no more than 5) before calling for help. Call 9-1-1, or get to a hospital right away.

Calling 9-1-1 is almost always the fastest way to get lifesaving treatment. Emergency medical services staff can begin treatment when they arrive, up to an hour sooner than if someone gets to the hospital by car. The staff is also trained to revive someone whose heart has stopped. You'll also get treated faster in the hospital if you come by ambulance.

IF THE POLICE ARRIVE

Sometimes the party becomes too noisy, driveways or reserved parking spots are blocked, or your neighbors are just far too uptight, and the police show up at your doorstep during your party. The first thing to try to remember is to talk to them just outside of your home with the front door closed. If you feel too inebriated to talk as clearly as you would like to the police, ask a friend to accompany you for this. Be polite and respectful when talking to them.

The police can only come into your home without your permission if they have a warrant to do so, there is an emergency, or they are in "hot pursuit." This last item is important to note, because if you or a drunken guest goes outside and disregards an officer's reasonable request and then turns back into the party, they can pursue. Having the door closed will help to keep the police from finding an excuse to declare that it's an emergency situation. They might ask to come into your home, but you do not have to let them in. State clearly, but pleasantly enough that everyone is fine, you don't need their assistance, and that they can't come in, if you don't want them. This is an especially good idea if there is something at your event that they might find problem with.

If the police ask, and you choose not to let them in, they may want to ask you questions. Answer their questions nicely without replying to any questions that seem incriminating. An incorrect answer will give them a reason to come into your home. If you do happen to receive a ticket for some violation, do not argue to vehemently, as it could get you arrested. Using the phrases "yes, sir" and "no, sir" can help a great deal.

Step 7 – After the Event

The last of the guests have left, and the party is finally over, now you've got to clean. There are things that *1)* are wise **to do before going to bed**; and *2)* things that **can wait until the next day**.

1) Some things **to do before you turn in for the night**:

- **Blow out the candles**.
- **Empty the ice chests** or move them outside so that there is not a problem with your floors from leakage or condensation.
- Take care of the **perishable food items**, either wrap it up and store it in the refrigerator or freezer for future use, or throw it out. Some food items can create some unpleasant aromas the next day if left unattended in your home.
- Make sure the **oven** has been turned **off**.
- Make sure that the **doors** and windows **are locked**.
- If you have used the **fireplace**, make sure that the fire has died down and the vents have been shuttered.

2) Some things to do that can wait until the **next morning** or next day:

- **After the party**, it's a good idea to **get some fresh air in your place** – Don't mind the outside weather, at least for a short while, and open some of your windows when you are cleaning after your party. The fresh air is a huge help in removing those unpleasant post-party odors.
- Finish **cleaning up**. Run the dishwasher. Take out the trash. Sweep. Be sure to look in nooks and crannies where food items might have fallen, and which might become malodorous in the coming days and weeks.
- Remember to **launder any towels**, napkins, etc. that were used.
- Check your yard and any other areas where your guests may have left trash.
- Process and distribute the **photos**.
- Apologize to the **neighbors**, if necessary.
- **Return** any **borrowed** and **rented items**. Borrowed items too often take a while to get back to their owners.

JUDGING THE SUCCESS OF YOUR EVENT

How do you know if your event has been a success, and does it really matter? It doesn't. If it didn't go as well as you would have liked, don't get discouraged from entertaining in the future. Not every party can be a complete success, much less perfect. For example, if it was a large or expensive soiree that you hosted, try the next time on a smaller and less elaborate scale. Practice helps, and it should be fun, too.

The most important thing to do after the party, after cleaning up and the other tasks outlined in the previous section, is that **you should be sure to learn from the event**. What went well? What didn't go well? Doing this you can avoid those pitfalls, and make your next event even better, and less stressful to plan. Don't overanalyze, or become too critical (unless things went very poorly). Though you want to learn from your recent event, you don't want to ruin the memory of it, and then possibly pull the trigger more slowly in the future when it comes time to think about entertaining again.

PARTY MISTAKES (AND HOW TO RECTIFY THESE)

Some common mistakes and how to avoid these for your next event include the following.

- **Attendance was far less than expected** – Some things that you can do are sending the invitations earlier; avoid potential conflicts when scheduling your event; and re-confirm with guests in the week leading up to the event. Next time, you might also want to more actively engage one of the people you know to be a social leader and possibly even ask them to host the event along with you.
- You **ran out of alcoholic beverages** – Review our suggestions on the provisioning alcohol in the chapter "Liquor for Your Event" on pages 82 to 89. Try to understand why your guests were thirstier than you hoped. Purchase more for a similar event next time. Also, identify the drinks that were preferred by your guests and take that into account when hosting future events.
- The **party ended earlier** than you had hoped – Try to understand why the guests left early: there was another event; it was a school night; they had to relieve the babysitter; you ran out of alcohol; or, it simply was not as enjoyable to them as it should have been. Then, rectify the problem for future events, or be content with typically short events.
- For singles who **didn't make desired progress with the opposite sex** – Try to be more attractive, more interesting, and wealthier in the future....
- **Guests made a mess** – Did you have enough easy-to-find trash cans? Were the trash cans emptied soon after they were filled? Are your friends slobs?

Part II – Background

These include topics related to entertaining that are good to know, information about specific types of events, and food and drink recipes that you might actually want to employ for a party.

Dinner Parties

When hosting a dinner party, your reputation (or lack thereof) as a cook might precede you, and guests might have fairly low expectations. This can be a good thing, and a great opportunity for you, noting this, to relax and prepare the meal with some confidence, as the bar has been set fairly low. If you provide something that is mostly palatable, most guests will enjoy it. Or, if you have a great reputation as a cook, your friends will be greatly anticipating your meal. In addition to possibly not expecting that much, they will certainly laud the effort regardless of the result, it's free food, after all, and the success of a dinner party really depends upon how much fun the guests have, not that they were served a gourmet meal. But, keep in mind that, while very enjoyable, hosting a dinner party can be a lot of work.

Necessary Tasks for Most Dinner Parties

Dinner parties are a special category since there is more to do, and the event is centered around the meal, typically the entrée. Dinner parties require some additional activities, which seems obvious enough, but might take some forethought. These general activities are: *1) devising the menu*; *2) shopping and cooking*; *3) setting the table*; and *4) seating guests*.

1) Devising the Menu

When choosing the menu for your dinner party, **you should throw your diet plans away**. It's not a good idea to impose those restrictions on your guests. In most cases your guests will be planning to take the evening off from their diets if they are planning to attend. Though you want to please your guests, planning a menu around the diet of one or two guests is not the way to do it, either, as the rest of the table will invariably be disappointed in the meal. It is also important to note that full-flavored and fatty foods are the most enjoyable.

Though you should ignore the dieting plans of you and your guests, what about religious restrictions of your guests? If you know that you will be hosting a guest or two who follows kosher dietary laws, or is a practicing Muslim, or pregnant, it might be wise to avoid pork or shellfish. For

Hindus, beef should probably be off limits. And, then there are the vegetarians. These are relatively easy to plan around ahead of time since there is a wide array of dishes to prepare that are not pork, beef or shellfish.

When devising the menu, it's a good idea to have hors d'ouevre or *antipasti* ready for your guests when they arrive. Many of these can be purchased. Cheese, olives and cured meats are ideally suited for this purpose. Giving your guests something to munch on while enjoying a drink will make them more social and amendable to waiting for the dinner. For the dinner, you might want to start with a soup or salad before proceeding to the entrée and sides. **Whatever you can make or mostly prepare beforehand will help** you a great deal getting everything ready on time, and allowing you to enjoy the party more. If you lack confidence in the kitchen, the more you can do beforehand, the more relaxed you can be. Find recipes that don't seem overly difficult for you, and practice, if possible. Slowly cooked dishes make for great entrées for dinner parties. Conversely, if you are good at the grill, quickly cooked items from the grill also work well. If you plan to grill, to keep the party going without a lull it's a very good idea to have a co-host or friend help in the matter. Sides that can be assembled beforehand and then cooked, or just heated are similarly useful.

For a dinner party it's often a good idea to serve dessert, coffee and an after dinner drink. Neither the dessert nor the after-dinner drink has to be elaborate. Port or a good whiskey for the latter will usually suffice for most guests. The after dinner drink might follow the theme of the dinner. For example, if the food is Italian-American, you might serve sambuca or *limoncello*; if it's Indian, you might want to serve scotch (really).

> **F**or an additional special or whimsical touch, especially for an elaborate meal, you might be interested in **creating printed menus** for your dinner party. This can easily be done with a word processing program and some high quality paper.

2) Shopping and Cooking

It is a good idea to begin these activities with plenty of time to spare.

3) Setting the Table

Knowing how to set the table in proper, or standard, fashion will give your guests the impression that you know what you are doing in terms of entertaining. And, it's a good idea to be able to set the table properly, at least when entertaining your boss and other people you might be trying to impress. You will only need to do this for a seated dinner party, i.e. not a buffet. Below and on the next page are generalized examples for both a basic and a more elaborate place setting.

BASIC PLACE SETTING

This is the type of place setting that can work for most dinner parties. The utensils in the foreground in this example of a simple place setting should be obvious; the fork, knife and spoon used for the main course. In the back are the fork and spoon for dessert. The larger glass is for water and the smaller one is for wine.

For any kind of place setting, the guidelines for selecting your utensils is to work from the outside in, with a different utensil or pair of utensils (one from each side) for each course. This is good to know, because as the host, guests will usually follow your lead. You can use this when dining in public, too. Some other tips in setting the table:

- **Cloth napkins** are preferable over paper napkins. In addition to being clean, the cloth napkins do not need to be ironed, just folded. If you do not have cloth napkins, high quality, thick paper napkins are a fairly good substitute for many occasions.
- It's a good idea to have **a pitcher of water** on or near the table.
- Have the **additional wine**, beer, etc. quickly **accessible**.
- Putting **condiments** (ketchup, butter, mustard, *sriracha*, etc.) **into small containers** or plates makes for a more formal and attractive setting. Remember to have utensils for dispensing each.
- Not just for condiments, but **every platter or bowl of food should have its own serving utensil**.

- You don't want to put out any utensil that is not going to be used.
- You might also want to **bring out the items for dessert and coffee just before it comes time for them**. This is a good idea with a cluttered table.

MORE ELABORATE PLACE SETTING

In this example of a more elaborate place setting above, the utensils on the left side of the plate are the salad fork, dinner fork and dessert fork. To the right of the plate are the dessert spoon and the knife for both salad and main course. The smaller plate is for bread, and the small knife above the dinner plate is the butter knife. The larger glass is for water and the smaller one is for wine.

4) Seating the Guests

When hosting a dinner party for friends, you do not need to worry about seating arrangements. And, they might think that you are somewhat pretentious if you try to seat them. On the other hand, in the cases where most guests do not know each other, providing some aid in seating is a good idea for a livelier gathering.

As at dinner parties, assigning seats to your guests is usually not necessary in most other informal social events. Seats are not even provided in many settings. There certainly is no need for it while meeting for drinks at a bar, a large evening party or the like. But, for some events, seating assignments can be a necessary hassle in certain situations to provide a more enjoyable atmosphere. The need to seat guests in some organized manner can especially arise in the following types of events: formal dinner parties; group dinners at restaurants; and rehearsal dinners.

Some tips on seating your guests for a small formal dinner party **when guests do not know others** are shown below. Again, these are just suggestions, and this is not something worth fretting about too much.

- **If a couple is newlywed or seemingly nervous**, it's probably a good idea to **seat them next to, or across from, each other**.
- For **singles with a date, it is a good idea to seat them together**, especially if the date does not know anyone.
- For **unattached singles, try to seat them next to someone that they might** possibly want to meet, or someone with whom they are comfortable.
- **Alternate** men and women, if possible.
- Seat **handicapped** or grossly obese people **at the corner**. This provides for easier access and more room for them.
- **Seat people together** who might have **common interests**.
- **Intersperse quiet** and **boisterous** guests.
- **24" of table width** per guest is a good rule-of-thumb to ensure enough space for everyone.

You can either direct the seating orally, or for a more formal touch, you can inscribe or type up place cards. The latter has the added benefit of being something that can be done beforehand, and it communicates your intent quite clearly.

If a guest or two is late in arriving, don't hold up the dinner too long. This could inconvenience the other guests. Wait for a short time, if possible, depending on your food, and begin without the late arrivals. Once they do show up, greet them politely, get them seated and served.

SOME SERVING SUGGESTIONS AT A TABLE

You don't have to think too hard about these, but these could help:

- As a host, **you will probably need to get things started**, as your guests will be likely waiting for you to do so.
- Try to notice when your guests might need their **drinks replenished**.
- **Try <u>not</u> to accept too much help when clearing**, as nearly all of the guests at a table might clear it themselves and leave the table empty of people.
- When serving dinner at a table, if you can remember to do so, **serve from the left**, and then **clean from the right**.

Guests that are very hungry or whose senses have been dulled by a fair amount of alcohol **will be less discriminating** when it comes to the food's quality. So, if you are wary of the outcome of your cooking, and can get away with it time-wise, you might want to have your guests wait for a while before serving the main dishes.

SOME SUGGESTIONS FOR BUFFET SERVICE

When thinking of buffet service for a party where you are providing the food, don't think that you have to compete with the copious, and often beautiful, spreads set out for Sunday brunch at expensive hotel restaurants. But, it's a good idea to note that people first taste with their eyes. So, even if you just have chips and dips, a tray of sandwiches, some deviled eggs and not much more, you can arrange this bounty so that it looks very appealing.

Below are some suggestions for setting up the buffet service:

- The first thing to do is **arrange the food on each platter** evenly and with some kind of consistent spacing and style (if it's hot food in a chafing dish, don't worry about this). A couple examples might be in simple rows or in a circle depending on the amount of items and the size of the serving platters. But, be creative and have fun with it.
- Another thing to do is **garnish the serving trays** with parsley, small peppers or cherry tomatoes. After all of the food has been artfully arranged on the serving trays, you can worry about dressing the table.

Easy garnishing ideas for a serving platter, not necessarily at the buffet:
- **Parsley** Bunches – The curly, not very tasty kind works well for this.
- **Sprigs of Fresh Herbs** – Basil, fennel, Italian parsley, tarragon, thyme, etc.
- **Lemons and Limes** – Sliced or whole.
- **Small Peppers** – Used whole.
- **Bell Peppers** – Hollowed and seeded then used as dip containers

- A nice and easy way to have an attractive buffet setting is by **creating various levels for presenting the trays** by placing a box or a stack of books on the table. With several trays you might want to create more than one level on the table or tables then cover each with a tablecloth.
- For quick, easy and effective decorations that go a long way, use **candles**, **flowers**, pieces or bowls of **fruit**, **wine bottles**, and even **dried leaves** and branches on the table. You can be fun and creative with this.
- **Make sure decorations aren't in the way** of the food otherwise the decorations will suffer at the hands of your hungry guests (if not the plastic food).

- Make sure that the **starting point of the buffet is obvious**. This is only problematic with larger spreads.
- With over 75 guests or so, setting up the buffet so that it can be **accessed from both sides** of the table might be a good idea.
- Place the items in a **logical and easy-to-reach format.** Salads, proteins and sides, then desserts; chips by the dips; meats by the bread and condiments, etc.
- At the starting point **place the plates along with the utensils**.

Here are some more practical tips for the buffet service:

- If possible and seemingly beneficial, have **the salad and / or soup served while seated before** the beginning the buffet service. This allows the lines at the buffet to be much more manageable since those served first with the salad or soup will be in the first group to attend to the chafing dishes in the buffet spread.
- If a very large group, you might need to **restock the food periodically**, and so, should keep on eye on it during the serving frenzy.
- As host, **make sure that you eat last** or there is definitely enough food for all of your guests before eating.
- Especially if it's a larger group, or a large buffet, be sure to **clean the serving area every now and then**.
- Be sure to **have a noticeable spot where guests can deposit their empty plates**. Otherwise, the plates are like to gather in a place that will be very much in the way, and become a distraction.

WINE FOR YOUR DINNER PARTY

Wine complements most types of food, helps to create a festive atmosphere, is expected for dinner parties, and so, is nearly requisite to purchase when hosting a dinner party. But, what type of wine might work best for what you are cooking? Matching food and wine can be difficult, especially given the wide array of cuisines and wines. After all, people train for years to understand how to do it properly, and there are numerous books on the subject. But, you should not worry too much about it for your dinner party. **The most important consideration is to drink what you like.** There is method to the madness of wine and food pairings, and a good wine and food match can enhance the enjoyment of both, but drinking what you like is a good fallback, or even starting point.

If you feel you need help picking the wine for your dinner party, a good suggestion is simply to ask a knowledgeable person at your local wine store. They are usually quite able and willing to help. If you are planning to go it alone, there are some factors that you should consider which can help a great deal. These are listed in order of importance below. For nearly all of these guidelines, you should take note of the sauce of the entrée, not just the underlying meat, chicken, seafood or other protein, as the sauce sets the tone for the dish. (*The factors underlined are shown in the hopefully informative table on the next page.*)

- **Weight** – Balancing the weight of the wine with that of the food, so that neither overwhelms the other, is probably the most important consideration, i.e. **light wines with light food, heavy wines with heavy foods.** Examples are a hearty red wine with a beef stew, and crisp light wine with a sautéed fish filet. A general rule of thumb is that heavy wines contain 13.5% alcohol and higher; light wines are 12% and lower.

- **Intensity of Flavor** – An **intensely-flavored light wine can provide a contrast** with rich and fatty foods, **or it can complement** highly flavored, but lighter fare such as many Thai or Japanese dishes. Examples are a Riesling, especially Spätlese or Auslese, with *sauerbraten* or roast duck, and Sauvignon Blanc with jambalaya.

- **Acidity** – The **acidity in the dish**, which is present courtesy of citrus juice, some other fruits, and vinegar in the cooking, **should be matched by a similar level of acidity in the wine.** Acidity is most prevalent in white grapes such as Riesling, Sauvignon Blanc and Chenin Blanc, grapes that are grown in cooler climates and wines that are not aged significantly in oak. Some lighter-bodied, young red wines also have decent acidity.

- **Saltiness** – **Salty dishes can pair well with sweet or fruity wines.** A classic example of the salt and sweet match is *prosciutto* and melon. On the other hand, the salt enhances the bitterness that is present in the tannins of most red wines.

- **Sweetness** – The **sweetness in the food should be matched by the sweetness in the wine.** Wines can be even sweeter than food and still be complementary. Conversely, comparatively dry white wines can clash with sweet foods.

- **Tannins** – Present to varying degrees in all red wines, **red meat provides a match**, as the substantial texture of the food can provide a partner that enhances the taste of the wine. Many high quality red wines can taste overly dry or austere without food, and only become complex and very enjoyable with it. Tannic wines work poorly with food with high levels of acidity, salt, and sweet and spicy dishes.

Very General Wine Characteristics – Whites then Reds (excluding dessert wines)

Weight	Flavor	Acidity	Tannins	Types of Wines
Light	Light	High	None	Pinot Grigio, Riesling Kabinett, Sancerre, Pouilly-Fumé, Pouilly-Fuissé, Vinho Verde
Med.	Med.	Med.	None	Gewürztraminer, champagne, Sauvignon Blanc (NZ), Vouvray, Riesling Spätlese
Med.+	Med.+	Med.+	None	Sauvignon Blanc (US), Chablis, Chardonnay, white Burgundy, vintage champagne
Heavy	Intense	Low	None	New World Chardonnay
Med.	Med.	High	Light	Chianti, Valpolicella, Beaujolais
Med.+	Med.	Med.	Med.	Pinot Noir, Barbera, Chianti Classico, Merlot, Malbec, Rioja Reserva
Med.+	Intense	High	Med.	red Bordeaux, red Burgundy, Super Tuscan, Barolo, Barbaresco, Hermitage
Heavy	Intense	Low	High	Cabernet Sauvignon, Shiraz, Petite Syrah, Zinfandel, Amarone

Don't fret about it too much. As the well-regarded English wine writer Jancis Robinson once wrote to the effect that **there might be the perfect wine for each food, but life is too short to worry about it.**

Some **food-and-wine pairings that have been recommended** by wine experts:

Dish / Food	Types of Wines
Steak	Cabernet Sauvignon, red Bordeaux, Malbec, Zinfandel, Merlot
Roast lamb	Bordeaux (Médoc), Cabernet Sauvignon, Rioja Reserva
Bouillabaisse	white Rhône, Viogner, Provençal rosé
Oysters, raw	Chablis, champagne
Grilled shrimp	Sauvignon Blanc, Riesling
Sautéed Flounder	Chablis, Sauvignon Blanc
Salmon	Pinot Noir, Chardonnay
Tuna, rare	Pinot Noir, Zinfandel
Italian-American	Chianti, Barbera, Zinfandel
Indian food	Gewürztraminer, champagne
Indian tandoori	Beaujolais, Rioja, Nero D'Avola, Pinot Noir
Chinese food	Riesling (Germany), Viognier, Lugana (white from Veneto)
Thai food	Gewürztraminer, Sauvignon Blanc, Grüner Veltliner
Japanese food	Riesling (from Germany)
Tempuras	Chablis, Pouilly-Fuisse (these feature un-oaked Chardonnay)
Olives, tapenade	Fino sherry, Manzanilla sherry

Some other practical considerations with wine at a dinner party:

- Light- and medium-bodied red wines with low tannins and noticeable acidity are the most enjoyable, and **work the best, for the greatest variety of foods.** Commonly-found wines that fit this description include **Chianti, Barbera, Valpolicella, red Burgundy, red Rhône,** and **Pinot Noir,** which all can work well in this capacity.

- Wine might **not** be the beverage of choice for the meal if most of the dishes are very spicy, or very acidic, especially if these dishes are not traditionally paired with wine. For example, beer and Margaritas are usually served with Tex-Mex, especially with plenty of fresh jalapeño-laden *pico de gallo* and cilantro present.

- It's practical, and much easier, to not worry about having a separate wine for each course. Simply **serve one wine during the meal that goes well with the main dish**.

- Since wine is drunk as an aperitif, during the meal, and after dinner, we recommend **provision nearly a bottle of wine per person**. Again, you can always drink the excess bottles at a future date.

There are some wine-and-food pairings that will actually **diminish the enjoyment of both the wine and the food**. Some pairings to avoid below:

Type of Wine	Type of Food	Problem
Heavy, Tannic Reds	Spicy (Thai)	Tannins clash badly with the heat
Heavy, Tannic Reds	Acidic (Salads)	Tannins and acids contrast badly
Heavy, Tannic Reds	Salty (Chinese)	Salt enhances tannins' bitterness
Heavy, Tannic Reds	Light Fish Dishes	Fish can taste metallic with tannins
Oaky Chardonnay	Not Creamy	Not enough acidity in the wine
Light or Sweet Wines	Red Meat	Body or flavor contrasts too starkly

Save the tannic red wines such as the hearty Cabernets for robust dishes featuring red meat or a hard cheese, and drink the big, oaky New World Chardonnays alone.

There is more practical information about wine in the following sections: "Wine Tasting Parties" beginning on page 134; "Wine for Your Event" on page 65; "The Wine Ritual" on page 143; and the numerous Glossary entries about wine starting on page 269.

Chilling a wine quickly – Fill a bucket with ice and water and insert the bottle. This works much more quickly than placing the bottle in the fridge.

AFTER-DINNER DRINKS

A choice of one or two after-dinner drinks can help extend the conversation at the dinner table or in another room, especially if the wine has run out. Some suggestions are: brandy, including its upscale French versions, cognac and armagnac, port, Bual or Malmsey Madeira, scotch, amaretto, Bailey's Irish Cream, sambuca, Grand Marnier, B & B and Drambuie. If looking to provision port, as we mention elsewhere, 10-year tawny port is usually the best value for the price. Tawny port also has the advantage that it can last much longer after it has been opened than vintage and late-bottled vintage port, both of which should be consumed within a month.

BEFORE-DINNER DRINKS

Since after-dinner drinks are mentioned, a few words should be spent on before-dinner drinks, or aperitifs. Though wine and beer usually do the trick for most dinner parties, you might be interested in serving a special drink before the meal. These aperitifs are typically light alcoholic drinks that are meant to stimulate the appetite. Champagne and *fino* sherry are classic examples. Prosecco, Kirs, and bottled beverages made specifically for the task such as Dubonnet, Lillet and Campari are other popular choices.

Cigars – Cigars might be welcome at a dinner party after a heavy and satisfying meal, even for the very casual cigar smoker. So, as a host you might want to have a few cigars on hand. For these infrequent cigar smokers, it's best to purchase cigars that are flavorful, but mild, and, overall, easy to smoke. Generally, **the lighter the color of the cigar, the more mild the taste**. Dominican tobacco is typically the mildest. The bigger the ring gauge (this is the measure of the diameter in increments of $\frac{1}{64}$ of an inch) the cooler the cigar will burn. Long and thin cigars will burn quickly, and will become bitter if not smoked at a fairly rapid clip. So, a recommendation for cigars for casual smokers is a **Dominican Robusto with a natural wrapper**. This cigar is about 4" to 5" long and thick enough to smoke coolly. In case your guests need reminding, with cigars, the smoke is not supposed to be inhaled as it is with cigarettes.

VINTNER-STYLE OR OENOPHILE DINNERS

You might want to take a cue from the vintner dinners that are held at numerous restaurants in which a different wine is paired with each course. This will take more of an effort than a typical dinner party, and you might need some help from your local wine store to match the courses, but it can be enjoyable, especially if your guests are as keen on wine as you. In addition to the information in the previous section above, it's also a good idea to offer the wines in a progression from lightest to heaviest. An example might be starting with a *fino* sherry to match with olives and prosciutto, a Pinot Gris for the soup or salad, a Beaujolais for a pasta dish, a Côtes du Rhône-Villages for a hearty meat dish, and then a tawny port for the dessert or cheese course. Another wishful example is starting with a brut sparkling wine with hors d'oeuvre, a Chardonnay with a stuffed crab appetizer, Pinot Noir with gumbo or turtle soup, and a Cabernet Sauvignon with beef tenderloin. A third begins with tuna carpaccio with Sauvignon Blanc, Chardonnay with a lobster tail braised in butter, grilled quail in a rich, truffle-laced gravy paired with a Pinot Noir, and a cheese plate filled with artisanal cheese, almonds and fruit served with a Syrah. The array of combinations is nearly endless. You can look to the nicer local restaurants for examples.

DINNER CLUBS

If you find that you enjoy throwing and attending dinner parties, you might want to try to form a dinner club with like-minded friends. With these, each member or member couple takes turns hosting the dinner party. Culinary expertise is not a requirement, just a desire to entertain, and to make an effort. There are a number of ways to run a dinner club such as having the hosts prepare all the food for the event. Or, since hosting an entire dinner party can be onerous, you might want to have the hosts prepare just the entrée, and have the other guests responsible for the appetizers, dessert and drinks, respectively.

WINE TASTING PARTIES

The less that you know about wine, the more reason there is to hold a wine tasting event, or events, to learn more.

ACCESSORIES FOR THE WINE TASTING

The basics for what you should have for any type of wine tasting are:

- **Crackers** or **Bread** – These help to cleanse the palate between wines.
- **Pitchers** – For water, used for cleaning glasses and drinking. You might also want to use a separate pitcher or pitchers for pouring the wines. For red wines, there is an additional benefit that the wines will aerate, at least slightly. For beer tastings, a pitcher for the beer to be tasted is a near necessity.
- **Spit Bucket** – Not really for spit, but for your guests to pour unfinished wine before refilling the glass with the next wine. An inexpensive plastic pail can do the trick.
- **Wine Glasses** – Simple, clear glasses work the best. You can find them very cheaply at IKEA, Target or a restaurant supply store.

Some additional items that you might consider are:

- **Appetizers** – Food is always a good idea with alcohol.
- **Cheese** – See the chapter beginning on page 163 for more information.
- **Paper Bags** or **Wrapping** – To obscure the wine labels when conducting a blind tasting.
- **Pens & Paper** – For your guests to jot down tasting notes. It could happen; more so early in the tasting. There are templates for tasting sheets in the References section on pages 370 and 371.
- **Wine Charms** – These help limit the number of glasses necessary, and can add a nice touch for your event. These are also quite inexpensive.

HOW TO CONDUCT A WINE TASTING

There are many different ways to conduct a fun wine tasting. Generally, there are: *1) the easy way; 2) a guided tasting; 3) a blind tasting;* and *4) a tasting with an expert*. One suggestion, no matter what type of tasting, is that if you are drinking a wide range of styles is **first arrange to taste the wines from the lightest-bodied to the heaviest. Second, from driest to sweetest.** For example, Pinot Grigio, Sauvignon Blanc, Chardonnay for white wines, and generally Pinot Noir, Merlot, Shiraz and Cabernet Sauvignon for reds.

Weight (or body) of popular wines from lightest to heaviest, generally –
Whites – Vinho Verde, Verdicchio, Orvieto, Soave, white Bordeaux, Pinot Grigio, Sauvignon Blanc (NZ), Sauvignon Blanc (California), Chablis, Kabinett, Gewürztraminer, Chardonnay, Auslese, Sauternes
Reds – Bardolino, Beaujolais Nouveau, Chianti, Beaujolais, Valpolicella, Pinot Noir, Barbera, Rioja, Rhône, Merlot, Barberesco, Barolo, Zinfandel, Shiraz, Cabernet Sauvignon, Amarone

1) The Easy Way – The easiest, and often the most fun, way to host an event centered around wine is simply to choose a wine style, and ask that your guests bring a bottle in that style. These could be a varietal such as Pinot Noir, Chardonnay, etc., a region like Bordeaux, Chilean Cabernet Sauvignon, or a theme like, "red wines under $12," or "summer whites." When the guests and the bottles arrive, simply open them, and people can serve themselves at their leisure. As a host, there is not much else left to do other than watch out for wine spills. With these parties, guests seem to get into the mood quite quickly, and much of the fuss and pretense associated with wine is removed. Encourage your guests to discuss the wines.

2) Guided Tasting – This involves having someone, usually you the host, leading a structured wine tasting. You certainly do not have to be a wine expert to lead one of these, though some rudimentary wine knowledge is necessary. You simply need to taste the wines in a proper order, from lightest to most full-bodied. If you have a decent wine store in nearby, a staff member will certainly help you pick out the wines and help to create a proper tasting structure. It is fairly easy. If you don't feel that you are up to the task, ask a more informed person to lead it. This **does not have to be done in lecture format**. Often, it's much easier to have the person leading the talk to briefly discuss each wine as it is being poured for an individual or small group. If someone wants to learn more about the wine, they can do so. In this way those that want to learn about the wines can, and those that just want to drink and socialize with others can do that, too, relatively unperturbed.

3) Blind Tasting – This takes a good deal more effort than the relatively easy tasting (and drinking) described above. But, it can be more rewarding for the serious wine drinker. You will need to select wines in the same general category (varietal, style or region), conceal the identities of the wines with brown paper bags or the like, and have at least one person to run the tasting. Be sure to have the bags numbered, and the wines properly cataloged. This can be a fun way to mix some value wines, popular moderately-priced wines, and high-end, obscure, or boutique wines. This type of tasting is usually easier to conduct on a smaller setting. A couple additional variations are:

- You can ask your **guests to try to guess each wine** and make this a friendly competition.
- Suited for more serious wine drinkers, you can pour the wines one at a time and get your **tasters to name as many of the key characteristics as possible** (country, region, major varietal, vintage and producer).

It is very difficult to guess a wine in a blind tasting. Wine writer Jancis Robinson relates that **trained tasters performed very poorly when they were asked to identify major varietals** in a blind format for a university study. Less than 40% could correctly identify Cabernet Sauvignon and less than 15% for Merlot.

4) Guided Tasting with an Expert – With this type of tasting you will need to engage a representative from a company that distributes wine, or a knowledgeable staff member at a local wine store, or a very informed friend. You will be surprised how receptive a wine distributor or wine importer will be for this, especially if you can get a decent-sized group, as it is a marketing opportunity for their wines. This person can discuss each wine that is being tasted, and it can make for a much more informative experience. Depending upon the liquor laws of your area, and more so the willingness of the wine importer, distributor or representative, this person's company might provide the wine for the tasting in the interest of marketing the wines.

A couple dimensions that you might want to consider adding to any of the types of tastings described above are a vertical tasting, or a horizontal tasting. In a **vertical tasting,** different vintages of the same wine are tasted. These should be wines that are meant to last at least several years, which are invariably not cheap wines. For example, this might consist of several vintages of a great Cabernet Sauvignon such as Robert Mondavi Reserve Cabernet Sauvignon, or a top Bordeaux such as Chateau Haut-Brion or Chateau Ausone. This is usually the domain of the aficionado or a restaurant or wine store, as it can be difficult, not to mention expensive to assemble these wines. In what is termed a **horizontal tasting,** different wines from the same vintage (and same region or style) are tasted in succession, such as Barolos from the great year of 1999. As with the vertical tasting, this can get pricey, but it doesn't have to be. A horizontal tasting can be done affordably with enjoyable, but moderately-priced wines such as Oregon Pinot Noirs, California Zinfandels or Chardonnays from a recently released vintage.

A wine with a comparatively **high alcohol content** will stand out in a **blind wine tasting**. Even if it's not the best wine in the lineup, it will have a good chance of being selected as the favorite.

HOW TO TASTE WINE

It's easy to drink, though there are some things to remember to do when you want to fully appreciate the nuances of a wine:

1. Hold the glass by the stem, not the bowl. **Why?** Holding by the stem will allow you to properly look at the wine in the glass to examine its appearance including the color and clarity. By not cradling the bowl you will keep the wine at the proper temperature.
2. Swirl the wine in the glass. (This is much easier to do with the base on a flat surface.) **Why?** This releases the wine's aroma.
3. Sniff the wine. (It's not necessary to stick your entire nose in the glass.) **Why?** Aromas are an important component to the wine.
4. Take a decent-sized sip of wine. Swirl it around your mouth. Open your mouth slightly and take a breath over your tongue, which is actually difficult to do without drooling wine. **Why?** Swirling the wine will allow you to experience more of the wine's characteristics. Taking a breath with wine in your mouth allows you to simultaneously taste and smell the wine. Doing these will allow you to more fully taste the flavors and nuances of the wine.
5. Spit the wine into the spit bucket, if you are sampling a number of wines, otherwise, this is not recommended. **Why?** To not get too drunk.

HOSTING A DINNER EVENT AT A RESTAURANT

Sometimes, for business, you are required to entertain at a restaurant. And, you might also want to entertain at a restaurant for purely social reasons. For many of these, you will want to choose a restaurant where the food is important (or just expensive) to denote some level of seriousness for a business meeting, or for enjoyment, to note an important social occasion.

Restaurants are more formal, and **offer a more serious place to conduct business with clients**. The level of expectation in terms of service and décor are generally much higher for business entertaining, especially when you might want to impress a client or customer. **Restaurants are also great for strictly social purposes** such as gathering a group of friends to enjoy good food and conviviality. At a restaurant, it can be pleasant and easy. You give up control for creating and serving the food, so the stress level is typically lower at a restaurant than at home (at least until the bill arrives).

SETTING UP THE EVENT AT A RESTAURANT

Some things that need to be done concerning arranging a dinner event at a restaurant are: *1) settling the basics; 2) selecting the restaurant; 3)* selecting the *type of service; 4) choosing the menu; 5)* setting up *drinks*; and *6) settling the bill*. When talking with the restaurant manager, be sure to understand that the restaurant will have the proper utensils, chairs and the like, and you usually shouldn't recommend recipes, as does actually occur.

1) Settling the Basics – These are what you need to consider first.

- Establish the **Budget** or general price per guest – If you decide to provide alcohol, understand that it will be a substantial portion of the budget (typically, 30 to 40%).
- Choose the **Date**.
- Choose the **Time and Function** – Lunch, Dinner, Brunch, etc.
- Choose the **Theme**, if desired.

2) Selecting the Restaurant – The first step in selecting a restaurant is settling the basics above, which will have to be satisfied for your event. Also, though you might be anxious and feel a need to confirm, the restaurant in question will have tables, chairs, dishware, glassware, etc.

- Does it fit in your **budget**?
- Is the **restaurant experienced** in hosting these types of events? In this regard you might want to be wary of recently opened restaurants.

- Do you need **privacy**? If so, the restaurant will have to have **a suitably-sized private room**.
- Is it the **right food** for the type of event? If the food quality, or type of food, is important, select a restaurant that you have confidence in from past experience.
- Have you **been to this restaurant before**? Or, **does it come highly recommended** for hosting your event?
- Does it have a **central location**, or one that is easily accessible for your guests? If guests are driving, is **parking adequate**?
- Is there a **separate sound system**?
- Is there the **ability to conduct a presentation**, if necessary?
- If interested in it, ask for the **restaurant's recommended florist** (for centerpieces and the like). If the restaurant does not have a source for flowers, ask if the florist you obtain can contact them to make the proper arrangements.

3) Type of Service – Some restaurants can aptly serve large groups with table service (where the dishes are brought to each person by a waiter), others cannot, and a buffet is preferable. If you have a large group, it is a good idea to ask the restaurant what type of service they recommend based on your needs. Below are some suggestions to help choose between the two with the emphasis on the quality of food.

When to choose table service:

- If there will be **less than 40 people** or so.
- If there will be a **presentation**.
- If the **food is a prime attraction**.
- If more **formality** is desired, as in most business situations.

When to choose a buffet:

- If there will be **more than 40 people** or so. It's our experience with groups of 40 or more that it's often difficult for most restaurants to provide very good food with table service. Kitchens can only handle a certain capacity, especially if it's serving only one or two types of entrées. We have experienced the proverbial rubber chicken dinners in large settings too many times. The same restaurant that will have difficulty with a large group in a traditional table service style can often prepare a much more flavorful meal buffet-style. Be sure to note that some foods, usually slow-cooked items, work much better than others when prepared beforehand and served from a chafing dish. The chef or banquet manager can guide you with this.

- When the **mixing of guests is paramount**.
- If the event is **casual**, or at least non-formal.

With groups numbering more than 15 to 20 receiving table service, we recommend that you ask the restaurant to bring entrées to the table when they are ready, rather than waiting for the all of the guests to be served at the same time. Kitchens can only prepare so many meals at one time, and serving each when ready will ensure that the dishes will taste much better than if they were sitting under heat lamps waiting for the other meals to be completed.

With buffet service, you might want to request salads and soups brought to the table. We like this because it reduces the mad rush to the buffet line while adding a slight bit more formality.

4) *Choosing the Menu* – Restaurants often like to have set menus with a group in a private dining room, in the belief that it facilitates service. Typically, this will consist of several appetizers to be shared, one soup or salad, a choice among several entrees, and maybe a choice among two or three desserts, plus coffee. Also, please don't try to provide any recipes to the chef, as the restaurant's kitchen will be mostly proficient, at least, in what they offer on a regular basis.

- **Appetizers**
- **Soups** and/or **Salads**
- **Entrées** – Especially for entrées remember that tastes vary, so it's wise to have a choice among three or so entrées. Though you should not necessarily provide a vegetarian option, ensure that the restaurant can meet that request, if necessary. Most will easily be able to accommodate for this. Below is a list of hot entrées and other dishes that seem to work especially well in **buffet settings**:

  - **Baked Pasta Dishes** – Lasagna, baked ziti, stuffed shells, etc.
  - **Casseroles** – Curries, *cassoulet*, paella; these refer to baked dishes that are cooked and served in the same dish
  - **Crab Cakes** – Especially when baked.
  - **Mashed Potatoes** – Always a good side.
  - **Meatballs** – Italian-style, Swedish, *keftedes*, etc.; all seem to do very well biding their time in chafing dishes before being eaten.
  - **Roast Beef** – An attended carving station is ideal, otherwise this will need to be sliced prior to display.
  - **Soups** – Hearty and flavorful soups such as gumbo can help reduce the reliance on a show-stopping entrée.

- **Stews** – Restaurants don't seem to serve many of these, though. Stewed or braised entrées found on restaurant and catering menus include *osso buco, beouf carbonade,* sauerbraten, *coq au vin,* and braised lamb shank.

- **Desserts** – Though sometimes overlooked with a buffet service, including dessert a very good idea.

5) *Drinks* – While alcoholic drinks might be offered because it is expected and possibly of little importance to your guests, these **will be a significant portion of the total cost**. If it might be of importance, aperitifs, wine, after-dinner drinks, and a specialty cocktail are some of the things that you might want to consider while planning your menu. You might also want to plan it around a special bottle of wine, for example.

- Consider providing **just beer and wine**, instead of a full bar. A full bar will greatly increase the final cost, especially at an evening event.
- **Select the wines** – An inexpensive red and white will usually suffice. The restaurant will help in this matter. Depending on the crowd, whose wine habits you might know, a ratio of two bottles of red to one of white is a safe estimate for most parties.
- Set a **limit on the amount of wine** – It's a good idea to limit the wine to be served. You can always order more upon your approval.
- **Include coffee and tea** – Most likely you will want to do this.

6) *Settling the Bill* – This might be the most important to you, as the host.

- Finalize the **desired price per guest**.
- **Gratuity** – This will usually be included by the restaurant. Be sure to ask about this. If gratuity is included, you will not need to tip above this unless you really want to.
- **Contract** – It might be wise to ask for one, for peace of mind at the very least, if the restaurant does not readily provide one. If it's a mom-and-pop type of establishment, and you desire a contract, you might want to create one yourself that both you and the restaurant can sign.

SETTING UP THE EVENT WITH YOUR GUESTS

If you are hosting a business dinner or are planning to treat your friends, this issue is moot. For social dinners where each person or couple is responsible for their share, here are some items to have covered before the event. Remember with large parties, restaurants rarely want to split the bill.

If they do, they will divide it evenly rather than trying to create a bill based on what each diner ordered.

- Determine if **non-drinkers** should pay as much as drinkers. It makes it easier, at least for the person running point for the bill, if everyone pays the same amount.
- What about **cocktails**? You can have a separate tab for cocktails, or have each person ordering them pay the waiter when served.
- If the restaurant has a **dress code**, be sure to communicate it to your guests beforehand.
- If you are the intermediary between the restaurant and guests, ask that the guests bring to the dinner the **proper amount in cash or a check**, so that you won't have to worry about the guests that have only brought credit cards.
- For a business event, be sure to **indicate that food will be served**. This should be obvious if the event is at a restaurant, but it helps to ensure that your guests, and potential clients or customers, know what to expect.

If a gratuity has been included in the bill for your group, as restaurants often do for parties of eight or more, should you tip any more? This can create some consternation, as you don't want to appear as a cheapskate by scribbling in zeroes in the tip section. Since this gratuity (or service charge) is typically 18%, above the average for normal service, do not feel compelled to tip any more unless you feel that the service has been exceptional.

Hosting an Event at a Restaurant

Some tips on being a successful host at a restaurant include:

- As the host, plan to **arrive early**. This is especially appropriate when hosting a business function with clients or customers.
- **Do not drink too much**, as obvious as this sounds.
- For a business dinner, especially, you might want to **give the waiter your credit card beforehand**, so that paying the bill is seamless and does not create an awkward pause.
- A tip for ensuring that the restaurant has served the correct number of bottles of wine is **to ask for the corks or the empty bottles** to be set aside for you. Otherwise, you might be surprised that the restaurant might have miscounted, seemingly always in their favor.
- If you as the host feel it's necessary to split the tab at the restaurant, you should **act as accountant** and be prepared to cover any deficits.

When setting up a social event, you certainly will have the enjoyment of your guests in mind, and you will hope to appease everyone. From our experience, unless the guests are all close friends who will be quick to overlook any foibles or minor mishaps, **someone will complain** if not entirely satisfied. A person might be in a bad mood during the event, be overly nitpicky, hold unrealistic expectations, or just be miserable. **Don't worry about it too much.** Set up the event the best that you can, for the majority of the guests. Understand that the restaurant is experienced in operating dinner events like yours, as they host them several times a week. Planning and organizing a social event is somewhat of a burden as it is, so don't let the inevitability of a couple of complaints or complainers worry you too much. It's wise to try to learn from the experience.

THE WINE RITUAL

Though less so now, in many "nice" restaurants in North America the presentation of wine has been accompanied with an aura of some formality and perceived ritual. Even if you are not a regular wine drinker, you should not be intimidated by the process. But, if you have ordered an unfamiliar wine, or don't like wine, ask someone else at the table to participate in the ritual instead. This might be the chance, in subtle fashion, to win points with your customer or client.

1. **The waiter will usually, or at least should bet, present the unopened wine bottle to the host at the table.** This is to ensure that you are receiving the wine that you ordered. That it should be unopened affirms that it is the correct wine, and that it has not been tampered with. Somewhat unscrupulous restaurants or waiters might pour a different (and invariably cheaper) wine than has been ordered, and it's difficult to send wine back once it has been consumed more than a few sips. Once the wine is presented, a simple acknowledgement is all that is necessary.

2. After that, **the waiter will open the wine, and then present the cork for inspection.** This is to ensure that the cork is in good condition. A cork that is crumbly, or is soaked all the way through, or nearly all the way through, can mean that the wine is "corked," or suffering from oxidation that will cause an off-taste in the wine. If the cork looks to have a fungus, there is another problem, and quite probably the wine will be bad. You don't have sniff the cork. The experienced oenophile might be able to detect mold in the cork, which will corrupt the wine, but you probably can't. Again a simple acknowledgement upon reception is fine, though if the cork looks bad, you should mention that.

3. After the cork ritual, **the waiter will pour a small amount of wine into your glass**.

4. Even if the cork looks bad, **swirl the wine in your glass** (which is much easier to do with the base of the glass on the table), **smell the wine**, as the aroma is a big part of the wine's quality. **Then take a small sip**

which you should drink slowly with a small breath of air. This might seem silly, but the swirling will help to get the wine in proper condition more quickly, and the small sip with a breath of air will allow you to taste the wine more accurately. It really does work. If the wine tastes fine, which in the vast majority of cases it will, tell the waiter it is fine, and it will then be poured for the rest of your party.

The Wine Spectator has written that up to 20% of wines may be somewhat tainted due to bad corks.

At restaurant events, especially non-seated affairs when guests are mingling throughout much of the time, **restaurants are notorious for having the wait staff fill guests' wine glasses when these become less than half-filled.** Since beers typically come as twelve ounce pours and mixed drinks are usually prepared individually at the bar, consumption of these beverages occurs at a more natural pace. But, wine lends itself easily to this hyped-up consumption. Doing this can greatly increase the amount of wine consumed, and your tab. Your guests can also become drunk fairly quickly, too. One way to short circuit the loss factor is to negotiate a price per bottle beforehand, and tell the restaurant not to pour wine until the glasses have only a sip or two left.

VERY BASIC ETIQUETTE

In addition to the very basics of chewing with your mouth closed and keeping your elbows off the table during dining, below is list of guidelines for dining etiquette that are common in North America, and are good to know when either a host or guest:

- With appetizers on toothpicks, after finishing, **do not deposit the toothpick back on the serving tray**.
- **Do not double dip**, at least in a public bowl of dip – Think Costanza.
- Your **water glass** is the one to **your right**.
- Your **bread plate** is to **your left**.
- **Cut enough butter** (with the butter knife if there) to be used for most of your bread then place that piece onto your bread plate.
- **Break the bread into bite-sized pieces** and butter each piece. Every single piece.
- Use the **utensils** from the **outside in**.
- If you **drop a utensil onto the floor, leave it**. Ask the waiter to bring you a replacement.
- When you have paused eating, **do not put the utensil on the tablecloth**. Put it on your plate so that the tablecloths will not get dirty.
- **Do not lift the soup bowl to your mouth** to drink the final drops, as tempting as it might be, unless you are in the confines of your own home

or don't care what others might think. But, there are exceptions depending on the cuisine; miso soup at a Japanese restaurant, for example.

- **Try <u>not</u> to make loud noises** (like slurping) when you eat.
- **Do <u>not</u> wear your napkin like a bib**. Wearing a bib is fine, for lobster, crabs and the like, when provided by the restaurant.
- If you need to **remove something from your teeth**, do so in the privacy of the **bathroom**.
- When leaving the table, **put your napkin on the table next to your plate**, not your chair. There is no need to refold it.
- When finished with your meal or course, **place your knife and fork together diagonally on your plate**. Doing this will let the wait staff know that you are done, and they can remove your plate and utensils.

These are just the basics. If really concerned, refer to a book on etiquette. Several suggestions are shown in the Resources section on page 359.

BUSINESS OR WORK-RELATED EVENTS

Sometimes the reason to entertain goes beyond your desire to have a good time, and you have to host an event for work. The steps to successfully host a work event are similar to those in planning any other social event, though more attention must be paid to several factors:

- When to **schedule** a business event.
- Choosing the **venue** to convey the proper level of importance.
- The potential need for **privacy** for a presentation, or a sales pitch.
- The need to **seat** your guests.

Then there is the company party, where the higher-ups feel the need to provide food, usually alcohol and sometimes activities under the guise of reward, team-building, or an excuse to show off their large homes. You might be involved with the planning of such an event.

WHEN TO SCHEDULE A BUSINESS EVENT

If possible, try to plan a business event during the week; Monday through Thursday evening, and Monday through Friday for lunchtime events. This applies for events with co-workers and customers. People do not want to take time away from their families and personal activities during the weekends, which is viewed as their time. An exception to this is a business event to which entire families are invited. Sunday afternoons seem to be better than Saturday afternoons, as fewer children's and family activities are planned on Sundays.

CHOOSING THE PROPER TYPE OF VENUE

When meeting with customers or clients, you will usually want to select a fine dining restaurant to convey the desired level of importance. Your customers or clients can be at least subtly swayed to what you are selling when you spend some money on them. And, it's not your money anyway. It's your company's. Conversely, if it can be construed that you are spending the client's money, a moderately-priced restaurant might not cause distress in them as might an expensive one.

THE POTENTIAL NEED FOR PRIVACY

If you are planning a presentation or need to conduct a discussion involving proprietary information, a private room is a must. If it's a more general meeting, it's still a good idea to have some privacy. So, you might want to ask the restaurant to arrange your table behind a partition or in a corner.

THE NEED TO SEAT YOUR GUESTS

If you are hosting the event for several people you will need to ensure that you, as the host, are sitting next to the most important person from the company you are hoping with whom to do business. Other than this fact, there is usually not a need to instruct your guests where to sit. Your customers will take care of themselves in this regard. If you are conducting a presentation with accompanying video, be sure that your customers can view it, which should be obvious enough.

SOME THINGS TO CONSIDER WHEN PLANNING THE COMPANY PARTY

The considerations for scheduling a company party are the same as outlined above. Some other considerations include the following:

- Try to make it easy for your co-workers to attend. There is a good chance that this event will be viewed as an obligation rather than a reward by many, and so, **try to make the event as enjoyable and undemanding as possible** on your co-workers.
- **Be sure to communicate clearly who is invited**: just the employee; spouses, too; or the entire family.
- When setting the time of the event during the week try to understand if the majority of your **co-workers will want to go home prior to the event, or head there straight from work**.
- For a site, try to **choose a central location** for most of your co-workers. Somewhere near the office is usually good, as everyone makes it to the office on a regular basis.
- **Try not to schedule a lengthy event**. Two or three hours are sufficient.
- If activities are to be involved, **try to choose activities that will be enjoyable** and easy to pick up for most.
- **If the entire family is invited be sure to have suitable activities for children**, if you know that children will be attending.
- If you are thinking about a pool party, be cognizant of the fact that many of **your co-workers might be skittish of appearing in a bathing suit** in front of their co-workers. If a pool must be included, maybe position it as a children's activity.
- Don't be stingy with the alcoholic beverages, but since there always seems to be at least one co-worker willing to over-indulge at a company party, **maybe just provision beer and wine**.

HOSTING AN EVENT AT A BAR

Why entertain at a bar in the first place? There are several reasons, if not already apparent, to plan an event in a nearby bar. Some of the better reasons are:

- You **don't have the room to entertain** as many people as you would like.
- You want to have **a lively atmosphere and setting**.
- You would rather **not** **have strangers** in your place.
- You want to provide **a central location** to ensure that more potential guests will show up.
- You don't want to worry about **setup or clean up**.
- You don't want the **cost burden of providing drinks and food** for everyone.

Of course, if it's just you and a few friends, and you don't need any special treatment from the bar, you don't need to approach the manager beforehand. But, for an event with a group that will be more than just a few friends, it's definitely in your best interest to pick a bar or restaurant that will not already be crowded during that time and day, notify the manager, and hopefully arrange some special treatment. The benefit of visiting a usually undercrowded bar is that your entire group will be able to mix and mingle, and the establishment will be more likely to work with you if you will be bringing business during a slow time. This will also give you an opportunity to ask for lower drink prices, complimentary appetizers or other food, or some other type of special treatment. Some questions that you might want to ask the bar's manager or owner:

- What can you do for us (in terms of **drink** and / or **food specials**) – It helps to have something in mind when you ask this question – $1 off drink prices, for example.
- Can you **extend the hours with happy hour prices for our group**?
- Can you provide us with **special drink prices** for certain drinks?
- Can you provide some **food**?
- May we play our own **music** (if really desired)?
- Can we **decorate** (if really desired)? If it is just a banner or some minimal decorations most bars will be fine with it.

There are a number of ways to set up your happy hour. Some options are:

- **Drink Tickets** – Each guest gets a ticket or several redeemable for drinks.
- **Cash Bar** – Everyone is responsible for paying for their own drinks.
- The **host purchases the first drink** or two.

- The **host purchases draft beer and house wine**. This will be appreciated by your guests, while helping to keep your costs reasonable.
- The **host purchases all** of the drinks. This can get expensive, of course. If you are going to do this it is best to set a time limit, such as free drinks until 9:00 PM.

Some **other venues** that can work for your event, in addition to a bar or restaurant:
- **Art Gallery** – You will certainly have to hire a bartender or bartending service, a caterer and probably security for this, though.
- **Bowling Alley** – More than just skinheads enjoy bowling.
- **Country Club** – A big benefit is that the staff at country clubs will be very experienced in handling large groups. If not a member, you might need to find a sponsor from that club.
- **Go Kart Track** – You will have to arrange this beforehand with the track, but this can make for a fun group outing.
- **Horse Track** – Many of these have private suites, which are great for entertaining.
- **Karaoke Club** – For anyone with pretensions of crooning, or as a group after a number of drinks, this can be a lot of fun.
- **Miniature Golf** – Taking over a golf course can be a lot of fun, especially when paired with plenty of beer.
- **Private Club** – Pretty much the same as the country club.
- **Public Park** – There is a good chance that you will have to make a reservation to ensure the spot you desire, and you will probably have to get a clearance from the municipality, at least regarding alcoholic consumption.
- **Sports Venues** – Getting a group together at a game can be a lot of fun, especially in a suite, which allows for the maximum amount of sociability. Many have group rates for seating outside of the suites.

If this is a work or sales event where a number of the guests will be from the company you are courting, purchasing most of their drinks, if not all, is a good idea. For this, when money is no object, usually meaning that you are not responsible for paying the bill, like for a company event, set up one tab for the party and be responsible (via the company) to pay for it. Using a company credit card is ideal for this.

Otherwise, most business events are similar to social happy hours. If you have a limited budget, a good way to proceed is to utilize drink tickets. For this you would give your guests a certain number of tickets that can each be redeemed for a drink. The establishment will certainly have something that can be used this purpose. One popular method, and the cheapest way for the host, is the cash bar. Yet another way is that the host can purchase the first drink for everyone, or have a limited tab that expires after a certain dollar amount, or a certain time. Then, after that, everyone will have to purchase their own drinks. But by then, most will be primed and ready to continue, and at their own expense.

Checklist to review with the manager when planning an event at a bar:

☐ Is the **room charge** included?

☐ Will there be any **food** provided?

☐ Has **sufficient staff** been arranged? Ideally, for larger groups, the wait staff will be employed exclusively for your party, and not used to service other patrons.

☐ **Exactly which items will you pay for?** Outline this with the manager. If you are paying for some, or all of the costs of the event, be sure to set a monetary limit and require that your approval be sought during the event if exceeded. The danger is that someone will order Macallan 25 or Remy Martin XO and charge it to your tab. Most bars categorize alcoholic drinks as well, call, premium and super-premium (the Macallan 25, etc.). You should consider excluding super-premium, and probably also premium liquors from the tab. A well run bar should easily meet this request.

☐ Is a **gratuity included**?

☐ How will the **check or checks** be handled?

☐ Who will be the **bar's contact** during the event?

HOW TO BE A GOOD GUEST

While at someone else's event, there are things that you can do to be a more welcome guest; before, during and when leaving.

BEFORE THE EVENT

"Fashionably late" is a phrase of malleable content that most of us have put into action at least once, if not always, when it comes to social events. It's applicable for cocktail parties, but almost never at dinner parties. If it's a very close friend that is hosting the dinner party, you might be able to plan on being slightly late, but with someone you don't know too well, it's best to be on time. The smaller the event, the greater the effort to be on time that you should plan to be. For a friend's event, you might even want to call just before leaving and ask if you can pick any items that they might have forgotten or under-stocked, as it is easy to forget an item or two, or to have run out of something during the preparations. Some other things you might want to do before heading to the party:

- Before it all begins, **respond to RSVPs** in a timely manner.
- **Try not to talk about the event to others who know the host**, unless you are sure that they have been invited in order not to embarrass them or put the hosts in a potentially awkward situation.
- **Try not to ask if you can bring an additional guest**, unless the hosts are good friends, or you are bringing a date. This is especially so when the event is a dinner party.
- **Do not bring children unless you are sure** they are welcome.
- **Do not bring a pet unless** you've cleared it beforehand with the hosts.
- When invited to a **dinner party**, be sure to arrive within thirty minutes of the **expected time**.
- At an event at someone's house **bring a bottle of wine** as a gift for the hosts, and neither ask nor expect that it be opened. In addition to wine, you might want to consider flowers as a gift.
- If you want to **bring some food, check with the host beforehand**. Remember, if you bring food other than finger food and utensils are required, this can be a burden on the host if all of the other food provided is finger food.
- **Dress according to the invitations**, and not too scantily (though personally we don't have a problem with women who can do so in fine fashion).

During the Event

Plan to enjoy the party. A good guest is a happy guest. Introduce yourself to the other guests that you don't already know. Do so with a pleasant attitude, and people will respond positively. An easy phrase to help break the ice is, "How do you know [the host's name]?" Alcohol can be your friend, up to a point. Have a drink, and loosen up. Another drink or two can let you enjoy yourself even if the other guests are personality-deficient and the music and food are less-than-palatable. After too many drinks, of course, you might become one of the guests that helps to liven the party in wrong way. Being a babbling buffoon or defecating indiscriminately is never the wise option, for example. Some other tips, which will hopefully seem somewhat obvious, are:

- **If you offer to help the host, and the offer is declined, don't feel bad**. And, it's less work for you.
- **Be pleasant**.
- **Mingle** with other guests.
- **Try not to talk about religion or politics**, if it will be contentious at all.
- **Try not to criticize the party** or the host; at least during the event.
- If you break, spill or otherwise ruin something at your hosts' house apologize and **do your best to fix or clean it.** Offer to pay for possible cleaning, repairs, or replacement.
- Again, **avoid getting get too drunk**.
- **Try not to use your cell phone too much**, or at all, as it gives the impression that this party is not that important for you. A vibrating ring is much less obnoxious to others than an audible ring. If you have to use the phone, go outside or find an empty room.
- **Don't monopolize the hosts' time**, as they have to mingle and host.
- **Flush** thoroughly (and, leave the seat down, guys).
- **Don't overstay your welcome**. You don't have to drink every last drop of your hosts' alcohol, for example.

Departure (or Escape) from the Event

Try not to be the last one to leave. If it's the party of a very good friend, and you are one of the last ones left standing, be sure to ask about helping clean up. It's easy to pick up the used cups, plates and other debris. When about to depart be sure to thank the host, especially at smaller gatherings. Some hosts will take a lack of a thank-you as a sign that the guest either did not enjoy themselves, or was ungrateful. When departing, try to say goodbye to as many folks as possible. At larger functions where you know many people, or have met many people with whom you would like to stay cordial, you should start the good-byes early. "I'm planning on leaving shortly, so if I don't get the chance to say 'goodbye' it was nice meeting you," is a good tact.

AFTER THE EVENT

If you had an exceptionally good time, if the hosts seemed to expend a lot of time or expense in planning and throwing the party, or if you felt that the hosts did a very good job in making you feel welcome, especially if you did not know them very well beforehand, you might want to thank them for their effort and mention that you had a good time via e-mail or with a brief phone call. A simple expression of appreciation can go a long, and can provide some additional validation to the hosts that their hard work was worth it. And, this can help get you invited to future events, too.

SOME MORE ABOUT SPIRITS

To stock a bar for entertaining or just enjoying yourself at home, it helps to know the basics about liquor. The term liquor and spirits are used interchangeably and refer to both hard liquor, which are typically at least 80 proof (vodka, whiskey, rum, gin, tequila and brandy), and liqueurs, which are highly flavored spirits with a generally much lower alcohol content.

THE BASICS OF THE HARD LIQUORS

Below is a very basic primer for the most popular types of hard liquor that are currently popular: **vodka**, **whiskies** (**scotch**, **Irish**, **Canadian** and **bourbon**), **rum**, **gin**, **tequila**, and **brandy**. What makes liquor what it is, is that it is a product of distillation involving water, yeast and some form of sugar, which has been converted via fermentation from a grain, sugar cane, a vegetable, or fruit, among other things. The recommended brands below have the best bang for the buck we believe. Keep in mind that brands and marketing concepts are always changing.

> **The retail price ranges** for standard-sized bottles (750 ml) of wine and **spirits** are: **$** ($0-$10), **$$** ($10-$20), **$$$** ($20-$30), **$$$$** ($30-$40), and **$$$$$** ($40-$50). You should probably save bottles over $50 for your own consumption.

Vodka is a clear, nearly neutral spirit that has become the most popular mixer for both men and women in North America. In Russia, Poland and the Baltic countries, the lands of its origin, vodka is usually consumed straight up, served chilled in small glasses. In the rest of the world, it's consumed mostly as part of a cocktail. The fact that it is neutral and only slightly flavored makes it a great mixer with just about anything, and is the biggest reason for its popularity. Vodka is made from mostly grains, corn, rye, wheat, and barley, and sometimes potatoes, beets or grapes. After fermentation of the sugars derived from the grains or potatoes, this "mash" is distilled at a very high proof, usually 190 (or 95% alcohol). This effectively eliminates most of its distinctive flavors, which are present in other liquors that are distilled to lower proofs. Vodka is then purified further by the treatment of the liquid with charcoal. The quality of the finished product is determined, in large part, by the quality of the water, which makes up more than half of the vodka, the method of distillation including the number of distillations, the type of charcoal used in the purification process, and the quality of the equipment used throughout.

Popular Drinks featuring Vodka – Apple Martini, Bay Breeze, Black Russian, Bloody Mary, Cape Cod, Colorado Bulldog, Cosmopolitan, Gibson, Greyhound, Hairy Navel, John Collins, Kamikaze, Madras, Martini, Salty Dog, Screwdriver, Sea Breeze, Sex on the Beach, *shot*, Vodka & Tonic, Vodka-Seven, Vodka-Soda, White Russian, Woo Woo

Recommended Brands of Vodka – **Regular** – Smirnoff ($$), Tito's ($$), Absolut ($$$), Belvedere ($$$), Ciroc ($$$), Grey Goose ($$$); **Flavored** – Finlandia Cranberry ($$), Finlandia Mango ($$), Smirnoff Orange Twist ($$), Absolut Citron ($$$), Absolut Mandrin ($$$), Stolichnaya Vanil ($$$)

Whiskey (or Whisky) – There are actually four very basic types of whiskies based on geography: **scotch, Irish, Canadian**, and American, of which the most important and most common is **bourbon**. Whiskies from each of the four areas have distinct general styles. Whiskies are also produced in other countries, most notably Japan and Australia, but these can safely be ignored unless you are traveling to either place.

Whiskey or Whisky? – You will find both spellings on labels, and both spellings are correct. "Whiskey" is used by most of the American and Irish producers, while "whisky" is used by the Scottish and Canadian companies. No one really seems to know why this has had occurred over the years, though it does not seem to have effected the quality of the whiskies (this plural is the same for both spellings).

Scotch whiskies are an acquired taste for most, and are generally much more popular with more mature drinkers. The distinctive smoky flavor is from the fact that the malted barley is dried over peat fires. Scotch is divided into two main types, **single malts** and **blends**. Single malt refers to the fact that the whisky was made at one distillery, has not been blended with any other whiskies, and barley malt was the only grain and the only fermentable material that was used. Single malt scotches meet these criteria, and blended scotches constitute everything else. The best blends are made solely with other scotch whiskies rather than any other liquor. The cheaper blends consist of single malt whiskies mixed with less flavorful liquors made with neutral grains. During the 1990s the number of single malts exploded, along with their popularity, and these scotches became the premium drink for many serious drinkers. Single malts have unique and more pronounced flavors, often of smoke and peat, more so than do the blends, which are generally smoother. Johnnie Walker, Dewar's and Cutty Sark are popular blended scotch whiskies. Both single malts and blends can be very good, and most benefit from aging in wood barrels. The quality of a particular brand of scotch is generally better the longer it has been aged, often 10, 12, 18 years and longer.

Each single malt scotch is an individual, often times as distinct from other single malts as they are from blends. Peat, partially carbonized vegetable material found in bogs, is the fuel for turning the barley into malt. The flavor of peat can be pronounced for some single malts, often its predominant flavor. There are four major regions for single malt scotches, each denoting certain regional characteristics: **Lowlands**, **Highlands**, **Campbeltown**, and **Islay**. **Lowland** whiskies, from the areas south of the large cities of Edinburgh and Glasgow, usually exhibit the pleasant taste of malt rather than the flavors of peat, or those of the coast (seaweed and brine) that can be evident in other regions. Whiskies from the Lowlands are often the most accessible of the single malts. The **Highlands** is the biggest region, and the whiskies vary widely among the general, unofficial areas of the west, north, Midlands, east, and Speyside. The western part of the Highlands produces whiskies that are generally firm and dry with the hint of some peatiness. The northern part of the Highlands produces whiskies that can be described as spicy (for whisky). The more temperate Midlands and East Highlands have whiskies that are comparatively fruity. Speyside whiskies are noted for their complexity and elegance, and exhibit two wide variations: the robust, sherry-flavored whiskies such as Macallan and Glenfarclas, and the lighter, subtle whiskies such as Glenlivet and Glenmorangie. **Campbeltown**, the smallest of the regions, consists of only three whiskies, which are distinctively briny with different levels of peatiness. **Islay**, which is an island off the southwestern coast of the mainland pronounced "eye-luh," produces whiskies that are noticeably full-bodied, peaty, smoky and with the flavor of seaweed. Excellent whiskies are produced on other smaller islands, such as Highland Park from Orkney, and Talisker on the Skye, both of which are described as Highland-like in character.

Popular Drinks featuring Scotch – Neat, On the Rocks, Rob Roy, Rusty Nail, Scotch & Soda
Recommended Brands of Scotch – **Blends** – Dewar's (**$$$**), Famous Grouse (**$$$**); **Single Malts** – Glenlivet 12 Year Old (**$$$$**), Craggenmore 12 Year Old (**$$$$$**), Glenmorangie Port Wood Finish (**$$$$$**), Highland Park 12 Year Old (**$$$$$**)

Irish Whiskey describes whiskies from Ireland. These generally do not have as complex a taste as most scotch whiskies, but are still of high quality, and comparatively inexpensive. Irish whiskey is made from a fermented mash of malted barley, unmalted barley, corn, rye and other grains. The malted grains in these whiskies are dried in closed kilns, rather than open peat-fueled fires, so the smoky and peaty flavors found in most scotch whiskies are not present. Irish whiskey is distilled three times and aged for three to nine years in reused oak casks. The resultant product has a smooth malty flavor that is more easily accessible than scotch whisky. Jameson and Bushmills are the two most common Irish whiskies found in North America. For what it's worth, Jameson is the "Catholic whiskey" and Bushmills is the "Protestant whiskey." That difference is very insignificant now, as both are owned by the same company.

Popular Drinks featuring Irish Whiskey – *Neat, On the Rocks,* Irish Coffee
Recommended Brands of Irish Whiskey – Bushmills (**$$$**), Jameson (**$$$**), Tullamore Dew (**$$$**), Bushmills Black Bush (**$$$$**), Bushmills 10 Year Irish Malt (**$$$$**)

Canadian Whisky is simply whiskey distilled in Canada. These are generally even more affordable than Irish whiskies, but are also usually quite well made. By law, Canadian whisky must be blended from the fermented mash of grains such as corn, wheat, rye and barley. Corn is by far the largest component for most. Canadian whiskies must be aged in oak casks for at least three years, though most are aged between six and eight years. After aging, the whiskey is blended and then aged a little longer. The final product is lighter-bodied and slightly sweeter than scotch and Irish whiskies, featuring a muted and smooth taste. Canadian whiskies generally make for good mixers, better, at least than their scotch and Irish cousins.

Popular Drinks featuring Canadian Whisky – *Neat, On the Rocks,* Crown & Cola, Manhattan, Old Fashioned
Recommended Brands of Canadian Whisky – Canadian Club (**$$**), Crown Royal (**$$$**), Forty Creek (**$$$**), Seagram's V.O. (**$$$**)

The best American whiskies are **bourbon** whiskies and its close cousins made in a slightly different process from Tennessee. These are the pride of American spirits. Bourbon whiskey must be made from between 51% and 79% fermented corn (mash at this juncture). Bourbon is straight whiskey, meaning no blending and nothing else is added after distillation other than water. It must be aged at least two years in new charred white oak barrels, but most are aged at least four years, and are sold at 80 proof. The sour mash method, which is often mentioned in discussions about bourbon, is a fermentation technique that employs part of the previous distillation in the current batch of fermenting mash. This allows for consistency among subsequent batches. Bourbon can be distilled anywhere in the U.S., but the great majority of it comes from Kentucky. The distillers claim that the very best water for their whiskey is why they stay at their original locations. Tennessee whiskey includes one more step in the production process than used for bourbon. After distillation, the liquid is filtered through charcoal made from maple trees to remove impurities before aging. This process either makes Tennessee whisky a smoother product than bourbon, or removes the flavor according to some bourbon partisans. Jack Daniel's and the boutique George Dickel are the only two distilleries left in Tennessee. In addition to bourbon and Tennessee whiskey, there is rye whiskey, in which rye makes up over half of the fermentable grains. Rye whiskey is the original American whiskey. It's similar in color to bourbon, but has a different, heavier and coarser taste. Then there is "blended American whiskey," which is not unlike the Canadian blended whisky. Seagram's 7 is the most popular brand of American blended whiskey and similar to the Canadian Seagram's V.O.

Popular Drinks with American Whiskey – Neat, On the Rocks, With a Splash of Water, Bourbon Old Fashioned, Bourbon Sour, Hot Toddy, Kentucky Cooler, Mint Julep, Sazerac, 7 & 7, Whiskey and Cola, Whiskey Sour
Recommended Brands of American Whiskey – Jack Daniel's Black ($$), Jim Beam ($$), Weller's 90 Proof ($$), Wild Turkey 101 Proof ($$), Makers Mark ($$$)

Rum is distilled from sugar cane or sugar cane molasses, and is popular for a wide range of drinks, including one of the easiest and most popular, the Rum & Cola. It's produced in tropical areas mostly around the Caribbean. There are three main types of rum: **light**, **dark**, and **flavored**. Light rums are usually produced in column stills to 160 proof and higher. The lowest level, white rum, spends at least one year in oak barrels. The second level, amber or gold, is aged for at least three years and has caramel added for the color. It's generally smoother and more flavorful than the basic white rum. The third level, *añejo*, is aged at least four years, and is the most flavorful of the light-bodied rums. The full-bodied dark rums are produced with a slightly different process, which includes capturing only the middle part of the distillation column, between 140 and 160 proof. This results in the most flavorful kind of basic rum, which is helped by an aging of at least five years in oak barrels. The popular rums from Jamaica are usually blended to achieve consistency. Flavored rums are typically light-bodied rums that are flavored with fruit juices or spices. These are generally more popular with younger drinkers.

Popular Drinks with Rum – Cuba Libré, Frozen Daiquiri, Hurricane, Mai Tai, Mojito, Piña Colada, Rum & Cola, Rum & Orange Juice, Rum & Pineapple Juice, Rum & Soda, Rum Runner, Rum Sour
Recommended Brands of Rum – **Light** – Castillo ($), Bacardi ($$); **Dark** – Barbancourt 5 Star ($$$), Myers ($$$); **Flavored** – Captain Morgan's Spiced Rum ($$), Malibu Coconut Flavor ($$)

Gin lost supremacy to vodka in the world of spirits years ago, even in the classic Martini, but it remains an essential for any well-stocked or somewhat-stocked bar. The long-popular London dry gin style, for which "gin" now usually refers, was created by distillers in England in the 19th century. This style is made with fermentable mash consisting of 75% corn, 15% barley malt, and 10% other grains, and is flavored with a number of spices, herbs and botanicals. The distinctive London dry gin flavor comes primarily from juniper berries, but many other items are used, including orange peel, cardamom, cassia bark, coriander, and angelica root. These are added to the liquid during the distillation process to produce the final product. After distillation, water typically is added to bring the gin to its marketed strength at 80 proof. There is not a huge taste difference among dry gins. Most gins sold are of this London dry style. The other, original, and somewhat rare, style is the Dutch sweet gin. In terms of value, dry gin remains a good buy, with acclaimed brands selling for under $20 per 750 ml bottle.

Popular Drinks with Gin – French '75', Gibson, Gimlet, Gin & Tonic, Gin Fizz, Gin 'n Juice, Gin Sour, Martini, The Perfect Cocktail, Ramos Gin Fizz, Singapore Sling, Tom Collins
Recommended Brands of Gin – Bombay ($$), Boodles ($$), Bombay Sapphire ($$$), Citadelle ($$$), Tanqueray ($$$), Hendricks ($$$$)

Not just the firewater with a worm in the bottle, mezcal describes the broad category of distilled spirits from the roasted heart of the agave plant. **Tequila** is a specific type of mezcal that was originally produced near the town of Tequila in the state of Jalisco. Tequila is legally produced in Jalisco and four other Mexican states. Tequila is made primarily from a specific variety of agave, the Agave Tequilana Weber, Variety Blue. Agave is not a cactus, but comes from its own botanical family called agavacea. Tequilas are generally divided among *mixto*, which can include *joven* (for "young" and to which caramel and sugar have been added for color and taste), that consists of at least 51% distilled agave juice blended with neutral spirits, and the three categories that are made with 100% distilled agave juice include *blanco* (that is bottled within 60 days of distillation), *repsosado* (which is aged from two to eleven months in oak), and *añejo* (aged for at least a year in small oak barrels). The more agave, the better. If in doubt, look for tequilas that are labeled "100% agave." The longer the tequila is aged, the darker the color becomes, the taste of the agave mellows, and the more noticeable the flavor of the oak becomes. Aged is not necessarily better, though aged tequilas are more expensive, and much more popular for drinking straight, or neat.

Popular Drinks with Tequila – *Shot*, *Neat*, Margarita, Paloma, Tequila Sunrise
Recommended Brands of Tequila – *Blanco* – El Tesoro Platinum (**$$$$**), Herradura Silver (**$$$$**), Gran Centenario *Blanco* (**$$$$$**); ***Reposado*** – Puerta Vallarta *Reposado* All Agave (**$$$**), Cazadores (**$$$$**), Chinaco *Reposado* (**$$$$$**), El Tesoro *Reposado* (**$$$$**), Gran Centenario *Reposado* (**$$$$$**); ***Añejo*** – Don Eduardo *Añejo* (**$$$$$**), Don Julio *Añejo* (**$$$$$**), Gran Centenario *Añejo* (**$$$$$**)

Brandy is the fermented juice of a fruit that is distilled and aged in wood. The most famous are made from grapes, but brandies are made from a wide range of fruits and even from the oils of flowers. It's a popular *digestif* and winter warmer. Brandies are made worldwide. The most famous are cognac and armagnac, both made from grapes. **Cognac** is from the Cognac region of southeastern France, and is the benchmark for brandies worldwide. It's made almost entirely from the Ugni Blanc grape (Trebbiano in Italy) in a three-tier production system. With this, there are distinct companies for wine-making, distillation, then aging and blending. For this reason cognacs show a great deal of similarity across the various brands. The designated categories refer to the amount of aging, though all cognacs are distilled twice in small copper potstills. Cognac is referred to as "Yak" in the hip-hop community. The term "Fine Champagne" that appears on some labels has nothing to do with the sparkling wine champagne. Instead, it refers to the fact that the cognac originated in the Petite Champagne districts of the Cognac region and contains at least 50% of its blend from the Grande Champagne district. Cognacs come in three basic quality designations based upon the time spent in oak casks. **VS** or **Three Star** are aged for a minimum of two-and-a-half years, though most are aged between four and seven years. **VSOP**, **VO (Very Old)**, or *Réserve* have a minimum aging is four-and-a-half years, however, most are aged between five and thirteen years. **XO**, **Extra**, **Napoleon**, and *Vielle Réserve* have a minimum aging of six years, but most are aged between seven and forty years.

Armagnac is similar to cognac, but is made in the smaller Armagnac region, is distilled only once instead of twice, made with one to four different grapes instead of just one, and often carries a vintage date. Though its production is much smaller than cognac, there is a comparatively greater range in tastes among the labels. **Calvados** is another notable type of brandy from France. From the cold and windswept Normandy where grapes will not readily grow, this distinctive brandy is made from apples. Calvados might be the most easily accessible brandy due to its comparatively mellow flavor. **Other brandies** include excellent brandies that are made in Spain and California. Cognac, the best known and probably the best type of brandy, is both enjoyed by most sophisticated drinkers, and the least sophisticated. It is best reserved for the former, since if you are going to mix it with something, a lesser brandy will work. There are also brandies made with a variety of other fruits such as peach and apricot that are common in Eastern Europe.

Popular Drinks with Brandy – *Neat*, Brandy Alexander, B & B, Brandy & Cola, Brandy & Soda, Incredible Hulks, Sidecar
Recommended Brands of Brandy – Fundador (Spain - **$$**), Courvoisier VS (**$$$**), Gabriel & Andreu Borderies (**$$$**), Hennessy VS (**$$$**), Martell VS (**$$$**), Courvoisier VSOP (**$$$$**), Hennessy VSOP (**$$$$**), Pierre Ferrand Ambré (**$$$$**), Cardenal Mendoza (Spain - **$$$$$**)

LIQUEURS AND CORDIALS

These two terms are used interchangeably. These refer to a flavored and often sweetened, packaged, commercial alcoholic beverage. These begin with a spirit such as rum, brandy, or whiskey that has been flavored with a variety of ingredients such as fruits, herbs, spices, nuts and leaves. There is a great amount of variety, but below are the major styles:

- **Anise-Flavored** – These highlight the flavor of anise, both the seed and leaf, and have a licorice flavor. Anisette, ouzo, sambuca, Pernod and pastis are several examples, along with absinthe. Some bottles that can be useful for entertaining are Molinari Sambuca (**$$$**) and Pernod (**$$$**).
- **Cream-Based** – These are made with real cream and liquor for a rich result. Though made with cream, it's not perishable. Bailey's Irish Cream (**$$$**) is the most well-known version. Nearly indistinguishable in quality are a few more affordable brands: St. Brendan's (**$$**); O'Leary's (**$$**); and Carolan's (**$$**). With a slightly different taste, but very flavorful is Amarula (**$$**) from South Africa.
- **Crème** – These do not have cream, but rather feature one dominant flavor such as crème de menthe, crème de cassis and the like. These are easily identifiable, as "crème" is in the name.
- **Fruit- , Bean-** and **Nut-Flavored** – These are made to highlight a type of fruit which becomes concentrated during the distillation process. Orange-flavored Cointreau (**$$$$**) and Grand Marnier (**$$$$**), coffee-based Kahlúa (**$$**) and the better value Kamora (**$$**), and almond-flavored amaretto (Amaretto di Amore - **$$**) are common versions.
- **Herbal-Based** – These were the first liqueurs usually created by religious communities in Europe and feature a number of local herbs. Chartreuse Green (**$$$$$**), Benedictine (**$$$$**), Strega (**$$**), and Jägermeister (**$$$**) are some widespread types.
- **Schnapps** – Usually from Germany or Central Europe, these are typically used as winter warmers, and often downed in a single gulp from a shot glass. Flavored with seeds, herbs or fruits, these come in a number of

flavors. Peach schnapps (DeKuyper - $$) is the one most commonly used in drink recipes. Other schnapps popular for parties are peppermint (Rumple Minze - $$$) and cinnamon Goldschlager ($$$).

Liqueurs can be proprietary, which are produced exclusively by a single distiller with secret formulas such as Southern Comfort, Benedictine, Drambuie, and Chartreuse. There are also generic liqueurs made by several producers following very similar recipes. Examples of generic liqueurs include amaretto, Irish cream liqueur, and crème de menthe.

For most parties, especially if you are not making any popular drinks using peach schnapps, and do not want to encourage shot-taking, you can get away without stocking any liqueurs. You will know your crowd, though.

CHEESE

Cheese makes for nearly completely pre-made appetizers, especially when paired simply with basic, bland crackers. The cheese provides the flavor and the crackers a contrasting, pleasing texture. Nearly everyone likes cheese, especially as an appetizer or a snack, except for those that believe they are lactose-intolerant. And, cheese is a great complement for beer and a historic accompaniment for wine. So, it's useful to know a few things about cheese when entertaining and shopping.

Popular types of cheese can be categorized by general style (some cheeses might fit more than one style). These styles are: *1) Fresh*; *2) Mild*; *3) Crème*; *4) Brie and Camembert*; *5) Swiss*; *6) Cheddar*; *7) Grana*; *8) Monastery*; *9) Goat*; *10) Sheep's Milk*; *11) Blue*; *12) Strong*; and *13) Flavored*. Somewhat common and popular cheeses (at least somewhere) are briefly described in the section below. Though not listed, there are many excellent artisanal cheeses that have begun to be produced in recent years throughout North America.

1) Fresh, Uncured Cheeses – These are unripened, and are slightly sweet in taste, which can be described as milky. High-quality cheeses in this category are well complemented by crisp-tasting lager beers and light, fruity white and rosé wines.

- **Cream Cheese** – A very soft, simple and slightly sour-tasting cheese that is most often used for spreading on crackers, bagels, and the like.
- **Mozzarella** – This is a relatively bland, fresh cheese that melts well, and is a necessity for pizzas, *Insalata Caprese* and many Italian-American dishes. The mozzarella sold in small balls (*bocconcini*) packed with water should be used if you are presenting it as an appetizer or desire a higher quality dish. Mozzarella is produced domestically, usually with cow's milk, or in its original format called *mozzarella di bufala* from outside of Naples, which is made from the milk of water buffaloes. The most commonly found versions at supermarkets that are packaged in bricks are comparatively horrible.
- **Scamorza** [skah-MOR-zah] – A soft, very mild, slightly nutty-tasting cow's milk cheese from Italy that is similar to mozzarella.

2) Mild Cheeses – These are grouped together because they have uncomplicated, mild flavors. The inexpensive versions that are industrially made are bland, and will need to be in the middle of a sandwich to provide much benefit. Crisp lager beers and lively, uncomplicated white and red wines are suitable matches for these cheeses.

- **Bel Paese** [bell pah-AY-say] – This versatile, mild creamy cheese from northern Italy melts well, and is good for both snacks and for dessert. Matches with light white wines like Orvieto, Soave, Chenin Blanc and Sauvignon Blanc.
- **Edam** – A firm, slightly rubbery textured cheese originally from Holland that has a mild, slightly buttery and tangy taste. It's a reliable cheese to purchase as it lasts for a very long time, and even more so, it's generally inexpensive. It goes well with crisp lager beers and light red and white wines.
- **Fontina** [fahn-TEEN-ah] – This is an excellent cheese from the northwestern Italian region of Valle D'Aosta that works well as a melting cheese and for the table. The texture is semi-firm and supple with a rich, herbaceous and fruity flavor. It pairs well with fruits. The Danish version is not nearly as flavorful.
- **Gouda** [GOOH-duh] – A mild, nutty cow's milk cheese from Holland that is a fine complement to most beers and red wines.
- **Monterey Jack** – An American mild, usually semi-soft cheese that works best as a complement to a wide variety of luncheon meats, breads and as a condiment on sandwiches. There are also aged versions that can work for grating purposes. Alone, it goes well with crisp white wines and light, fruity red wines.
- **Muenster** [MUHN-stehr] or **American Münster** – A very light, mild and inoffensive, but pleasant-enough commercially-produced cheese that bears no resemblance to its Alsatian namesake.
- **Neufchâtel** [nohf-CHAH-tel] – A very mild, simple-tasting cream cheese originally from Normandy. Best consumed when young. Watch out for a gray-colored rind and an overly salty taste. Light and fruity red wines are a good match for this.
- **Robiola** [roh-beeh-OH-lah] – A soft, mild cheese from northern Italy. The ones labeled Robiola Lombardia is very similar to Taleggio.
- **Taleggio** [tah-lay-GEEH-oh] – A soft, mild and flavorful cheese that is eaten as a snack, appetizer or as a dessert in its native Italy. It is past prime if it sports a pungent aroma. Matches well with fruity, light white wines such as Soave and Chenin Blanc.
- **Tilsit** [TIHL-ziht] – This is a mild, firm cheese, not unlike Gouda.

3) Crème Style Cheeses – Not to be confused with cream cheeses, these cheeses feature the addition of cream during the production process that raises the butterfat content to 60% for double-crème cheeses and up to 75% for triple-crème cheese. These cheeses are soft, creamy, mild, and very rich. The different brands have very similar tastes. All match well with off-dry, flavorful white wines such as Spätlese and Auslese.

- **Boursault** [boohr-SOHLT] – A brand of triple-crème cheese.
- **Boursin** [boohr-SEH] – A popular brand covered in pepper or flavored with garlic and herbs.
- **Brillat-Savarin** [breeh-LAH sahv-ah-RAH] – Another popular unflavored brand from France. It sports a somewhat sharp taste, and is named after the famous gourmet and food writer of the early nineteenth century.
- **Cambozola** [kam-boh-ZOH-lah] – This is a creamy cheese from Germany that tastes much like a cross between Gorgonzola and Camembert. Its white triple-crème interior contains streaks of blue.
- **Explorateur** [ex-plohr-AH-tehr] – A brand of triple-crème cheese.
- **Pierre-Robert** [peeh-EHR roh-BEHR] – Tripe-crème cheese from France that sports noticeable mineral and grassy flavors.
- **Saint-André** [sahn ahn-DRAY] – Another brand of triple-crème cheese.

4) Brie and Camembert Style Cheeses – These are characterized by the soft, moist and flavorful texture of the interiors and the slightly less soft mold-covered rinds. Fruit-forward, quality red wines and high quality whites are good complements to brie and Camembert.

- **Brie** [BREE] – A popular soft cheese that features a creamy interior with a mild flavor covered with a white, edible rind. Good when just opened or when heated before eating. Brie should be used within a few days after purchase. Champagne is the classic pairing for brie.
- **Camembert** [KAM-uhm-behr] – This is a classic, creamy and spreadable cow's milk cheese with a white rind and a milky and tangy flavor. The ones from Normandy and elsewhere in France are usually of higher quality.

The rinds of brie are edible. Tell your guests, too.

---

5) Swiss Style Cheeses – These are generally hard-textured cheeses with a mild, but nutty taste and are very good for eating alone. For wines, light- and medium-bodied white wines such as Riesling, Gewürztraminer, and Sauvignon Blanc go well with these, as do most beers, especially crisp-tasting lagers.

- **Beaufort** [boh-FOHR] – A Swiss-style cheese from France that has a fruity and slightly sweet but clean taste. It is a very good cheese for melting.
- **Boerenkaas** [bor-EN-kahs] – This is aged Gouda that has developed noticeable nutty flavors.

- **Comté** [kom-TAY] – Made in France, this is a smooth, firm cheese with a sharp, nutty flavor that is similar to Beaufort and Gruyère. Melts well.
- **Emmental** [EM-mahn-tahl], **Emmentaler**, **Emmenthaler** – A pale cheese with a light buttery taste that is made from skimmed cow's milk. Replete with holes, this is the cheese that gave name to the much more generic and much less flavorful cheeses labeled as "Swiss Cheese." The best versions are from Switzerland and France, and are very versatile.
- **Fontina** [fahn-TEEN-ah] – This is an excellent cheese from the northwestern Italian region of Valle D'Aosta that works well as a melting cheese and for the table. The texture is semi-firm and supple with rich, herbaceous and fruity flavor. It pairs well with fruits. The Danish version is not nearly as flavorful.
- **Gruyère** [groo-YEHR] – A cow's milk cheese from Switzerland and France that has a very good, rich and nutty flavor that makes for a great eating cheese. Melts well, too.
- **Jarlsberg** [YAHLZ-berg] – A mild, nutty and buttery cheese from Norway that is fairly versatile.
- **Raclette** [rah-KLET] – A mild but flavorful hard cheese from Switzerland that becomes even more enjoyable when melted for the famous Swiss dish of the same name. Somewhat similar to Gruyère.

6) Cheddar Style Cheeses – This hard cow's milk cheese is the most popular type of cheese in the world. It can range in flavor from very mild to quite sharp. Beers go best with these, but full-bodied red wines such as Cabernet Sauvignon provides a fitting complement for high quality sharp cheddars and other strong-tasting versions of these cheeses. The milder tasting ones match better with lighter-bodied wines with pronounced fruit flavors.

- **Asiago** [ahs-eeh-AH-goh] – A tangy cheese from Italy that tastes pleasant and mild when young, and becomes more flavorful with age.
- **Caciocavallo** [kah-chah-kuh-VAHL-oh] – A cow's milk cheese from southern Italy that is mild when young. The young versions are usually served with fruit. Fruity and light-bodied wines, both red and white, work well as a complement for the younger versions of this cheese.
- **Cheddar** – This is the most widely made cheese in the world, and the one that nearly everyone seems to enjoy, even though much of the mass-produced cheddar cheese is bland and rubbery, bordering on tasteless. From the better producers, young cheddar has a taste that starts off fairly mild and sweet with notes of nuts, often with a salty tang. Older cheeses have a wonderfully nutty taste with a real piquancy to it that makes for a fine match with robust red wines and ports.
- **Cheshire** – An English cheese with production centered around the town of Cheshire. It comes in two styles, referred to as Red and Blue. The Red

is a mild and flavorful cheddar-style cheese. The Blue is a blue cheese with a richer and stronger taste than the Red. Goes well with beer, especially English styles, and fruity red wines.

- **Colby** – An American spin on cheddar that is softer and more moist than the original English style, but also more mellow, often to the point of blandness.
- **Derby** – A mild cheddar-style cheese from England that is an enjoyable, if not memorable, snacking cheese with beer or light-bodied fruity wines.
- **Gloucester** [GLOHW-ster] – A flavorful cheddar-style cheese from England that is known as a good eating cheese. The cheeses labeled "Double Gloucester" are tastier than the ones labeled "Single." Beers and most red wines match well with both versions.
- **Leicester** [LES-ter] – A rich, orange-colored cow's milk cheddar cheese made in and around Leicester, England that goes well with ciders, red wines, and most beers, especially the pepper-infused versions.
- **Provolone** [proh-voh-LOHN] – A very mild, sometimes almost bland, firm cow's milk cheese that originated in southern Italy, though most versions sold here are produced in North America. Most commonly found in sandwiches and inexpensive cheese trays.
- **Tillamook** – High quality, sharp-tasting cheddar cheeses made in a cooperative dairy in Tillamook County, Oregon.

7) Grana Style Cheeses – These are the very hard, sharp-flavored cheeses that are used primarily for grating, though these can also be a very good eating cheese, especially with wine, when in good condition. Parmigiano-Reggiano is the best of this type of cheese. Full-bodied and flavorful red wines from northern Italy, especially the nebbiolo-based wines of Barolo, Barberesco, Valtellina and Gattinara, plus Barberas and the piquant Amarones are nice choices when eating these cheeses. Zinfandels and Malbecs might be good New World substitutes.

- **Asiago** (aged) [ahs-eeh-AH-goh] – When aged this is a hard cheese with a tangy taste, somewhat similar, if not nearly as flavorful, as Parmigiano-Reggiano. The aged versions go well with full-bodied red wines.
- **Caciocavallo** (aged) [kah-chah-kuh-VAHL-oh] – A cow's milk cheese from southern Italy that is tangy and flavorful when aged. The older versions are used as a grating cheese.
- **Dry Jack** – This is aged Monterey Jack that has a rich and nutty flavor, and was created during the First World War for Italian-Americans as a substitute for the unavailable Parmesan and Romano.
- **Grana Padano** [grahn-NAH pah-DAH-noh] – Very similar to Parmigiano-Reggiano, this is becoming more common in upscale supermarkets as a slighter cheaper alternative.

- **Montasio** [mohn-TAH-seeh-oh] – A cow's milk cheese from northeastern Italy that has sharp flavor and firm texture when aged, similar to Asiago. It is very mild, almost bland, when young.
- **Parmigiano-Reggiano** [pahrm-mee-JAHN-oh ray-jeeh-AHN-oh] – Hard cheese that has been made since at least the eleventh century in a strictly controlled area in northern Italy. The flavor is subtle, complex and enticing. It's an excellent eating cheese when aged for a shorter period, and always good for grating and cooking. High quality Grana Padano is the nearest substitute. American made Parmesan is a pale imitator, though. In addition to the rich, red wines, Chardonnay-based wines also pair well.
- **Pecorino-Romano** [pek-ohr-EEN-oh roh-MAHN-oh] – This is a hard, sharp-tasting sheep's milk cheese made that is mostly found in the aged version. This is popular as a grating cheese, but is not as flavorful or complex as the similar-looking Parmigiano-Reggiano. In Italy it is also enjoyed when fresh, and eaten with bread, *salame* and red wine. The first name of the cheese, "Pecorino" means "from sheep milk." The second name, the place, "Romano" designates the area around Rome. Pecorino Romano doesn't qualify the best version of this cheese. The *Abruzzese, Sardo, Marchigiano, Toscano, Umbro,* and *Molisano* are tastier than the Romano itself, though are much less widely available in North America.
- **Provolone** (aged) [proh-voh-LOHN] – Flavorful aged versions from Italy work well as a grating cheese.
- **Sbrinz** [ZBRIHNZ] – A hard cow's milk cheese from the central mountains of Switzerland with a nutty, rich flavor. Used for grating, cooking and as a table cheese.

8) Monastery Style Cheeses – This broad general style originated in French and Belgian monasteries, and features semi-soft cheeses with often very pungent aromas, even if these are often mild tasting. This is a wide-ranging category that usually calls for beer, though a light-bodied, fruity wine can also work.

- **Havarti** [hahv-RAHR-tee] – A slightly tangy, but mildly flavored semi-soft cheese from Denmark that matches especially well with clean-tasting, light lager beers.
- **Morbier** [mohr-bee-AY] – This is a semi-soft cow's milk cheese that has a mild but buttery flavor, which is not unlike that of good Fontina. Light, fruity red wines are a good match for this.
- **Münster** [MOON-ster] – A flavorful cheese with a noticeable aroma and earthy, herbaceous taste from Alsace. Becomes very pungent when aged. A great complement for a wide range of beers and white wines from either side of the Rhine.

- **Port-Salut** [port sah-LOOH] or **Port-du-Salut** – This is a soft and mild cow's milk cheese with a creamy texture, which is its greatest characteristic. Pairs well with fruity wines, both red and white.

9) Goat Cheeses – Made from the milk of goats rather than cows, these all have a similar creamy texture and a tangy flavor that is similar to sheep's milk cheeses. For most goat cheeses, a hearty, simple red wine will work well.

- **Chèvre** [SHEHV] – Cheese made from goat's milk that features a popular tart flavor and usually a thick creamy texture. Light-bodied whites complement most chèvres such as Sancerre and most other Sauvignon Blancs.
- **Garroxta** [gah-ROWKS-tah] – A goat's milk cheese from Catalonia, Spain that has a mild, but earthy nut-like flavor and a semi-firm texture, firmer than most goat cheeses, and a unique gray rind. It's good for appetizers, and pairs with wines like Albariño and Spanish reds.
- **Monte Enebro** [mon-TAY en-AY-broh] – A tangy goat's milk cheese from Spain with intense herbal flavors.
- **Montrachet** [mohn-truh-SHAY] – A goat's milk cheese from Burgundy that has a very creamy and soft texture and a mild, slightly sour, but rich and attractive flavor. Though named after the famous white wine, this matches better with a fruity red wine like Beaujolais, which is produced down the road.

10) Sheep's Milk Cheeses – These are made from the milk of sheep rather than cows or goats. These can range widely in flavor, from mild to somewhat sharp tasting, and in quality. Some, like the Pecorino-Romano, have a salty character because it's cured in brine. For this and feta, a good beverage pairing is a tasty lager beer, or a simple wine. For the less salty cheeses, you will want a straightforward red wine such as an inexpensive Chianti, Rioja or Zinfandel.

- **Brin d'Amour** [BRIN dah-MOR] – A tangy, aromatic cheese from Corsica that is covered with herbs.
- **Feta** – A salty, tangy flavored style, which is integral to Greek cuisine.
- **Idiazabal** [ih-dee-ah-THAH-bol] – A salty, sharp and crumbly cheese. What is available in North America is usually smoked and aged. It's a good cheese to grate in salads, melt, or eat with crackers and sherry, though it does seem to clash with most other wines.
- **Manchego** [mahn-CHAY-go] – The sheep milk's cheese from Spain features a firm texture and a rich flavor. Works great on a cheese plate,

and might be the best all-around cheese to complement a wide range of wines, though a sturdy red might be the best match.

- **Pecorino-Romano** [pek-ohr-EEN-oh roh-MAHN-oh] – A hard, sharp-tasting cheese made near Rome that is mostly found in the aged version, which is popular as a grating cheese. Not as flavorful or complex as the similar-looking Parmigiano-Reggiano.
- **Teleme** [tell-uh-MAY] – This is a soft cheese with a slightly lemony flavor that was created by Greek immigrants in San Francisco in the 1920s. It works well as a snacking cheese, and also melts well.

11) Blue Cheeses – These have blue or blue-ish colored veins of mold, usually of the Penicillium variety, within a semi-soft to semi-hard texture. The tastes are sharp and unique. Many full-bodied red wines are good matches with the harder versions, or with dishes featuring blue cheese. Sweeter wines such as dessert wines, ports and Madeiras go well the creamier ones. Port and Stilton is considered a classic pairing.

- **Blue** or **Bleu Cheese** – This is the generic name for cheeses with internal molds, which are noticeable with veins that are typically blue or blue-ish in color. With the exception of Roquefort and Cabrales, most blue cheeses are made from cow's milk.
- **Cabrales** [kah-BRAH-lez] – A very high quality Spanish blue cheese with intense flavors and aromas that is primarily made from goat's milk. It matches well with the sweet Pedro Ximenez sherry for dessert.
- **Cambozola** [kam-boh-ZOH-lah] – This is a creamy cheese from Germany that tastes much like a cross between Gorgonzola and Camembert. Its white triple-crème interior contains streaks of blue.
- **Fourme d'Ambert** [for-MAY dahm-BEHR] – A French-made cheese with a buttery taste that is much like Stilton.
- **Gorgonzola** [gohr-guhn-ZOH-lah] – An excellent, very creamy cow's milk blue cheese from northern Italy. *Dolce* denotes mild flavored; *naturale* is strongly flavored.
- **Maytag Blue** – A fine American blue cheese made from cow's milk.
- **Roquefort** [ROHK-furht] – A sheep's milk blue cheese from southwestern France that has been produced since at least Roman times. As with other blue cheeses it works well on canapés, on salads, or alone with ports and other dessert wines. Sauternes is the classic pairing.
- **Shropshire** – A blue cheese from England with an orange interior spiked with blue veins and having sharp and grassy flavors.
- **Stilton** – A cow's milk blue cheese from England. It is considered the classic complement for port, though it goes well with other rich red wines.

12) Strong Cheeses – These are pungent and intensely flavored. As odiferous as these are you might want to avoid using these for an event, especially one indoors. If you plan to serve them, you should place them on separate plates from the other cheeses. Avoid placing these cheeses on wood cheeseboards, as the wood might absorb the smell of the cheeses, and be difficult to cleanse. Full-bodied, aromatic red wines, flavorful white wines such as Gewürztraminer and especially malty beers such as Oktoberfest or Scottish ales, all can provide suitable pairings for these.

- **Époisses** [AY-pwah-sehs] – This is a very creamy cheese with fruity and pungent aromas and a spicy and rich flavor when aged.
- **Farmhouse Tilsit** [TIHL-ziht] – This is a much more flavorful version of Tilset. It is very pungent, nearly as much as Limburger.
- **Liederkranz** [lee-der-KRANTS] – Despite the Germanic name, this cheese was invented in the U.S. (albeit by a German-speaking Swiss immigrant). A pungent, strong-tasting, but creamy and very tasty cheese that is perfectly suited to flavorful beer. The name comes from its popularity in the late nineteenth century with a New York singing society, Liederkranz Hall. Often used as a less stinky substitute for Limburger.
- **Limburger** – This is a very stinky cheese that is strongly flavored, but a tasty cheese, especially when consumed with beer. Given its almost rank odor, you might wonder if the cheese has gone bad. If the rind is cracked and the cheese runny, it most likely has.
- **Münster** (aged) [MOON-ster] – A flavorful cheese with a noticeable aroma and earthy, herbaceous taste from Alsace. Becomes very pungent when aged. A great complement for a wide range of beers and white wines from either side of the Rhine.

13) Flavored Cheeses – In this category are cheeses with some flavorings added, such as spices, herbs, nuts, olives, jalapeños, and truffles, plus smoked cheeses. These have become more common in recent years as variations on popular cheeses such as Cheddar, Havarti and especially Monterey Jack, which has provided the base for a wide array of interesting flavored cheeses.

- **Leyden** [LIE-dn] – A mild, tangy and very flavorful eating cheese from Holland that is spiced with caraway and cumin seeds. Goes well with lager beers and light-bodied and fruity red and white wines. Similar to *Nökkelost*.
- **Nökkelost** [nowk-UH-loohs] – A mild, but slightly spicy and flavorful Scandinavian cheese that is spiced with cloves and either, or both, caraway and cumin seeds. It's popular for snacks and sandwiches, and melts well for cooking. Also called *kuminost*, and very similar to Leyden.

- **Pepato** [peh-PAH-toh] – This is sharp-tasting Pecorino cheese containing whole black peppercorns resulting in a spicy flavor.
- **Pepper Jack** – This is Monterey Jack studded with bits of jalapeños or another pepper. This can be a wonderful snacking cheese, especially when paired with lager beer.

MATCHING WINE AND CHEESE

When matching wines and cheeses, try to have the flavors either complement or contrast. Of course, with a cheese plate where there are several types of cheeses and one wine, some of the matches will do neither. But, even the less-than-perfect matches are not that bad and most are less than perfect. Award-winning wine writer Joanna Simon has even written that **"cheese is one of the trickiest foods to choose wine for."** Even so, having cheese to nibble on with wine is somewhat expected at most social functions, and the accompanying bread or crackers can help to cleanse the palate between the wine and cheese. And, not incidentally, cheese is readily affordable and easy to provide.

Some classic or **recommended wine and cheese combinations** are:

Cheese	Best Wine Match	Other Wine Matches
Brie	Brut champagne	White Burgundy, Chablis, Beaujolais
Cheddar	Cabernet Sauvignon	Zinfandel, Merlot, Chardonnay
Chèvre	Sancerre	Sauvignon Blanc
Parmesan	Amarone	Chianti, Zinfandel, Chablis, Chardonnay
Roquefort	Sauternes	Bual Madeira, Tawny Port
Stilton	Tawny port	Rioja Reserva, Cabernet Sauvignon

Good, hard cheeses match best with the greatest array of wines. **Manchego** from Spain has been described as the most wine-friendly cheese. Some other excellent hard cheeses that should work well when providing cheese as an appetizer or after-dinner course are: **Parmigiano-Reggiano** (Parmesan), the similar **Grana Padano**, artisanal **Cheddar**, **Gruyère**, **Dry Jack**, and a couple of English farmhouse cheeses, **Double Gloucester** and **Leicester**. In lieu of a cheese plate with a variety of cheeses, **you might want to just provide a well-made version of one** of these cheeses.

Though there has been far more ink given to matching wine and cheese, **beer is generally a much better match with cheeses** (and not just because beer drinkers might be less discriminating).

ABOUT THE RECIPES

The recipes that we have chosen have most of the following characteristics: these can be prepared beforehand; can serve a large group; are easy to serve or are self-serve; are generally easy to make; and many are easy-to-eat.

The somewhat eclectic group of recipes we provide has the added benefit that each is quite flavorful. (Indeed, that's the goal of any recipe collection, or it should be, at least.) Many recipes feature a fair amount of tasty fat, which will make them more readily enjoyable for your guests. Fat does add flavor, after all. Low fat (or low carbohydrate or low calorie) foods and recipes should generally be avoided when entertaining, or used judiciously. It's a party, after all. **It's not a good idea to impose any severe food constraints on your guests** that you might have unless they are good friends and know what to expect.

The recipes that we have included have been tested many times over, both in the hands of talented and not-so-talented cooks, oftentimes under the influence of a fair amount of alcohol. So, **these recipes will be fairly easy to prepare for the vast majority of home cooks**. These are aimed at the novice, casual or intermediate cook. So, if you are a budding Thomas Keller, Bocuse or Lagasse, these recipes might seem simple. In any case, we recommend that you cook at the level that you are comfortable, or just slightly above.

These recipes are not meant to be exhaustive in any way in terms of what you might want to use for your event. We aren't that presumptuous. But, in addition to being useful and tasty, these might provide help in bringing to mind other dishes that might work well. In the References section we have included a list of recommended cookbooks that should provide some help, especially for those who could benefit from some added confidence in the kitchen.

Unless it is a baked pasta dish such as lasagna or baked ziti, avoid pastas for a party. Pastas featuring boiled noodles topped with a sauce (linguine with clams, Pasta Carbonara, Fettuccine Alfredo, etc.) are meant to be eaten immediately after cooking and become far less edible afterwards. In his Italian-American cookbook, noted food writer John Mariani relates a story of a dinner with Luciano Pavarotti, who became very agitated while waiting for the entire party to be served before eating. "Pasta waits for no man," he exclaimed after his pasta became clumpy and had to be redone. The aforementioned not-so-delicate baked pasta dishes, conversely, work very well for large social events.

Most of our recipes will have a south Louisiana, New Orleans and Gulf Coast flavor to them. These types of dishes are very popular both in

Louisiana, and neighboring areas. Depending on where you live, these dishes might provide a level of exoticism. These are party-tested and from **a region that lives for good food and celebrating in fine fashion,** so give them a try. If you are more comfortable with dishes from your area, so be it. **There is no one type of dish or cuisine that works exclusively well for social events.** People do celebrate and entertain differently across the globe. The list of foods good for entertaining purposes is nearly limitless.

Many of the recipes provided are mostly authentic New Orleans and Cajun family recipes. This type of food is usually hearty and often zesty. It's not fiery, which is a common mistake that many make concerning Cajun food. As it is done in south Louisiana, our recipes do not call for a lot of pepper-based ingredients, the source of much of the heat. Your guests can adjust the heat of their individual dishes by providing them with condiments such as the indispensable Louisiana-style pepper sauce, such as the popular Tabasco brand, or Tony Chachere's seasoning (pronounced "saah-shuh-REE"), which may or may not be available near you. If not, you can order it on-line.

We include several recipes for easy-to-prepare condiments or sauces, which we believe can be very useful for entertaining. Freshly prepared condiments and sauces can provide some more diversity in flavors when paired with roasted beef and pork, which are often the centerpiece dishes for decent-sized dinner parties. Having two sauces for a single entrée is almost like providing two entrées. In addition to providing additional flavors, it can also help cover up some minor (or not-so minor) mistakes when cooking the meat.

The recipes are meant to be helpful and used, and used at your own discretion. Like our thoughts concerning templates for parties, we thought it was a waste of time to suggest entire menus, as these are seemingly never put into practice. Parties, including dinner parties, are individualistic and timely affairs, after all.

THE FOOD RECIPES

APPETIZERS

Bacon & Tomato Tartlets
Beef Satay
Bruschetta, Texas-Style
Bruschetta with Feta
Cajun Crawfish Cornbread
Cajun Seafood Dip
Cheddar & Chutney Sandwiches
Chile con Queso
Marinated Mozzarella
Red Pepper Hummus
Red Sauce & Goat Cheese Dip

ENTRÉES

Beef Tenderloin with Bourbon
Chicken & Sausage Gumbo
Chicken Marengo, Illinois
Easy Beef Tenderloin
Easy Roast Beef
Easy Standing Rib Roast
King Ranch Chicken
New Orleans-Style Barbecue Shrimp
Pork Loin with Mustard & Rosemary
Red Beans & Rice

CONDIMENTS / SAUCES

Caper Sauce
Green Peppercorn Sauce
Red Wine-Ginger Sauce
Soy-Ginger Sauce
Tomato-Basil Sauce

SIDES

Cheese-Battered Tomatoes
Chilled Asparagus with Sesame
    Vinaigrette
Chilled Zucchini with Fresh Mint

Maque Choux
Mashed Potatoes & Variations
Potato & Stilton Gratin
Roasted Potatoes with Garlic
Sautéed Fresh Corn
Spinach Gratin

DESSERTS

Bread Pudding à la Fuselier
New Orleans Peanut Butter Pie
Strawberries with Marsala

BACON & TOMATO TARTLETS ────────

APPETIZER

This a very easy appetizer that works well hot, warm and even lukewarm, so it's a perfect fit for party situations, especially with a beer or a glass of wine.

Serves – 8 or more as an appetizer

Ingredients:

Bacon – 8 slices
Tomato, seeded and chopped – 1
Swiss or Monterey Jack Cheese, shredded – 4 ounces
Parmesan Cheese, shredded or grated – ⅓ cup
Mayonnaise – ½ cup
Refrigerated Flaky Biscuit Dough – 1 can; Hungry Jack brand works well.
Dried Basil – 1 teaspoon
Dried Thyme – 1 teaspoon
Dried Oregano – ½ teaspoon
Garlic Powder – 1 teaspoon
Salt - Dash

Assembly Steps:

1. Preheat oven to **350° F** (177° C). Lightly grease a mini-muffin pan.
2. In a skillet over **medium** heat, cook bacon until evenly brown. Drain on paper towels.
3. Crumble bacon into a medium mixing bowl, and mix with tomato, cheeses, mayonnaise and herbs, garlic and salt.
4. Separate biscuits into thirds horizontally. Place each third into cups of the prepared mini-muffin pan. Fill each tartlet cup with the bacon mixture.
5. Bake for 10 to 12 minutes.

To Serve:

Simply arrange artfully on a plate or serving tray.

BEEF SATAY

APPETIZER

This dish can add some interesting flavors to the appetizer plates while being surprisingly easy to create, and works well when you desire that meat appetizer.

Serves – 8 or more as an appetizer

Ingredients:

For the Marinade:

Green Onion, finely chopped – 1
Ketchup – ⅓ cup
Soy Sauce – ⅓ cup
Brown Sugar – 3 tablespoons
Lime Juice – 3 tablespoons
Peanut Oil – 1 teaspoon
Ginger, grated – 1 teaspoon
Garlic, finely chopped – 3 cloves
Red Pepper Flakes – ¼ teaspoon
Water – ¼ cup

For the Rest of the Dish:

Top Round or Beef Tenderloin – 1 ½ pounds
Creamy Peanut Butter – ⅙ cup

Assembly Steps:

1. In a bowl whisk together all of the marinade ingredients.
2. Trim the excess fat from the beef, and cut into ¾ inch cubes.
3. Place the cubes in a re-sealable plastic bag and pour in the marinade.
4. Press the air from the bag and seal it. Refrigerate it for 1 to 2 hours.
5. Remove the meat from the bag, reserving the marinade.
6. Thread the cubes onto skewers, leaving a small space between the cubes. Allow to sit at room temperature for twenty to thirty minutes.
7. Grill or broil the meat over direct, high heat until it is cooked to medium-rare, and set aside.

8. Pour the reserved marinade into a small saucepan. Bring to a boil over **high** heat for 1 minute. Add the peanut butter, and return the mixture to a boil. Whisk while cooking until the sauce thickens.

To Serve:

Pour the sauce over the beef skewers, or serve it separately in a bowl.

BRUSCHETTA, TEXAS-STYLE

APPETIZER

This is an easy way to prepare the popular appetizer, bruschetta, with a Southwestern twist. (If you want to appear more sophisticated be sure to tell your guests that this is supposed to be pronounced "broo-SKEH-tah." They might believe that these taste better, too). In the name of convenience, we do away with the traditional step of rubbing the toasted bread with a clove of garlic.

Serves – 8 or more as an appetizer

Ingredients:

For Preparation:

Garlic, finely chopped – 6 cloves
Roma Tomatoes, ripe, diced – 3
Red Onion, diced – ¼ onion
Serrano Peppers, seeded and diced – 2
Cilantro, chopped – 2 tablespoons
Black pepper, freshly ground – To taste
Extra Virgin Olive Oil – 6 to 10 tablespoons
Basil, freshly torn – 4 leaves; *Optional*
Dried Oregano – ½ teaspoon; *Optional*

For Serving:

Baguette – 1, sliced and toasted

Assembly Steps:

1. With the exception of the olive oil, mix all of the chopped ingredients in a small bowl.

2. Add enough oil to coat all of the ingredients without being runny.

Note – The amount of garlic, onion and cilantro can be adjusted to taste.

To Serve:

Serve in a bowl accompanied with toasted baguette slices.

BRUSCHETTA WITH FETA

APPETIZER

This is another easy recipe for bruschetta that could possibly be found at a functional Greek-owned Italian restaurant.   This has a greater tomato-quotient than the previous bruschetta recipe.

Serves – 8 or more as an appetizer

Ingredients:

For Preparation:

Garlic, finely chopped – 4 cloves
Roma Tomatoes, ripe, diced – 4
Chives, finely chopped – ¼ bunch
Feta Cheese, crumbled – ½ cup
Lemon Juice – ½ a lemon
Salt – ½ teaspoon
Extra Virgin Olive Oil – 6 to 10 tablespoons; enough to coat.
Kalamata Olives, seeded, sliced – 6 to 8; *Optional*
Capers – 1 teaspoon; *Optional*
Dried Oregano – ½ teaspoon; *Optional*

For Serving:

Baguette – 1, sliced and toasted

Assembly Steps:

1. With the exception of the olive oil and lemon juice, mix all of the ingredients together in a small bowl. Add the olive oil and lemon juice and toss again.
2. Apply mixture to each piece of toasted bread.

To Serve:

Arrange on a tray.

CAJUN CRAWFISH BREAD ————————————————

APPETIZER OR SIDE

Crawfish has become more readily available over the years, seemingly throughout much of the country. Though the tastier Louisiana or Texas crawfish is preferred for use in this dish, frozen Chinese crawfish will also work. For the cornbread, any recipe will do. You can also use cornbread mix and simply follow the instructions on the box. Most mixes require only the addition of milk or water.

Serves – 8 or more as an appetizer

Ingredients

Cornbread Mix – A 16 ounce box; you will need milk or water with this
Crawfish Tails – 2 pounds; thawed
Garlic, finely chopped – 3 cloves
Butter, unsalted – 8 ounces (1 stick)
Onion – 1 large, finely chopped
Celery, diced – 2 stalks
Cajun Spices – ½ cup; you should be able to find this in the spice section
    with this name or as "Creole Seasonings."
Green Bell Pepper, seeded and diced – 1
Red Bell Pepper, seeded and diced – 1
Yellow Bell Pepper, seeded and diced – 1

Cooking Steps:

1. Melt the butter over **medium** heat in a saucepan.
2. Add the crawfish tails, peppers, onions, garlic and ¼ cup of the Cajun spices to the pan and cook until the onions are translucent.
3. Drain.
4. Add the remaining Cajun spices and the sautéed items to the cornbread mixture and mix well.
5. After coating a baking dish with oil, add the cornbread and crawfish mixture then follow the baking instructions on the box.
6. When finished baking and cooled, cut into squares.

To Serve:

On a plate or a tray. This works well as a side when served warm, as a fork is needed. For an appetizer, it should be cooled or even slightly chilled so that it can properly solidify and be cut and then eaten as finger food.

CAJUN SEAFOOD DIP (OR CRAWFISH DIP) ————

APPETIZER

This recipe is from our good friend Hank Fuselier, originally from Morgan City, Louisiana. This dish has been a big hit over the years for casual get-togethers, especially when Hank is also cooking some freshly-caught fish from the Gulf of Mexico. Shrimp can be substituted for the crawfish, though the flavor will be somewhat different.

Serves – 8 or more as an appetizer

Ingredients

For Cooking:

Crawfish Tails – 1 pound; thawed if frozen
Garlic, finely chopped – 6 cloves
Butter, unsalted – 8 ounces (1 stick)
Heavy Cream – 4 ounce (1 cup)
White Onion – 1 large, finely chopped
Celery, diced – 4 stalks
Cream Cheese – 16 ounces (2 - 8 ounce blocks); near room temperature
Lemon Juice – 1 lemon
Cayenne Pepper – 1 teaspoon
Salt – To taste
Black Pepper, freshly ground – To taste

For Serving:

Baguette – 1, sliced and toasted; works better than crackers; OR
Saltine Crackers

Cooking Steps:

1. Melt the butter over **medium heat** in a saucepan.

2. Sauté the garlic until it's golden. Be careful not to burn it.
3. Add the crawfish tails, and cook at least five minutes, until done.
4. Remove the crawfish and garlic with a straining spoon, leaving as much of the liquid in the pan as possible (for disposal), and transfer to a food processor.
5. Add the heavy cream to the crawfish mixture and run the food processor until it's finely chopped, but not liquefied. Add more cream if the mixture appears too lumpy.
6. In a large mixing bowl add in the cream cheese, crawfish mixture, onions, celery, cayenne pepper, juice of the lemon, and salt and pepper to taste. Mix thoroughly.
7. Refrigerate for at least an hour.

To Serve:

Serve in a bowl, or bowls, with crackers or toasted baguette slices.

CHEDDAR & CHUTNEY SANDWICHES —————

APPETIZER

This is an easy adaptation of the popular British combination of cheddar cheese and a popular style of chutney. The Brits are well versed in finger foods that complement a wide variety of alcoholic beverages.

This will make 40 little sandwiches. Each is very easy, and can be done well before the event. Be sure to purchase fresh, high quality rolls and very good cheddar for this. There are excellent versions of cheddar made in New York, Vermont along with those made in England. A flavorful cheddar cheese marries well with slightly sweet mango-flavored Major Grey's chutney. In case you don't know, Major Grey's is a style rather than a brand, or a person. It comes in several variations, and labels. The sweet mango flavor well complements the sharpness of the cheddar cheese. Tomato chutney also works.

Serves – A couple dozen, or so

Ingredients:

Small Rolls – 40
Major Grey's Chutney – 2 jars
Extra-sharp Cheddar Cheese, thickly sliced – 1 ½ pounds

Assembly Steps:

1. Cut each roll in half sideways, so it will make a little sandwich.
2. Spread chutney on the bottom half of each roll.
3. Place a slice of cheddar cheese on top of the chutney and cover with the top half of the roll.

To Serve:

Just put these on a plate or platter once assembled.

CHILE CON QUESO [CHIL-EEH KON KAY-SO] ———

APPETIZER

For a great many Texans, this gooey, messy mixture is a taste of home. Though Velveeta will not be found in *Larousse Gastronomique*, it helps ensure a creamy and appealing texture. Note that freshly-made *pico de gallo* (about 6 to 8 ounces) can substitute for the onion, tomato, jalapeño and cilantro.

Serves – 8 or so

Ingredients:

For Cooking:

Jalapeño, seeded and chopped – 1
Tomato, chopped – ¼ cup
Onion, finely chopped – ¼ cup
Cilantro, chopped – 1 tablespoon
Cheddar Cheese, grated – 1 cup
Velveeta Cheese, cut into pieces – 1 cup
Heavy Cream **or** Milk – ½ cup
Butter – 4 tablespoons (½ of a stick)
Lemon **or** Lime – ¼ of the fruit

For Serving:

Tortilla Chips

Cooking Steps:

1. Mix together the jalapeño, tomato, onion and cilantro in a bowl. Squeeze lemon or lime over the mixture if you would like.
2. Melt the butter on **high** heat.
3. Put the mixture into a skillet and sauté for 30 seconds.
4. Put both of the cheeses into the skillet, stirring often.
5. When the cheeses have melted, add the cream and stir until the mixture is smooth.
6. Transfer to a serving medium; a crockpot works the best.

To Serve:

Serve warm with tortilla chips. The cheese mixture becomes far less appealing when it gets cold. The easiest way to keep the *queso* warm is in a crockpot.

MARINATED MOZZARELLA ──────────

APPETIZER

This works well alone, or as part of an *antipasti* plate. It is a palate refresher between bites of salami. Use fresh, artisan-made, or imported mozzarella, not the tasteless stuff that comes in a brick.

Serves – 8 or more as an appetizer

Ingredients:

For Assembly:

Mozzarella – 1 pound
Red Pepper Flakes – ½ teaspoon
Flat Leaf Parsley, chopped – 1 tablespoon
Basil, chopped – 4 tablespoons
Extra Virgin Olive Oil – ¼ cup
Lemon Juice – 3 teaspoons

For Serving

Bread, crusty French or Italian – 1 loaf

Assembly Steps:

1. Cut the mozzarella into ¾ inch cubes and place in a bowl along with the parsley, basil and red pepper flakes.
2. Pour in the olive oil and lemon juice, and mix together.
3. Let marinate for at least 2 hours at room temperature before serving.

To Serve:

Put in a serving tray, and serve with slices of French or Italian bread.

RED PEPPER HUMMUS

APPETIZER

This dip will be popular even for those who believe they don't like Middle Eastern food.

Serves – A dozen, or so

Ingredients:

For Assembly:

Garlic, finely chopped – 2 cloves
Chickpeas (garbanzos) – 15 ounce can
Tahini Sauce – ⅓ cup; you can find this in most grocery stores now
Lemon Juice – ⅓ cup
Roasted Red Peppers – ½ cup; the jarred version works well.
Salt – To Taste
Black Pepper – To Taste
Olive Oil – 1 tablespoon, or so

For Serving:

Pita Bread

Assembly Steps:

1. Into a food processor add the garlic, chickpeas, tahini and lemon juice and process until smooth
2. Add the red peppers and process until these are fully chopped.
3. Season with salt and pepper.

4. Refrigerate
5. When ready to serve, drizzle the top with olive oil.

To Serve:

Serve in a bowl with pita bread, crackers or even tortilla chips.

RED SAUCE & GOAT CHEESE DIP ─────────

APPETIZER

This amazingly simple recipe never fails to please guests. This was inspired by a similar dish at the very popular Carrabba's restaurant on Kirby Drive in Houston that begat the national chain.

Serves – 8 or more as an appetizer

Ingredients:

For Cooking:

Goat Cheese (like chèvre) – 4 ounces
Bottled Spaghetti Sauce – 1 jar, 32 ounces
Basil, freshly torn – 3 leaves; *Optional*

For Serving:

Baguette, sliced into pieces

Cooking Steps:

1. Put the sauce and goat cheese into a bowl.
2. Microwave until the cheese is melted, which might be between 3 and 5 minutes depending upon the size of the serving bowl.

To Serve:

Serve the sauce and cheese mixture with slices from a baguette or Italian-style bread, toasted or otherwise

BEEF TENDERLOIN WITH BOURBON ————

ENTRÉE

This is a surprisingly easy main course. Not cheap, though.

Serves – 8

Ingredients:

Beef Tenderloin – About 5 pounds
Olive Oil – 1 cup
Red Wine Vinegar – 1 cup
Bourbon Whiskey – 1 cup

Cooking Steps:

1. Mix together the olive oil, red wine vinegar and bourbon.
2. Pour the mixture over the tenderloin and massage into the tenderloin.
3. Marinate in the refrigerator for at least 1 hour.
4. Preheat the oven to **500°F** (260°C).
5. Cook on a roasting or baking pan for 30 minutes for rare.
6. Remove beef from oven, cover with aluminum foil and let rest for at least 1 hour before serving.

To Serve:

If there is a string holding together the tenderloin, remove it, slice and serve.

Note – This recipe does not work well when pork is substituted for beef.

CHICKEN & SAUSAGE GUMBO (SOUTH LA-STYLE) ——

ENTRÉE

The LA here stands for Louisiana. Andouille [ahn-DOOH-eeh] is south Louisiana-style spicy, smoked pork sausage that helps to give this a more authentic taste. Garlic-laden pork sausage can be used if you cannot find andouille. Tasso is a lean piece of cured and seasoned pork.

Serves – At least a dozen

Ingredients:

For Cooking:

For the Roux:
Butter, unsalted – 8 ounces (1 stick)
Flour, all purpose – 8 ounces (1 cup)

For the stock:
White Onion, diced – 2 large onions
Celery, diced – 6 stalks
Bell Peppers, seeded and diced – 2
Salt – 2 teaspoons
Black Pepper, freshly ground – 1 tablespoon
Worcestershire Sauce – 1 tablespoon
Andouille Sausage, sliced – 1 pound
Tasso, finely chopped – 8 ounces; salt pork can be substituted.
Chicken Breasts, de-boned, cut into 1 inch cubes – 1 pound
Chicken Stock – 2 quarts
Water – 2 quarts

For Serving:

White Rice, steamed – 10 cups; more rice will extend the number of servings.
Green Onions, chopped – 4
Your favorite Pepper Sauce
Crusty Bread

Cooking Steps:

1. *First you make the roux….* In a two-gallon stock pot with a thick bottom, melt the butter over **high heat**; gradually add the flour, about a quarter of a cup at a time; keep stirring; cook the mixture until it is a milk chocolate color. This will probably take at least ten minutes. Partaking in a drink while stirring makes these ten minutes or so go much more quickly. For those steeped in classic French cooking the ten minutes for the roux is not a misprint. Long-cooked roux is a staple of Louisiana cooking.
2. Add the onions, celery and bell pepper. Do so carefully, as it is easy to get burned.
3. Add the salt and pepper, and stir for a few minutes.
4. Add all of the chicken stock and water, and the Worcestershire sauce.
5. Add the sausage and tasso, cover and let come to a boil.

6. Uncover, **reduce the heat slightly** so a gentle rolling boil continues, and cook for at least an hour. Stir occasionally to keep items from becoming burned on the bottom.
7. Add the chicken and cook for at least 30 minutes.

Note – The rice is cooked separately; a rice cooker is perfectly acceptable, and much easier to use.

To Serve:

1. Serve from the stovetop or a bowl heated by sterno.
2. Ladle into an individual bowl half-filled or so with steamed white rice. Be sure to scoop from both the top and bottom, since the sausage will be at the top, and the chicken on the bottom.
3. Top with the chopped green onions and your favorite pepper sauce, if desired. Crusty bread is a near necessity to serve with the gumbo.

CHICKEN MARENGO, ILLINOIS

ENTRÉE

This is a very easy variation on the classic Chicken Marengo, which was originally created by Napoleon's chef to celebrate the French victory over the Austrians in the Battle of Marengo (in northern Italy, not northern Illinois) in 1803. That initial creation used an entire chicken and included eggs and crawfish as the finishing touches, both of which are omitted for ease of use in this recipe. Inexpensive and flavorful chicken thighs make it even a little easier. Oregano replaces tarragon and additional garlic is included to give it a more Italian-American taste.

Serves – 8

Ingredients:

Chicken Thighs – 4 pounds; you can substitute a whole chicken that is cut into pieces or chicken breasts (if using boneless breasts, you might need to reduce the cooking times)
Olive Oil – ⅓ cup
Butter – 4 tablespoons
Dried Oregano – 2 teaspoons
Pepper – 1 teaspoon
Salt – 1 teaspoon
White Wine – 1 ¼ cups

Flour – ½ cup
Mushrooms, sliced – 8
Garlic, finely chopped – 6 cloves
Canned Peeled Tomatoes, chopped – 1 large can (28 ounces)
Flat-Leaf Parsley, finely chopped – 3 tablespoons

Cooking Steps:

1. Preheat the oven to **350 °F** (177° C).
2. Sprinkle the flour with the salt, pepper, and dried oregano, then dredge the chicken in it. Keep the flour.
3. Heat the oil and butter in a large pan and brown the chicken thighs in a pan over **medium** heat, about 4 minutes per side. This will probably have to be done in batches.
4. Put the browned chicken into a large casserole dish.
5. Put in an additional 5 tablespoons of the reserved flour into the pan and slowly pour in the wine while stirring. When this sauce (or roux at this point) is thick and smooth, which should be less than a minute, pour it over the chicken in the casserole dish.
6. Add the tomatoes, mushrooms and garlic on the chicken and cover.
7. Bake in oven for 45 minutes or so, until the chicken is tender and thoroughly cooked.
8. Before serving, sprinkle the chopped parsley over the dish.

Note – This can be prepared up to the point of baking ahead of time and refrigerated. If refrigerated, increase the baking time by 10 to 15 minutes. This can also be baked and kept warm until serving.

To Serve:

This works well with mashed potatoes, rice or pasta to soak up the extra sauce.

Easy Beef Tenderloin

Entrée

This is another surprisingly easy main course, albeit not inexpensive.

Serves – 8 to 10

Ingredients:

Beef Tenderloin – About 5 pounds; trimmed lean by the butcher, if possible
Butter, unsalted – 4 tablespoons (1 stick); at room temperature
Sea Salt – 1 tablespoon
Black Pepper, freshly ground – 1 tablespoon

Cooking Steps:

1. Preheat the oven to **500 °F** (260°C).
2. Place the filet on baking sheet. Remove the excess moisture from the exterior of the filet with a paper towel.
3. Slather the butter on the beef. Sprinkle with the pepper and salt.
4. Cook for 25 minutes for medium rare.
5. Remove beef from oven, cover with aluminum foil and let rest for at least 20 minutes before serving.

To Serve:

If there is a string holding together the tenderloin, remove it, slice and serve.

EASY ROAST BEEF ───────────────────

ENTRÉE

Yet another easy one; a meat thermometer will assure more accurate cooking, so use one if you have it.

Serves – 20, or so

Ingredients:

For Cooking:

Roast Beef – 15 pounds

For the Rub:

Lawry's Seasoned Salt – ½ cup
Black Pepper, coarsely ground – ¼ cup
Garlic Powder – ¼ cup
Onion Powder – ¼ cup
Cayenne Pepper – 2 tablespoons
Thyme, dried – 2 tablespoons

Cooking Steps:

1. Take the roast out of the refrigerator an hour or two before you want to cook. This allows the entire roast to come to near room temperature, and is more likely to cook evenly.
2. Preheat the oven to **250° F** (121°C). If you have a pizza stone, place it in the oven. This will even the heat, and diminish the effects of your oven's "hot spots."
3. Mix together all of the ingredients of the rub into the roast beef ten to fifteen minutes before placing into the oven. Season with salt and pepper immediately before cooking.
4. Place the roast in the lower half of the oven and cook for about 3 hours, or until the internal temperature reaches 130° F (54.5° C). Check the temperature periodically. If you want to expedite the cooking process, once the internal temperature reaches 110° F (38° C), turn the oven to **500° F** (260° C) and cook for 45 more minutes.
5. Remove beef from oven, cover with aluminum foil and let rest for at least 20 minutes before serving. This allows the juices to distribute throughout the roast.

To Serve:

Cut and serve. This size roast will work in a carving station.

EASY STANDING RIB ROAST ─────────────

ENTRÉE

This is easy, too. A meat thermometer will assure more accurate cooking, so use one if you've got it. When purchasing the meat, provision one rib for two people, i.e. six ribs should serve a dozen people.

Serves – Variable; two people per pound is a decent estimate.

Ingredients:

Standing Rib Roast or Bone-In Prime Rib

Cooking Steps:

1. Let the meat stand for an hour or two at room temperature before cooking.
2. Preheat the oven to **500°F** (260°C).

3. Place the meat in a rack in a pan with the fat side up, then place in the oven.
4. Reduce the oven temperature to **325°F** (163°C).
5. Cook, uncovered with a meat thermometer. Baste every half-hour.
6. Cook until the meat thermometer is at the following temperatures for the desired doneness: **Rare** – 115° F (46.1° C); **Medium-Rare** – 125° F (51.7° C); **Medium** – 135° F (57.2° C); **Well-Done** – 145° F (62.8° C).
7. Remove from oven, cover loosely with aluminum foil, or the like, and let stand for at least 15 minutes. The meat will continue to cook during this time.

To Serve:

Slice and serve.

KING RANCH CHICKEN ────────────────

ENTRÉE

This dish is a staple in home kitchens across the state of Texas. Though a variety of recipes exist, this comparatively easy and certainly flavorful version is from our friend Shannon Caldwell, a very good home cook, who also supplied the Bacon & Tomato Tartlets recipe.

Serves – 8

Ingredients:

Corn Tortillas – 8 to 10
Cream of Mushroom Soup – 1 can (14 ½ ounces)
Cream of Chicken Soup – 1 can (14 ½ ounces); lighter versions work fine.
Chicken Broth – 1 can (14 ½ ounces); or, broth from poaching the chicken.
Rotel Brand Tomatoes with Green Chilies – 1 can (14 ½ ounces)
Chopped Green Chilies – 1 can (14 ½ ounces)
Onion, chopped – 1
Butter – 2 tablespoons
Cheddar **or** Monterrey Jack – 2 cups; a combination of these also works well.
Chicken Breasts – 4
Vegetable Oil – 2 tablespoons; just to coat a casserole dish; PAM works, too.

Cooking Steps:

1. Poach the chicken in water, then shred into bite-sized pieces.

2. Heat the corn tortillas in a pan over **low** heat until all are softened.
3. Preheat oven to **375° F** (191° C).
4. In a large saucepan or pot, sauté onion in butter until tender. Mix in the soups, Rotel, chilies and broth. Heat until warm, but not boiling.
5. Line the sides of a large casserole dish with oil. Tear or cut tortillas into pieces and spread one layer of tortillas in pan. Layer with shredded chicken. Top with the sauce from the pan. Repeat with the tortilla, chicken and sauce until you are out of ingredients. Make sure that the sauce is the layer on top.
6. Bake for 30 to 40 minutes until done.
7. Sprinkle with shredded cheese and return to oven until melted.

Note – This can be assembled ahead of time and refrigerated. If refrigerated, increase the baking time by 10 to 15 minutes.

To Serve:

This works well with mashed potatoes, rice, or as a one-pot dish.

NEW ORLEANS-STYLE BARBECUE SHRIMP ———

ENTRÉE

Barbecue is a misnomer here, as this dish is actually baked, not barbecued. A version of this dish was originally created at the New Orleans restaurant Pascale Manale's some years ago. This amazingly flavorful dish is surprisingly easy, and great for parties, since most of the work is done beforehand. Though shrimp is commonly sold without heads these days, it's better to find whole shrimp for this dish. There is a lot of flavor in those heads. If you want to use pre-peeled shrimps, let's say for finger food, just increase the marinade time at least another hour or so.

Serves – 8 to 10

Ingredients:

Large Shrimp (uncooked & heads-on) – 4 to 6 pounds
Butter – 3 sticks
Olive Oil – ½ cup (4 ounces)
Garlic, finely chopped – 4 cloves
Bay Leaves, crumbled – 2
Lemon Juice – 4 tablespoons; use the juice from freshly-squeezed lemons.
Worcestershire Sauce – 2 tablespoons

Flat-Leaf Parley, finely chopped – 1 tablespoon
Oregano, dried – 2 teaspoons
Paprika – 2 teaspoons
Cayenne Pepper – 2 teaspoons
Louisiana-style Hot Sauce – 1 teaspoon
Black Pepper, freshly ground – 2 teaspoons
Chili Sauce – ½ cup (4 ounces)
Lemons, thinly sliced – 4

Cooking Steps:

1. Place the butter in the saucepan over **medium-low heat**. As the butter melts add all of the remaining ingredients, except for the shrimp. Simmer for 10 minutes.
2. Place the shrimp in a large baking dish and then pour the butter mixture over it. Arrange the thin lemon slices in rows over the shrimp. Cover the dish with plastic wrap and then store in the refrigerator for at least 2 hours. The longer the better.
3. Preheat the oven to **300°F** (149°C).
4. When nearly ready for your guests, put it in the oven at **300°F** (149°C) and cook for 20 to 30 minutes.

To Serve:

Serve with steamed rice and crusty French bread. For more casual settings, the bread alone will suffice.

PORK LOIN WITH DIJON MUSTARD & ROSEMARY ——

ENTRÉE

This is amazingly easy, and inexpensive.

Serves – 8

Ingredients:

Pork Loin – About 3 pounds
Dijon Mustard – 2 tablespoons
Onion, finely chopped – 1
Garlic, finely chopped – 2 cloves
Salt, preferably sea salt – 2 tablespoons
Black Pepper – ½ teaspoon

Rosemary, dried – 2 tablespoons

Cooking Steps:

1. Preheat the oven to **350 °F** (177° C).
2. Rub the mustard over the pork loin.
3. Cover the top and sides of the pork loin with the onion and garlic, then the salt, pepper and dried rosemary.
4. Cook on a roasting or baking pan for 90 minutes or so for rare.
5. Remove beef from oven, cover with aluminum foil and let rest for at least 15 minutes before serving.

To Serve:

Slice and serve.

RED BEANS & RICE ─────────────────

ENTRÉE

Its praises have been sung throughout the years by artists with such diversity in talent as New Orleans native Louis Armstrong and Sir Mix-A-Lot. Along with the crawfish dip and gumbo recipes, this version is from Hank Fuselier, the "Executive Chef" for the annual Big Crawfish Boil held since the early 1990s at the landmark West Alabama Ice House in Houston. During that event over the years, this recipe has helped provide sustenance for thousands of guests, while collecting donations for a charity that helps the homeless. If you cannot find Louisiana-style Andouille sausage in your area, substitute a garlicky pork and beef sausage.

Serves – 8 to 10

Ingredients:

For Cooking:

White Onion, diced – 1 large
Bell Pepper, seeded and diced – 1
Garlic, finely chopped – 3 cloves
New Orleans-style Red Beans, dry – 2 pounds
Andouille Sausage, sliced – 1 pound
Salt Pork, cubed – 8 ounces
Water – Enough to cover the beans

Salt – To taste
Black Pepper, freshly ground – 1 tablespoon

For Serving:

White Rice, steamed – 4 cups
Green Onion, chopped – 1
Your favorite pepper sauce
Tony Chachere's – To taste

Cooking Steps:

1. Sauté the salt pork on **medium-high** heat until the fat is liquefied in a large stockpot. This will be about seven to ten minutes.
2. Add the onions, pepper, and garlic, and mix thoroughly. Cook until the onions are clear, which is probably between ten and fifteen minutes.
3. Add the beans.
4. Add enough water to cover the beans, and turn the heat to **high**, and cook until it boils.
5. Add the sausage and the black pepper. Reduce the heat to **medium**, and cook for at least an hour until the mixture thickens. The longer the cooking, the thicker the resulting dish.

Note – The rice is cooked separately; a rice cooker is perfectly acceptable, and much easier.

To Serve:

1. Serve the red beans & rice and the steamed white rice in separate bowls.
2. Have the guests ladle into individual bowls, half-filled or so with steamed white rice.
3. Top with the chopped green onions and your favorite pepper sauce and Tony Chachere's, if desired.

Tony Chachere's is a flavorful and somewhat spicy dried seasoning consisting of salt, black pepper, cayenne pepper, sweet paprika and garlic powder. If not found at your local grocer, Tony Chachere's can be ordered at www.tonychachere.com.

CAPER SAUCE ──────────────

CONDIMENT / SAUCE

A good complement to roasts, too.

Serves – Variable

Ingredients:

Butter – 2 tablespoons
Flour – 2 tablespoons
Beef Stock – 1 cup; chicken or veal stock can also be substituted
Horseradish – ½ tablespoon
Capers – 2 ½ ounces

Cooking Steps:

1. Heat the beef stock until it boils for at least a minute.
2. Melt the butter in a saucepan over **medium** heat.
3. Add the flour, stir and cook for about 1 minute without browning the flour.
4. Add all of the hot beef stock. Stir vigorously with a whisk until the sauce is smooth and thick.
5. Add the horseradish and capers and blend in gently.

To Serve:

Ladle on the sliced beef or another main dish when serving.

GREEN PEPPERCORN SAUCE ──────────

CONDIMENT / SAUCE

This goes very well with roasts.

Serves – Variable

Ingredients:

Butter – 1 ounce
Shallot, finely chopped – 1
Green Peppercorns – ⅛ cup

Brandy – 1 tablespoon
Chicken Stock – ⅛ cup
Heavy Cream – ⅝ cup + ¼ cup
Cornstarch – 1 tablespoon

Cooking Steps:

1. Melt the butter in a heavy saucepan over **medium** heat.
2. Add the chopped shallots and cook for 45 seconds.
3. Add the green peppercorns, brandy, and chicken stock; bring to a boil.
4. Add ⅝ cup of the heavy cream and bring to a boil again.
5. In a separate bowl, mix ¼ cup more of the heavy cream and the cornstarch then stir to form a smooth, lump-free mixture.
6. Add the cream-cornstarch mixture to the pan, and cook until the contents of the pan reach a fairly smooth consistency then remove from the heat.

To Serve:

Ladle on the sliced beef or another main dish when serving.

RED WINE-GINGER SAUCE

CONDIMENT / SAUCE

Another sauce that complements roasted beef and similar dishes.

Serves – Variable

Ingredients:

Red Wine – 1 cup
Red Wine Vinegar – ⅓ cup
Shallots, finely chopped – 1 tablespoon
Heavy Cream – ⅙ cup
Butter – ⅔ pound
Ginger, grated – ⅔ tablespoon
Lemon Juice – ½ a lemon
Salt – Pinch
White Pepper – Pinch; black pepper can be substituted

Cooking Steps:

1. Combine the red wine, red wine vinegar and chopped shallots in a sauce pan over **medium** heat and cook until the contents have reduced to about ¼ cup.
2. Add the heavy cream, salt and pepper and mix well.
3. Reduce the heat to **low**. Add the butter slowly, stirring constantly, and cook until all of the butter is melted.
4. Add the lemon juice and ginger and mix well.
5. Hold the sauce in bowl in a warm water bath or the like until serving, so that the sauce will not separate.

To Serve:

Ladle on the sliced beef or another main dish when serving.

SOY-GINGER SAUCE ──────────────

CONDIMENT / SAUCE

This is extremely easy to make, and works really well with pork (especially a tenderloin), pork chops, and baked or grilled salmon entrées. Steamed white rice is a fitting accompaniment for both the meat or fish and this sauce. There is no cooking, and this can be made well ahead of time.

Serves – 8 to 10

Ingredients:

Soy Sauce – ½ cup
Lemon Juice – 4 teaspoons; this from about ½ a lemon.
Ginger, grated – 1 teaspoon; use more, if you would like, it works well.
Sugar – 3 teaspoons

Assembly Steps:

Just mix all of the ingredients together.

To Serve:

Ladle on pork, salmon or another main dish when serving. And, it works very well with steamed white rice.

Note – Light lager beer or a light-bodied Pinot Noir go well with this sauce. A Riesling Spätlese is an even better choice.

TOMATO-BASIL SAUCE

CONDIMENT / SAUCE

This also goes well with roasts. Creating this is similar to the sauce above.

Serves – Variable

Ingredients:

Red Wine – 1 cup
Red Wine Vinegar – ⅓ cup
Shallots, finely chopped – 1 tablespoon
Heavy Cream – ⅙ cup
Butter – ⅔ pound
Lemon Juice – ½ a lemon
Basil, chopped – ⅔ bunch
Tomatoes, seeded, peeled and chopped – 3
Tomato Paste – 1 ounce
Salt – Pinch
White Pepper – Pinch; black pepper can be substituted.

Cooking Steps:

1. Combine the red wine, red wine vinegar and chopped shallots in a sauce pan over **medium** heat and cook until the contents have reduced to about ¼ cup.
2. Add the heavy cream, salt and pepper and mix well.
3. Reduce the heat to **low**. Add the butter slowly, stirring constantly, and cook until all of the butter is melted.
4. Add the lemon juice, tomatoes, basil and tomato paste and mix well.
5. Hold the sauce in bowl in a warm water bath or the like until serving, so that the sauce will not separate.

To Serve:

Ladle on the sliced beef or another main dish when serving.

CHEESE-BATTERED TOMATOES

SIDE OR APPETIZER

This dish should be served hot. So, you should prepare it after the guests arrive, at least the final cooking of it.

Serves – 8

Ingredients:

Eggs, large – 4
Parmesan Cheese, grated – ½ cup
Basil, finely chopped – 2 tablespoons
Tomatoes, large ripe – 4
Flour – 1 cup
Olive Oil – ½ cup
Salt – To Taste
Black Pepper, freshly ground – To taste

Cooking Steps:

1. Beat the eggs in a bowl then mix in the Parmesan cheese and basil. Let sit for 30 minutes at room temperature.
2. Slice off both the top and bottom of the tomatoes. Then cut into four slices of equal thickness (not quartered).
3. Season the flour with salt and pepper.
4. Heat the olive oil in a heavy skillet over **medium** heat.
5. Dust the tomato slices on both sides with the seasoned flour, then dip into the egg mixture. **Note** – You can stop at this point and refrigerate the coated tomatoes, saving the frying until the guests are ready for them.
6. Place the tomatoes in the skillet, turning once, and cook until golden brown on both sides.
7. Drain on paper towels and serve hot.

To Serve:

This works as a side or as an appetizer.

Chilled Asparagus with Sesame Vinaigrette —

Side

This is easy and can be made the day beforehand.

Serves – 8

Ingredients:

Asparagus, trimmed – 2 pounds
Sesame Oil – 2 tablespoons + 2 teaspoons
Rice Vinegar – 1 tablespoon + 1 teaspoon
Soy Sauce – 1 tablespoon + 1 teaspoon
Sugar – 1 teaspoon
Salt
Pepper
Sesame Seeds, toasted – 1 teaspoon, or so

Cooking Steps:

1. Cook asparagus in a large skillet filled with salted boiling water until just tender enough, which is about 4 minutes.
2. Rinse the asparagus with cold water and drain well.
3. Pat dry, and arrange on a platter.
4. Mix the sesame oil, rice vinegar, soy sauce and sugar in a bowl. Season to taste with salt and pepper. **Note** – If preparing the night before, store the asparagus and dressing separately, just cover each and refrigerate.
5. Spoon dressing over the asparagus. Sprinkle with the toasted sesame seeds and serve.

To Serve:

Serve as a side.

CHILLED ZUCCHINI WITH FRESH MINT ——————

SIDE

This is another easy one that is made well before guests arrive, typically the night before. This dish seems to work best in the warmer months, where it can provide a tart and refreshing contrast to the entrée.

Serves – 8

Ingredients:

Zucchini, sliced into ⅛" slices – 2 pounds; five to eight zucchinis.
Extra Virgin Olive oil – ½ cup + 2 tablespoons
Garlic, finely chopped – 3 cloves

Red Wine Vinegar – 3 tablespoons
Mint, chopped – 6 to 8 leaves
Salt – 1 teaspoon

Cooking Steps:

1. Heat the olive oil in a large pan over **medium** heat.
2. Cook the zucchini slices until golden and firm, turning once, which is about six to eight minutes total. Be careful not to break the slices.
3. Move the zucchini to a serving dish, and let cool to nearly room temperature.
4. Add the mint, garlic, vinegar, salt, and extra olive oil.
5. Refrigerate for at least 4 hours.

To Serve:

Serve as a side. This works well as a leftover, too.

MAQUE CHOUX [MOCK-SHOO] ───────────

SIDE

As above, this is best in the late summer or early autumn when corn is at its best. This is the classic south Louisiana take on corn. The addition of the optional hot pepper gives it a southeast Texas twist and some more heat.

Serves – 8

Ingredients:

Corn, ears – 8
Tomatoes, diced – 2
Onions, chopped – 1
Green Pepper, chopped – ½ pepper
Jalapeño **or** Serrano Pepper, seeded and finely chopped – 1; *Optional*
Butter, unsalted – 4 tablespoons
Salt – ½ teaspoon
Black Pepper, freshly ground – ½ teaspoon

Cooking Steps:

1. Remove the cobs of corn from the husks, and trim kernels from the cob.
2. Melt half the butter in a large sauté pan over **medium-low** heat.

3. Add the corn, tomatoes, onions and pepper(s) and bring to simmer for 10 minutes, stirring constantly.
4. Add the remaining butter, salt and pepper and cook for another 5 minutes, or until done.

To Serve:

This can be made an hour or two beforehand and kept warm, covered in the oven on **very low** heat, just don't let it dry out. Tony Chachere's or Louisiana-style pepper sauce goes naturally with this.

MASHED POTATOES & VARIATIONS ————————

SIDE

Serves – 8

OK, mashed potatoes are certainly nothing unusual, but there are several different ingredients you can add to give an interesting and flavorful twist. Several variations are shown below, but the possibilities are nearly endless.

Ingredients:

Potatoes, peeled and cubed – 8; medium-sized (about 1 ½ pounds each)
Onion, cut in half – 1
Milk, whole – 2 cups
Butter, unsalted – 4 tablespoons (this is ½ of a stick)
Salt – 1 tablespoon
Black Pepper, freshly ground – ½ teaspoon

Variation – Blue Cheese Mashed Potatoes – Additional Ingredients:
Blue Cheese, crumbled – ½ cup

Variation – Cream Cheese Mashed Potatoes – Additional Ingredients:
Cream Cheese, cut into small cubes – 5 ounces

Variation – Gruyère Mashed Potatoes – Additional Ingredients:
Gruyère Cheese, grated – ½ cup

Variation – Horseradish Mashed Potatoes – Additional Ingredients:
Horseradish – 1 tablespoon; this will result in a horseradish subtle flavor.

Variation – Wasabi Mashed Potatoes – Additional Ingredients:

Wasabi – 1 tablespoon; paste will work, but freshly grated is best.

Cooking Steps:

1. Peel the potatoes and cut into cubes.
2. Put the potatoes and onion halves into a pot with salted boiling water, and cook until the potatoes are tender but not mushy.
3. Discard the onions, and drain the potatoes, and mash thoroughly with a fork, potato masher or mixer.
4. Place in a large pan over **low** heat. Add the butter, and slowly add the milk while stirring the potatoes. Cook until all of the ingredients meld and the potatoes are at the desired consistency.
5. Season with salt and pepper.

Variations

6. Add the additional ingredient and stir until mixed in thoroughly.

To Serve:

Serve as a side.

POTATOES & STILTON GRATIN ━━━━━━

SIDE

There is plenty of potato and cheesy goodness with this fairly rich dish that will make a fitting match to one of the roasts. Though there are many steps, it is an easy recipe to follow. If you are an inexperienced cook, serving something called a "Gratin" should impress your guests.

Serves – 8

Ingredients:

Russet Potatoes, unpeeled, thinly sliced – 3 pounds
Chicken Broth – 3 cups
Heavy Cream – 1 ½ cups
Shallots, thinly sliced – 4
Salt – To Taste
Black Pepper, freshly ground – To Taste
Stilton, crumbled – 3 cups

Cooking Steps:

1. Preheat the oven to **400° F** (204° C).
2. Put potatoes, chicken broth, cream and shallots in a large, heavy skillet, and bring to a simmer.
3. Reduce heat to **medium-low**, cover and cook for about 10 minutes, stirring occasionally.
4. Using a slotted spoon, transfer half the mixture to a baking dish and season with salt and pepper.
5. Sprinkle 1 cup of the cheese on it.
6. Transfer the remaining potato mixture to the baking dish, and then pour the cooking liquid over it.
7. Season with salt and pepper then sprinkle another cup of cheese on top.
8. Cover with foil and bake for 45 minutes.
9. Uncover and sprinkle the last cup of cheese on top.
10. Bake until the liquid is nearly completely absorbed, about 1 hour.
11. Cool 20 minutes before serving.

To Serve:

Serve as a side.

ROASTED POTATOES WITH GARLIC

SIDE

Everyone likes potatoes as a side dish, and the contrasting colors of beige, red and green will make this dish seem more involved than it really is.

Serves – 8

Ingredients:

Red Potatoes, small, unpeeled – 3 pounds
Extra Virgin Olive Oil – ⅓ cup
Garlic, finely chopped – 6 to 8 cloves
Salt – 2 teaspoons
Black Pepper, freshly ground – 1 teaspoon
Flat-Leaf Parsley, finely chopped – 2 tablespoons

Cooking Steps:

1. Preheat the oven to **400° F** (204° C).

2. Cut the potatoes into eighths.
3. Place the potatoes in a large bowl or casserole dish with the olive oil, garlic, salt and pepper and toss until all of the potatoes are well coated.
4. Bake in the oven until the potatoes are crisp and browned, which will be at least an hour. Flip the potatoes at least a couple of times during the baking for consistent browning.
5. When finished, serve with the chopped parsley.

To Serve:

This can be made an hour or two beforehand and kept warm covered in the oven on **very low heat**.

SAUTÉED FRESH CORN

SIDE

This is best in the late summer or early autumn when corn is at its best.

Serves – 8

Ingredients:

Corn, ears – 8
Butter, unsalted – 4 tablespoons (1 stick)
Salt – 1 teaspoon
Black Pepper, freshly ground – ½ teaspoon

Cooking Steps:

1. Remove the cobs of corn from the husks, and trim kernels from the cob.
2. Melt the butter in a large sauté pan over **medium-low** heat.
3. Add the corn, pepper and salt and cook for 8 to 10 minutes, stirring occasionally.

To Serve:

This can be made an hour or two beforehand and kept warm covered in the oven on **very low** heat. For an extra kick, sprinkle a little Tony Chachere's or Louisiana-style pepper sauce on top of the corn.

SPINACH GRATIN

SIDE OR APPETIZER

Serves – 6 to 8

You can do all but the final baking a day beforehand, if you need to save time. This also works as a spinach dip.

Ingredients:

Frozen, Chopped Spinach, defrosted & drained well – 3 pounds (five 10 ounce packages)
Onions, chopped – 2
Heavy Cream – 1 cup
Milk, whole – 2 cups
Parmesan Cheese, grated – 1 cup
Gruyère Cheese, grated – ½ cup
Butter, unsalted – 4 tablespoons (this is ½ of a stick)
Flour – ¼ cup
Nutmeg, grated – ¼ teaspoon
Salt – 1 tablespoon
Black Pepper, freshly ground – ½ teaspoon

Cooking Steps:
1. Preheat the oven to **425° F** (218° C).
2. Melt the butter in a large sauté pan over **medium** heat. Add the onions and cook for about 15 minutes, until the onions are shiny.
3. Add the nutmeg and flour and cook for 2 more minutes while stirring.
4. Add the milk and cream and cook for several more minutes, until the mixture has thickened. Remove from the heat.
5. Drain the spinach well. Then add the spinach, half of the Parmesan cheese and the salt and pepper to the sauce and mix well.
6. Transfer it all to a baking dish, top with the rest of the Parmesan and all of the Gruyère cheese.
7. Bake for 20 minutes, until the cheese on top is bubbling.

To Serve:

Serve as a side. Or you can use it as a dip with pieces of bread.

DESSERT IDEAS

Purchase desserts if you want to save effort and time. Tasty desserts are readily available from bakeries, dessert shops, and even most supermarkets. At most dinner parties, your guests won't begrudge the fact that you might not have made the dessert from scratch. Additionally, seasonal fresh fruits such as strawberries, raspberries, blueberries and such are often the best choice for dessert, especially when the meal is rich and the portions generous. Serving fresh berries with whipped cream is an easy way to dress these up.

A good idea for dessert, especially in the cooler months is the classic combination of **port and Stilton cheese** served with pears and English-style water crackers. Cooled, crisp Granny Smith apples are another good choice. Other high quality blue cheeses can be substituted for Stilton. A high-quality sharp cheddar cheese also works well. **Tawny port is the best value**, especially when entertaining more than a few folks. There are several types, and the 10-year tawny is the best combination of quality and value for entertaining.

In case you feel compelled to create a dessert from scratch, we have provided a few ridiculously easy and very satisfying recipes.

BREAD PUDDING À LA FUSELIER ————————

DESSERT

Don't be concerned by the number of steps in the production process; this dish is actually quite easy to make. It is recommended that you use a good quality baguette or the like, since the better the bread, the better the result. The bourbon sauce is a classic accompaniment.

Serves – 8 to 12

Ingredients:

For the Pudding:

Baguette – 1
Butter, unsalted – 3 tablespoons
Eggs, large – 3
Milk, whole – 4 cups
Sugar – 2 cups

Vanilla – 2 tablespoons
Cinnamon – 1 tablespoon

For the Bourbon Sauce:

Butter, unsalted – 8 tablespoons
Sugar – 1 cup
Bourbon Whiskey – ¼ cup
Nutmeg, grated – ¼ tablespoon
Salt – ⅛ teaspoon
Egg, large – 1

Cooking Steps:

For the Pudding:

1. **Leave the bread out for a couple of hours** if possible to harden. This will enable the bread to soak up the liquid mixture like a sponge.
2. Break up the French bread into 1" pieces.
3. Spread the butter over a standard-size glass baking dish (13" x 9" x 2").
4. In a large mixing bowl whisk the eggs until frothy.
5. Whisk in the milk, sugar, vanilla, and ground cinnamon.
6. Pour the liquid over the bread and let it soak in overnight; if that is too long, let it sit at least an hour, no less. Every once in a while, push the bread down in the mixture with a spatula.
7. Preheat oven to **375° F** (191° C).
8. Bake uncovered for 50 minutes, or until the top is lightly browned.

For the Bourbon Sauce:

1. Melt the butter in a small, heavy saucepan over **medium-low** heat.
2. Stir in the sugar, bourbon, the freshly grated nutmeg, salt, and 2 tablespoons water.
3. Cook and stir until the sugar is dissolved and everything is blended.
4. Remove from heat, and whisk until frothy.
5. Whisk the egg into the hot mixture vigorously. Set mixture over **medium** heat and stir gently until it simmers. Cook for about 1 minute until thickened. Serve at once.

To Serve:

This can be made an hour or two beforehand and kept warm covered in the oven on **very low heat**.

NEW ORLEANS PEANUT BUTTER PIE ——————

DESSERT

Do not be dismayed by the number of ingredients, as this recipe is very easy. This is a hit with anyone who likes peanut butter, even just a tad. The whipped cream (or topping) works as a very good complement to the peanut butter filling. Though this dessert does not contain any alcohol, it is indeed from New Orleans.

Makes – 2 pies; 16 people

Ingredients:

For the Crust: Using a pre-made pie crust is perfectly acceptable and time-saving, but if not:

Vanilla Wafers, crushed – 3 cups; this the entire contents of a 12 ounce box
Butter – 8 tablespoons; 1 stick

For the Pie Filling and Topping:

Cream Cheese, softened – ½ pound
Peanut Butter, creamy – ½ cup
Sweetened Condensed Milk – 7 ounces; half of the standard 14 ounce can
Powdered Sugar – 1 cup
Whipped Topping, thawed – 10 ounces

Optional Toppings and Garnishes:

Semisweet Chocolate Shavings
Unsalted Peanuts
Chocolate Candies, small-sized – 6 ounces

Cooking Steps:

1. If making the crust – In a large bowl, mix together the softened butter and vanilla wafer crumbs to moisten the latter. Form a thin layer of the mixture on the bottoms and sides of two standard (9 inch) pie pans. Bake at **350° F** (177° C) for 10 to 15 minutes, until done.
2. Allow the crusts to cool.
3. For the filling – In a large bowl, beat together the cream cheese, peanut butter and sweetened condensed milk until well-mixed and frothy.

4. Add the powdered sugar gradually to the filling mixture.
5. Fold in about 80% of the whipped topping.
6. Pour the mixture into the pans with the pie crusts. Smooth the top.
7. Add the rest of the whipped topping to the top of the pies. Garnish.
8. Refrigerate until chilled.

To Serve:

This can be made several days beforehand. This may even be made weeks beforehand and frozen then mostly defrosted before serving.

STRAWBERRIES WITH SWEET MARSALA

DESSERT

This is ridiculously simple to prepare, and very tasty. It's a sweet and fairly light way to end the meal. Quarter the strawberries if these are very large. Be sure to use sweet Marsala rather than dry Marsala.

Serves – 12

Ingredients:

Strawberries, trimmed and halved – 3 pounds
Sweet Marsala – ½ cup
Sugar – ⅓ cup

Assembly Steps:

1. Trim and cut the strawberries.
2. Toss and mix all of the ingredients together until the sugar is dissolved.
3. Let sit for at least 45 minutes at room temperature for the ingredients to properly come together.

To Serve:

Serve alone, with vanilla ice cream or sugar cookies.

ABOUT THE DRINK RECIPES

To help satisfy every type of party situation, the drink recipes that are provided in this book fall into several categories, and geared toward: *1)* satisfying **groups**; or *2)* just **one** guest at a time. Our aim isn't to list every conceivable concoction, but to provide drink recipes that you might actually use, or at least consider using.

1) Drinks Recipes for Several or More:

- **Pitcher-sized** – These drink recipes are for the standard-sized pitchers, which are a half-gallon (64 ounces). Also helpful, is that most of these recipes call for an entire bottle of liquor, either 750 milliliter or one liter size. If you have a very large crowd, it's a good idea to make a recipe several times over.
- **Frozen** – If you just have to have these. The recipes provided are for a standard-sized blender pitcher (48 ounces - 6 cups).
- **Super-sized** – This recipe might come in handy.
- **Infusions** with vodka can be an interesting addition to your event.

2) Drink Recipes for One:

- **Individual-sized** – Some drinks are best made just one at time. The recipes provided instruct you to make drinks the Marfreless way, with a healthy two ounces of alcohol. The list of recipes is not meant to be complete, or even nearly so. For that, you probably have a cocktail book at home with hundreds of obscure recipes, almost all of which you will never attempt to use.
- **Simple Combinations** – These are straightforward, but worth mentioning when it comes to entertaining, especially when thinking about a self-service bar.
- **Shooters / Shots** – These can get the party started, or ended.

A note about the drink recipes – When ice is listed in a recipe, it refers to the normal ice cubes that you can get from your freezer. If crushed ice or something else should be used, it's mentioned specifically.

THE DRINK RECIPES

PITCHER-SIZED DRINKS

Bellini – *La Gran Bellini*
Cajun Martini
Eggnog, Fresh & Easy
Ginger & Vodka Punch
Hurricane
Margarita
Mojito
Sangria
Super Bowl Punch
Tequila Sunburst
Waste Basket Punch

FROZEN DRINKS

Frozen Margarita
Frozen Screwdriver
Green Ernie
Piña Colada
Strawberry Daiquiri

SUPER-SIZED DRINKS

Trash Can Punch

VODKA INFUSIONS

Pineapple Infusion
Very Berry Infusion

INDIVIDUAL-SIZED DRINKS

B & B
Bay Breeze
Black Russian
Bloody Mary
Bourbon Old Fashioned
Bourbon Sour
Brandy Alexander
Cape Cod
Champagne Cocktail

Chocolate Martini
Colorado Bulldog
Cosmopolitan
Cuba Libré
French '75'
Frozen Daiquiri
Fuzzy Navel
Gibson
Gimlet
Gin & Tonic
Gin Fizz
Gin Sour
Green Apple Martini
Greyhound
Hairy Navel
Hot Toddy
Irish Coffee
John Collins
Kamikaze
Kentucky Cooler
Kir
Kir Royale
Madras
Mai Tai
Manhattan
Margarita – West Coast Version
Martini
Melon Ball
Michelada
Midori Sour
Milk Punch
Mimosa
Mint Julep
Old Fashioned
Paloma
The Perfect Cocktail
Pimm's Cup
Piña Colada
Planter's Punch
Ramos Gin Fizz
Rob Roy

Rum Sour
Rusty Nail
Salty Dog
Sazerac
Screwdriver
Sea Breeze
Sex on the Beach
Sidecar
Singapore Sling
Tequila Sunrise
Tom Collins
Vodka & Tonic
Whiskey Sour
White Russian
Woo Woo

SIMPLE DRINK COMBINATIONS

SHOOTERS / SHOTS

Apple Pie
B-52
Bull Blaster
Buttery Nipple
C & L
Chocolate Covered Banana
Chocolate Covered Cherry
Cotton Candy
Creamcicle
Jack's Panty Dropper
Jell-O Shot
Kamikaze
Lemon Drop
Mind Eraser
Raspberry Kamikaze
Red-Headed Slut
Red Snapper
Sex with an Alligator
Slippery Nipple
Three Wisemen
Water Moccasin

PITCHER-SIZED DRINKS

These recipes are easy to make beforehand and are also very tasty, and so are great when you want to go beyond beer and wine, and maybe have somewhat of a communal beverage for your event.

BELLINI — LA GRAN BELLINI

Maybe a fraction less elegant than the original version made at Hotel Cipriani in Venice, this one is almost as easy to make, as it is to enjoy. And, it has somewhat of a kick.

Makes – Half-Gallon (64 ounces)

Ingredients:

Peach Nectar – 12 ounces; it should be easy to find cans of this juice.
Peach Schnapps – 6 ounces
Vodka – 6 ounces
Prosecco – 1 bottle (750 ml)
Ice
Raspberries – *Optional*; a few

Mixing Steps:

1. Mix all of the ingredients together in a pitcher except the ice.
2. Stir.

To Serve:

Pour into glasses over ice.

CAJUN MARTINI

The inspiration for this is a similar drink that is served in oversized Martini glasses at Paul Prudhomme's K-Paul's restaurant in the French Quarter in New Orleans.

Makes – More than a quart

Ingredients:

Dry Gin – 750 ml bottle, **or** Vodka – 750 ml bottle
Dry Vermouth – 2 tablespoons
Serrano Peppers, seeds removed and sliced - 4
Pickled Tomatoes – *Optional*; for garnish
Pickled Chayote (or Mirlitons in Louisiana) – *Optional*; for garnish

Mixing Steps:

1. In the bottle of gin or vodka pour in the vermouth and the sliced peppers. Re-seal the bottle.
2. Store at least overnight in the refrigerator.

To Serve:

Pour into Martini glasses to serve straight up, or into lowball glasses over ice, and garnish with the pickled tomatoes or chayote, as you like.

EGGNOG — FRESH & EASY

This is tasty, and much better than the commercial versions, but considered seasonal and only popular during the Christmas holidays.

Makes – Half-Gallon (64 ounces)

Ingredients:

Eggs, separated – 8
Powdered Sugar – ⅙ cup
Milk – 1 pint
Heavy Whipping Cream – 1 ½ quarts
Vanilla – ½ teaspoon
Nutmeg, grated – ½ teaspoon, or so
Rum **or** Brandy – *Optional*

Mixing Steps:

1. Whip the egg whites and set aside.
2. Whip the egg yolks with sugar then add the milk, cream and vanilla.
3. Fold the egg whites into the egg yolk mixture and then refrigerate.
4. Serve when chilled.

To Serve:

You can add an ounce or so of rum or brandy to individual-sized drinks or the entire batch. Serve either version with grated nutmeg.

GINGER & VODKA PUNCH ──────────

This is another very easy and refreshing punch.

Makes – Half-Gallon (64 ounces)

Ingredients:

Lime Juice – From 10 limes (10 ounces)
Limes, sliced – 2
Ginger, peeled and cut into ¼ inch pieces – 6-inch stalk
Brown Sugar – 1 cup
Vodka – 1 liter
Ginger Ale – 48 ounces
Ice

Mixing Steps:

1. Put the ginger, sugar, lime juice and vodka in a gallon-sized pitcher.
2. Mash the ginger, which will release its oils.
3. Stir vigorously.
4. Add the ginger ale and ice.

To Serve:

Serve in glasses over ice.

Note – Less ice can be used, so less dilution results if the vodka had been stored in the freezer, and the ginger ale in the refrigerator.

HURRICANE ──────────────

This is another very easy and refreshing punch.

Makes – Half-Gallon (64 ounces)

Ingredients:

Passion Fruit Nectar – 1 cup; guava nectar can be substituted for this.
Orange Juice – 1 cup
Pineapple Juice – 1 cup
Lemon Juice – ¼ cup
Grenadine Syrup – ¼ cup
Dark Rum – 1 cup
Light Rum – 1 cup
Ice
Orange Slices – *Optional*; for garnish
Maraschino Cherries – *Optional*; for garnish

Mixing Steps:

1. Combine all ingredients into a blender and process until smooth.
2. Pour into glasses over ice and garnish.

To Serve:

Serve in glasses, preferably hurricane glasses if available, over ice.

MARGARITA ——————————————————————

This is one of the many ways and sizes of this popular concoction. *Blanco* tequila tastes more of agave than the *reposado* and *añejo tequilas*, and so, seems to work best with the flavor of lime, and work better in margaritas.

Makes – Half-Gallon (64 ounces)

Ingredients:

Tequila, *blanco* – 750 ml bottle
Triple Sec **or** Cointreau – 1 to 2 cups
Lime Juice – 1 cup
Salt, coarse (kosher-type) – 1 tablespoon
Ice

Mixing Steps:

1. Fill the pitcher about ⅓ the way with ice, and pour the tequila, 1 cup of the triple sec and lemon juice and stir vigorously.

2. Taste and add more of the triple sec if you think your margaritas need more orange flavor to balance the other flavors.
3. Chill the pitcher and its contents in the refrigerator.

To Serve:

Stir vigorously before pouring, and serve in salted glasses over ice.

MOJITO

Bring the boozy Batista era back to your home.

Makes – Half-Gallon (64 ounces)

Ingredients:

Mint Leaves – 75 or so; the standard-sized 0.67 ounce package will work.
Club Soda – 4 tablespoons
Sugar – 15 tablespoons
Rum – 1 liter; this is the bottle just bigger than the standard 750 ml bottle.
Limes, cut into quarters – 4
Lime Juice – 8 ounces; this is in addition to the limes from above.
Ice

Mixing Steps:

1. Muddle the mint with the sugar and a splash of club soda. This quick crushing of the mint leaves with the pestle helps to release the flavor of the mint. It's best done in a mortar and pestle then dump the contents into the pitcher. Depending on the size of the mortar, this might take several times.
2. Squeeze each of the lime quarters into the pitcher
3. Pour in the lime juice and the rest of the sugar.
4. Pour in the rum and stir vigorously.
5. Add the ice and stir again.

To Serve:

Serve in glasses over ice.

Note – This can be stored in the refrigerator for several hours before your event.

SANGRIA ─────────────────────────────

Make this several hours beforehand. The night before is even better, allowing the fruit juices, sugar and wine to properly meld. When chilled and served over ice with club soda, this goes down amazingly quickly. You might want to make several pitchers of this before your party, or expand the recipe for a much larger container. The apple slices are great to eat afterwards. For the wine, use a medium-bodied, dry red wine with fruity flavors like a Garnacha- or Tempranillo-based Spanish wine, a Chianti, Valpolicella, a light-bodied red wine from southern France, or a Pinot Noir.

Makes – Half-Gallon (64 ounces)

Ingredients:

For Mixing:

Red Wine – 2 bottles, 1.5 liters; see above
5 liters; see above
Orange Juice – 4 ounces
Oranges, cut into quarters or eighths – 2
Lemons, cut into quarters or eighths – 4
Apples, cut into eighths – 2
Sugar – 2 tablespoons

For Serving:

Club soda
Ice

Mixing Steps:

1. Squeeze each of the orange and lemon slices into the pitcher, and then drop in.
2. Pour in the sugar and orange juice, and stir.
3. Pour in the wine, and the apples. Stir again.
4. Cover the top in plastic and let sit in the refrigerator for at least six hours.

To Serve:

In a glass with a few ice cubes, fill about one-third of it with club soda. Then pour the sangria over the ice and club soda.

SUPER BOWL PUNCH

This easy and tasty punch was created with help from an expert mixologist, Jack Thetford, our favorite bartender *cum* attorney. This drink debuted at a cooking class about entertaining for the Super Bowl that Mike led at the bounteous Central Market just before the 2004 event. The sparkling wine hinted at the festivity of the event, and the tequila and lime provided a Southwestern flair for this Houston-hosted Super Bowl.

Makes – Half-Gallon (64 ounces)

Ingredients:

Lime Juice – from 4 limes (4 ounces)
Orange Juice – 12 ounces
Pineapple Juice – 2 ounces
Tequila, preferably 100% agave – 4 ounce
Asti Spumante (most any brand will do) – 1 bottle (750 ml); this stuff is
    fairly inexpensive, cheaper than champagne
Ice

Mixing Steps:

1. With the exception of the Asti Spumante, mix in all of the ingredients, and stir thoroughly.
2. Before serving, mix in the Asti Spumante, and pour over ice into a punch bowl or the like.

To Serve:

Serve in glasses over ice.

TEQUILA SUNBURST

This is another use for tequila. The cleaner-tasting *blanco* tequilas work best.

Makes – Half-Gallon (64 ounces)

Ingredients:

Orange Juice – 24 ounces
Pineapple Juice – 6 ounces
Sugar – 4 tablespoons

Tequila, *blanco* – 750 ml bottle
Limes, cut into slices – 2
Ice

Mixing Steps:

1. Put the sugar in a half-gallon-sized pitcher
2. Squeeze each of the lime quarters into the pitcher.
3. Pour in the orange and pineapple juices.
4. Pour in tequila
5. Add the ice and stir again.

To Serve:

Serve in glasses over ice.

WASTE BASKET PUNCH ───────────

This is a pitcher-sized version of trash can punch. This can be made ahead of time, and is even better the more fruit that is used, and when it has been given at least a couple of hours for the flavors to meld.

Makes – Half-Gallon (64 ounces)

Ingredients:

Vodka – 12 ounces
Rum – 6 ounces
Pineapple Juice – 20 ounces
Fruit Punch – 24 ounces
Limes, cut into slices – 2
Oranges, cut into slices – 1
Ice

Mixing Steps:

1. Pour all the liquids into the pitcher. Stir vigorously.
2. Add ice and the slices of fruit. Chill.
3. Stir again before serving.

To Serve:

Serve in glasses over ice.

FROZEN DRINKS

Frozen drinks can be messy, time-consuming and distracting for the host to provide, and often seem to turn out poorly. For these reasons, we caution against offering these. But, if you want to, these several recipes are well-tested. Just follow the directions explicitly and you shouldn't have a problem. These recipes are all geared toward the standard 48 ounce blender pitcher, and should serve four adults.

FROZEN MARGARITA

It's our experience that following directions on the back of a bottle of Margarita mix will ensure a tasty, but weak concoction. Simply increase the amount of tequila by at least 50%, though you might even want to double it. *Variation* – For a Strawberry Margarita, add 3 or 4 ounces of trimmed strawberries to the blender. It's that easy.

FROZEN SCREWDRIVER

This is ridiculously easy to make.

Makes – 48 ounces; serves 4

Ingredients:

Vodka – 8 ounces
Frozen Orange Juice Concentrate – 10 ounces
Ice – 4 cups

Mixing Steps:

Pour all the liquids into the pitcher. Blend until thoroughly mixed. Pour into pint glasses.

GREEN ERNIE

This concoction is courtesy of the very prodigious Koch family of Texas. It should taste like a lime sherbet with just a hint of alcohol.

Makes – 48 ounces; serves 4

Ingredients:

Vodka – 8 ounces; substitute grain alcohol for a very serious wallop.
Frozen Limeade Concentrate – 2 ounces
Lime Sherbet – 2 cups
Ice – 2 cups

Mixing Steps:

Pour all the liquids into the pitcher. Blend until thoroughly mixed. Pour into pint glasses.

PIÑA COLADA

Makes – 48 ounces; serves 4

Ingredients:

Light Rum – 4 ounces
Pineapple Juice – 4 ounces
Cream of Coconut – 4 ounces; Coco Lopez brand should be easy to find.
Ice – 2 cups

Mixing Steps:

Pour all the liquids into the pitcher. Blend until thoroughly mixed. Pour into pint glasses.

STRAWBERRY DAIQUIRI

Makes – 48 ounces; serves 4

Ingredients:

Light Rum – 6 ounces
Sour Mix – 4 ounces
Strawberries, trimmed – 3 or 4 ounces
Ice – 2 cups

Mixing Steps:

Pour all the ingredients into the pitcher. Blend until thoroughly mixed. Pour into pint glasses.

SUPER-SIZED DRINKS

Some parties, like those with a beach theme, encourage the creation of a communal alcoholic beverage. Maybe wearing a brightly-colored, or otherwise loud, aloha shirt creates the desire in many for a brightly-colored and brash drink, consumed in prodigious amounts.

TRASH CAN PUNCH

When you feel the need to make a big batch of high-octane fruit punch, here is a recipe that has worked wonders in the past. A useful suggestion is to make a few batches of ice cubes from additional packages of the fruit punch the night before. With these the punch will not taste as diluted as when using plain ice cubes. Though "Trash Can Punch" is a descriptive name for this, you might want to bestow a more festive one on it for your event.

Makes – Trash Can Size

Ingredients:

Vodka – 1.75 liters; the contents of an entire handle
75 liters; the contents of an entire handle
Rum – 750 ml
Everclear, or other 190 proof grain alcohol – 375 ml
Pineapple Juice – 20 ounces
Fruit Punch – The contents of 2 package mixes
Limes, cut into slices – 12
Oranges, cut into slices – 6
Apples, cut into slices – 2; *Optional*
Pineapple, cut into chunks – 1; *Optional*
Ice

Mixing Steps:

Pour all the liquids into a large container. A *new* plastic trash can lined with a plastic trash bag will work if nothing else is available. Stir vigorously. Add ice and the slices of fruit. Chill. Stir again before serving.

To Serve:

Serve in 16 ounce plastic cups over ice.

Vodka Infusions

Vodka Infusions can be a great party addition. These are simple, inexpensive, delicious and decorative. These concoctions need to be prepared at least twenty-four to forty-eight hours in advance. The perfect receptacle for these is a glass jug with a spout for pouring at the bottom. If you can't get your hands on such a vessel, a large glass jar will suffice. The basic notion behind these is that pieces of fruit, mixed with vodka for a few days will meld and become a very tasty beverage. Simple enough.

Not all fruit is compatible. Apples and pears turn an unattractive brown color. Mangoes simply exude sugar and so produce a sweet-flavored vodka drink. This is decent enough, but does not taste like mango. The best fruits to use are pineapple and berries (strawberries, raspberries, blackberries, and the like). Vodka is the best liquor to use because it's generally neutral in flavor. In a subtle fashion it complements the fruit juices and provides a backbone for the drink.

Pineapple Infusion

Makes – Varies; depends on the size of the vessel chosen

Ingredients:

Pineapples – 2 to 4
Vodka – Varies; enough to nearly fill the vessel.
Vanilla Beans, slice each bean in half lengthwise – *Optional*; standard-size jar
Maraschino Cherries – *Optional*; for garnish

Assembly Steps:

1. Trim and cut the pineapples. You can get creative and cut these into small cubes, rings, triangles, etc.
2. Place the pieces of pineapple into the glass vessel.
3. If using the vanilla beans, slice each bean in half lengthwise, scrape the beans out of the shell and into the infusion. Drop the shells in as well, and stir.
4. Pour in the vodka almost to the top, cover, and let sit for two or three days before serving.

To Serve:

Before the event, be sure to taste the finished product. It will be very tasty and resplendent with the fresh pineapple, but might be quite strong. If so, be sure to serve with plenty of ice, and you also might want to have pineapple juice to further cut it. Garnished with a slice of pineapple or a cherry, and it's ready for an event.

Note – Don't eat the pineapple slices, as these will have developed an off-taste. Or, if you want to play a joke on someone....

VERY BERRY INFUSION

Makes – Varies, as it depends on the size of the vessel chosen.

Ingredients:

Strawberries – Varies; enough to fill an inch, or several, across the container.
Raspberries – Varies; enough to fill an inch, or several, across the container.
Bluberries – Varies; enough to fill an inch, or several, across the container.
Vodka – Varies; enough to nearly fill the container.

Assembly Steps:

1. **Thoroughly rinse** the strawberries, raspberries and blueberries.
2. **Remove the stems and leaves** from the strawberries.
3. Cut the **strawberries in half**, and place in jar until it fills an inch or several or so.
4. Place the **raspberries and blueberries on top** of the strawberries, so that it creates a layered effect.
5. **Pour in the vodka** to nearly fill the container, cover, and let sit for two or three days before serving.

To Serve:

Before the event, be sure to taste the finished product. It should be very tasty and filled with flavor of fresh berries, but that flavor might be overly concentrated. If so, be sure to serve with plenty of ice, and you also might want to cut it with a splash of sour mix.

INDIVIDUAL-SIZED DRINKS

This following listing of recipes for individual cocktails is not meant to be comprehensive, but rather to provide you with tasty, popular or well-worn, and fairly easy-to-make drinks that will be sure to please a wide range of guests.

Sour Mix is needed in several recipes. If you are a purist and want to make everything from scratch, or simply forgot to purchase sour mix, the following recipe works:

1 ounce **sour mix** = **lemon juice** from ½ a lemon + 1 teaspoon **sugar**

Shake this in a shaker thoroughly with ice and the other cocktail ingredients.

B & B

Benedictine and Brandy is a classic cocktail, even if it's something that you can't use right now. The better the brandy, the better this cocktail will be. This mixture is also sold commercially.

Ingredients:

Brandy – 1 ounce
Benedictine – 1 ounce

Mixing Steps:

Preferably in a cordial glass or a brandy snifter, pour in the Benedictine. Take care to pour in the brandy slowly, letting it run down the inside of the glass. If done correctly, the brandy will float on top of the Benedictine.

BAY BREEZE

Though some guys might have some difficulty ordering this in a bar, it can be a very tasty cocktail.

Ingredients:

Vodka – 2 ounces
Pineapple Juice – 7 ounces
Cranberry Juice – Splash
Ice

Mixing Steps:

Pour the vodka and pineapple juice into a highball glass over ice. Stir a few times then add a splash of cranberry juice before serving.

BLACK RUSSIAN ──────────────────

Maybe not as popular as it once was, it nonetheless still deserves some attention.

Ingredients:

Vodka – 1½ ounces
Kahlúa **or** other Coffee Liqueur – 1 ounce
Ice

Mixing Steps:

Pour the vodka and Kahlúa over ice into a highball glass and stir.

BLOODY MARY ──────────────────

This is the classic morning drink, and often synonymous with the "hair of the dog" for many.

Ingredients:

Vodka – 2 ounces
Tomato Juice – 3 ounces
Lemon Juice – 1 teaspoon
Tabasco Juice – Dash
Worcestershire Sauce – Dash
Black Pepper – Pinch
Celery Stalk – For garnish
Ice

Optional:
Horseradish
Clamato Juice – A mixture of tomato juice and the juice from clams, this can
    be used as an interesting substitute for regular tomato juice. Made with
    Clamato Juice instead of tomato juice creates a Bloody Caesar.
Beef Bouillon Cubes – for a variation on the Bloody Mary, the Bloody Bull
Cumin, ground – Dash

Dill, dried – Dash

Mixing Steps:

Pour all the liquids into a shaker with crushed ice. Shake vigorously, and then strain into an Old Fashioned glass with ice. Alternatively and simpler, pour the liquids into a glass and stir until well mixed. Garnish with the celery stalk, and top with freshly ground pepper.

BOURBON OLD FASHIONED

This is definitely an old-fashioned type of drink. Barkeeps from the hip-hop community refer to this as a Bourbon Old School.

Ingredients:

Bourbon – 2 ounces
Bitters – 2 dashes
Sugar – 1 teaspoon
Water – 1 teaspoon
Ice
Lemon Peel – 1
Maraschino Cherry – For garnish
Orange Slice – *Optional*; for garnish

Mixing Steps:

Into an Old Fashioned glass, of course, pour in the sugar, the dash of bitters and a teaspoon of water. Mix well. Add the whisky, lemon peel, and ice cubes. Garnish with the cherry and a slice of orange, if you would like.

BOURBON SOUR

This is a more specific, and slightly sweeter, version of the Whiskey Sour.

Ingredients:

Bourbon – 2 ounces
Sour Mix – 4 ounces
Orange Slice – For garnish
Ice

Mixing Steps:

Pour the bourbon and sour mix into a shaker and shake several times. Strain over more ice and garnish with an orange slice.

BRANDY ALEXANDER

Great for after the dinner party, if you haven't already consumed enough calories. Vanilla ice cream may be substituted for the heavy cream, and when mixed together in a blender makes for a delicious after-dinner cocktail and dessert.

Ingredients:

Brandy – 2 ounces
Crème de Cacao – 1 ounce
Heavy Cream – 1 ounce
Nutmeg, grated – Pinch
Ice

Mixing Steps:

Pour the liquids into a shaker, and shake. Strain into a brandy snifter and sprinkle the nutmeg on top.

CAPE COD

This is another popular pink drink that works well as a refresher. And, this is an example of adding a slice of lime to a very simple combination, and requiring a new and fancier name.

Ingredients:

Vodka – 2 ounces
Cranberry Juice – 6 ounces
Lime Wedge – 1
Ice

Mixing Steps:

Pour the vodka and cranberry juice into a highball glass over ice. Stir a few times. Garnish with a lime wedge.

CHAMPAGNE COCKTAIL ——————————————

Very old school, but a favorite among modern-day strippers.

Ingredients:

Champagne – 4 ounces
Bitters – 2 dashes
Sugar – 1 teaspoon
Lemon Peel – For garnish

Mixing Steps:

Place the sugar into a champagne flute. Add the bitters, then pour in the champagne. Garnish with a lemon peel.

CHOCOLATE MARTINI ——————————————

A popular choice to satiate both the chocolate and alcohol cravings.

Ingredients:

Vodka – 2 ounces
Crème de Cacao – ½ ounce
Ice

Mixing Steps:

Combine the ingredients in a shaker. Shake and strain into a Martini glass.

COLORADO BULLDOG ——————————————

None of these ingredients are from Colorado, but it is still a fitting name.

Ingredients:

Vodka – 1 ounce
Kahlúa **or** other Coffee Liqueur – 1 ounce
Milk – 3 ½ ounces
Cola – ½ ounce
Ice

Mixing Steps:

Pour all into a highball glass over ice. Stir a few times.

COSMOPOLITAN (OR COSMO)

This drink is popular for a reason. The version below will make for a healthy drink.

Ingredients:

For Mixing:

Orange-flavored Vodka – 2 ounces
Triple Sec **or** Cointreau – 1 ounce
Cranberry Juice – 1 ounce
Lime Juice – ½ ounce
Orange Juice – Dash
Lime Slice – For garnish

Mixing Steps:

Shake hard with cracked ice, strain, and pour into a Martini glass. Garnish with a lime wedge.

CUBA LIBRÉ [KOO-BUH LEE-BRAY]

This is pretty much a more sophisticated way to order a rum-and-coke, and another example of how the presence of a slice of lime requires a cocktail to receive a new and more obtuse name.

Ingredients:

Rum – 2 ounce
Cola – 6 ounces, or so
Lime – quarter
Ice

Mixing Steps:

Squeeze the lime into a glass, and then deposit the rind there, too. Add ice, the rum, and then fill with cola. Stir lamely.

FRENCH '75'

OK, no one at your event might order this unless there happens to be some spry veterans of the Great War, but it still is a tasty drink. This cocktail is from the second decade of the last century, and takes its name from the main French artillery piece, the 75-millimeter-barreled '75,' which was the best artillery piece of the war, used by both the French and American forces during World War I. American officers probably used the name because this concoction drinks easily, and carries a wallop.

Ingredients:

Gin – 2 ounces
Champagne – 5 ounces, or so
Sour Mix – 2 ounces
Ice
Lemon Slice – *Optional*; for garnish
Orange Slice – *Optional*; for garnish
Maraschino Cherry – *Optional*; for garnish

Mixing Steps:

Put in the ice, then the gin and sour mix then fill with champagne. Stir a couple of times. Garnish with a lemon or orange slice and a maraschino cherry.

FROZEN DAIQUIRI

Oh yeah, oh yeah... Though there are non-frozen versions, the Frozen Daiquiri is the one that is ordered the most. A recipe for the more popular frozen Strawberry Daiquiri is shown on page 226. To make this a fruit-flavored daiquiri, simply add 2 ounces of a fruit. Strawberries, and also, bananas, melon and mango work well.

Ingredients:

Rum – 2 ounces
Triple Sec – 1 tablespoon
Lime Juice – 1 ½ ounces
Sugar – 1 teaspoon
Ice – 1 cup
Maraschino Cherry – *Optional*; for garnish

Mixing Steps:

Combine all of the ingredients into a blender, and mix at low speeds for about five seconds or so. Then, blend at a high speed until the mixture is firm. Pour into a glass, and garnish with a maraschino cherry if would like.

FUZZY NAVEL

You might want to reference the Hairy Navel, too.

Ingredients:

Peach Schnapps – 3 ounces
Orange Juice – 3 ounces
Lime Wedge – For garnish
Ice

Mixing Steps:

Pour into a glass over ice and stir a few times. Garnish with a lime wedge.

GIBSON

This is simply the classic gin Martini (see below) garnished with one to three pickled pearl onions instead of olives or a lemon peel twist.

Ingredients:

Gin – 2 ounces
Dry Vermouth – ¼ ounce; less vermouth makes it drier, of course.
Ice
Olives **or** Lemon Peel, twist – For garnish

Mixing Steps:

Pour the gin, then the vermouth over ice in a shaker. Shake vigorously then strain into a chilled Martini glass. This is referred to as "straight up" and most preferred, but Martinis can also be served on the rocks.

GIMLET

Old school drink that is more popular during the warmer months. When properly made, this becomes a quick way to ingest gin very quickly and somewhat unknowingly.

Ingredients:

Gin – 2 ounces
Lime Juice – ½ ounce
Powdered Sugar – 1 teaspoon
Ice

Mixing Steps:

Shake with ice and strain or pour into Old Fashioned glasses for neat and on the rocks, respectively.

GIN & TONIC

For the sake of completeness…. This is a very good summer cooler.

Ingredients:

Gin – 2 ounces
Tonic Water – 4 ounces, or so
Lime Wedge
Ice

Mixing Steps:

Pour the gin into a glass filled with ice. Fill the rest with tonic water. Squeeze the lime wedge into the glass, and stir a couple of times.

GIN FIZZ

It's fizzy….

Ingredients:

Gin – 2 ounces
Sour Mix – 4 ounces

Powdered Sugar – 1 ½ tablespoon
Club Soda – 1 ounce
Orange Slice – For garnish
Maraschino Cherry – For garnish
Ice

Mixing Steps:

Pour the gin, sugar and sour mix into a shaker with ice. Shake then strain into a Collins glass over more ice. Add the club soda. Garnish with the orange slice and cherry.

GIN SOUR

For those aficionados of gin and sour mix.

Ingredients:

Gin – 2 ounces
Sour Mix – 4 ounces
Orange Slice – *Optional*; for garnish
Maraschino Cherry – *Optional*; for garnish
Ice

Mixing Steps:

Pour the gin, sugar and sour mix into a shaker with ice. Shake then strain into a Collins glass over more ice. Garnish with the orange slice and cherry.

GREEN APPLE MARTINI

This is a popular twist on the classic Martini, and it must have some added health benefits since an apple a day keeps the doctor away, or so they say. Several might attract unwanted attention if attempting to drive afterwards.

Ingredients:

Vodka – 2 ounces
DeKuyper Apple Pucker brand Liqueur – 1 ounce
Sour Mix – 1 ounce
Granny Smith Apple, slice – *Optional*; for garnish

Mixing Steps:

Pour the vodka, then the apple liqueur and sour mix over ice in a shaker. Shake vigorously then strain into a chilled Martini glass, straight up.

GREYHOUND

Great most mornings, this is the same thing as the Salty Dog, without the salt.

Ingredients:

Vodka – 2 ounces
Grapefruit Juice – 5 ounces, or so
Ice

Mixing Steps:

Pour the vodka into a glass over several ice cubes. Fill the rest with grapefruit juice, or to taste. Stir several times.

HAIRY NAVEL

This is the drink that is often mistakenly called the Fuzzy Navel. The difference is that there is vodka in this one.

Ingredients:

Vodka – ¾ ounce
Peach Schnapps – ¾ ounce
Orange Juice – 6 ounces
Lime Wedge – For garnish
Ice

Mixing Steps:

Pour into a glass over ice and stir a few times. Garnish with a lime wedge.

HOT TODDY

Best during those colder months....

Ingredients:

Rum – 1 ounce
Boiling Water – 4 ounces
Sugar – 1 teaspoon
Cloves – 3
Cinnamon Stick – 1
Lemon Slice, thinly sliced – 1
Nutmeg, grated – Pinch

Mixing Steps:

Put the sugar, cloves, cinnamon stick and lemon slice into a heat-resistant glass or mug. Add 1 ounce boiling water and stir. Let stand for five minutes. Add the bourbon and 3 more ounces of boiling water. Stir well then sprinkle with grated nutmeg.

IRISH COFFEE

This is even popular on warm nights. The stronger and more flavorful the coffee, the better. Though not part of the original "Irish" version, you can add Kahlúa, or an Irish cream liqueur, or both, for a flavorful effect.

Ingredients:

Irish Whiskey – 2 ounces
Coffee – 4 ounces, or so
Whipped Cream, chilled – A dollop
Crème de Menthe – Dash; *Optional*

Mixing Steps:

In a coffee cup or a sturdy stemmed glass pour in the whiskey. Fill to about a ½ inch to the rim with the coffee, then top with the whipped cream. For a prettier effect, drizzle some crème de menthe on top as a final step.

JOHN COLLINS

This is now more popular than the classic Tom Collins. This might also be referred to as a Vodka Collins.

Ingredients:

Vodka – 2 ounces
Lemon Juice – ½ a lemon
Powdered Sugar – 1 teaspoon
Soda Water
Lemon Slice – For garnish
Ice

Mixing Steps:

Put sugar, vodka and lemon juice into a shaker with ice, and shake vigorously. Strain into a Collins glass. Add ice and fill the rest with the soda water. Decorate with the lemon slice.

KAMIKAZE

This is usually consumed as a shot, but it can also work as a regular cocktail, drunk quickly, of course. Several of these can help you make that last flight….

Ingredients:

Vodka – 1 ounce
Rum, 151 proof – ½ ounce
Triple Sec **or** Cointreau – ½ ounce
Sour Mix – 1 ounce
Ice

Mixing Steps:

Put all into a shaker and shaker vigorously. Strain into a lowball glass for a shot, or serve on the rocks if drinking at a moderate pace.

KENTUCKY COOLER

If you like this, Formula One probably isn't your favorite form of racing.

Ingredients:

Bourbon – 1 ½ ounces
Rum – ½ ounce
Orange Juice – ¼ ounce

Lemon Juice – ¼ ounce
Grenadine – 1 dash
Ice

Mixing Steps:

Pour all into a shaker and shake vigorously. Strain into a Collins glass over more ice.

KIR [KEER]

Named after a popular mayor of the Burgundian town of Dijon, this is an easy drink that gives the impression of some level of sophistication.

Ingredients:

White Wine – 3 ounces; a dry, not overly oaky wine is preferred
Crème de Cassis **or** Chambord – ¾ ounces, or so
Lemon Slice

Mixing Steps:

Pour the wine over ice in a wine glass. Add the crème de cassis and lemon slice then stir.

KIR ROYALE [KEER ROY-AL]

The substitution of champagne for the usually simple white wine raises this cocktail to royal status.

Ingredients:

Champagne – 3 ounces, or so
Crème de Cassis **or** Chambord – ¾ ounce, or so
Lemon Slice

Mixing Steps:

Pour the champagne over ice in a champagne flute. Add the crème de cassis and lemon slice then stir.

MADRAS

These are geared toward the warmer summer months just like the shirts of the same name.

Ingredients:

Vodka – 2 ounces
Orange Juice – 3 ounces
Cranberry Juice – 3 ounces
Ice

Mixing Steps:

Pour into a Collins glass or a pint glass, and stir several times.

MAI TAI [MY TIE]

Originally from Trader Vic's in California, not Tahiti or some exotic locale. It is still a good drink, though. The story of the name was that Vic Bergeron, the proprietor of Trader Vic's, in the 1940s, gave this drink to two Tahitian friends who exclaimed, "Mai Tai!," Tahitian for "out of this world!" It's probably somewhat more involved than the type of drink that most make at home, but it can be fun, especially when a proficient bartender is on hand.

Ingredients:

Rum – 2 ounces
Triple Sec – 1 ounce
Orgeat Syrup – 1 tablespoon; this is an almond-flavored syrup.
Grenadine – 1 tablespoon
Lime Juice – 1 tablespoon
Sugar – ½ teaspoon
Ice
Maraschino Cherry – For garnish
Pineapple Wedge – For garnish
151 proof Rum – Splash; *Optional*

Mixing Steps:

Pour all the ingredients together with the ice and shake. Strain into an Old Fashioned glass. Garnish with a cherry and pineapple for effect. If this is not enough alcohol, finish the drink with a float of 151 proof rum, and sip through a straw. For a cheesier result, add a toothpick umbrella.

MANHATTAN

This is a true classic in the world of cocktails, even if the popular recipe has changed over the years. This was originally made with rye, but it's much more common to use Canadian whisky or bourbon these days. By the same token, dry vermouth has replaced sweet vermouth. A Dry Manhattan uses only dry French vermouth. A Perfect Manhattan uses dry and sweet vermouth in equal portions of ¼ ounce.

Ingredients:

Blended, Canadian Whisky or Bourbon – 2 ounces
Dry Vermouth – ½ ounce
Bitters – Dash
Ice
Maraschino Cherry – *Optional*; for garnish

Mixing Steps:

Stir together in a cocktail glass. Garnish with a maraschino cherry if desired.

MARGARITA – WEST COAST VERSION

This version comes from the expertise of renowned mixologist Jack Thetford, who grew up amidst the orange groves and the John Birch Society in Orange County, California long before the pretty people arrived. The better the tequila, the better the result, though good quality *blancos* and *reposados* work better than most *añejos*, which have a distinctive oaky flavor. For a more expensive and much sweeter touch, Grand Marnier can be substituted for the triple sec.

Ingredients:

Tequila, *blanco* – 2 ounces
Triple Sec – ⅓ ounce
Fresh Lime Juice – 1 ounce
Ice, cracked or shaved

Mixing Steps:

Pour the tequila, the triple sec and the lime juice over the cracked or shaved ice in a shaker. Shake vigorously then strain into a chilled Martini glass to serve straight up.

MARTINI

Though now a Martini means almost any alcoholic concoction that is shaken then strained into a Martini glass, the drink gained popularity and renown as a simple combination. The classic version is made with gin, though vodka is currently more popular. The original recipe called for half gin, half dry vermouth. In the early 1940s, the portion of vermouth began to decline to two or three parts gin to vermouth. By the late 1970s, it had become five-, six-, and eight-to-one. In case you don't know, the drier the Martini, the greater the ratio of gin (or vodka) is to vermouth. A Dirty Martini features at least a splash of the juice from a jar of olives.

Ingredients:

Gin – 2 ounces
Dry Vermouth – ¼ ounce
Ice
Olives **or** Lemon Peel, twist – For garnish

Mixing Steps:

Pour the gin, then the vermouth over ice in a shaker. Shake vigorously then strain into a chilled Martini glass. This is referred to as "straight up" and most preferred, but Martinis can also be served on the rocks.

Some purists believe that a Martini should be stirred rather than shaken, but the shaker is commonly referred to as a "Martini shaker" after all.

MELON BALL

It's sweet, but delicious, nutritious, as well as fun to drink.

Ingredients:

Vodka – 1 ounce
Midori – ½ ounce; this a melon-flavored liqueur from Japan.
Orange Juice – 5 ounces

Ice

Mixing Steps:

Pour into a glass over ice, and stir several times.

MICHELADA [MEE-CHAH-LAH-DAH] —————————

Created either in the port cities of Veracruz or New Orleans many years ago, this is actually popular throughout much of Mexico, in the *taquerias* in Houston and in similarly humble establishments throughout the Southwest. Some recipes leave out either or both the soy sauce and the Worcestershire sauce. A Mexican bottled hot sauce can be substituted for the Tabasco sauce. This drink is not for everyone, but it can work well, especially as a thirst quencher. Plenty of freshly-squeezed lime juice is the key to this drink.

Ingredients:

Lighter Lager Beer, preferably Mexican like Carta Blanca – 12 ounces
Lime, with juice – 1 teaspoon
Worcestershire Sauce – 2 dashes
Soy Sauce – 1 dash
Tabasco Sauce – 1 dash
Black Pepper – Pinch
Salt
Ice

Mixing Steps:

Salt the rim of a pint glass. Pour in the rest of the ingredients over ice and stir a few times. You might want to serve this with a straw.

MIDORI SOUR ————————————————————

This is one of the sweeter drinks in the sour family. You can make this an Amaretto Sour by substituting amaretto for the Midori. If you are lazy, you can substitute 3 or so ounces of sour mix for the lemon juice and sugar.

Ingredients:

Midori – 3 ounces
Lemon Juice – From 1 lemon, this is about 1½ ounces.
Powdered Sugar – 2 teaspoons

Maraschino Cherry – *Optional*; for garnish
Ice

Mixing Steps:

Mix the lemon juice and sugar in the bottom of the glass to create the sour effect. Put in the ice then the Midori and stir several times.

MILK PUNCH

This is good for those with tender stomach. It is popular in country clubs in an expanded format.

Ingredients:

Brandy **or** Canadian Whisky – 2 ounces
Milk – 8 ounces
Sugar – 1 teaspoon
Nutmeg, grated – Pinch
Ice

Mixing Steps:

Pour all into a shaker with ice. Shake vigorously, strain into a highball or pint glass.

MIMOSA

This is a great way to get rid of that really cheap sparkling wine.

Ingredients:

Sparkling Wine – 2 ounces
Orange Juice – 2 ounces

Mixing Steps:

Pour into the champagne then the orange juice into a champagne flute. That's it.

MINT JULEP

This is a classic late spring and summer refresher, and a requisite for those Kentucky Derby-watching parties.

Ingredients:

Bourbon – 2 ounces
Mint Leaves – 6
Sugar – 1 teaspoon
Water – 1 teaspoon
Ice

Mixing Steps:

Mash the mint, sugar and water in an Old Fashioned glass. Add half of the bourbon and stir. Fill the rest of the glass with crushed ice and then add the rest of the bourbon.

OLD FASHIONED

This is definitely an old-fashioned type of drink and another classic that has stirred debate over the proper way it should be made. Some prefer a splash of soda, among the several popular variations.

Ingredients:

Blended **or** Canadian Whisky – 2 ounces
Bitters – Dash
Sugar – 1 teaspoon
Ice
Lemon Peel
Orange Slice – *Optional*; for garnish

Mixing Steps:

Into an Old Fashioned glass, of course, pour the sugar, the dash of bitters and a teaspoon of water. Mix well. Add the whisky, lemon peel, and ice cubes. Garnish with a slice of orange, if you want.

PALOMA

A staple at clubs in Mexico, this is a very easy, and fun, way to become *borracho*. Squirt is a grapefruit-flavored soft drink that can be found in Mexican grocery stores. If you can't find it, Fresca is a decent substitute. If using Fresca, you might want to add a teaspoon or so of sugar.

Ingredients:

Tequila, *blanco* – 2 ounces
Squirt – 6 ounces, or so
Lime Slice – 1
Ice

Mixing Steps:

Pour in tequila and Squirt into a glass or cup over the ice. Squeeze the lime and deposit, then stir a few times.

THE PERFECT COCKTAIL

Maybe not, but a good drink, nonetheless, and very old school.

Ingredients:

Gin – 1 ½ ounces
Dry Vermouth – 1 ½ teaspoons
Sweet Vermouth – 1 ½ teaspoons
Bitters – Dash
Ice

Mixing Steps:

Pour the ingredients together into a glass or a shaker. Stir or shake well with ice cubes. Strain into a cocktail glass.

PIMM'S CUP

If you like gin, you might like this, as Pimm's is a gin-flavored liquor.

Ingredients:

Gin – 1 ½ ounces
Pimm's – ½ ounce
Sour Mix – 4 ounces
Cucumber Slice – For garnish
Ice

Mixing Steps:

Pour together, mix and garnish.

PIÑA COLADA

Though one of the cheesiest pop songs in history was written about this drink, ("…if you're not into yoga, if you have half a brain….") it can be a tasty cocktail, nonetheless.

Ingredients:

Light Rum – 3 ounces
Coconut Milk – 3 tablespoons
Pineapple, chopped – 3 tablespoons
Ice – 2 cups

Mixing Steps:

Combine all of the ingredients into a blender. Blend at a high speed until the mixture is firm, which should be within ten or fifteen seconds, or so. Pour into a glass, and serve with a straw.

PLANTER'S PUNCH

This recipe arrives with a little help from a Myers rum bottle label.

Ingredients:

Myers Dark Rum – 2 ounces
Orange Juice – 3 ounces
Lemon Juice – From ½ a lemon
Grenadine – Dash
Sugar – 1 teaspoon
Orange Slice – For garnish

Maraschino Cherry – For garnish
Ice

Mixing Steps:

Pour all, except the fruit garnishes, into a shaker. Shake vigorously, and then pour into a Collins glass. Garnish with the slice of orange and maraschino cherry.

RAMOS GIN FIZZ ──────────────

This is one of several famous drinks to have originated in the Crescent City ("The City that Forgot Care").

Ingredients:

Gin – 2 ounces
Lemon Juice – ½ a lemon
Powdered Sugar – 1 teaspoon
Egg White – 1
Heavy Cream – 1 tablespoon
Orange Juice – teaspoon
Club Soda
Ice

Mixing Steps:

Pour all into a shaker. Put a couple of ice cubes into a highball glass. Shake several times then strain into the glass. Fill the rest with the club soda.

ROB ROY ──────────────────

Two first names, and one interesting, and old-fashioned, drink.

Ingredients:

Scotch Whisky – 2 ounces
Sweet Vermouth – ¾ ounce
Bitters – 1 or 2 dashes; *Optional*
Ice

Mixing Steps:

Pour all into a glass and stir.

RUM SOUR

It's very simple.

Ingredients:

Light Rum – 2 ounces
Sour Mix – 4 ounces
Club Soda – 2 ounces, or so
Lemon Slice – *Optional*; for garnish
Ice

Mixing Steps:

Put sugar, rum, sour mix into a shaker with ice, and shake vigorously. Strain into a Collins glass. Add ice and fill the rest with the soda water. Decorate with the lemon slice.

RUSTY NAIL

Just hearing the name should make you want one....

Ingredients:

Scotch Whisky – 2 ounces
Drambuie – ¼ ounce
Ice

Mixing Steps:

Pour the whisky over a few ice cubes into an Old Fashioned glass. Then, pour the Drambuie over it. Don't stir.

SALTY DOG

Great most mornings, this is the same thing as the Greyhound, but with the salted rim.

Ingredients:

Vodka – 2 ounces
Grapefruit Juice – 5 ounces, or so
Salt – ¼ teaspoon
Ice

Mixing Steps:

Salt the rim of a low ball glass. Pour the vodka into a glass over several ice cubes. Fill the rest with grapefruit juice, or to taste. Stir several times.

SAZERAC [SAZ-ER-RACK]

This was invented at the bar of the old Roosevelt Hotel, now the Fairmont, in the Central Business District in New Orleans, a stone's throw from the French Quarter and across the street from the city's first Jesuit church. It's a very sweet drink that is very conducive to hangovers if you can manage more than a couple.

Ingredients:

Bourbon – 2 ounces
Pernod – 3 dashes
Sugar, granulated – 1 teaspoon
Bitters – 2 dashes; Peychaud's, preferably
Ice

Mixing Steps:

Pour the bourbon into a mixing glass, then add the sugar and bitters and stir until the sugar is dissolved. Pour the Pernod into an Old Fashioned glass. Add the ice then the bourbon mixture.

SCREWDRIVER

This is great most mornings.

Ingredients:

Vodka – 2 ounces
Orange Juice – 5 ounces, or so
Ice

Mixing Steps:

Pour the vodka into a highball glass over several ice cubes. Fill the rest with orange juice, or to taste. Stir several times.

SEA BREEZE

This is another winning combination of juices and vodka.

Ingredients:

Vodka – 2 ounces
Grapefruit Juice – 7 ounces
Cranberry Juice – Splash
Ice

Mixing Steps:

Pour the vodka and grapefruit juice into a highball glass over ice. Stir a few times then add a splash of cranberry juice before serving.

SEX ON THE BEACH

This can be fun, and you don't have to worry about the sand.

Ingredients:

Vodka – 1 ½ ounces
Peach Schnapps – ¾ ounce
Cranberry Juice – 3 ounces
Pineapple Juice – 3 ounces
Ice

Mixing Steps:

Pour the liquids in the glass over ice and stir so it's mixed thoroughly.

SIDECAR

This cocktail from the Roaring Twenties, was supposedly created at Harry's New York Bar in Paris soon after World War I, and named for an eccentric

American Army Captain who showed up regularly in a chauffeur-driven motorbike sidecar.

Ingredients:

Brandy – 2 ounce
Triple Sec – 1 ounce
Lemon Juice – From ½ a lemon
Ice

Mixing Steps:

Pour all into a shaker with ice. Shake then strain into a cocktail glass.

SINGAPORE SLING

This classic from the British colonial era is a wonderfully refreshing drink during the warmer months.

Ingredients:

Gin – 2 ounces
Lemon Juice – ½ a lemon
Powdered Sugar – 1 teaspoon
Club Soda – 4 ounces
Wild Cherry Brandy – ½ ounce
Fruit, fresh, sliced – *Optional*; for garnish
Ice

Mixing Steps:

Put sugar, gin and lemon juice into a shaker with ice, and shake vigorously. Strain into a Collins glass. Add ice and fill the rest with the club soda. Float ½ ounce of Wild Cherry Brandy. If desired, decorate with fresh seasonal fruit slices and serve with a straw.

TEQUILA SUNRISE

This is an easy way to drink tequila, though drinking tequila at sunrise is probably not a recommended way to get your day started.

Ingredients:

Tequila, *blanco* – 2 ounces
Orange Juice – 4 ounces
Grenadine – Splash
Crème de Cassis – Splash
Ice

Mixing Steps:

Pour in tequila and orange juice into a glass with ice, and stir. Add the Grenadine slowly, allow to sink, then settle. Don't stir. Serve with a straw so that it looks like a sunset while drinking.

TOM COLLINS

This drink originated in mid-19th century London, though sour mix was probably not used in the first version.

Ingredients:

Gin – 2 ounces
Sour Mix – 4 ounces
Club Soda – 2 ounces, or so
Lemon Slice – *Optional*; for garnish
Ice

Mixing Steps:

Put sugar, gin and Sour Mix into a shaker with ice, and shake vigorously. Strain into a Collins glass. Add ice and fill the rest with the soda water. Decorate with the lemon slice.

VODKA & TONIC

Another one included for the sake of completeness. This is just like the Gin & Tonic, but with vodka instead of gin.

Ingredients:

Vodka – 2 ounces
Tonic Water – 4 ounces, or so
Lime, slice – 1

Ice

Mixing Steps:

Pour the vodka into a glass filled with ice. Fill the rest with tonic water. Squeeze the lime slice into the glass, and stir a couple of times.

WHISKEY SOUR

This is the manliest member of the sour family, along with the Bourbon Sour.

Ingredients:

Blended **or** Canadian Whisky – 2 ounces
Sour Mix – 4 ounces
Club Soda – 2 ounces, or so
Maraschino Cherry – For garnish
Lemon Slice – *Optional*; for garnish
Ice

Mixing Steps:

Put sugar, whiskey and sour mix into a shaker with ice, and shake vigorously. Strain into a Collins glass. Add ice and fill the rest with the soda water. Decorate with the cherry and lemon slice.

WHITE RUSSIAN

Easy on the stomach, so it's more palatable than other drinks if you are nursing an ulcer. Note that half & half or cream work much better than milk.

Ingredients:

Vodka – 2 ounces
Kahlúa **or** other Coffee Liqueur – 2 ounces
Half & Half – 6 ounces
Ice
Nutmeg, ground – Pinch

Mixing Steps:

Pour in the liquids over ice, and stir several times, then top with the grated nutmeg.

Woo Woo

Yes, it's a silly name, but not a bad drink. And, it's fun to say. This tends to be drunk quite quickly, too.

Ingredients:

Vodka – 1 ounce
Peach Schnapps – 1 ounce
Cranberry Juice – 6 ounces
Ice

Mixing Steps:

Pour in the liquids over ice, and stir several times.

SIMPLE DRINK COMBINATIONS

Shown below are some simple but popular drink combinations that are good to know, especially if you are provisioning a self-service bar at your event. **Brandy**, **rum**, **Canadian** and **American blended whiskies**, and **vodka** seem to mix the best with just one mixer over ice. Canadian whiskies, which have a smooth and delicate flavor, are a natural for mixing. The nearly neutral soda water works as a good mixer for most types of liquor since it dilutes the alcohol, and the effervescence of the soda aids in the enjoyment. **Cola** provides sweetness along with its flavor and both complement the residual sugar in brandy, rum and whiskey. **Lemon-lime soda**, most commonly Seven-Up brand, works well with the taste of Seagram's 7 Whiskey, and also provides some sweetness to the neutral taste of vodka. The sweetness and acidity of many citrus juices (especially **orange juice**, **grapefruit juice** and **pineapple juice**) go well with both rum and vodka.

These drinks are made in the same way: fill the glass or cup with ice; pour in about two ounces of the spirit; add the mixer; stir a couple of times; and, drink readily.

Easy combinations that might be made at your event at home:

- **Brandy & Cola** – It's usually a waste to use an expensive brandy such as most cognacs and armagnacs when mixing with cola, but to each, his own.
- **Brandy & Soda** – Same as above.
- **Rum & Cola** – This is more sophisticated when a lime slice is added, making it a *Cuba Libré*.
- **Rum & Orange Juice** – People do drink this.
- **Rum & Pineapple Juice** – Same as above.
- **Rum & Soda** – This can be surprisingly cooling on a hot day.
- **Whiskey & Cola** – This is usually ordered as a Jack & Coke, Bourbon & Coke, or Wild Turkey & Coke, specifying each fluid. Most of those who order these are particularly loyal to their brand of whiskey, and the fact is that the mixer must be Coca-Cola rather than Pepsi, RC, and the local supermarket brand of cola. If the type of whisky is not specified, the basic Canadian blended whiskey (Seagram's VO, Canadian Club, etc.) will make for a sufficient drink. Or, at least that is our experience.
- **7 & 7** – This refers to Seagram's 7 brand blended whiskey and Seven-Up soda, as you should know. Seagram's VO and Sprite can be substituted for only a slight change in taste.
- **Vodka & Pineapple Juice** – Vodka does pair well with most citrus juices.
- **Vodka & Seven** – With its neutral flavor, vodka also goes well with most common mixers such as Seven-Up, the uncola. Regular cola might be the exception.
- **Vodka & Soda** – This can be quite refreshing, especially with a slice of lime.

SHOOTERS / SHOTS

The liquors that lend themselves readily to shots, or are popular, at least, are vodka, bourbon and its Tennessee cousins, Canadian whisky, Jägermeister, Southern Comfort, Tuaca, nearly every variety of schnapps, and tequila, of course.

If you want to shoot something smoother, below are recipes for some well-tested, useful and colorfully-named shots.

APPLE PIE

Ingredients:

Vodka – ½ ounce
Apple Pucker brand Apple Liqueur – 1 ounce
Cinnamon Schnapps – ½ ounce
Sour Mix – Splash
Ice

Mixing Steps:

Shake and strain into a lowball glass.

B-52

Ingredients:

Coffee Liqueur – ½ ounce
Grand Marnier – ½ ounce
Irish Cream Liqueur – ½ ounce
Ice

Mixing Steps:

Layer the coffee liqueur, Irish cream liqueur and then Grand Marnier into a small glass. It also tastes very good when shaken well over ice and strained before imbibing.

BULL BLASTER

Ingredients:

Jägermeister – 1 ½ ounces
Red Bull brand energy drink, chilled – ½ can (3 ounces)

Mixing Steps:

Fill a standard jigger (1 ½ ounces) with the Jägermeister. Fill a glass with the Red Bull (and no ice) then pour in the Jägermeister.

BUTTERY NIPPLE

Ingredients:

Irish Cream Liqueur – 1 ounce
Butterscotch Schnapps – 1 ounce

Mixing Steps:

Layer into a lowball glass by pouring in schnapps first, and then slowly adding the Irish cream liqueur.

C & L

If melon-flavored vodka is not on hand, simply use ¾ ounce of vodka and up the amount of melon liqueur from ½ to ¾ of an ounce.

Ingredients:

Melon-flavored Vodka – 1 ounce
Melon Liqueur – ½ ounce
Grenadine – Splash
Red Bull energy drink – ½ ounce
Ice

Mixing Steps:

Shake and strain into a lowball glass.

CHOCOLATE COVERED BANANA ───────────

Ingredients:

Vanilla-flavored Vodka – ½ ounce
Crème de Banana – 1 ounce
Irish Cream Liqueur – Splash
Cream – Splash
Ice

Mixing Steps:

Put all into a shaker and shake vigorously. Strain into a lowball glass.

CHOCOLATE COVERED CHERRY ───────────

Ingredients:

Kahlúa **or** other Coffee Liqueur – ½ ounce
White Crème de Cacao – ½ ounce
Amaretto – ½ ounce
Grenadine – Drop or two
Ice

Mixing Steps:

Put all but the grenadine into a shaker and shake vigorously. Strain into a lowball glass then add the drop or two of grenadine.

COTTON CANDY ──────────────────

Ingredients:

Vanilla-flavored Vodka – 1 ounce
Raspberry-flavored Vodka – 1 ounce
Pineapple Juice – Splash
Grenadine – Splash
Ice

Mixing Steps:

Shake and strain into a lowball glass.

CREAMCICLE ─────────────────────

Ingredients:

Vanilla-flavored Vodka – 1 ½ ounce
Crème de Cacao White – Splash
Orange Juice – ½ ounce
Ice

Mixing Steps:

Put all into a shaker and shake vigorously. Strain into a lowball glass.

JACK'S PANTY DROPPER ─────────────────

Ingredients:

Everclear, or other 190 proof grain alcohol – 2 ounces
Grand Marnier – 1 ounce
Sour Mix – 2 ounces
Ice

Mixing Steps:

Shake and strain into a lowball glass.

JELL-O SHOT ──────────────────────

Ingredients:

Vodka – 1 cup (8 ounces)
Jell-O brand mix – 3-ounce package
Water – 1+ cup
1 ounce paper cups

Assembly Steps:

1. Stir in 1 cup of boiling water into a bowl with the Jell-O mix and stir for at least 2 minutes, until the mix is entirely dissolved.
2. Stir in 1 cup of cold water, and 1 cup of vodka
3. Pour into 1 ounce paper containers and place in the freezer for at least a couple hours, or until firm.

Note – Variations on this simple recipe are to put complementary fruits into each of the containers. For example, strawberries with strawberry-flavored Jell-O, raspberries in raspberry-flavored mixes, and the like.

KAMIKAZE

Ingredients:

Vodka – 1 ounce
151 proof Rum– ½ ounce
Triple Sec **or** Cointreau – ½ ounce
Sour Mix – 1 ounce
Ice

Mixing Steps:

Put all into a shaker and shake vigorously. Strain into a lowball glass.

LEMON DROP

Ingredients:

Vodka, chilled – 1 ½ ounce
Lemon Juice – From 1 wedge
Lemon Slice
Sugar – For the rim of the glass and the lemon slice
Ice

Mixing Steps:

Sugar the rim of the glass. Sugar the lemon wedge. Pour the vodka and lemon juice with the ice into a shaker, shake vigorously and then strain into a lowball glass. Have the sugared lemon wedge to add to the lemony sensation.

MIND ERASER

Ingredients:

Vodka – 1 ½ ounces
White Crème of Cacao **or** Coffee Liqueur – ¾ ounce

Club Soda – 1 ½ ounces
Ice

Mixing Steps:

Pour the liquids with the ice into a shaker, shake a few times and then strain into a lowball glass.   Shaking with the club soda included will produce a frothy effect.

RASPBERRY KAMIKAZE

Ingredients:

Vodka – 1 ounce
151 proof Rum – ½ ounce
Chambord – ½ ounce
Sour Mix – 1 ounce
Ice

Mixing Steps:

Put all into a shaker and shake vigorously. Strain into a lowball glass.

RED-HEADED SLUT

Ingredients:

Jägermeister – 1 ounce
Canadian Whisky – 1 ounce
Cranberry Juice – 1 ounce
Amaretto – Dash
Ice

Mixing Steps:

Put all into a shaker and shake vigorously. Strain into a lowball glass.

RED SNAPPER

Ingredients:

Canadian Whisky – 1 ounce

Peach Schnapps – 1 ounce
Cranberry Juice – 1 ounce
Ice

Mixing Steps:

Put all into a shaker and shake vigorously. Strain into a lowball glass.

SEX WITH AN ALLIGATOR ─────────────

This is a fun, layered shot that is quite effective.

Ingredients:

Vodka – 1ounce
Melon Liqueur – 1 ounce
Chambord – ½ ounce
Jägermeister – ½ ounce
Ice

Mixing Steps:

Put the vodka and Melon liqueur into a shaker with ice and shake vigorously. Strain into a lowball glass. Pour in the Chambord, which will sink to the bottom. Slowly add the Jägermeister, which will float on top.

SLIPPERY NIPPLE ──────────────────

This is a variation on the Buttery Nipple that contains a hint of licorice.

Ingredients:

Irish Cream Liqueur – 1 ounce
Peach Schnapps – 1 ounce
Sambuca – Dash
Ice

Mixing Steps:

Shake and strain into a lowball glass.

THREE WISEMEN

If not the tastiest of shots in its various forms, it is quite effective.

Ingredients:

Jägermeister – 1 ounce
Goldschlager – 1 ounce
Rumple Minze – 1 ounce
Ice

Mixing Steps:

Shake and strain into a lowball glass.

WATER MOCCASIN

Ingredients:

Canadian Whisky – 1 ounce
Peach Schnapps – 1 ounce
Pineapple Juice – 1 ounce
Ice

Mixing Steps:

Shake and strain into a lowball glass.

Part III – Glossary

The purpose of this Glossary is to define some commonly heard terms that arise in association with entertaining in its many guises. These can be useful in decoding menus, recipes, wine labels, in the aisles of the liquor store, and when dealing with restaurant and event staff. Some knowledge of these terms can help to impress your guests, even if these are used nowhere other than in conversation. This is not meant to be exhaustive, as there are plenty of other terms associated with wining and dining and the like, but we have aimed to capture the most useful. For ease of use this is divided among easy-to-use headings:

- Wines & Wine Styles
- Wine Characteristics
- Other Wine-Related Terms
- Beer
- Spirits & Cocktail-Related Terms
- Cheese
- Snacks, Appetizers, Entrées & Desserts
- Sauces & Condiments
- Ingredients – Herbs & Spices
- Ingredients – Vegetables & Some Fruits
- Basic Cooking Terms
- Miscellaneous – Non-Drink & Non-Food Entertainment Terms

WINES & WINE STYLES – Popular Grapes, Varietals and Regional Wines

- **Aglianico** [ah-LYAH-neeh-coh] – This is a red wine grape in southern Italy that can make a quality, robust wine.
- **Albariño** [ahl-bahr-REEN-yoh] – The name for the grape, wines and the wine region in northwestern Spain were these grapes are grown and wines made. These white wines are dry, delicate and interesting. These are the same grapes that are used across the border in Portugal for the lighter and less serious Vinho Verde.
- **Amarone** [ahm-ahr-OH-nay] – The full name for this wine is Recioto della Valpolicella Amarone, which is made from ripe Valpolicella grapes that once picked are allowed to dry and shrivel. The wine is fermented slowly to a very high alcoholic content, roughly 16.5%. The resultant fairly pricey wine is strong, tannic and bitter, usually in a good way.
- **Arneis** [ahr-NAYS] – An ancient white wine grape from Piedmont that makes a flavorful dry wine.
- **Asti Spumante** – A generally sweet sparkling white wine made from the muscat grape in the bulk charmat method. It takes its name from the

town of Asti in the Piedmont region of Italy. Often used as an inexpensive substitute for champagne.

- **Barbera** [bar-BEHR-ah] – This makes for full-bodied, dry red wines with high acidity that are very food-friendly, especially for hearty foods such as stews and roasts. These wines are typically labeled with their locations of origin in towns in Piedmont in northwestern Italy such as Barbera d'Asti, Barbera d'Alba, etc.
- **Barberesco** [bar–buh-RAY-skoh] – A full-bodied, silky and tannic red wine from Piedmont in northwestern Italy made from the fickle Nebbiolo grape. Too expensive for most gatherings.
- **Bardolino** [bar-doh-LEE-noh] - A light-bodied, usually fruity and always uncomplicated red wine from the Veneto region in northeastern Italy outside of Venice. Inexpensive, it can be a decent wine for a large gathering.
- **Barolo** [bah-ROH-loh] – Like Barberesco above and also made from the Nebbiolo, but even richer and long-lasting. These distinctive wines are some of the world's best.
- **Beaujolais** [boh-zhah-LAY] – Light- and medium-bodied red French wine that is dry and fruity. It has become a good buy. Part of the greater Burgundy region, these wines are vinted from the distinctive Gamay grape. Regular Beaujolais is a much more flavorful, richer, and longer-lived wine than the Beaujolais Nouveau.
- **Beaujolais Nouveau** [boh-zhah-LAY noo-VOH] – This is a simple, fruity and (should be a) very inexpensive wine similar to regular Beaujolais that should be consumed before the end of the year of its release.
- **Bordeaux** [bor-DOH] – This refers to both the large famous wine region in southwestern France and the wines that are produced there. Some of the world's best and most expensive hearty reds come from here, as well as one of the best sweet dessert wines, Sauternes, and some very good still white wines. Most of the red wines, which make up about three-quarters of all wines produced here, are based primarily on Cabernet Sauvignon and, to a lesser extent, Merlot, along with some other grapes (Cabernet Franc, Malbec and Petit Verdot). Sauternes are based on Sémillon grapes. The still, dry whites are from Sauvignon Blanc grapes, including the well-regarded Graves appellation.
- **Bracchetto** [brah-KET-oh] – This is a red grape that makes a sweet red effervescent wine. Bracchetto wines such as Bracchetto d'Acqui have become more popular as dessert wines in North America.
- **Burgundy** – Located in eastern France, this is one of the most famous wine regions in the world, and produces very high quality, and expensive, reds and whites, both known for their sublimity and complexity. Pinot Noir is the primary grape for the red wines outside of

the southern Beaujolais region, which uses the Gamay grape. Chardonnay is the primary grape for the white wines.

- **Cabernet Sauvignon** [cab-er-NAY sauv-in-YAWN] – A popular red varietal that can produce dry, full-bodied, tannic, complex and rich wines with flavors of blackcurrant that achieve prominence as the primary grape in Napa Valley, the Médoc and Graves areas of Bordeaux, and Chile. A great match for roasts and steak.
- **Cahors** [ka-HORS] – This refers to the often high quality red wines and the ancient wine region in southwestern France from where these wines are made.
- **Cannonau** [kahn-NON-ow] – These are Grenache-based wines from the island of Sardinia.
- **Carignan** [cahr-in-YAHN] – This is the most widely planted red grape in France, and especially popular in southern France. It is mostly used in inexpensive wines where it is blended to soften its edge. It is also grown in South America and California, where it is known as "Carignane."
- **Carmenére** [kar-men-EHR] – This grape and wine is growing in popularity in Chile since it produces a flavorful, medium- to full-bodied, easy-drinking wine. The grape is French in origin.
- **Cava** [KAH-vah] – The Spanish sparkling wine that is usually made in the champagne method, and which is often an excellent value.
- **Chablis** [shah-BLEE] – True Chablis is a white wine made from the Chardonnay grape near the town of Chablis in the Burgundy region of France. Dry and crisp with a noticeable hint of minerals, Chablis is generally a much better food wine than its new world Chardonnay counterparts. Though not as expensive as other whites from Burgundy, Chablis will probably be too pricey for most get-togethers unless you are considering the very *faux* likes of "Mountain Chablis" and the like.
- **Champagne** [sham-PAYNE] – This is sparkling wine from the Champagne region made in the *méthode champenoise*, an expensive process that includes a secondary fermentation in the bottle. Sparkling wine, even if produced by this same process, with the same types of grapes, and commonly referred to as champagne is not champagne, as Champagne denotes a sparkling wine made from this specific region. Sparkling wine from outside the Champagne region can be excellent and comparatively good values, but never match the top champagnes in terms of refinement, suppleness, cost or cachet. Champagnes and their brethren can range in taste from very dry to very sweet. The label will indicate the level of sweetness: brut, natural, extra dry (or extra sec), sec, demi-sec, and doux. Demi-sec and doux are dessert wines.
- **Chardonnay** [shar-doh-NAY] – An excellent and very versatile white grape that produces dry wines of the same name in California and most of the rest of the New World and Italy. It's also the primary grape for the

famous, highly-rated white wines of Burgundy. Generally, with the heavy use of oak casks, the New World Chardonnays are described as buttery and creamy with noticeable fruit, and work better when drunk alone than when paired with food. These Chardonnays are the most popular white wines at bars and social events.

- **Châteuaneuf-du-Pape** [sha-toh-nuhf-doo-PAHP] – Most of the production of this famous wine from the southern Rhône valley consists of dry, full-bodied reds made from up to thirteen types of grapes. White versions are made in more limited quantities.
- **Chenin Blanc** [SHEN-in BLAHNK] – This is a grape that produces slightly sweet and piquant wines from Loire valley in France such as Vouvray, Saumur, and Côteaux de Layon. New World versions are less common, and are named after the grape. These are often made in the style of a simple, but refreshing wine.
- **Chianti** [kee-AHN-tee] – This is a dry red wine, usually medium-bodied, from the Chianti area of Tuscany in central Italy. It can be an excellent food wine, or enjoyable on its own. There are seven Chianti regions. Chianti Classico is the best, after which Rufina (labeled as "Chianti Rufina") is a usually reliable buy in North America, and generally better than regions that are sold simply as "Chianti." *Riserva* Chiantis are aged in oak for at least three years and are full-bodied, longer lasting and demand more robust food.
- **Cirò** [chee-ROH] – A historic wine region in Calabria in southern Italy that produces reds, whites and rosés of often decent quality.
- **Colombard** [kol-UHM-bard] – This is a widely planted white grape that is fragrant and acidic. It is used mostly for blends though also bottled as a varietal.
- **Corvo** [KOR-voh] – The brand name of a successful winery in Sicily.
- **Dolcetto** [dohl-CHAY-toh] – A fruity, even grapey, red wine from Piedmont that has become more alcoholic and international in style since the 1990s. It is often labeled as one from of the areas from where the wines are made such as Dolcetto d'Alba, Dolcetto di Diano d'Alba, Dolcetto di Monferrato, etc.
- **Frascati** [frah-SKAH-tee] – A light-bodied, fragrant, usually dry and uncomplicated white wine from near Rome.
- **Fumé Blanc** [fooh-MAY BLAHN] – This is another name for Sauvignon Blanc.
- **Gamay** [gam-AYE] – The grape used for Beaujolais, where it makes light-bodied and fruity red wines whose tastes are often described as grapey.
- **Gevry-Chambertin** [zhev-REE cham-behr-TAN] – A highly regarded red Burgundy that is one of the longest lasting reds. This is too expensive to serve for nearly any occasion.

- **Gewürztraminer** [guh-VURTZ-trah-mee-ner] – This white grape produces wine of the same name that exhibits crisp, clean, yet spicy flavors, coupled with an unusual aroma. Originally from the Alsace region, currently in France, this wine is also produced with success in Germany, California and the Pacific Northwest. The non-dessert versions can be excellent accompaniments to somewhat spicy food such as Thai and Vietnamese cuisines.
- **Graves** [GRAHV] – This is an important area in Bordeaux that can produce great red and white wines. It usually refers to the dry whites.
- **Grenache** [gren-AHSH] – A red wine grape that is found in southern France, Spain (where it's called Garnacha), Sardinia and more commonly in Australia. In Europe it is usually used as a blending grape to add fruity flavors and additional alcohol.
- **Grüner Veltliner** [grooh-NER felt-LINE-er] – This is a fruity, acidic white wine from Austria that are named after the grape.
- **Hermitage** [ehrm-eh-TAJH] (or **Ermitage**) – A famous region in the northern Rhône valley that produces red and white wines made for aging.
- **Lambrusco** [lahm-BROO-skoh] – A pale red wine (though white and rosé version also exist) from the Emilia-Romagnan region of central Italy. It's usually slightly sweet, effervescent, uncomplicated and low in alcohol (about 6%). Referred to in Italy, as the "Italian cola," it is best utilized in washing down the rich food of its home region, or as an easy quaffer.
- **Languedoc** [lahn-gwah-DOK] – The area in southern France whose wine industry has undergone dramatic improvements that became noticeable in the 1990s, it's an area for well-made inexpensive wines usually exported as popular varietals such as Merlot and Cabernet Sauvignon.
- **Madeira** [muh-DAIR-uh] – Fortified wines made in the Portuguese islands of the same name in the Atlantic. The four main styles, from lightest and driest, to heaviest and sweetest, are: **Sercial** [sehr-SEE-ahl], **Verdehlo** [vehr-day-LOH], **Bual** [BOOL], and **Malmsey**. The lighter versions can work as aperitifs, while the Bual and Malmsey are excellent after dinner drinks similar to port. Madeira is also used in many culinary creations. The Founding Fathers toasted the signing of the Declaration of Independence with Madeira.
- **Malbec** – A rich, red and tannic grape originally from France where it is a major grape in the Cahors region and a very minor one in Bordeaux. However, it has reached it greatest form in Argentina where it makes smooth but meaty wines that are fitting complements to red meats.
- **Margaux** [mar-GO] – A large region in Bordeaux that produces many excellent wines.
- **Marsala** [mahr-SAH-lah] – A fortified wine from western Sicily somewhat like sherry, port and Madeira. It comes in dry and sweet styles. Though some good versions exist it is not regarded nearly as

highly as the other three great fortified wines, and is mostly used in this country for cooking (Veal Marsala, *zabaglione*, etc.).

- **Médoc** [may-DOK] – An area within Bordeaux. Wines labeled *Appellation d'Origine Médoc Contrôlée* will be less interesting than wines that sport the name of a town within the Médoc.

- **Merlot** [mehr-LOH] – A red wine grape that produces dry, full-bodied wines that are slightly more mellow, less complex and tannic than the similar Cabernet Sauvignon grapes. Used both as a blending grape in Bordeaux where it originated, and in the New World, it is now commonly bottled as a wine of its own. Many wine snobs are not big fans of Merlots.

- **Meursault** [mehr-SOH] – Based on the Chardonnay grape, this designation produces some of the best white wines in the world. Expensive.

- **Montepulciano d'Abruzzo** [mohn-tay-pool-chee-AHN-oh duh-BROOTZ-oh] – A rich, fruity red wine from eastern Italy that continues to improve in quality, and often a good value. Not related to the similarly named Vino Nobile di Montepulciano.

- **Moscato di Pantelleria** [moh-SKAH-toh DEE pahn-tell-ay-REE-ah] – These are white and dessert wines from the Muscat grape that are produced on the tiny island south of Sicily, close to Africa. The dessert wines are highly prized.

- **Mourvèdre** [mohr-VEDD] – A red wine grape that is very common, and used mostly for blending, in the Rhône and elsewhere in southern France and southeastern Spain (where it is known as Monastrell). It has also become popular in Australia.

- **Muscadet** [muh-skah-DAY] – A dry, simple white wine from the lower Loire region of France.

- **Muscat** [mus-KAT] and **Moscato** [moh-SKA-toh] – A generic name for over 200 similar varieties of grapes that are often used for sweet wines.

- **Nebbiolo** [nay-beeh-OH-loh] – This is the red wine grape used for the famous Barolo and Barberesco wines, as well as the lesser known and less regarded wines from Spanna, Valtellina, Nebbiolo d'Alba, and Nebbiolo della Langhe.

- **Negroamaro** [nay-gro-ah-MAHR-oh] – A red wine grape from Apulia in southeastern Italy that produces hearty red wines such as Salice Salentino.

- **Nero d'Avola** [nehr-OY duh-ahv-OH-lah] – Sturdy red wine grape from Sicily that has been bottled as a varietal in fairly recent years.

- **Orvieto** [or-veeh-EHT-oh] – A famous wine from the area near the town of the same name in central Italy. These wines are light-bodied and made either semi-sweet or dry, of which the dry is most often exported.

- **Penedés** [pe-nay-DEZ] – Spanish wines from the region southwest of Barcelona. The reds are made mostly from the local clones of Tempranillo and Mourvèdre can be rich and flavorful, while the whites fruity and crisp tasting.

- **Petite Sirah** [peh-TEET sur-AH] – A Californian varietal that originated from the obscure French Durif grape. Not related to the similarly named Syrah, it can make some pleasant, beefy reds that are often good values. Well-made Petite Sirah has intense blueberry and eucalyptus flavors, along with a lot of tannins, which can make it tough to drink before a few years of age. The wines are highly aromatic, yet not at all subtle. For the sake of classification, Petite Sirah is Durif, an obscure French grape that itself was a cross between Syrah and Peloursin, another obscure Rhône grape.

- **Pinotage** – A quality red wine grape from South Africa that was derived from the Pinot Noir and Cinsault grapes.

- **Pinot Blanc** [peeh-NOH BLAHN] – A white wine grape originally from Alsace in northeastern France. Often used for blending with other grapes, but can make some interesting white wines with low acidity on its own.

- **Pinot Grigio** [peeh-NOH greeh-GHEEH-OH] – A white Italian grape that is identical to the French Pinot Gris. Typically makes a light, dry, acidic wine, often with hints of lemon and lime flavors. The Alsatian Pinot Gris styles are usually more distinctive than their Italian cousins.

- **Pinot Noir** [peeh-NOH NWAHR] – A red French grape that makes wines that are typically low in tannins, fruity aromas and light- to medium-bodied. In Burgundy especially, Pinot Noir is responsible for some of the world's greatest wines. Generally, a very good wine for a wide variety of foods.

- **Pomerol** [poh-MEHR-ahl] – A small area in Bordeaux that produces many excellent wines that predominately feature the Merlot grape, including one of the world's most expensive wines, Chateau Petrus.

- **Port** – A fortified wine from northern Portugal that comes in four basic varieties: vintage, tawny, ruby and white. The tawny ports, which can last for a while after opening, are also probably the best value versions. All but the white ports are commonly drunk as an after-dinner drink.

- **Pouilly Fuissé** [pooh-WEE fooh-SAY] – This can be fun to say. A white Burgundy, so made with the Chardonnay grape.

- **Pouilly Fumé** [pooh-WEE fooh-MAY] – Along with the Pouilly Fuissé, the name is fun to pronounce, at the very least. Made with the Sauvignon Blanc grape.

- **Primativo** [prim-ah-TEEH-voh] – This is the Zinfandel grape that is grown in southern Italy, most proficiently in the southeastern province of Puglia, where it makes full-bodied, hearty and straightforward red wines.

- **Prosecco** [proh-SAY-koh] – Both the grape, and the generally inexpensive and well made light-bodied, dry sparkling wine from northeastern Italy. Works well as an aperitif and a cheap substitute for champagne.

- **Retsina** [reht-SEE-nuh] – This is wine from Greece that has been treated with resin from pine trees, resulting in a very distinctive flavor, at its worst, not unlike turpentine. It should be served very cold, and with some trepidation to non-Greeks, as it is very much an acquired taste.
- **Rhône** [RHON] – The large wine region in southern France around the Rhône River valley that produces high-quality, food-friendly reds, whites and rosés. The vast majority of the wines imported to North America are red and generally full-bodied and fairly concentrated. The ones from the northern Rhône (Hermitage, Crôzes-Hermitage, Saint Joseph, Cornas, and Côte-Rôtie) are made primarily from the Syrah grape. The reds from the southern Rhône (Châteuaneuf-du-Pape, Côte du Rhône, Côte du Rhône Villages, etc.) are made with a greater number of grapes, the most prominent ones of which are Grenache, Mourvèdre, and Carignan. Some of the southern Rhône wines can be excellent values, mostly red, but some good value-priced whites, too.
- **Ribera del Duero** [ree-BEHR-ah DEL dwehr-OH] – Some excellent, velvety red wines are made in the Spanish region, including Vega Sicilia, Spain's most expensive wine.
- **Riesling** [RHEEZ-ling] – One of the top white grapes in the world, it produces excellent wines from dry to very sweet in Germany, plus excellent mostly dry wines in the New World, especially in the Pacific Northwest. The flavor can often be described as complex, fruity (such as hints of mangoes, melons or green apples) with floral notes and a long finish. But, it produces different flavors everywhere that it is produced. For German Rieslings, the types of wines from driest and light (and most inexpensive) to sweetest, most viscous and most expensive are: Kabinett, Spätlese, Auslese, Beerenauslese, Trockenbeerenauslese. In California, Johannisberg Riesling is the same Riesling grape that is used in Germany.
- **Rioja** [ree-OH-hah] – A famous wine-making region in Spain known for sturdy, smooth reds and in recent years, also crisp, whites.
- **Roussanne** [rooh-SAHN] – A white wine grape from France's northern Rhône where it makes light and delicate wines when blended with the Marsanne grape. It is also an important component in the white Hermitage and white Châteuaneuf-du-Pape wines, and in other simpler wines from southern France.
- **St. Emilion** [SAINT aye-MEEH-leeh-own] – A famous region in Bordeaux that produces a wide range of red wines based on the Merlot grape. Though the top wines can age well, most are notable for the fact that among red Bordeaux wines that they are ready to drink soon after release.
- **Sancerre** [sahn-SEHR] – A white wine from the Loire Valley in France that is made with the Sauvignon Blanc grape. This wine is a good match for most seafood that is simply grilled.

- **Sangiovese** [sahn-joe-VAY-zay] – A red wine grape that predominates in Tuscany as the biggest contributor to the Chianti blend. It is also grown and bottled, but without the same success, under the "Sangiovese" name in the Emilia-Romagna and Abruzzo regions of Italy, California and Argentina.
- **Sauternes** [saw-TERN] – A famous region in Bordeaux that produces great sweet and very rich white wines from the Sémillon grape that are a traditional match for *foie gras*. Its top winery, Chateau d'Yquem produces one of the most expensive wines in the world.
- **Sauvignon Blanc** [sauv-in-YAWN BLAHN] – A white wine grape that produces dry table wines with grassy and citrus flavors. It is the primary grape used for white Bordeaux in Graves and Sancerre of the Loire Valley, Pouilly Fumé, and other excellent wines, especially in New Zealand and California.
- **Sémillon** [sem-MEE-yohn] – This is the white wine grape that is used in the Sauternes in Bordeaux, and frequently blended with Sauvignon Blanc in the New World to provide some additional sweetness.
- **Sherry** – One of the classic fortified wines that is made around the southern Spanish town of Jerez, which gives this beverage its name, as "sherry" is the English corruption of Jerez. There are four basic styles of sherry. **Fino** is the lightest and most dry. It works very well as an aperitif especially when chilled. **Manzanilla** is also dry, though with a fuller body. These are often served chilled with seafood. **Amontillado** has a medium body and a nutty and sweeter flavor than the fino and manzanilla. **Oloroso**, which is sometimes labeled as **Cream**, are sweet and full-bodied.
- **Shiraz** [shir-RAHZ] – The Australian name for the Syrah grape, and a wine of the same name. See "Syrah." These are usually easy to drink without accompaniment, especially at the lower end of the price scale.
- **Soave** [swah-VAY] – A medium-bodied dry, clean-tasting white wine from northeastern Italy that can range from insipid to very good.
- **Super Tuscan** – Very high quality wines from Tuscany that usually blend Cabernet Sauvignon with the native Sangiovese grapes in red wines.
- **Syrah** [sir-RAH] – A red wine grape that originally came to prominence in the Rhône valley of southern France, especially in the northern Rhône area where it is the primary grape for the often expensive wines of Cornas, Hermitage, Croze-Hermitage, Côte-Rôtie, and Saint Joseph. It also produces excellent wines in Australia under the Shiraz name, and in California. The wines from Syrah are rich, and tannic, with peppery and plum flavors.
- **Tavel** [tah-VELL] – This is a rosé produced in the Rhône region, and is regarded as a serious wine, unlike most other rosés.

- **Tawny Port** – This is the type of port that you are most likely to purchase. There are five common styles: basic, 10-year-old, 20-year-old, 30-year-old, and 40-year-old. The taste becomes progressively less fruity, drier and more complex in the older versions. The 10-year-old is much better than the basic style, and probably the best value among the tawny ports.

- **Thunderbird** – A syrupy-sweet beverage marketed to the economically- and spiritually-depressed. A jingle associated with it ran, "what's the word, it's 'Thunderbird,' what's the price, it's fifty-thrice; why we drink it, 'cause it tastes nice." Not recommended.

- **Tokay** [toh-KAY] (or **Tokaji**) – The great sweet dessert wine from Hungary. The level of sweetness and quality is measured on *puntos* (or *puttonyos*) from one to six, six being the best and expensive.

- **Trebbiano** [tray-bee-AHN-oh] – A generally light-tasting, bland, but acidic, family of Italian white grapes that is used mainly for blending. Called Ugni Blanc in France, the basis for cognac.

- **White Zinfandel** – A usually slightly sweet and simple wine that is favored by new wine drinkers. Bears almost no resemblance to regular Zinfandel.

- **Valpolicella** [vahl-poh-lee-CHAY-lah] – A fruity red wine with a light or medium body and low tannins from northeastern Italy that can make for a fine value wine with food or to be drunk on its own. *Recioto* and *Ripasso* versions made with dried grapes in some fashion, have more body and deeper flavors.

- **Verdicchio** [vehr-deek-EEH-oh] – A white grape and wine from the central Italian region of the Marches. It usually produces light dry wines.

- **Vermentino** [vehr-men-TEE-noh] – This is a white grape and wine grown and produced in Sardinia and Liguria in northwestern Italy. The wines are typically medium-bodied and flavorful.

- **Vernaccia** [vehr-notch-CHEE-ah] – A white grape and wine from the Tuscany in central Italy and the island of Sardinia. The wines are usually light, dry and fragrant.

- **Vinho Verde** [veen-YO vehr-DAY] – Wines from a region in northwest Portugal that are made from barely ripe grapes, and have to undergo a special secondary fermentation. Though both red and whites are produced, the whites are typically all you will find on shelves. These wines are very light-bodied, low in alcohol, crisp and usually effervescent. Carrying a low price, these make for great summer quaffers.

- **Vino Nobile di Montepulciano** [vee-NOH noh-BEE-lay DEE mohn-tay-pool-chee-AHN-oh] – A rich, flavorful red wine with a difficult multi-syllabic name for non-Italian speakers that is produced in Tuscany from a clone of the Sangiovese. It's not related to the similarly named Montepulciano d'Abruzzo from across the Italian peninsula.

- **Vin Santo** – Dessert wine from central Italy that is usually on the sweet side and a great accompaniment to *biscotti*.
- **Viognier** [vee-oh-en-AY] – A grape originally from the northern Rhône that produces distinctly soft and perfumed white wines.
- **Vouvray** [voo-VRAY] – White wines made the Chenin Blanc grape from near the town of Vouvray in France's Loire Valley. These can range widely in style from dry to sweet and still to sparkling, and in terms of quality and expense.
- **Zinfandel** – [zin-FAHN-dell] – A unique, tannic, red wine with hints of spice and jam that has excelled in northern California. It's usually made in highly alcoholic versions that can reach roughly 17% alcohol by volume, or higher. The Primativo grape that is grown in the Apulia region of southwestern Italy is the same grape as Zinfandel, though it doesn't produce nearly as good wines there.

WINE CHARACTERISTICS – Common or useful adjectives used to describe a wine; aroma, appearance and taste. Don't laugh, as these are often useful terms to characterize a wine.

- **Acidic** – This refers to a high level of acidity in a wine. Acid is present in grapes, and is essential for enjoyable wines. It can be identified with a sharp taste, or tartness. Malic, tartaric and lactic acids are the most prevalent in wines. Overly high acidity causes excessive sharpness or sourness, while very low acidity results in a wine that is bland and flavorless.
- **Aftertaste** – This is the taste left in the mouth after you swallow the wine, which is synonymous for finish and length. The longer the aftertaste lingers in the mouth, the finer the quality of the wine, provided that it's an enjoyable taste.
- **Aroma** – This can simply be how the wine smells, and is often used interchangeably with "bouquet." When used with bouquet, aroma refers to the relatively straightforward smell of the grape variety, and bouquet is the portion of the fragrance that develops through fermentation and aging.
- **Astringent** – This is evident when your mouth begins to pucker, as when drinking some red wines. The level of astringency relates to the level of tannins. A moderate level of astringency is desirable in many types of red wines.
- **Balance** – This refers to when the concentration of fruit, level of tannins, and acidity are in harmony within in the wine. No single flavor dominates. It is one of the most desired traits for a wine to have.
- **Big** – This refers to full-bodied wines that seem full and intense on the palate, and are typically fairly high in alcohol.

- **Body** – This is the tactile impression of weight on the palate; the viscosity. Used interchangeably with the term, "weight." Light-bodied wines tend to be low in alcohol, residual sugar, or for red wines, tannins. Full-bodied wines are usually higher in alcohol and can be sweet or tannic.
- **Bouquet** [boo-KAY] – This is the wine's aroma or fragrance that develops complexity because of fermentation and then bottle and barrel aging.
- **Buttery** – This is a sensation of a smooth creaminess not unlike melted butter. This can be present in Chardonnay-based wines that have undergone some aging in oak barrels.
- **Citrus** – These flavors are usually found in white wines, such as Sauvignon Blanc, and some lighter-style Chardonnays.
- **Color** – Comparison with the expected color is one of the important factors in determining a wine's quality. For example, a white wine that is brown usually indicates that the wine is well past its prime.
- **Dry** – When wine features fairly low residual sugar (less than 1%). Most popular wines can be described as dry, and are more acidic, or tart, than sweet.
- **Earthy** – Robert Parker describes this trait as "a positive aroma of fresh, rich, clean soil." It's more often associated with French and Italian wines.
- **Finish** – This refers to the length of time the feel and flavor of the wine last after the wine has been swallowed. Generally, the longer the finish, the higher quality the wine.
- **Fruit-Forward** – This is a term typically used for wines that have immediate and noticeable fruitiness, and can be used both for complex, well-made, mature wines and unbalanced, often young wines.
- **Fruity** – This is used to describe the aroma and taste of fresh grapes, and is usually associated with younger wines.
- **Herbaceous** – Specific herbal aromas under this descriptor are commonly thyme, rosemary, oregano, basil and fennel.
- **Maderized** – This is the brown color of white wines that is caused by age or poor storage.
- **Oaky** – A distinctive flavor usually used for the New World Chardonnays. It comes from the oak barrels that are used for aging.
- **Oxidized** – Denotes decay in wine that is caused by exposure to air.
- **Rich** – This denotes wines that are high in flavor and fruit intensity.
- **Spicy** – Wines that are described as spicy have pungent aromas commonly of pepper, cinnamon, and some other spices.
- **Sweet** – Opposite of dry, this refers to a certain level of sugar in the wine. Depending on the type of wine, this description is used for wines ranging from a lightly sweet finish to syrupy-sweet dessert wine. Sugar is sometimes used in winemaking to hide defects in lesser quality wines, which is why very cheap wines are usually somewhat sweet.

- **Tannic** – Wines that have a high level of tannins, an astringent substance found in red wine and tea, will make your mouth pucker at least slightly. Tannins help give body and potentially long life to red wines. Tannins can create overly bitter flavors in some young red wines. There are no tannins in white wines.
- **Unctuous** [unk-SHUS] – This is used for rich, intense, very flavorful wines with layers of concentrated fruit notes. A great adjective to fit into a casual conversation, especially with those who seem to take wine too seriously.

OTHER WINE-RELATED TERMS – You might find these on wine labels, in marketing literature, and in discussions about wine. Some familiarity with these terms can help to demystify wine.

- **Appellation d'Origine Contrôlée** – Often abbreviated as AOC or AC, this is a legal designation for French wines that guarantees the wines origin and certain quality production methods. This helps to ensure a certain level of quality in the most famous wineries in France.
- **Auslese** [owz-LAY-zeh] – This is the German term for "selected." This refers to top quality wine that is made from selected bunches of ripe grapes. These wines are normally sweet; sweeter than Spätlese.
- **Beerenauslese** [behr-en-owz-LAY-zay] – This is the German term for "berry selection." These are the sweet and very expensive type German white wines made with overripe botrytis-affected grapes.
- **Blanc de blanc** [BLAHN DUH BLAHN] – The French term that denotes that the wine is made from white grapes. On champagne labels it means that it's made only from the Chardonnay grape. These champagnes are generally slightly sweeter than the common brut style.
- **Blanc de noir** [BLAHN DUH NWAHR] – This is the French phrase that means the white wine is made from dark-colored grapes. For champagne it denotes that it's made from solely the Pinot Noir grape.
- **Blush** – This refers to pink-colored wines made from red grapes. This term usually refers to inexpensive plonk like White Zinfandel. It's often used synonymously with the term rosé.
- **Botrytis cinerea** [boh-TRI-tis sihn-EHR-eeh-uh] – This is a fungus that attacks grapes in cold and wet weather. Though very harmful to red grapes, in can, in white grapes produce the "noble rot." This is when the grape is shriveled and the sugar is greatly concentrated. Low yielding and more expensive to pick these grapes, this is responsible for many of the great sweet dessert wines such as Sauternes and Trockenbeerenauslese.
- **Brix** [BREE] – A measure of sugar levels in grape juice and wines. High levels of brix denote a sweeter wine.

- **Brut** – The French term for "unsweetened," which is used mostly for sparkling wines. This is drier than "Extra Dry."
- **Carneros** – This is a cool area that straddles the southern portion of both Napa and Sonoma counties, and is known for its high quality Chardonnay, Pinot Noir and sparkling wine.
- **Central Coast** – This is the well-regarded area near Santa Barbara. Its cool and foggy climate is suited for Pinot Noir and Chardonnay, which are generally lighter and less intense than similar wines from northern California. This area is also home to many good quality Syrah and Viognier wines.
- **Central Valley** – Though you won't find this term used for marketing purposes, this enormous valley that runs roughly two-thirds the length of the state of California produces 70% of the state's wine. All varietals and other blending grapes are grown here. Wines from here are usually labeled as "California" wine.
- **Charmat** – This is a method for making sparkling wine in bulk. It produces wines that are generally not as refined or flavorful as wines made with the traditional champagne method, *méthode champeniose*.
- **Chateau** [sha-TOH] – This is used to refer to a wine estate, which would include all of the property's buildings, vineyards. Used most often in regards to Bordeaux. Chauteaux is the plural.
- **Claret** [klair-EHT] – The British term for red Bordeaux wines.
- **Classico** – The term for Italian wines that are from a specific area, usually the original one, within a larger DOC region. These wines are usually better than the similar wines without the "Classico" designation.
- **Clos** [KLOH] – This is the French term for a vineyard that was once or still is, enclosed by a wall. This term is usually associated with Burgundy.
- **Coonawarra** [koon-ah-WAHR-ah] – This is an important wine region in South Australia that produces excellent wines from Shiraz and Cabernet Sauvignon plus high quality ones with Chardonnay and Riesling.
- **Corked** – This is wine that has been oxidized and spoiled by a cork that has dried up or otherwise been defective. Wines that have been "corked" exhibit a very noticeable stale and moldy odor, and should be discarded.
- **Côte** [COAT] – This is the French term for "hillside," which is used in the name of many wine areas.
- **Crémant** [KRAY-mahn] – Sparkling wine made by the champagne method, usually outside of the Champagne region.
- **Crianza** [kree-AHN-zah] – The Spanish word that denotes that the wine has been aged at least two years, with one being in oak. *"Sin crianza"* means that the wine has not been aged.
- **Cru** [KROO] – This is the French term meaning "growth." This refers to wines from a single vineyard and denoting additional quality.

- **Cuvée** [kooh-VAY] – Commonly refers to a wine that is blended from different grapes, vineyards, or regions.
- **Decanter** – In practical terms, a decanter can be nearly any glass pitcher or carafe that holds wine. Typically, it's made of clear glass and features a narrow neck. In addition to holding wine from another vessel, be it a large format bottle or a box that might be unyielding and unattractive for your guests, a decanter allows wine to aerate, which usually enhances its flavors.
- **Demi-sec** [dem-EE SEK] – The French term for signifying a sweet wine, usually used in terms of champagne. The literal translation is "half dry," but tastes in wine have moved considerably drier in the many decades since the term came into usage.
- **Denominación de Origen** – Abbreviated as DO. This is the Spanish equivalent of the French AOC regulations.
- **Denominazione di Origine Controllata** – Abbreviated as DOC. This is the Italian equivalent of the French AOC regulations.
- **Denominazione di Origine Controllata Garantita** – Abbreviated as DOCG. This is for the very best traditional Italian wine regions. These wines are usually of high quality.
- **Doux** [DOOH] – The French term for "sweet." These wines will be very sweet.
- **Eiswein** [eyez-WINE] – This is the German term for "ice wine," and refers to wines made from grapes that are traditionally picked after the first freeze. These very expensive and very sweet dessert wines are made in Germany, Austria, Canada, and in at least a couple of northern US states.
- **Estate Bottled** – This refers to wine that is bottled where it has been made.
- **Fortified Wine** – This is wine that in which extra alcohol is added. These are relatively high in alcohol, and can last for a while after the bottle has been open, unlike other wines. Sherry, Madeira, port and Marsala are the four most famous fortified wines.
- **Frizzante** [freeh-ZAHN-tay] – The Italian term for "semi-sparkling."
- **Grand Cru** [GRAHN KROOH] – This is a French phrase appearing on labels in Burgundy, Alsace, Champagne and Bordeaux that means "top quality." It has the greatest significance in Burgundy.
- **Gran Reserva** [GRAHN ray-SEHR-vah] – This is a designation for Spanish wines. These red wines have a minimum aging of five years; the white wines a minimum of four years.
- **Half-Bottle** – This bottle can hold half the contents of a normal bottle of wine, 375 milliliters or 12.7 ounces. This equates to about two large glasses of wine.
- **International (Style)** – This style is typified in wines that have prominent fruit, non-distinct *terrior*, are fairly alcoholic (13.0% and greater), often

noticeably aged in oak, and ready to be drunk soon after release. To the chagrin of many traditionalists, these are the hallmarks of many New World wines, and have been replicated with success in the market by many producers in Europe.

- **Kabinett** – This is the lightest and driest category of quality German wines. These are typically low in alcohol and fairly dry; drier than **Spätlese**.
- **Maderization** – This is when white wines turn brown in color due to poor storage conditions or age.
- **Magnum** – A bottle that is the size of two normal-sized bottles, 1.5 liters.
- **Malolactic Fermentation** – This is secondary fermentation (after the primary alcoholic fermentation) where unpleasant malic acid is converted into carbon dioxide and more palatable lactic acid. This process can improve red wines by reducing acidity and softening the wines. It's used only in more expensive white wines to create wine with more complexity and a fuller flavor.
- **Meritage** [mehr-ih-TAJH] – This is a trademarked term used to described expensive Bordeaux-style blends from California that are made with Cabernet Sauvignon, Merlot, Cabernet Franc, Petit Verdot and Malbec. Dominus and Opus One are two well-known versions.
- **Méthode Champeniose** [METH-awd sham-pahn-WAZ] – The traditional and most expensive way to make sparkling wine in which carbonation is induced in each bottle.
- **Mulled Wine** – This is wine mixed with different citrus fruits, spices (commonly cinnamon, nutmeg and cloves) and often sugar and a spirit then heated. Most frequently encountered during the cooler months.
- **Napa** – Though it produces only 4% of the California's wine, this is the most well-known and probably best wine region in the U.S. Many excellent wines are produced here, especially Cabernet Sauvignon, Chardonnay and Zinfandel. Many of the most famous American wineries are located here.
- **Négociant** [neeh-go-SEE-ahn] – A company that purchases grapes or wines to create, blend and sell the finished wines as their own. Most famously, the Burgundy wines are handled by négocians. More recently, négociant firms emerged in California to take advantage of the wine and grape glut of the early part of this century. The fairly new négocians in California can produce inexpensive wines that are great values.
- **New World** – In terms of wine this refers to the wine-producing regions of the U.S., mostly California and the Pacific Northwest, Chile, Australia and Argentina.
- **Old World** – In terms of wine this means the classic wine producing regions of Europe: France, Italy, Germany and Spain, and to a lesser extent, Austria and Switzerland, and the Tokay wines of Hungary.

- **Plonk** – A derogatory term for wine of low quality.
- **Reserva** [ray-SEHR-vah] – The label on Spanish wines that denotes a red wine that has been aged for at least three years; a white wine for at least two years. More concentrated and longer-lasting than similar wines without the *Reserva* designation.
- **Residual Sugar** – This is the amount of sugar that remains in the wine after the fermentation process has ended. Dry wines have low levels of residual sugar; sweet wines have comparatively high levels.
- **Riserva** [reeh-SEHR-vah] – The Italian term for DOCG and DOC wines that have been aged a minimum amount of time depending upon the type of wine. More concentrated and longer-lasting than similar wines without the *Riserva* designation.
- **Rosé** [row-ZAY] – Any of a number of wines that are made from red grapes and are pink in color. Meant to be consumed chilled, these generally feature a light-bodied and uncomplicated character. **Rosado** [row-SAH-doh] and **Rosato** are the Spanish and Portuguese, and Italian terms for rosé.
- **Sediment** – This is residue that accumulates in the bottom of the wine bottle as the wine ages. Much more so in red wines, this residue consists of tartrates, pigments and tannins (in red wines).
- **Sonoma** – This is probably the second most well-known wine region in American after its neighbor just to the east, Napa. Its often foggy and cool climate makes it an excellent source of Chardonnay, Pinot Noir and Merlot. Just 3% of California's wine production comes from here.
- **Spätlese** [shpate-LAY-zay] – This is the German term for "late-harvested" wine. These are typically slightly sweet.
- **Split** – A 6.3 ounce (or 187 milliliter) bottle, most often used for champagne.
- **Spritzer** – This is a combination of white wine, originally German wine, and club soda.
- **Spumante** [spooh-MAHN-tay] – This is the Italian term for "sparkling." Wines labeled as such are usually slightly sweet.
- **Still wine** – This term means that the wine is non-sparkling.
- **Sulfites** – Sulfur dioxide (a sulfite) is used around the globe to clean equipment, kill undesirable micro-organisms, and protect wine from spoiling. A very small amount typically remains in each bottle.
- **Table wine** – This refers to non-sparkling wines meant for the table, and is often used synonymously with the "still wine." It is commonly used to refer to everyday wines as opposed to high dollar wines.
- **Tannins** – These are an astringent substance found in red wine and tea, which will make your mouth pucker at least slightly. Tannins help give body and potentially long life to red wines. Tannins can create overly

bitter flavors in some young red wines. There are no tannins in white wines.

- **Tartrates** – This is the crystal sediment you might find in the bottom of wine bottles. This is caused by the tartaric acid present in the wine, and sometimes calcium. It's tasteless and harmless.
- **Terroir** [tehr-WHAHR] – The French term that refers to an area of terrain, usually very small, whose particular soil and microclimate give the wine its distinctive quality. This term is usually used in contrast to technological aspects championed for the quality of many New World wines.
- **Trockenbeerenauslese** [trock-en-behr-en-owz-LAY-zay] – These are the sweetest and most expensive category of quality German wine. These are made from individually selected, late-harvested grapes that are infected with noble rot. These wines are very expensive.
- **Varietal** – Used to describe wines made chiefly from a single grape. Popular red wine varietals are Cabernet Sauvignon, Merlot, Zinfandel, Pinot Noir, Syrah (Shiraz), and Malbec. Popular white wine varietals are Chardonnay, Sauvignon Blanc, Pinot Grigio, Riesling, Gewürztraminer, and Chenin Blanc.
- **Vin Gris** – [VAHN GREE] – This is rosé made from Pinot Noir.
- **Vintage** – The year on wine bottles that denotes the year of the grape harvest for that wine.

BEER – Beer styles and other terms associated with beer.

- **Ale** – All beers are broadly classified by the type of yeast used in the primary fermentation process. If top-fermenting yeast is used, it is an ale. Bottom-fermenting yeast results in lager beer (see below). To generalize, ales are generally fruitier and often hoppier than lager beers. Ales are best served at warmer temperatures than are lagers.
- **Amber** – This is a term used most often by American microbrewers that refers to beer that is generally amber-colored and hoppy, usually with the flavor of the distinctive Cascade hops. These make for a different taste than similarly colored English ales.
- **Barley** – This is the grain that is generally the most suitable for making beer. After malting, it provides flavor, body, head, and color to beers. Beers made with 100% barley malt and no adjuncts such are corn and rice are more flavorful. The malt is what the yeast consumes to produce alcohol as a by-product.
- **Barley Wine** – These are very strong ales usually sold in small bottles. Too strong for most parties, not to mention too pricey.
- **Beer Bong** – An apparatus favored by many college-aged and younger students consisting of a funnel attached to a decent-sized tube. This

allows for a beer or beers to be ingested very quickly. Extended use during a party will result in vomiting and drunkenness.

- **Black and Tan** – Though some bottled beers are labeled as this, the term commonly refers to a mixture of a dry stout, usually Guinness, and Bass, a well known English ale, that when poured has a bottom half that is brown (or tan) and a top that is black. Though very popular in Irish bars, an order of "Black and Tan" can offend some sensitive sorts of Irish descent who believe that the name comes from the uniform colors of the hated irregular constabulary during the "Troubles" in Ireland in the 1910s and 1920s. The name, however, dates to a commercial product from 1900, or before, that was inspired by a foxhunt in Limerick, Ireland.
- **Bitter** – This is the British term for a hoppy ale, which is widely available on tap in pubs in England. Bitter also refers to the tangy or sharp taste of a beer, which is a product of the hops added during the brewing process.
- **Bock** – This is the German term for a strong beer, which usually means a lager with an alcoholic level of over 6% per volume. Outside of Germany, this is usually a dark colored beer with a somewhat lower amount of alcohol.
- **Chimay** [shih-MAY] – A brand of very flavorful, rich beers made by Trappist monks in Belgium since the 1860s. Three versions are produced, referred to the red, white and blue, which contain progressively more alcohol. The red has become widely available in North America, even in kegs, which is not quite as flavorful as in bottles, but still excellent.
- **Doppelbock** – This is the German term for a "double bock," a very strong, flavorful and slightly sweet lager. The names of these beers from their original Bavarian producers usually ends in "-ator" such as Salvator, Optimator, and Celebrator. Due to their strength, these are not a good idea for most parties outside of Munich.
- **Draft** (or **Draught** [DRAFT]) – This is beer drawn from a keg or a cask.
- **Forty Dog** (or **Forty**) – Refers to inexpensively made, and priced, but fairly highly alcoholic beer known as malt liquor that is bottled in economical forty ounce bottles. More popular in depressed communities, these were featured prominently in many rap videos of the 1990s and early 2000s. Serving these can add some urban flavor to your party.
- **Gimmick Beer** – Beer styles that seem to originate in the marketing departments of the largest breweries, becoming faddish and then disappearing from the shelves. Ice beer, dry beer, beers featuring red animals in their names and low carbohydrate beers are several of the styles of beers that fit this definition from the 1990s on.
- **Guinness** – A very popular brand of Irish dry stout that is available around the world. The draft and draft-enabled cans and bottles versions are rich, creamy, flavorful and contain a relatively moderate amount of

alcohol. The Extra Stout versions, usually just found in bottles, are less creamy, but hoppier and more alcoholic.

- **Hops** – These are the dried ripe cones from the female flowers of a kind of climbing vine. The resin, when used in the brewing process, adds bitter flavors, and also acts as a preservative. There are many different types of hops that used in a variety of beers.
- **IPA** – This stands for "India Pale Ale," a style of ale that is medium-bodied, highly hopped and bitter, that was created to withstand the long voyage from England to India during colonial times.
- **Lager** – Refers to a style of beer made with bottom-fermenting yeast. The result is a generally clean-tasting beer. This style originated only in the 1820s, but is now the most popular style worldwide. Most popular American beers are lagers. The term "lager" means "store," which means that these beers have to be stored in a cold environment for several weeks before the beer is ready.
- **Lambic** – This is a style of beer made with wild yeasts that are unique to a small area southwest of Brussels. Several distinct styles are made, the most popular are those flavored with fresh fruit such as raspberry (*framboise*) and cherry (*kriek*).
- **Lawnmower Beer** – This is a somewhat facetious term that is used to describe beers with very little body and not much taste that work well as a thirst-quencher after mowing the lawn on a hot day. The phrase has been embraced by the Saint Arnold Brewery in Texas for their popular light-bodied, but flavorful, Kölsch-style beer.
- **Malt** – For beers, this usually refers to malted barley. This grain is steeped in water, which then begins to sprout, and is dried in a kiln.
- **Mash** – This is ground malt that is soaked in water to begin the fermentation process.
- **Malt Liquor** – This is the term used for strong, cheaply made beers from American breweries that are often dispensed in 40 ounce bottles. The laws in some states require excellent high alcoholic imports to also to be labeled as malt liquor, but these are easy to distinguish from the cheap stuff (by the price).
- **Oktoberfest Beer** – This is a lager beer style with a malty taste, medium body and a higher than average alcoholic content (5.5% by volume or so). In Bavaria this type of beer was originally brewed in March (hence its other name, *Märzen*) and lagered during summer and finished in late September. It has since become identified with Oktoberfest celebration in Munich, and now worldwide.
- **Pale Ale** – This denotes a beer that is copper-colored, or bronze, rather than dark brown or black, and is usually fairly hoppy.
- **Pilsner** [pilz-NER] – A clear, hoppy and fragrant lager beer style that originated in the town of Pilsen in Bohemia, the Czech Republic in the

1840s, and that has now become the most widely imitated and popular beer style in the world. The original version (Pilsner Urquell), when fresh, is one of the best beers in the world, as is the slightly sweeter Budweiser Budvar brewed in southwestern Bohemia. Very good versions exist in the Central European regions of Bohemia, Moravia, Slovakia and Bavaria. The large-scale commercial versions brewed in the New World from the major brewers are comparatively very pale, pathetic imitations.

- **Porter** – Top-fermented beers that are usually roasty in flavor and black or dark brown in color. Similar to stout these are lighter and generally less creamy, and often found in brewpubs around North America.

- **Shotgun** – In case you have forgotten, this refers to punching a hole near the bottom of a can of beer while it is horizontal, putting your mouth around the opening, moving the can upright, then opening the pop top to force the beer down your throat. This is a good way to force a lot of beer into your system quickly, if not to enjoy the brewmaster's art.

- **Skunky** – The off-aroma and taste of a beer that is faintly like that of a skunk. This is usually caused by photosynthesis, when the container is exposed to light. Though this can affect all beers that have been damaged, imported Heineken is most often associated with this sensation. It can be reduced by pouring the beer into a glass.

- **Stout** – This popular, hearty, nearly black beer made with top-fermenting yeasts and darkly roasted malts, comes in several different styles: dry, milk or sweet, Imperial, oatmeal, and chocolate. The ubiquitous Guinness is an example of a dry stout.

- **Trappist Ale** – These are strong, complex beers brewed by Trappist monks in five breweries in Belgium and one in the Netherlands. Chimay is a brand that is widely available in North America.

- **Wheat Beer** – This is a beer that is made with typically at least 50% wheat (most top beers are 100% barley malt) and a top-fermenting yeast that, in Bavaria, produces a refreshing, slightly sweet beer with flavors of citrus and sometimes cloves and bananas. There are also Belgian wheat beers (see below). The popular Bavarian wheat beers are served in versions with yeast sediment (*hefe-*), filtered (*kristal*), dark (*dunkel*), and the rare bock styles. These beers, especially the *hefe-* and *kristal* versions, make for great summer thirst quenchers, and are especially popular among women. These are even more refreshing when served with a slice of lemon. *Weisse, Weissbier, Weizen,* and *Weizenbier* are some of the names on the labels of these German beers.

- **White Beer** – This term is used mostly for Belgian wheat beers, which have a distinctive creamy style different than the more common Bavarian wheat beers. *Witbier* and *Bièrre Blanche* are other names for these beers.

SPIRITS & COCKTAIL-RELATED TERMS

- **Absinthe** [AB-sinth] – This is a highly alcoholic, bitter spirit that is distilled from wormwood and flavored with a number of herbs. Primarily tasting of anise (or licorice), it really needs to be cut with water and mixed with sugar to be palatable. The reputed cause of several instances of violent insanity, resulted in it being banned during the early part of the twentieth century in much of Europe and the U.S., where it's still not allowed to be sold. But, bottles occasionally do make it to North America.
- **Aguardiente** [ah-gwahr-dee-AYN-teeh] – In South America, especially Colombia and Ecuador, this refers to a rough liquor made from sugar cane and usually flavored with aniseed. In Spain and Portugal it refers to an often harsh brandy made from grape skins and other excess from the wine-making process, akin to the Italian grappa and the French marc.
- **Amaretto** [ahm-ahr-RET-oh] – An almond flavored liqueur from Italy that mixes especially well with coffee, and women.
- **Angostura Bitters** – This is a long popular brand of bitters produced in Trinidad that is used widely for cocktails such as the Manhattan and Old Fashioned and in cooking. It's roughly 90 proof and is made with primarily angostura bark, gentian root and rum.
- **Anisette** [ahn-eh-ZET] – A licorice-flavored liqueur from France.
- **Amer Picon** [ah-MEHR peeh-KAWN] – A bitter French brand of aperitif that is flavored primarily with oranges and gentian root plus other ingredients that are the basis for quinine. Often mixed with soda, a splash of grenadine and served on the rocks. Also just called Picon.
- **Aperitif** [ah-pehr-uh-TEEF] – A usually light and dry alcoholic drink served before a meal to ostensibly enliven the palate prior to a meal. Most drinks will work though traditionally it would be a *fino* sherry, kir, dry champagne, and a category of branded products such as Dubonnet or Campari that are created specifically for the purpose. A drink before dinner sounds more sophisticated when called an "aperitif." *Apertivo* is the Italian word for this, and are served in upscale Italian restaurants.
- **Applejack** – This is liquor distilled from apple cider in North American that is somewhat similar to the French calvados, if not quite that quality.
- **Armagnac** [ar-man-YAK] – A highly-regarded French brandy that comes from the Gascony region. In addition to the fact that it's made in another area, the other significant differences between it and the more well-known cognac are that armagnac uses wine from up to four grapes instead of one, is distilled once instead of twice, and is often vintage-dated while cognac is not. Armagnac's flavor is smooth but full-flavored.
- **Aquavit** [ahk-kwuh-VEET] – Colorless distilled spirit that is produced throughout Scandinavia. Produced from grain or potatoes to between 70

and 100 proof. The most common style is caraway flavored. It's meant to be served very cold and consumed in a single gulp.

- **Bailey's** – This is a popular brand of Irish crème liqueur, a viscous blend of Irish whiskey, cream and honey that was created in the 1970s. Usually served on the rocks or as a mixer with coffee.
- **B & B** – Both a combination produced commercially since the late 1930s using Benedictine liqueur and brandy that is dry and piquant but flavorful, and a cocktail of the same creation.
- **Benedictine** – A sweet, cognac-based liqueur made in the French region of Normandy by monks of the Benedictine order. With a delicate flavor that hints of honey and citrus, this has long been a popular after-dinner drink.
- **Bitters** – This refers to liqueurs that have a bitter or bittersweet taste, and are used in cocktails. These are also drunk alone as an aperitif or after-drink, used as digestion aid, as an appetite stimulant, and even as a hangover aid. Angostura is the most widely found brand in North America, though Peychaud's from New Orleans is popular there, and provides a slightly sweeter and less bitter flavor that will give more authenticity to those numerous New Orleans-bred cocktails. Other brands or versions include orange bitters, Amer Picon, Fernet Branca, Unicum and Abbott's.
- **Blended Whiskey** – This is a blend of one or more straight whiskies and neutral grain spirits that results in straight whiskey accounting for at least 20% of the blend with a proof of at least 80.
- **Bourbon** – Refers to the sweet, flavorful bourbon whiskey, named for Bourbon County, Kentucky. Bourbon whiskey must be made from between 51 and 79% fermented corn, and is a straight whiskey that is sold at 80 proof. It can be distilled anywhere in the U.S., but the great majority of it does come from Kentucky.
- **Branch Water** – This is often used in regards to whiskey. Branch refers to a branch of a stream. It's an archaic and romantic way of stating that fresh, stream water should be used if you require water with your whiskey. Any cold, clean drinking water will work if branch water is called for.
- **Brandy** – This is the distilled fermented juice of a fruit. The most famous are made from grapes, but brandies are made from a wide range of fruits and even from the oils of flowers. Cognac and armagnac are the two most well-known types of brandies. But, there are also excellent brandies from Spain and California, plus the distinctive apple brandy from Normandy, calvados.
- **Cachaça** [kah-cha-SKAH] – Brazilian liquor, similar to rum, made from distilled sugar cane juice. This main difference is that most rum is distilled from molasses, while cachaça is distilled directly from the juice

of the unrefined sugar cane, and retains a scent of this in the finished products. Cachaça is the liquor in the famous caiprinha, and the most popular booze of the Brazilian poor.

- **Call (Drink)** – This means that the customer "calls" for a specific brand of liquor to be used. It's not too expensive, as this is typically the middle tier of pricing and quality for drinks at a bar or restaurant (well, call, then premium, and sometimes super-premium, in terms of increasing quality and cost), and it usually includes the popular brands such as Jack Daniel's, Smirnoff, Gordon's, Dewar's, etc.

- **Calvados** [kal-vah-DOHS] – A dry, apple-based brandy that is made around the town of Calvados in the Normandy region of France. It is regarded as one of the classic brandies. Probably more accessible than cognac and armagnac.

- **Campari** [kahm-PAHR-ee] – Bright red liquor from Italy that is popular mostly in Italy, though displayed prominently in many Italian-American restaurants. Regular Campari has a bitter and bittersweet flavor. The sweet Campari is, well, sweet. These are usually mixed with soda, mixed in cocktails, or even consumed alone. You will probably not need to provision this for a party unless you are expecting a throng of northern Italians.

- **Chambord** [sham-BORD] – A raspberry-flavored liqueur. Raspberry schnapps is similar, if not quite as smooth, nor as complex, but is typically one-third of the cost.

- **Chartreuse** [shar-TROOSE] – Spirits containing some 130 herbs and spices created by Carthusian monks in France initially in the 16th century, though commercial production did not begin until the mid-19th. The famous green-hued version is 110 proof and has given its name to the color, chartreuse. The yellow version is less alcoholic and has a slightly different flavor, though both are certainly acquired tastes on there own as after-dinner drinks.

- **Cinzano** [chin-ZAHN-oh] – A popular brand of vermouth from Italy that is flavored with orange and angostura bitters (from the bark of a South American tree). This is commonly served over ice with a lemon twist.

- **Cognac** [kon-YAK] – This is brandy from the Cognac region of southeastern France, and is the benchmark for brandies worldwide.

- **Cointreau** [KWAN-tro] – A famous orange liqueur from France that has an interesting, slightly bitter orange flavor. It is made from the peels of sour oranges from the Caribbean island of Curaçao and sweet oranges from Spain.

- **Collins** – A cocktail consisting of a citrus juice, sugar, club soda, ice and a liquor that is traditionally served in a tall thin glass, which is called a Collins glass.

- **Cordial** – A sweetened, packaged alcoholic beverage. These begin with a spirit such as rum, brandy, or whiskey, which is then flavored with a variety of ingredients such as fruits, herbs, spices, nuts and leaves. Common cordials include Benedictine, Southern Comfort, amaretto, Cointreau, and Grand Marnier. Used interchangeably with "liqueur" in North America.
- **Curaçao** [KOO-rah-soh] – The term for orange-flavored liqueurs that are made with peels of the sour oranges found on the Caribbean island of Curaçao in the Netherlands Antilles. Cointreau, Grand Marnier and triple sec are other orange liqueurs.
- **Dash** – Liquid that is obtained by a quick pour of the bottle. This usually pertains to ingredients like bitters, etc. Officially, it should be ¹/₃₂ of an ounce.
- **Digestif** [dee-zhay-STEEF] – An after dinner drink that supposedly aids in digestion after a meal. Popular ones include brandy, B & B, scotch, etc. *Digestivo* is Italian for this.
- **Drambuie** [dram-BOO-ee] – This is a liqueur consisting of scotch whisky, honey and various herbs, usually consumed as an after-dinner drink.
- **Dry** – This is used in connection with basic gin and vodkas referring to the comparative lack of vermouth. These days, a "Dry Martini" might be gin or vodka mixed between an 8-to-1 or 20-to-1 ratio with vermouth.
- **Dubonnet** [dooh-buh-NAY] – This is a fortified wine-based liqueur that is flavored with herbs. There are two styles, Rouge and Blanc. The former is flavored with quinine, and is the richer of the two. The Blanc is drier, and similar to vermouth.
- **Eau-de-vie** [OH-DAY-VEEH] – This is the term for a range of distilled spirits, brandies, which are usually quite strong. The literal translation from the French is "water of life."
- **Falernum** – This is a type of syrup made from mixed fruits with lime, ginger and almond being the most pronounced flavors. From the Caribbean, it contains little or no alcohol, and is used to sweeten and flavor cocktails. Strangely, it is named after a famous wine made during Roman times.
- **Fernet Branca** [FAYR-nay BRAHN-kah] – A very astringent, and highly alcoholic, brand of bitters from Italy that is often consumed as a *digestif*, though it also is used as an aperitif and a hangover cure. It is usually consumed straight or with ice.
- **Fifth** – This refers to a standard 750 milliliter bottle, which contains 25.4 ounces. In its initial, pre-metric size, the bottle was almost exactly ⅘ of a quart, or "a fifth" short of an entire quart of liquor. 1 liter bottles are also popular for spirits.
- **Frangelico** [frahn-JEL-ih-koh] – A hazelnut-flavored 48 proof liqueur that works especially well in coffee.

- **Galliano** – This is a unique brand of liqueur from northern Italy that comes in a distinctively tall, thin bottle. It has a sweet, spicy and slightly vanilla flavor, and is seemingly rarely found in cocktails these days.
- **Genever** (or **Jenever**) – This is the original gin that was first distilled in Holland, and which remains its last outpost. These are rich in aromatic oils and don't seem to mix well in cocktails. Also called Dutch, Holland, Geneva and Scheidam gin. The common London-style dry gin long ago eclipsed it for most of the world's perception of gin.
- **Gin** – A spirit made primarily from grain that is distilled a second time with juniper berries, additional herbs and other items. The ubiquitous dry gin has an understandably dry and aromatic in flavor.
- **Glayva** [glah-VAH] – A brand of liqueur from Scotland that is based on that lands' whisky and is flavored with honey and herbs.
- **Goldschlager** – 107 proof cinnamon-flavored schnapps containing flecks of gold from Switzerland that is popular shooter.
- **Grappa** – An Italian spirit distilled from the leftover matter of the wine-making process such as stems, skins, and grape must. Pretty much the same thing as the French *marc*, and *aguardiente* from the Iberian peninsula, it is often sold in attractive and expensive bottlings. But, grappa is, nonetheless, seemingly only enjoyed by aged male peasants in northeastern Italy, usually in the morning to make their *café corretto*.
- **Grand Marnier** [GRAHN mahr-NYAY] – A cognac-based liqueur from France made with vanilla and bitter oranges. Excellent as a *digestif*, it is also popular in top-shelf Margaritas.
- **Grenadine** – A sweet liqueur with little or no alcohol made from pomegranates used almost solely for flavoring cocktails. "Grenadine" is the French word for pomegranates.
- **Handle** – This refers to a 1.75 liter bottle of liquor, which has a handle.
- **Hard Liquor** – These are liquors with a high alcoholic content, typically at least 80 proof. Whiskey, rum and vodka are referred to as hard liquor rather than liqueurs, which are often around 40 proof.
- **Hypnotiq** [hip-not-IK] – A very bright blue and very sweet, fruity 34 proof liqueur that is favored by the hip-hop community.
- **Jägermeister** [YAYG-er-my-ster] – A very bitter, complex, sometimes described as harsh, liqueur from Germany. Most often consumed as shots, these go down much more smoothly when the Jägermeister is served from the freezer. The name means "hunt master" in German.
- **Jigger** – A shot-sized glass, and a common measurement used in cocktail recipes, that contains 1½ ounces in standard size. It also refers to the amount of 1½ ounces.
- **Kahlúa** [kah-LOOH-uh] – A popular brand of coffee-flavored liqueur that is 40 proof.

- **Lillet** [leeh-LAY] – These are brands of French vermouths that work well as aperitifs. There is a dry version that has a hint of orange, and a sweet red version.
- **Liqueur** [li-KYEER] – A sweetened commercial alcoholic beverage. These begin with a spirit such as rum, brandy, or whiskey that has been flavored with a variety of ingredients such as fruits, herbs, spices, nuts and leaves. Common liqueurs include Benedictine, Southern Comfort, amaretto, Cointreau, and Grand Marnier. Used interchangeably with cordial throughout North America.
- **Liquor** – This is any alcoholic beverage that is made by both fermentation and distillation. Whiskey, rum, gin, vodka and brandy are popular types of liquor. Beer and wine are just fermented.
- **Maceration** – A term that you will find on the labels of many liqueurs, and refers to the process of steeping fruit in alcohol to extract the flavor.
- **Maraschino** [mehr-ah-SHEE-noh] – A cherry liqueur originally from western Croatia that used be commonly used in an array of cocktails.
- **Marc** [MARK] – This is the French version of grappa.
- **Metaxa** [may-TAKS-uh] – Brand of sweet, aromatic brandy from Greece.
- **Mezcal** [mez-KAHL] – This describes the broad category of distilled spirits from the roasted heart of the agave plant. Tequila is a specific type of mezcal that was originally produced near the town of Tequila in the state of Jalisco. Much of what is labeled as mescal can be very bad.
- **Midori** [mih-DOOR-ee] – A bright green liqueur from Japan that tastes like a honeydew melon.
- **Muddle** – To mix and mash with some harshness, which can be with a mortar and pestle, so that the oils are released from the herbs or spices.
- **Mull** – These are drinks that are heated, in part, to ensure the ingredients are thoroughly integrated.
- **Neat** – The term for serving a drink straight without any mixers or ice. Scotch, other whiskies and tequila are most commonly served neat. The term "straight up" is sometimes used for this same purpose when referring to whiskies or other liquors.
- **Noilly Prat** [noh-WEEH PRAHT] – This is brand of very dry vermouth from Marseilles, France that works well in Martinis and as an aperitif.
- **Orgeat** [ohr-ZHAY] – Non-alcoholic almond-flavored syrup that is used primarily as an ingredient in Mai Tai's.
- **Ouzo** [ooh-ZOH] – A licorice-flavored liquor of 80 proof from Greece.
- **Pastis** [pahs-TEEH] – This is a licorice-flavored absinthe substitute that is especially popular in the south of France. There are several brands, each with a somewhat more pronounced licorice taste than the similar Pernod.
- **Pernod** [pehr-NODE] – A brand of anise-flavored liqueur from France that has long been used as a substitute for absinthe.
- **Pimm's** – This is a unique form and brand of English gin.

- **Pisco** [PEE-skoh] – A brandy made from grapes and very popular in Peru, Chile and Bolivia. The Pisco Sour cocktail is a common method of consumption. The Peruvians rightly claim superiority for their piscos.
- **Poire Williams** [pwhar WEEL-yahms] – Brandy made from Williams pears; top brands feature a pear that has grown within that bottle. This is done by placing the bottles on the trees over the maturing fruits.
- **Pousse-Café** [poos kah-FAY] – A mixed drink made with at least two liqueurs and often cream. A key attraction of these drinks, if made properly, is that the different liquids settle in separate levels according to the specific gravity of each. This can be an overly attractive and fussy drink for many.
- **Premium (Drink)** – This denotes that it is an esteemed brand of liquor. This is typically the highest tier of quality at a bar or restaurant among popularly sold brands (well, call, premium in terms of increasing quality and cost), and it usually includes such liquors as Bombay Sapphire (gin), Grey Goose (vodka), and Glenlivet (single-malt scotch). There can be, of course, higher quality and more expensive liquors in each category. These are the "super premium" brands.
- **Proof** – An indicator of the amount of alcohol. In North America, this number divided in half is the percentage of alcohol. For example, 80 proof denotes that the beverage is 40% alcohol.
- **Rickey** – A cocktail featuring either lemon or lime juice, club soda and usually gin, though another liquor can be used.
- **Rock and Rye** – This is a 60 to 70 proof liquor made with rock candy syrup, rye, grain and sometimes fruits.
- **Rumple Minze** [rum-PEL MINTZ] – A well-regarded brand of 100 proof peppermint schnapps from Germany that is most widely used as a shooter.
- **Rye Whiskey** – Though barley and wheat are most often used in the fermentable mash, rye whiskey must contain at least 51% rye. It has a color similar to bourbon, but a fuller and coarser flavor that can be fairly spicy. Straight rye whiskies are from a single distiller. Blended rye whiskies are combinations of several rye distilleries.
- **Saké** [sah-KAY] – This is a Japanese drink of fermented rice with a very long tradition. It technically is a beer, since it is not distilled, nor is it made from grapes. It can be drunk either warm or cold. Heating the saké both releases the aromas and can hide the off-flavors of cheap versions. Saké is fairly perishable and should be consumed within a year of purchase, and soon after opening a bottle.
- **Sambuca** [sahm-BOOK-ah] – A viscous anise-flavored liqueur from central Italy that is a pleasant *digestif*, or *digestivo*.

- **Schnapps** [SHNAHPS], **Schnaps** – These are a wide array of strong alcoholic drinks usually flavored with seeds, spices, herbs or fruits for a distinctive taste that can be either dry or sweet.
- **Scotch** – This refers to whisky from Scotland. It is made primarily from malted barley instead of the corn that is typically used for North American whiskies. Scotch has a distinctive malty and smoky flavor. The two main types of labeling of scotch whiskies are as blended or single malt. Blended refers to whiskies that are blended with many individual (single) malt whiskies, plus possibly whiskies made with grain other than malted barley, such as corn, wheat and unmalted barley, which are all more inexpensive. Single malt scotch is whisky that is produced and bottled at a single distillery and is not blended with any other whiskies. These single malts can be idiosyncratic and vary widely in style and price.
- **Shaker** – Most are three-piece utensils, consisting of a stainless steel top that fits a glass or metal tumbler, and usually a strainer, which are used to mix drinks. This is essential in creating many cocktails.
- **Shooter** (or **Shot**) – Any one of a number of cocktails meant to be consumed in a single gulp.
- **Simple Syrup** – This is a solution of sugar and water, which is cooked over a low heat until it is clear, and then boiled for about minute. For drink recipes, the ratio is three parts water to 1 part sugar. It is also called "sugar syrup."
- **Sloe Gin** [SLOH JIHN] – Not gin at all, but a liqueur of usually around 50 proof made from sloe berries, which are from the blackthorn bush.
- **Straight Up** – Refers to a cocktail shaken with ice, which is then strained and usually served in a Martini glass. For cocktails that are not shaken, this is same as "neat."
- **Sour** – A type of cocktail made with lemon or lime juice, sugar and a liquor usually served in a short glass. Whiskey Sour is the most common.
- **Southern Comfort** – A 70 proof liqueur that provides a very sweet montage of fruit flavors, primarily peach. This was invented as a mixer to make bad quality bourbon drinkable.
- **Straight Whiskey** – This is whiskey that has not been blended with other whiskies, liquors or anything else, other than water, after distillation.
- **Strega** [STRAY-gah] – An Italian liqueur brand that has a rich and distinctively sweet, spicy taste that sometimes makes it into cocktails or as an after-dinner drink.
- **Sweet-and-Sour** – This is a mixture of lemon juice, sugar, and sometimes egg whites that is a component in a wide variety of cocktails. It's available commercially bottled or in powdered mix form, and is often called "sour" or "bar" mix.
- **Tequila** – This is a specific type of mescal, made with the roasted heart of the Agave Tequilana Weber, Variety Blue, which was originally produced

near the town of Tequila in the state of Jalisco, though now also made in four additional Mexican states. Tequilas are generally divided among *mixto*, (at least 51% distilled agave juice blended with neutral spirits), and the three categories that are made with 100% distilled agave juice; *blanco* (bottled within 60 days of distillation); *repsosado* (aged from two to eleven months in oak); and *añejo* (aged for at least a year in small oak barrels).

- **Tia Maria** – This is a brand of coffee liqueur from Jamaica made with rum, and is slightly drier than the popular Kahlúa.
- **Toddy** – Traditionally this is a hot drink made with sugar, spices such as cinnamon and cloves, spirits, and garnished with a lemon peel.
- **Top Shelf** – Used in the same fashion as Premium, though usually in respect to Margaritas.
- **Triple Sec** – A liqueur flavored with the peels of bitter and sweet oranges, it is most commonly used as an ingredient in Margaritas.
- **Vermouth** [ver-MOOTH] – A flavored fortified wine originally from Italy and France that is made with an array of different botanicals. Vermouth is either sweet or dry. Sweet vermouth, which is somewhat sweet, is used mostly as an aperitif. Dry vermouth is, well, drier, and is best known as a component in the classic Martini. In older cocktail books, you will find recipes specifying French and Italian vermouth. French vermouths were originally dry and Italian sweet, though each style has been made in each of the countries for many years now.
- **Vodka** – A clear liquor that can be distilled from a wide variety of plants including beets, grapes and potatoes, though grain is the most popular. Because of its generally neutral flavor, vodka has become the most popular liquor used in cocktails. Flavored vodkas have become more common in recent years in North America. When drunk alone, vodka is tastier when it's served very cold, preferably from the freezer.
- **Well (Drink)** – This means it comes from the "well" of the bar. This is typically the lowest tier of quality at a bar or restaurant (well, call, premium in terms of increasing quality and cost), and it usually denotes industrially-made brands that are usually only marketed at bars and restaurants. Never order well scotch.
- **Whiskey, Whisky** – An alcoholic beverage distilled from a fermented mash of grains such as barley, corn, and rye. Distinctive styles are produced in Ireland, Scotland, which is known as scotch, Canada, and in the U.S., of which bourbon and the similar Tennessee whisky are the most famous styles.

CHEESE

- **Asiago** [ahs-eeh-AH-goh] – A hard tangy cheese from Italy that tastes pleasant, if mild, when young, and like Parmesan when aged. Goes well with full-bodied red wines when aged. American asiago is very bland.
- **Bel Paese** [bell pah-AY-say] – A very mild, soft and creamy Italian cheese. A versatile cheese that melts well, and is good for both snacks and for dessert. Matches with light white wines like Orvieto, Soave, Chenin Blanc and Sauvignon Blanc.
- **Beaufort** [boh-FOHR] – A Swiss-style cheese from France that has a fruity and slightly sweet, but clean taste. It is a very good cheese for melting.
- **Boerenkaas** [bor-EN-kahs] – This is aged Gouda that has developed noticeable nutty flavors.
- **Blue** (or **Bleu**) **Cheese**– This is the generic name for cheeses with internal molds, which are noticeable, with veins that are typically blue or blue-ish in color. With the exception of Roquefort, most blue cheeses are made from cow's milk.
- **Boursault** [boohr-SOHLT] – A common brand of French triple-crème cheese.
- **Boursin** [boohr-SEH] – A popular brand of French triple-crème cheese that is covered in pepper or flavored with garlic and herbs.
- **Brie** [BREE] – A popular soft cheese that features a creamy interior with a mild flavor covered with a white, edible rind. This works well for nearly any events' cheese platter, and it's also good when heated before serving. Brie should be used within a few days after purchase. Works well to end a meal, especially with a flavorful, rich red wine that is somewhat fruity, such as a good-quality Beaujolais, red Burgundy or Cabernet Sauvignon.
- **Brillat-Savarin** [breeh-LAH sahv-ah-RAH] – Another popular brand of triple-crème cheese from France, evoking the refinement associated with the name of the famous gourmet and food writer of the early nineteenth century. It has a somewhat sharp taste.
- **Brin d'Amour** [BRIN dah-MOR] – A tangy, aromatic goat's milk cheese from Corsica that is covered with herbs.
- **Cabrales** [kah-BRAH-lez] – A very high quality Spanish blue cheese with intense flavors and aromas that is primarily made from goat's milk. It matches well with the sweet Pedro Ximenez sherry for dessert.
- **Caciocavallo** [kah-choh-kuh-VAHL-oh] – A cow's milk cheese from Southern Italy that is mild when young, and tangy and more flavorful when aged. The young versions are usually served with fruit, while the older versions are used as a grating cheese. Fruity and light-bodied wines, both red and white, work well as a complement.

- **Cambozola** [kam-boh-ZOH-lah] – This is a creamy cheese from Germany that tastes much like a cross between Gorgonzola and Camembert. Its white triple-crème interior contains streaks of blue.
- **Cantal** [kahn-TAHL] – A semi-firm cheese from France made from the milk of cows that has mild and nutty flavor, similar to that of Cheddar cheese. It's a reliable party-pleaser, as it's mild, but with enough complexity of flavor to make it interesting. This cheese has been made since pre-Roman times.
- **Comté** [kom-TAY] – Made in France, this is a smooth, firm cheese with a sharp, nutty flavor that is similar to Beaufort and Gruyère. Melts well.
- **Cream Cheese** – A very soft, simple and slightly sour-tasting cheese that is most often used for spreading on crackers, bagels, and the like.
- **Camembert** [KAM-uhm-behr] – This is a classic, creamy and spreadable cow's milk cheese with a white rind and a milky and tangy flavor. The ones from Normandy and elsewhere in France are usually of higher quality.
- **Cheddar** – This is the most widely made cheese in the world, and the one that nearly everyone seems to enjoy, though much of the mass-produced cheddar cheese is bland and rubbery, bordering on tasteless. From the better producers, young cheddar has a taste that starts off fairly mild and sweet with a note of nuts, often with a salty tang. Older cheeses have a wonderfully nutty taste with a real piquancy to it that make for a fine match with robust red wines and ports.
- **Cheshire** – An English cheese with production centered around the town of Cheshire. It comes in two styles, referred to as Red and Blue. The Red is a mild and flavorful cheddar-style cheese. The Blue is a blue cheese that is not quite as tangy or pungent as Stilton, England's most famous blue cheese. Goes well with beer, especially English styles, and fruity red wines. The Blue will complement a full-bodied red wine.
- **Chèvre** [SHEHV] – Cheese made from goat's milk that features a popular tart flavor and usually a thick creamy texture.
- **Colby** – An American spin on the original English-style cheddar that is softer and more moist, but also mellower, often to the point of blandness.
- **Derby** [DAHR-beeh] – A mild cheddar-style cheese from England that is an enjoyable, if not memorable, snacking cheese with beer or light-bodied fruity wines.
- **Dry Jack** – This is aged Monterey Jack that has a rich and nutty flavor, and was created during the First World War for Italian-Americans as a substitute for the unavailable Parmesan and Romano.
- **Edam** – A firm, slightly rubbery textured cheese originally from Holland that has a mild, slightly buttery and tangy taste. It is a reliable cheese to purchase as it lasts for a very long time. It goes well with crisp lager beers and light red and white wines.

- **Emmental** [EM-mahn-tahl] (or **Emmentaler** or **Emmenthaler**) – A pale cheese with a light buttery taste that is made from skimmed cow's milk. Replete with holes, this is the cheese that gave name to the much more generic and much less flavorful cheeses labeled as "Swiss Cheese." The best versions are from Switzerland and France, and are very versatile.
- **Époisses** [AY-pwah-sehs] – This is a very creamy cheese with fruity and pungent aromas and a spicy, rich flavor when aged.
- **Explorateur** [ex-plohr-AH-tehr] – A brand of French triple-crème cheese.
- **Feta** – A salty, tangy-flavored style of sheep's milk cheese that is integral to Greek cuisine. Matches well with most wines and beers.
- **Fontina** [fahn-TEEN-ah] – This is an excellent cheese from northwestern Italian region of Valle D'Aosta that works well as a melting cheese and for the table. The texture is semi-firm and supple, with rich, herbaceous and fruity flavor. It pairs well with fruits. The Danish version is comparatively flavorless.
- **Fourme d'Ambert** [for-MAY dahm-BEHR] – A French-made cheese with a buttery taste that is much like Stilton.
- **Garroxta** [gah-ROWKS-tah] – A goat's milk cheese from Catalonia, Spain that has a mild, but earthy nut-like flavor and a semi-firm texture and a unique gray rind. It's good for appetizers, and pairs with wines like Albariño and Spanish reds.
- **Gloucester** [GLOHW-ster] – A flavorful cheddar-style cheese from England that is known as a good snacking cheese. The cheeses labeled "Double Gloucester" are tastier than the "Single" ones. Beers and red wines match well with both versions.
- **Gorgonzola** [gohr-guhn-ZOH-lah] – An excellent cow's milk blue cheese from northern Italy. Doesn't improve after purchase, so use quickly.
- **Gouda** [GOOH-duh] – A mild, nutty cow's milk cheese from Holland that is a fine complement to most beers and red wines.
- **Grana Padano** [grahn-NAH pah-DAH-noh] – Very similar to Parmigiano-Reggiano, this is becoming more common in upscale supermarkets as a slighter cheaper alternative. A good match for many wines.
- **Gruyère** [groo-YEHR] – A cow's milk cheese from Switzerland and France that has a very good, rich and nutty flavor. A great eating cheese, Gruyère goes well with most beers and red wines.
- **Havarti** [hahv-RAHR-tee] – A slightly tangy, but mildly flavored semi-soft cheese from Denmark that matches very well with clean-tasting lager beers.
- **Idiazabal** [ih-dee-ah-THAH-bol] – This is a salty, sharp and crumbly cheese made with raw sheep's milk. What is available in North America is usually smoked and aged. It's a good cheese to grate in salads, melt, or eat with crackers and sherry.

- **Jarlsberg** [YAHLZ-berg] – A mild, nutty and buttery cheese from Norway that is fairly versatile. Crisp lager beers and fruity wines match well.
- **Leicester** [LES-ter] – A rich, orange-colored cow's milk cheddar cheese made in and around Leicester, England that goes well with ciders, red wines, and most beers.
- **Leyden** [LIE-dn] – A mild, tangy and very flavorful eating cheese from Holland that is spiced with caraway and cumin seeds. Goes well with lager beers and light-bodied and fruity red and white wines.
- **Liederkranz** [lee-der-KRANTS] – Despite the Germanic name this cheese was invented in the U.S. A pungent, strong-tasting, but creamy and very tasty cheese that is perfectly suited to beer. The name comes from its popularity with a New York singing society, Liederkranz Hall. Often used as a substitute for Limburger.
- **Limburger** – This is a very stinky cheese that is strongly flavored, but a tasty cheese, especially when consumed with beer. Given its almost rank odor, you might wonder if the cheese has gone bad. If the rind is cracked and the cheese runny, it most likely has.
- **Manchego** [mahn-CHAY-go] – This is a Spanish sheep milk's cheese that features a firm texture and a rich flavor. Works great on a cheese plate, and might be the best all-around cheese to complement a wide range of wines, though a sturdy red might be the best match.
- **Maytag Blue** – A fine American blue cheese made from cow's milk.
- **Montasio** [mohn-TAH-seeh-oh] – A cow's milk cheese from northeastern Italy that has sharp flavor and firm texture when aged, similar to Asiago. It is very mild, almost bland, when young.
- **Monte Enebro** [mon-TAY en-AY-broh] – A tangy goat's milk cheese from Spain with intense herbal flavors.
- **Monterey Jack** – A mild, usually semi-soft cheese originally from California that works best as a complement to a wide variety of luncheon meats, breads and condiments on sandwiches. There are also aged versions, marketed as Dry Jack, which works well for grating purposes. Alone it goes well with crisp white wines and light, fruity red wines.
- **Montrachet** [mohn-truh-SHAY] – A goat's milk cheese from Burgundy that has a very creamy and soft texture and a mild and slightly sour, but rich and attractive, flavor. Though named after the famous white wine, this matched better with a fruity red wine like Beaujolais, which is produced down the road.
- **Morbier** [mohr-bee-AY] – This is a semi-soft cow's milk cheese that has a mild but buttery flavor, which is not unlike that of good Fontina. Light, fruity red wines are a food match for this.
- **Mozzarella** – This is a relatively bland, fresh cheese that melts well, and a necessity for pizzas, *Insalata Caprese* and many Italian-American dishes. The mozzarella sold in small balls (*bocconcini*) packed with water should

be used if you are presenting it as an appetizer or desire a higher quality dish. Mozzarella is produced domestically, usually with cow's milk, or in its original format called *mozzarella di bufala* from outside of Naples, which is made from the milk of water buffaloes. The most commonly found versions at supermarkets that are packaged in bricks, are comparatively horrible.

- **Muenster** [MUHN-ster] (or **American Münster**) – A very light, mild and inoffensive, but pleasant-enough commercially-produced cheese that bears no resemblance to its Alsatian namesake.
- **Münster** [MOON-ster] – A flavorful cheese with a noticeable aroma and earthy, herbaceous taste from Alsace. Becomes very pungent when aged. A great complement for a wide range of beers and white wines from either side of the Rhine.
- **Neufchâtel** [nohf-CHAH-tel] – A very mild, simple-tasting cream cheese originally from Normandy. Best consumed when young, watch for a gray-colored rind and an overly salty taste. Light and fruity red wines are good match for this.
- **Nökkelost** [nowk-UH-loohs] – A mild, but slightly spicy and flavorful Scandinavian cheese that is spiced with cloves and either, or both, caraway and cumin seeds. It is popular for snacks and sandwiches, and melts well for cooking. Also called kuminost.
- **Parmesan** – The American word for Parmigiano-Reggiano, which often refers to a poor imitation of the original northern Italian version.
- **Parmigiano-Reggiano** [parm-eeh-JON-oh ray-geeh-AHN-oh] – Hard cheese that has been made since at least the eleventh century in a strictly controlled area in northern Italy. The flavor is subtle, complex and enticing. It is an excellent eating cheese when younger, and always good for grating and cooking. Full-bodied red wines are the best wine match. High quality Grana Padano is the nearest substitute. American-made Parmesan is a pale imitator, though.
- **Pecorino-Romano** [pek-ohr-EEN-oh roh-MAHN-oh] – This is a hard, sharp-tasting sheep's milk cheese made that is mostly found in the aged version. This is popular as a grating cheese, but is not as flavorful or complex as the similar-looking Parmigiano-Reggiano. In Italy it is also enjoyed when fresh, and eaten with bread, *salame* and red wine. The first name of the cheese, "Pecorino" means "from sheep milk." The second name, the place, "Romano" designates the area around Rome. Pecorino Romano doesn't qualify the best version of this cheese. The *Abruzzese*, *Sardo*, *Marchigiano*, *Toscano*, *Umbro*, and *Molisano* are by far better than the Romano itself, though are much less widely available in North America.
- **Pepato** [peh-PAH-toh] – This is sharp-tasting Pecorino cheese containing whole black peppercorns resulting in a spicy flavor.

- **Pepper Jack** – This is Monterey Jack studded with bits of jalapeños or another pepper. This can be a wonderful snacking cheese with lager beer.
- **Pierre-Robert** [peeh-EHR roh-BEHR] – Tripe-crème cheese from France that sports noticeable mineral and grassy flavors.
- **Port-Salut** [port sah-LOOH] (or **Port-du-Salut**) – This is a soft and mild cow's milk cheese with a creamy texture, which has been its greatest attraction. Matches well with fruity wines, both red and white.
- **Provolone** [proh-voh-lohn] – A very mild, bordering on bland in many cases, firm cow's milk cheese that originated in southern Italy, though most versions found here are produced in North America. Most commonly found in sandwiches and inexpensive cheese trays. Flavorful aged versions from Italy work well as a grating cheese.
- **Raclette** [rah-KLET] – A mild but flavorful, hard cheese from Switzerland that becomes even more enjoyable when melted for the famous Swiss dish of the same name. Somewhat similar to Gruyère, and goes best with crisp lager beers and white wines.
- **Ricotta** [rih-COHT-tah] – This is rich, moist and indispensable in many Italian dishes such as manicotti, lasagna and cannoli. In its original form it is made from the whey obtained during the process of cooking mozzarella, which is then cooked again (ricotta means "re-cooked). Since it made from a cheese by-product, it is technically not a cheese.
- **Robiola** [roh-beeh-OH-lah] – A soft, mild cheese from northern Italy. The ones labeled Robiola Lombardia are very similar to Taleggio.
- **Roquefort** [ROHK-fohr] – A sheep's milk blue cheese from southwestern France that has been produced since at least Roman times. As with other blue cheeses it works well on canapés, on salads, and alone with ports and other dessert wines.
- **Saint-André** [sahn ahn-DRAY] – A popular French brand of triple-crème cheese. This is a very rich cow's milk cheese that has a creamy texture and simple, easily enjoyable flavor. Matches well with off-dry or slightly sweet white wines such as a Spätlese or Auslese, as well as fruity red wines.
- **Sbrinz** [ZBRIHNZ] – A hard cow's milk cheese from the central mountains of Switzerland with a nutty, rich flavor. Used for grating, cooking and as a table cheese.
- **Scamorza** [skah-MOR-zah] – A soft, very mild, slightly nutty-tasting cow's milk cheese from Italy that is similar to mozzarella.
- **Shropshire** – A blue cheese from England with an orange interior spiked with blue veins and having sharp and grassy flavors.
- **Stilton** – An excellent cow's milk blue cheese from England. It is considered the classic complement for port, though it goes well with other rich red wines, also.

- **Taleggio** [tah-lay-GEEH-oh] – A soft, mild and flavorful cheese that is used primarily as a dessert cheese in its native Italy. It is past prime if it sports a pungent aroma. Matches well with fruity, light white wines such as Soave and Chenin Blanc.
- **Teleme** [tell-uh-MAY] – This is a soft cheese with a slightly lemony flavor that was created by Greek immigrants in San Francisco in the 1920s. It works well as a snacking cheese, and also melts well.
- **Tillamook** – High quality, sharp-tasting cheddar cheeses made in a cooperative dairy in Tillamook County, Oregon.
- **Tilsit** [TIHL-ziht] – This is a mild, firm cheese, not unlike Gouda. **Farmhouse Tilsit** is more flavorful and very pungent, nearly as much as Limburger.
- **Triple-crème** – This is a very rich cow's milk cheese that has a creamy texture and simple, easily enjoyable flavor. Matches well with off-dry or slightly sweet white wines such as a Spätlese or Auslese, as well as fruity red wines.

SNACKS, APPETIZERS, ENTRÉES & DESSERTS – The number and diversity of food terms continues to grow as the world becomes smaller and the variety of foods available becomes larger. These are some terms that you might encounter on a restaurant menu or a nearby food market.

- **Amuse-Bouche** [ah-mewz-BOOSH] – A very small appetizer meant to help awaken the palate; usually served complimentary at a restaurant.
- **Andouille** [ahn-DOOH-eeh] – This is a spicy, smoked pork sausage that is used in Cajun cooking.
- **Antipasti** [ahn-TEE-pah-stee] – Basically, this is the Italian term for appetizers, either hot or cold. The singular is *antipasto*, which is commonly used for plural in North America. This is fine, as we are not in Italy after all.
- **Au Jus** [AH ZHOO] – This is a French term for "with juice" and it denotes a meat, or sometimes a fish, that is served with or in its own juices.

- **Baba Ganoush** (or **Ghanoush** or **Ghanouj**) [BAH-bah gah-NEWSH] – A popular purée of eggplant, olive oil, garlic, lemon juice and tahini sauce. Great as an appetizer spread, especially with pita bread.
- **Biscotti** [bis-KOH-tee] – This is the plural form of the dried hard small biscuits that are commonly served accompanying coffee at the end of an Italian meal, or with tea in the afternoon, or for breakfast.
- **Bottarga** [boh-TAHR-gah] – This is the compressed, dried and salted roe of the gray mullet or tuna that is popular in coastal communities of Italy where it is usually shaved or grated over dishes like pastas, or served in thin slices with lemon juice and oil.
- **Bresaola** [bres-ay-OH-lah] – This is salted and air-cured beef fillet that originated in northern Italy. It's typically served as an appetizer when thinly sliced, and drizzled with olive oil and lemon juice. Very flavorful, it is very expensive, especially when you are feeding others.
- **Brochette** [broh-SHET] – This typically refers to food cooked on a skewer.
- **Bruschetta** [brew-SKEH-tah] – Originally from the Tuscan region of Italy, this now refers to almost any toasted slice of hearty bread topped with minimal toppings such as chopped tomatoes, basil and garlic. Traditionally, this is made with slices of toasted bread that are rubbed with cloves of garlic, drizzled with olive oil, salted and peppered, heated and served warm with a variety of simple toppings.
- **Canapé** [kan-uh-PAY] – These are small and usually decorative pieces of bread, toast, crackers or pastry that are topped with a savory spread. Cheese, anchovies and pâté are common toppings. Can be served either hot or cold, and nearly always before dinner as an appetizer, with cocktails. Canapés are a type of hors d'oeuvre.
- **Caponata** [kap-oh-NAH-tah] (or **Camputina** [kahm-puh-TEE-nah]) – This is a useful appetizer from Sicily, usually served at room temperature, that features eggplant, tomatoes, onions, garlic, celery, olives, sugar, vinegar and sometimes pine nuts, which is cooked in olive oil. Though it can work as a side dish, it is best utilized in party situations as a topping for bread, toast and the like. And, it is best made several days beforehand.
- **Caviar** – Most properly, and most expensively, this refers to the lightly salted roe or eggs of the sturgeon. The three types of caviar, which take their name from the species of sturgeon, are, in order of (considerable) expense, beluga, osetra and sevruga. Caviar is very perishable and must be refrigerated from the time it's removed from the fish. Other kinds of fish roe that are often labeled caviar, though much less expensive, are lumpfish, whitefish, salmon, red, and paddlefish.
- **Charcuterie** [shar-kooh-tuhr-EE] – This usually refers to pork specialties such as pâtés and dried sausages. It's a good word to throw out at a party, for example, "Did you enjoy our *charcuterie*?" when referring to the slices of inexpensive salami that you have laid out for your guests.

- **Chutney** [chut-NEE] – A spicy Indian condiment that is made from vinegar, sugar, fruit, herbs and spices. Ranging in flavor from sweet to fiery hot, these can be a fitting accompaniment for cheeses and as a dipping sauce for breads.
- **Confit** [kohn-FEEH] – This derives from the traditional method of preserving meat in the Gascony region of France. The duck, goose or pork meat is salted, slowly cooked in its own fat, then packed into a container and covered with some more of the fat.
- **Cornichon** [kor-neeh-SHOHN] – These are crisp, tart pickles made from the small gherkin cucumbers. These are commonly served with pâtés.
- **Couscous** [KOOZ-kooz] (or **Cous Cous**) – This is small durham wheat (or semolina) grain originally from North Africa that appears on restaurant menus as a side dish in North America.
- **Crème Fraîche** [KREHM FRESH] – This is a thickened cream with a usually rich texture and a creamy and slightly tangy and nutty flavor. It is often used for dessert, ladled over fresh fruit or served with puddings or cobblers. Since it can be boiled without curdling, it is a common addition to thicken and enrich soups and sauces.
- **Crostini** [croh-STEEH-neeh] – This is similar to bruschetta; toast topped with various ingredients. Crostini is thinner and brushed with olive oil before toasting.
- **Crudités** [kroo-dee-TAY] – These are raw fresh vegetables that are often served with a dipping sauce as an appetizer. Another class of hors d'oeuvre.
- **Edamame** [eh-dah-MAH-may] – This is the Japanese word for green soybeans that is popularly used to refer to these when boiled and usually salted. Edamame can make for an easily prepared and different appetizer.
- **En croûte** [EHN KROOT] – This refers to an entrée wrapped in a pastry and then baked.
- **Escabèche** [es-keh-BEHSH] – This is a fish that is cooked then covered with a spicy marinade and chilled for at least a day, after which it is most often served cold as an appetizer. **Escovitch** is its Jamaican name.
- **Farro** [fah-ROH] – An ancient grain from Italy that is used in soups and sides. Spelt is the English name for this.
- **Foie Gras** [FWAH GRAH] – This usually refers to goose liver from a specially bred bird that is soaked overnight then marinated with armagnac or a fortified wine and seasonings, and finally baked. Foie gras is very rich and is usually served chilled with thin slices of toast. **Pâté de foie gras** is at least 80% pureed goose liver made with other ingredients such as pork liver or eggs. **Purée de foie gras** is similar, but must contain at least 55% goose liver.

- **Fricassee** [frik-ah-SEE] – A stew consisting of meat sautéed in butter and further cooked with vegetables, and often wine.
- **Gravlax** [grahv-LOKS] – This is thinly-sliced raw salmon that is cured in a mixture of sugar, salt and dill. Originally from Sweden, this is popular as appetizer, often served on slices of dark bread.
- **Gumbo** – A soup originally from southern Louisiana that begins with a dark roux and can have a variety of ingredients. The two most popular versions are one with chicken and andouille sausage, and the other with seafood, primarily shrimp and crab. The word gumbo is from a west African word for okra, though many versions do not contain these vegetable. Gumbo can be made in advance, and so can be very useful when entertaining.
- **Hors d'oeuvre** [or-DERV] – These are small appetizers served before the meal, usually with drinks (cocktails and aperitifs for the more sophisticated). These can be hot or cold, and are small, typically one- or two-bite sized. The literal translation is (dishes) "outside the work" (meal). "Hors d'oeuvre" can be used for a single appetizer or many. The other plural is "hors d'oeuvres."
- **Hummus** – A popular Middle Eastern dish that is made of pureed chickpeas, lemon juice, garlic and olive oil. It's commonly accompanied with pita bread and used as a dip.
- **Jambalaya** [juhm-buh-LYE-uh] – This is a Cajun and Creole dish of rice cooked with an array of ingredients that includes green peppers, onions, tomatoes and meat or shellfish.
- **Jamon Serrano** [hah-MOHN sehr-RAH-noh] – Excellent cured ham from Spain that is similar to *prosciutto*.
- **Lardo** – On restaurant menus this refers to the white fat from the rump of the pig that has been cured in salt brine with a variety of herbs and spices. It is served in thin slices atop bread or even pizzas in Italy. Lardo can also mean fatback, the fresh layer of fat that runs along the pig's back.
- **Lavash** – This is a round, thin and crunchy bread that is usually sold in sizes of between 6 inches and a foot in diameter that make for a good accompaniment for dips and sauces.
- **Lox** – This is cold-smoked salmon that has been brine-cured. A staple of Jewish-American cuisine, especially when paired with bagels and cream cheese, it is usually saltier than other types of smoked salmon.
- **Napoleon** – This was originally a dessert featuring layers of puff pastry, but is often used to refer to any creation featuring layering of some sort.
- **Noisette** [nwah-ZEHT] – This is a small round slice of meat from the rib or loin. It also means hazelnut in French.
- **Pancetta** [pan-CHEH-tah] – This is Italian-style bacon that is cured with salt and spices, but not usually smoked. Flavorful, leaner and saltier than

American bacon, it must also be cooked prior to serving. Smoked and seasoned versions can be found in the depths of large Italian food stores.

- **Panko** [PAHN-koh] – These are Japanese-style breadcrumbs, used to create especially tasty and crisp crusts with fried foods, and are coarser than those found in Western cuisines.
- **Pâté** [pah-TAY] – Flavorful pureed food preparations that can be either hot or cold, and are usually served as an appetizer with toast or crackers. These are traditionally made with meat, often liver, though versions made with vegetables are also common. High quality store-bought pâtés can be found in most cities and can be an easy addition to the pre-dinner spread.
- **Prosciutto** [proh-SHOO-toh] - High quality cured ham sliced in paper-thin slices makes for a classic appetizer solo, or as a component in an array of cold appetizers such prosciutto and melon, prosciutto and fig, etc. Excepting its cost, often more than $20 a pound, it works especially well for parties because it is ready to serve after purchase. *Prosciutto* is now the default name for several types of cured hams including the Spanish *jamon serrano* and the German Westphalian ham.
- **Pu pu** [POOH POOH] – The Hawaiian term for appetizers. A exotic and seemingly sophisticated term to use for your guests if you present an array of vaguely Polynesian, Chinese or other Asian array of pre-dinner small bites.
- **Quinoa** [KEEN-wah] – A very nutritious grain that was the staple of the Incan empire and often appears as a side dish on menus. Its flavor is very light and is commonly used as a substitute for rice.
- **Ragoût** [rah-GOOH] – This is a thick, heartily seasoned and rich stew of meat, fish or vegetables.
- **Red Beans & Rice** – A slowly-cooked, hearty dish from southern Louisiana featuring red kidney beans, some form of pork, and long-grained white rice that can make for easy and tasty party sustenance. Its praises have been sung throughout the years by New Orleans native Louis Armstrong and Sir Mix-A-Lot ("red beans and rice didn't miss her; baby got back...").
- **Roulade** [rooh-LAHD] – This is the French term for a thin slice of meat that is rolled around a filling, secured with a toothpick or string, and is typically browned before being baked or braised. *Braciola* is the Italian term for this.
- **Savoury** [SAY-vuh-ree] – This is a British term that originally described dishes that were served after dessert as a palate cleanser. It now refers to small dishes that work as appetizers or heartier ones served for lunch, tea, and even supper.
- **Tasso** – A lean piece of pork that has been seasoned with garlic, red pepper and other ingredients, then smoked; a Cajun specialty.

- **Terrine** [teh-REEN] – Often used interchangeably with pâté. See **Pâté**.
- **Tournedo** [TOOR-nih-doh] – This refers to a slice of steak from a beef tenderloin, which is typically about an inch thick and a couple of inches in diameter. These are usually served with a sauce.
- **Westphalian Ham** [west-FAY-lee-an] – High-quality ready-to-eat ham produced in Germany that is cured and then smoked. It is somewhat similar to *prosciutto*.

SAUCES & CONDIMENTS

- **Aïoli** [ay-OH-lee] – Strongly flavored garlic-infused mayonnaise originally from the south of France that works well as a condiment for vegetables, meat and seafood.
- **Béarnaise** [behr-NAYZ] – This rich French sauce is made with a reduction of wine, vinegar, shallots, tarragon, egg yolks and butter. It's used with a wide range of dishes, meat, seafood, vegetables and eggs.
- **Béchamel** [BEH-shuh-mehl] – This is the traditional French white sauce that is made by stirring milk into a roux of flour and butter, and can be made into varying thickness. It's one of the four "mother sauces" of classic French cuisine.
- **Beurre Blanc** [burr BLAHN] – This is a thick, smooth sauce made of wine, vinegar, shallots and butter. It works very well with seafood, poultry and vegetables. The name means "white butter" in French.
- **Bordelaise** [bohr-duh-LAZE] – This a sauce made with wine, brown stock, shallots, parsley, a variety of herbs and in the classic French version, bone marrow. It works as a fine accompaniment for broiled red meats.
- **Chimichurri** – A condiment originally from Argentina that is an uncooked mixture of chopped parsley, olive oil, vinegar, garlic, salt and black pepper plus often oregano, onion and cayenne. In Argentina, it is a requisite accompaniment to grilled meats. It also works well for dipping plantain chips.
- **Coulis** [koo-LEE] – A term that usually refers to a thick sauce or puree.
- **Demi-glace** [DEHM-eeh glahs] – This begins with a rich brown sauce that is slowly cooked with beef stock and sherry or Madeira until it is reduced by at least half. This result is very viscous and intense. It is used mostly as a base for other sauces. Jarred versions are available.
- **Harissa** – A very spicy sauce originally from Tunisia that usually contains chiles, caraway, coriander, cumin, garlic and olive oil. It is traditionally served with couscous, but is also used in stews and soups.
- **Hoisin** [HOY-sin] – This viscous dark brown sauce is a combination of soybeans, garlic, chiles and several spices, and is used widely in Chinese cuisine mostly as a condiment for poultry, meat and seafood dishes.

- **Hollandaise** [HOL-uhn-dayz] – This white, smooth, creamy and very rich sauce comprised of butter, egg yolks and lemon juice is a staple of French cooking as a condiment for a variety of dishes.
- **Marguery** [mahr-guh-RAY] **Sauce** – A sauce made from a mixture of fish stock, white wine, butter and egg yolks that is reduced. It is commonly served with a mild-flavored fish such as sole.
- **Mornay** – This is béchamel sauce with cheese, often Parmesan, which has been added. It is served with dishes of seafood, chicken, eggs and vegetables.
- **Mostarda** [moh-STAHR-dah] – This is a preserve made from various fruits into a sweet-and-sour condiment originally from the northern Italian city of Cremona. It is used as an accompaniment to boiled meats.
- **Niçoise** [neeh-SWAHZ] – This refers to a sauce made with tomatoes, black olives, garlic and usually anchovies originally from Nice, France.
- **Pesto** – In its original form from the coastal Liguria region in northwestern Italy this is an uncooked sauce made with a mortar and pestle consisting of basil, garlic, olive oil, pine nuts, salt and a hard cheese such as Parmigiano-Reggiano or Pecorino. Walnuts are sometimes included, though in more recent examples any number ingredients might be used in something called a pesto.
- **Pistou** [pees-TOOH] – This condiment of crushed basil, olive oil and garlic is the French version of pesto.
- **Ponzu** – This is a dipping sauce from Japan that consists of soy sauce, saké, seeweed, dried flakes of bonito (a tuna), and either rice vinegar or lemon juice.
- **Red Sauce** – A staple of Italian-American cooking, this is made from long-simmered tomatoes, which have been peeled and seeded (usually from a can), garlic, dried oregano, basil, and sometimes other ingredients.
- **Rémoulade** [ray-muh-LAHD] – In its original French version, it is a chilled sauce of mayonnaise, mustard, capers, herbs, chopped gherkins and anchovies. In the more common incarnation from New Orleans, it is a spicier sauce based on tomato or ketchup with onions, celery and mustard, often used to accompany shrimp.
- **Romesco** [roh-MEHS-koh] – This is sauce made from a mixture of finely ground red bell peppers, tomatoes, onions, almonds, garlic and olive oil that originated in the Catalonia region of Spain. It is usually served with grilled poultry or fish.
- **Soy Sauce** – An integral part of Chinese and Japanese cuisines this is made from boiled soybeans fermented with roasted barley or wheat. This nearly black, salty sauce is used in marinades, sauces, and to flavor vegetables, meats and fish dishes.
- **Sriracha** [shree-RAH-chuh] – A very flavorful, bright reddish-orange-colored commercially-produced hot sauce that consists of chiles, garlic,

sugar, and vinegar and a natural complement to many Vietnamese and other dishes from Southeast Asia.

- **Tapenade** [TAH-puh-nahd] – This is a thick paste classically made with olives, capers, anchovies, olive oil, and lemon juice used as a condiment. It originated in the southern French region of Provence.
- **Vinaigrette** [vihn-uh-GREHT] – This is a sauce in its most basic form consists of three parts oil to one part vinegar seasoned with salt and pepper, and one of the four "mother sauces" in class French cooking.

INGREDIENTS – HERBS & SPICES – You might want to review this before your next business dinner, or if you get stumped by a cookbook. Herbs are the leaves of plants. The often more pungent spices come from an array of sources such as seeds, stems and roots.

- **Achiote** [ah-chee-OH-tay] – This is the ground seed of the annatto tree that is used to provide a fant earthy flavor; also used as a coloring agent.
- **Allspice** – Native to the Caribbean and South American, this is the small berry of evergreen pimiento tree that has a taste described as a combination of nutmeg, cloves and cinnamon.
- **Anise** [AN-iss] – This licorice-flavored spice is used primarily in Vietnamese and Chinese cooking to flavor soup, pork and poultry.
- **Basil** – A member of the mint family, this is a prime component in Mediterranean cooking, especially in regions around Naples and Genoa. There is also anise basil, cinnamon basil, clove basil and lemon basil, which have aromas and flavors similar to the respective names.
- **Bay Leaf** – Pungent, but used to give a subtle bitter flavor to dishes, the two main varieties are the Turkish and California. The Turkish one is smaller, featuring oval leaves, and has a less assertive flavor. Fresh bay leaves are difficult to find, but have much more flavor than the dried versions.
- **Bouquet Garni** [booh-KAY gahr-NEEH] – Dried herbs that are placed in a cheesecloth bag or tied together for easy removal before serving and used for flavoring soups and stews. The traditional consists of thyme, parsley and bay leaf.
- **Caper** – A flower bud from a shrub native to southern Europe that is sun-dried and either pickled in a vinegar or packed in salt. These can add a unique, identifiably Mediterranean flavor and a bit of heat to a dish.
- **Caraway** – This aromatic herb has a mildly spicy flavor and is a popular addition to Central European sauerkraut, soups, breads, and cakes.
- **Cardamom** – A spice that is native to India and related to ginger, which has a spicy, yet sweet flavor. A small amount goes a long way.

- **Chive** – Similar to an onion, these have mild, slightly sweet taste that is used to provide a complementary flavor and crunchy texture when used in its fresh form.
- **Cilantro** – The dark green leaves of the coriander plant, which is a staple of Mexican, Indian and Vietnamese cooking. Very pungent and flavorful, this can be an acquired taste for those accustomed to mild cuisines. The flavor of the leaves and the seeds are completely different.
- **Clove** – This is a dried, unopened flower bud of the tropical evergreen clove tree that has a spicy and sweet flavor. One of the most important spices, it is cooked with pork, sweet potatoes, squash and mulled wine.
- **Coriander** – This refers to dried ripe fruit (commonly and mistakenly referred to as the seeds) of the plant, a relative of parsley. These are mildly aromatic and have a taste described as a combination of sage, caraway and lemon.
- **Cumin** [KYOO-mihn] – These nut-flavored and aromatic seeds are the dried fruit of a member of the parsley family, and available as whole seeds and ground. There are actually three types: amber, white and black. The amber and white taste nearly the same, while the black is more complex and flavorful.
- **Curry Powder** – This is a ground blend of up to twenty different herbs, seeds and spices. Some of the most common ingredients are cardamom, chile peppers, cinnamon, cloves, coriander, cumin, black pepper, nutmeg, saffron and turmeric. It is integral to Indian cooking, and varies widely depending on the regions and desire of the cook.
- **Dill** – The distinctive flavor of fresh dill has been used in Europe for thousands of years, and is integral to Scandinavian cooking. It loses it flavor quickly when heated, so its stems are best added near the end of cooking. Powdered dill weed is also available.
- **Fenugreek** [FEHN-yoo-greek] – Native to southern Europe and Asia, the seeds, with its sweet and bitter taste, are used in teas and curry powders.
- **Fines Herbs** [FIN EHRB] – This is a mixture of fresh herbs that usually includes chervil, chives, parsley and tarragon. It is used to flavor egg dishes, butter, soup and meats.
- **Galangel** [gah-LAHN-guhl] – Popular as a seasoning in Thai cooking, this has a spicy, peppery and ginger-like flavor.
- **Garam Masala** – A staple of Indian cooking, this is a blend of dry-roasted and ground spices which can include a variety of ingredients, sometimes as many as a dozen, such as cardamom, chiles, cinnamon, cloves, coriander, nutmeg and pepper. It's usually used at the end of cooking.
- **Ginger** – A pungent root that can provide a subtlety and sweet flavor to a dish is a key ingredient to a number of Asian cuisines.
- **Green Peppercorn** – This is the underripe berry that is often preserved in salt. It's soft in texture and is less pungent than black or white

peppercorns. These are often found in the spice section away from the other peppercorns.

- **Herbes de Provence** [EHRB duh proh-VAWNZ] – This is a variety of dried herbs, often including **basil**, **fennel** seed, **lavender**, **marjoram**, **rosemary**, **sage** and **thyme**, that are meant to reflect the flavors of the south of France. This is used to season a range of dishes.
- **Kaffir Lime Leaf** – This is a fragrant, floral-scented leaf used both fresh and dried in the cuisines of Southeast Asia.
- **Lavender** – An aromatic mint relative that is used in salads and teas.
- **Mace** – Made from the covering of the nutmeg seed. It is ground and has a similar, but more subtle flavor than nutmeg.
- **Marjoram** – A delicately flavored herb most often used both fresh and dried, at the end of cooking to flavor veal, lamb and vegetable dishes. Part of the mint family, there are many varieties, the most common being sweet marjoram. This is the marjoram that is used the most.
- **Mint** – A widely grown aromatic herb with a distinctive cool flavor.
- **Mustard Seed** – In addition to being the basis for the condiment, this provides a hot, sharp taste, and is used widely in Indian cooking.
- **Nutmeg** – This is a spice made from the seeds of the fruit of the nutmeg tree. The slightly spicy and sweet flavor of grated nutmeg has long been popular in European cooking, and is a natural complement to cream-based dishes, eggnog and vegetables like spinach and squash.
- **Oregano** – This herb is part of the mint family and related to thyme and marjoram, of which it has a similar, but stronger and less sweet flavor. It's most often used in its dried form, and is integral to Sicilian, Neapolitan, Italian-American and Greek cooking. Mexican oregano has a stronger and different taste than the Mediterranean variety.
- **Paprika** – This is finely ground red peppers that provide piquancy to a dish. It originated in Hungary, and is integral to Hungarian cooking.
- **Rosemary** – A very aromatic herb that is used fresh or dried, and is popular in many Mediterranean cuisines.
- **Saffron** – The most expensive spice in the world due to labor involved in its picking and drying, it is very aromatic and used to color and flavor dishes such as paella, risotto Milanese and bouillabaisse. Fortunately, a small amount goes a long way.
- **Sage** – This Mediterranean herb is used both fresh and dried most frequently in dishes featuring pork, stuffing for chicken and game, and most noticeably in saltimbocca.
- **Savory** [SAY-vuh-ree] – This is an herb related to the mint family with a strong, piquant flavor that is somewhat similar to both mint and thyme, used for meats, fish and pâtés. There are two similar types, summer and winter. The winter is slightly stronger. Savory is used both in its dried and fresh forms.

- **Sorrel** [SOR-uhl] – This is any one of several varieties of an herb that belongs to the buckwheat family. All varieties have a sour flavor. The most mild is the **dock sorrel**. The strongest-flavored is the **garden sorrel**. When sorrel is young and less sour, typically in the spring, it is used in salads and cooked as a vegetable. The more sour leaves are used in soups and to accompany vegetables and meats.
- **Star Anise** [AN-iss] – This is the seed from a star-shaped pod of a small evergreen tree that is native to China. In Asian cuisines it is used as a spice including part of the Chinese five-spice powder. In Western cuisines, it's mostly found in baked desserts and as a flavoring in cordials.
- **Sumac** – These are dried berries, usually ground, with a tart and fruity flavor, and used in a wide variety of Middle Eastern and Persian dishes.
- **Tarragon** – This strongly aromatic herb has a hot, licorice-like flavor, and is integral to southern French cooking. It is used both fresh and dried.
- **Thyme** – An herb that is a member of the mint family, of which there are several varieties with similar flavors and uses. It is used in a wide array of dishes as a flavoring agent including meats, seafood, soups and cream sauces. It is used both fresh and dried.
- **Turmeric** [TER-muh-rik] – Used to add color and flavor to food, this is a root of a tropical plant, related to ginger. It is pungent, bitter and a bright yellowish orange. It is used in curries and gives American-style mustard its obnoxious yellow color.
- **Wasabi** [WAH-sah-bee] – This is the Japanese version of horseradish with a very sharp flavor and is used fresh, powdered and as a paste, mostly as a condiment.

INGREDIENTS — VEGETABLES, FRUITS, MUSHROOMS, ETC. – As with the above listing, you might want to review this before your next visit to a restaurant or to the gourmet food store.

- **Arugula** [ah-roo-GOO-lah] – A strong-tasting salad green with a bitter, slightly peppery flavor. Sometimes appears as "rugula," or "rucola," and called "rocket" by the British.
- **Blood Orange** – These are oranges with a bright red or red-streaked interior. The taste is sweeter and more tart than most oranges. These are both eaten fresh, while the more acidic varieties are used more so in cooked sauces.
- **Bok Choy** – A mild-tasting vegetable with tender green leaves and a crunchy white stalk. Used raw and cooked, usually stir-fried.
- **Cèpe** [SAYP] – This is the French term for porcini mushrooms. Mushrooms labeled as porcini seem to taste better, though. Cèpes are usually found in dried form in North America (usually labeled as porcini), and provide added richness and a woodsy flavor to a dish.

- **Champignon** [sham-peen-YOHN] – Though it usually refers to button mushrooms, it is the French term for any edible variety.
- **Chanterelle** [shan-tuh-REL] – This is a wild mushroom with a distinctive trumpet shape that has sublime fruity and nutty flavor. When using during cooking, it is best to add near the end, as these become overly tough when overcooked.
- **Chayote** [chi-OY-tay] – Similar to squash, it has a mild flavor that is used raw in salads or baked. These are called mirliton in Louisiana.
- **Chervil** [CHER-vul] – This is a mild, anise-flavored member of the parsley family, which is best enjoyed when fresh.
- **Chicory** – A relative of endive that has curly, bitter leaves, which are cooked as greens, usually in southern cooking, or eaten raw in salads. Radicchio is red-leafed variety originally from Italy.
- **Citron** [SIH-tron] – This is a semi-tropical fruit that is grown almost solely for its lemon-scented peel, which is candied used in baking.
- **Cremini** [cray-MEEH-nee] – These are the darker, firmer, and slightly more flavorful version of the basic, cultivated white mushrooms. The Portobello is the fully grown version of this.
- **Daikon** [DYE-kon] – This is a large radish from Japan with a sweet, slightly crisp flavor eaten raw or cooked.
- **Duxelles** [doh-SEHL] – A thick paste used in sauces and soups, and as a garnish that consists of a mixture of finely chopped shallots, mushrooms and herbs cooked in butter.
- **Endive** – A green that is used mostly raw in salads. The three main varieties are curly endive, Belgian endive and escarole. Related to, but different, from chicory.
- **Escarole** [EHS-koh-rohl] – Part of the endive family that has broad light green leaves and a flavor that more mild than curly or Belgian endive.
- **Fennel** – An aromatic plant with bright green leaves and a light green, crisp stalk. There are two main varieties, the Florence fennel and the common fennel. The former has a bulb, the latter does not, though the tastes of each are similar. The bulb and stems can be eaten raw or cooked.
- **Frisée** [free-ZAY] – A green with a slightly bitter flavor, which is a member of the chicory family. Used mostly in salads.
- **Guava** [GWAH-vah] – This is a sweet, tropical fruit native to South America which is eaten fresh and made into juices, preserves and sauces.
- **Haricot Verts** [ahr-EEH-coat VEHRT] – These are thin, short, crisp and tender French-style green beans.
- **Hearts of Palm** – This is the inner part of the stalk of the cabbage palm tree that is grown in Florida and other tropical regions. These delicately-flavored and firm-textured vegetables are popular additions to salads, either fresh, or more often, from a can.

- **Huitlacoche** [weet-lah-KOH-chee] – A strong-tasting fungus that grows on corn, and is considered a delicacy in Mexican cooking.
- **Jicama** [hik-uh-MAH] – This is a bulbous root vegetable with crunchy texture and mild somewhat nutty flavor. It's eaten raw and cooked, and appears in Mexican and South American cooking.
- **Kale** – Hearty greens that are both cooked and used raw in salads.
- **Kohlrabi** [kol-RAH-bee] – This is a type of turnip. Its bulb has a mild, but slightly sweeter taste than a regular turnip. Its leaves can also be eaten.
- **Leek** – Native to the Mediterranean and related to the onion, its mild and enjoyable flavor has been eaten for thousands of years, both cooked and eaten raw in salads.
- **Lemon Grass** – This herb is integral to Vietnamese and Thai cooking where its firm white stalk provides a sour lemony flavor to dishes.
- **Litchi** [lit-CHEE] – A sweet-tasting fruit grown in subtropical areas in the U.S. and Asia and enjoyed in China for over two thousand years. It's eaten as a snack, in fruit salads, as a dessert, and increasingly in drinks.
- **Mâche** [MAYSH] – These are delicate, small-leafed lettuce greens with a peppery taste.
- **Mesclun** [MEHS-klun] – This is a mix of different types of young salad greens, such as arugula, dandelion greens, oak leaves, radicchio, sorrel and others.
- **Morel** – These is a fungus related to the truffle that features a honeycombed top with an earthy, smoky flavor and hints of nutmeg. The dried versions have a more intense flavor than the fresh ones.
- **Nori** [NOH-ree] – This is dark-colored thin sheets of dried seaweed that are mostly used in Japanese cuisine for wrapping sushi. When thinly sliced it can be used as a garnish or seasoning.
- **Parsnip** – This starchy white root can be cooked in a variety of ways to result in a somewhat sweet taste.
- **Passion Fruit** – This purple-skinned tropical fruit has a sweet and tart flavor that is most often eaten fresh as a dessert or used to make drinks, sauces and ice cream.
- **Plantain** – This is a firm variety of banana that is extremely popular in tropical Latin American cuisines where it is typically sautéed or fried and served as a side dish.
- **Porcini** [pohr-CHEE-neeh] – See **Cèpes**.
- **Quince** [KWINS] – This is a yellow-skinned fruit with a very tart flavor that is related to the apple. It is most often cooked into jams and other preserves rather than eaten raw.
- **Radicchio** [rah-DEEK-eeh-oh] – Used both raw and cooked, it has a bitter flavor. Its primarily red leaves provide a colorful addition to most plates.
- **Rutabaga** – A cross between a cabbage and a turnip, and is cooked liked a turnip.

- **Scallion** – This term is used for several members of the onion family including very young onions (or green onions), young leeks, the tops of shallots, and true scallions. All have a similar flavor, though the real scallions have the mildest, and all can be used interchangeably. The white base and the thin, bright green stalks are both edible.
- **Shallot** – A member of the onion family that look much more like garlic. These have subtle mild onion flavor, and are used in cooking much as onions.
- **Shiitake** [shih-TAH-kay] – Originally from Korea and Japan, this mushroom has a firm consistency and a woodsy flavor. It can be used fresh or dried, and works well in a variety of cooking methods.
- **Swiss Chard** – Greens with a tart taste that are commonly sautéed when young, and braised when older. These taste similar to bok choy when cooked. The heartier stems are usually cooked separately from the leaves.
- **Taro Root** – This is a potato-like tuber with a grayish flesh and a bland, slightly nutty flavor when cooked. It is basis for the Hawaiian poi.
- **Water Chestnut** – This is the tuber of an aquatic plant originally from Southeast Asia. Its interior is crunchy and juicy with a bland flavoring and a touch of sweetness. It is most often employed for its texture.
- **Watercress** – A member of the mustard family with small dark green leaves. It has a bitter and somewhat peppery taste, and is used raw in salads and sandwiches, cooked, and as a garnish.
- **Yucca** [yoo-KUH] – This bland-tasting, crisp root is popular in South American cooking and a staple in much of western Africa. It comes in two main categories, sweet and bitter. The latter is poisonous until cooked. Also called cassava and manioc, it is used to make tapioca.

BASIC COOKING TERMS

- **Barbecue** – A method of cooking, usually meat on a spit or in a pit, employing low heat from an indirect source, that is either hardwood or coals, and a long cooking time. You typically grill from your barbecue pit, though it can be used for barbecuing if you cook slowly from six to eighteen hours or longer.
- **Baste** – This is moistening foods during the cooking process with a liquid, usually a sauce, in order to prevent it from drying out and to add additional flavor.
- **Blanch** – This is to immerse a vegetable, or fruit, into boiling water in order to cook it very slightly, so that it retains much of its original flavor and texture.
- **Boil** – This is cooking in a liquid, usually water, which is boiling. This is when bubbles are breaking on the surface, 212° F (100° C) for water at sea level. A rolling boil refers to a vigorous boil, when the bubbles are large.

- **Broil** – This is cooking directly from a heat source. Food is typically broiled from above in an oven, and from below with an outdoor grill.
- **Deglaze** – This is heating a small amount of liquid, often wine, liquor or a stock, in the same pan used to sauté meat while stirring to loosen the leftover fat and food. The resulting mixture becomes the sauce or the basis for the sauce to be served with the meat.
- **Deep Fry** – This is cooking in hot fat that completely covers the food being cooked. A high smoke point for the cooking oil is necessary for deep frying, so lard, shortening and most vegetable oils are much preferable to butter or margarine.
- **Flambé** [flahm-BAY] – This method of cooking, which is employed usually for dramatic effect after sautéing, is where a liquor is added to the food, ignited, and the flame quickly suppressed, all just prior to serving.
- **Fold** – This is a technique for combining a light liquid, often egg whites, with a heavier liquid, such as custard or cream. The lighter liquid is placed on top of the heavier one in a bowl and with a gentle and thorough stirring, the two liquids will successfully blend.
- **Fry** – This is cooking in a good amount of fat over moderate to high heat. This is similar to sautéing, though more cooking fat is used.
- **Glaze** – This is a thin, glossy coating for both hot and cold dishes. For an entrée a glaze might be a meat stock, while for a dessert it might be a thin layer of chocolate.
- **Gratin** [GRAH-tin] – This refers to a dish topped with a combination of cheese, breadcrumbs and butter that is finished in the oven until the top is brown and crisp.
- **Grill** – Cooking food on a metal grate over a heat source.
- **Julienne** [joo-LEE-ehn] – This is to cut food, usually vegetables, into long thin rectangular pieces.
- **Papillote** [pah-peeh-YOHT] – Commonly seen as *"en papillote,"* which refers to food, usually seafood, baked within parchment paper. The paper puffs up as the baking food lets off steam. This is how it is served, and the paper is cut and peeled off to eat the dish.
- **Parboil** – This is to boil food until it is partially cooked, which is just about the same as blanching. Though when the term "parboil" is used it usually denotes that there will be additional cooking to finish the dish.
- **Poach** – This is cooking food in a liquid that is heated just below the boiling point, which is when the liquid's surface is quivering, but bubbles are not forming. Poaching helps to produce delicate flavors and imparts some of the liquid's flavor to the ingredients.
- **Roast** – To cook food in an oven in an open pan, which should produce a dark brown exterior and a moist interior when finished. Tender pieces of meat are necessary for proper roasting.

- **Roux** [ROOH] – This is a French term for a mixture of flour and fat that is cooked over low heat and used to thicken soups and sauces. The color of the roux is determined by the length of cooking. Those used in Creole and Cajun cooking, such as for gumbo, are cooked much longer and are richer than those used in French cooking.
- **Sauté** – This is cooking food in a relatively small amount of fat in a pan over a direct heat source.
- **Scald** – This is to cook something in water that is very close to boiling, which is at the point when bubbles are just forming (just after the poaching stage).
- **Sear** – Browning or charring a meat with high heat to seal in the juices.
- **Simmer** – This is cooking food in a liquid at temperature that causes small bubbles to break the surface, but just before boiling, about 185° F (85° C).
- **Steam** – This is a cooking method in which the food is placed in or on a container over boiling or simmering water. Steaming results in cooked food that is preserved in a more natural state than does cooking by poaching or boiling.
- **Steep** – This is to let food rest in a hot liquid in order to enhance the flavor of the item being cooked, or to extract flavor of a component ingredient. An example is a tea bag in boiling water.
- **Stew** – This is cooking in which food is covered in liquid that is simmered for a long period, usually in a covered pot. Stewing is a preferred method for cooking tough pieces of meat, which also effectively blends the myriad of ingredients.
- **Stir-Fry** – This is cooking small pieces of food in a large pan like a wok over high heat while it is being stirred. A staple method for many Chinese cuisines, this requires a small amount of cooking fat and results in food that retains its crisp textures.
- **Timbale** [tihm-BAHL] – This is a dish baked in a dome-shaped mold resulting in a dome-shaped dish.

MISCELLANEOUS — NON-DRINK, NON-FOOD ENTERTAINMENT TERMS

- **Bacchanalia** [bak-uh-NAY-luh] – Drunken revelry. If your party is particularly drunken, wild, or just fun, it might be described as "bacchanalian."
- **Bon Vivant** [bon VEE-vahnt] – Someone, usually male, who enjoys parties, often too much, but usually is just a few steps from rehab.
- **Crunk** – Hip-hop term that entered the parlance during the 1990s to describe a good party, among other things. Quite possibly derived as a contraction of the complimentary phrase "crazy drunk."
- **Fête** [FET] (or **Fete**) – A fancy word from the French for "party."

- **Hair of the Dog** – This refers to drinking alcohol while suffering from a hangover. This can actually be beneficial if you are up to it.
- **Hippie Dance** – The semi-rhythmic swaying of people, often well into middle age and beyond, to the oftentimes barely rhythmic and nearly undanceable music of the rock genre of the late 1960s through the mid-1970s, plus that of the Grateful Dead and Phish. You see this at live music venues, though at your event it's probably not something that you will want to encourage.
- **Joie de Vivre** [JWAH deh VEEH] – Literally means, "joy of life" in French. Usually describes someone who is energetic and joyful, or maybe just a happy drunk at a social event.
- **Life of the Party** – Usually a person exhibiting *joie de vivre* or an amusing level of alcohol consumption.
- **Lurker** – Someone who stays well past the time the party has ended. Also, a particularly useless guest. Successfully parodied in a classic (John) Belushi-era Saturday Night Live skit, "The Thing that Wouldn't Leave."
- **RSVP** – *Repondez s'il vous plait*, which is French for "please respond." What it really means is that many of your guests will ignore that you want a response from each of them about whether or not they are attending.
- **Savoir Faire** [sav-WAH FAIR] – It's not everywhere, but you might often hope to exhibit some while entertaining guests.
- **Technicolor Yawn** – This is colorful way to say vomit; and usually used to refer to a particularly colorful vomit.
- **Tête-à-tête** [TET-UH-TET] – A sophistic, or sophisticated, phrase to describe a private conversation between two people. For a successful social event, you want your guests to mingle rather than engaging in this, or maybe you do.
- **Wall Dancing** – When a person, usually female, prefers to dance alone on or near a wall. This originated in the mid-1980s before ecstasy was declared illegal.
- **White Elephant Party** – A party where guests are expected to bring inexpensive, and often humorous or otherwise crappy gifts. Exchanging them is the object of the party, which can be fun, if done right. This might also be referred to as a Chinese Gift Exchange. When hosting, be sure to let your guests know if they are expected to bring truly bad gifts or gifts that are under a certain dollar amount. As a guest, be sure to ask the host if you are not sure, as embarrassment can often ensue.

Part IV – References

CHECKLIST FOR HOSTING AN EVENT AT HOME

This master checklist is to help you prepare for your event. Don't feel that you need to check off every box. The steps (1 through 7) refer to the different stages of the Social Event Life Cycle, which are associated with bringing your event to fruition. These are explained in the Introduction and the subsequent chapter entitled "Initial Planning of Your Event."

I. TO DO WELL BEFORE THE EVENT

INITIAL PLANNING – STEP 1

- ☐ Decide upon the **type of event**.
- ☐ Set your general **budget**.
- ☐ Determine the **need for co-hosts** and contact, if necessary.
- ☐ **Determine if your place is sufficient to host** the event you have in mind; if not; determine what you need to do, or find an outside venue.
- ☐ Set the **date and time**.
- ☐ Determine the desired **duration** (two hours, four hours, etc.).
- ☐ Determine the **guest list**.
- ☐ **Plan the menu.** Keep in mind your capabilities for storing the prepared food, heating it and serving it.

INVITATIONS – STEP 2

- ☐ Determine **how you will communicate the event** – Printed invitations, e-mail, etc.?
- ☐ **Obtain all of the proper addresses** (physical or e-mail).
- ☐ Ensure that you include all of the **necessary information** such as time, theme and expected dress, but also directions, a map, instructions for parking, etc.
- ☐ **Send** the invitations.

DETERMINING WHETHER OR NOT YOU NEED TO HIRE HELP – STEP 3

- ☐ Determine **whether or not you need to hire professional help** – Caterers, bartenders, entertainment, parking staff, etc.
- ☐ **Hire** necessary help.

☐ If hosting the event at your place, you might want to schedule a special visit from a **maid** to aid in cleanup. You might schedule the maid for cleanup after the event, too.

PURCHASING SUPPLIES AND ACCESSORIES — STEP 4

☐ Purchase the non-food and drink **supplies and equipment** (plastic cups, plates, etc.) you will need for your event.
☐ Determine and **purchase the drinks that are needed** – Wine, beer, liquor;
☐ **Purchase** or order the **food** for the event.
☐ Purchase **insect repellant**, if any part of the party is outside.

PREPARATION — STEP 5

☐ Prepare the **vodka infusions**, if necessary.
☐ Make the **Jell-O Shots** the night before, if using.
☐ Where appropriate, remember to **marinate, thaw, and make desserts** if the recipes chosen entail multi-day activities.
☐ Have an **extra cooler** or several for beer, soft drinks, bottled water, and extra ice, as the refrigerator will not be large enough if you have more than a dozen guests.
☐ Make sure that you have **all of the necessary equipment** to cook and serve the food and drinks.
☐ **Call a friend or two to aid in the final preparations**, or at least show up early to help you greet the early the guests.
☐ Arrange with **a friend** (possibly the same one) **to call before they leave** for your event **so that they might bring any items** that you have forgotten. It's seemingly very common to forget smaller items such as napkins and lemons, or to run out of ice, for example.

CLEANUP / SETUP — STEP 5

☐ If you have a lawn that needs **mowing**, and part of the event is outside, be sure to do that **a day or two beforehand**.
☐ The same goes for the large-scale **insect spraying**.
☐ Do any **touch-up painting** that you might want to do.

II. TO DO HOURS BEFORE THE EVENT

CLEANUP / SETUP — STEP 5

☐ **Clean all of the rooms** and areas where guests might be.
☐ Clean the **bathrooms**.

- ☐ Ensure that is there enough **toilet paper** in each bathroom.
- ☐ Place an **ashtray** or ashtrays out for your guests who smoke.
- ☐ Set out an **extra trash can**, or cans, if needed.
- ☐ Place an **extra trash bag** or two with each trash can.
- ☐ **Make the punches** and large drinks.
- ☐ **Purchase ice**, if you need to.
- ☐ **Ice the beverages**.
- ☐ **Make sure that the oven is clean**, and so, won't smoke when the oven is turned on.
- ☐ **Do as much of the cooking as you can**, well before your guests arrive.
- ☐ Run the dishwasher to **clean the glasses** for dust, water spots, etc.
- ☐ If you don't have a dishwasher or time for that, be sure to **check, and rinse if necessary, the glasses to be used for dust and water spots**. Wine glasses seem to readily attract these.
- ☐ Try to have a **plunger** in each bathroom.
- ☐ If you have appetizers that utilize toothpicks, **have a trashcan or a tabletop receptacle for the toothpicks within eyesight**. If not, toothpicks might end up anywhere.
- ☐ **Slice lemons and limes**.
- ☐ Make sure that the **bar is self-sufficient**, or, very nearly so.
- ☐ **Marinate**/thaw/prepare the **meat** or **fish**.
- ☐ **Open up** some of **the red wine** to aerate.
- ☐ If you are planning to use a **fireplace, be sure to open the flue**.
- ☐ Turn down the **air conditioning**. With more people than usual in your place, it can warm up surprisingly quickly and then be tough to cool down during the event.
- ☐ Do you need to **mark your home to help guide your guests with something distinctive such as a sign** or balloons.

III. To do Immediately before the Event

Setup – Step 5

- ☐ Place a **candle in each bathroom**?
- ☐ **Dim** the lights.
- ☐ Put out the **ice bucket**.
- ☐ Put out the **appetizers**.
- ☐ Have a place for guests' **coats and purses**.

Decorations – Step 5

- ☐ Arrange the **flowers**.

- [ ] Light **candles**.
- [ ] Tidy or fix the **other decorations**, if necessary.

Drinks – Step 5

- [ ] Have the **initial round** of beer, wine and soft drinks readily available.

Food – Step 5

- [ ] **Prepare the food** (including to remember to turn on the oven for those baked or roasted dishes).
- [ ] Put out the **appetizers**.

Preparation for Spills and other Mishaps – Step 5

- [ ] Have the **club soda** easily accessible for those spills.
- [ ] Have **white towels** handy for cleanup.

Personal Preparation – Step 5

- [ ] You will know your guests, or should know most of them, so you can **prepare for any potential unpleasantries** beforehand.
- [ ] **Shower early** so you are not rushing. You want to try to avoid greeting your guests with wet hair.
- [ ] For men, **shave early**. Your blood is thinner when you are excited and more apt to bleed freely when nicked.
- [ ] As per the old adage that "it ain't a party until something is broken," it's a good idea to **mentally prepare for the fact that something might get broken**, stained or otherwise ruined. Don't fret too much when it does happen.

III. During the Event – Hosting – Step 6

- [ ] **Greet each guest** upon arrival (if crowd is a manageable size).
- [ ] Make sure guests have **drinks and access to drinks**.
- [ ] **Introduce guests to each other**.
- [ ] **Replace the hand towels** in the bathroom (or ensure extras are on hand).

IV. after the Event

Cleanup – Step 7

- [ ] Have you **blown out all of the candles**?

- ☐ Clean the **dishes.**
- ☐ **Clean everything else.**
- ☐ **Check the area outside your home for any trash** that your guests might have left.
- ☐ Throw out the **trash.**
- ☐ **Open the windows** to air out those rooms.

PHOTOS – STEP 7

- ☐ **Process** the **photos.**
- ☐ **Distribute** the photos.

MISCELLANEOUS – STEP 7

- ☐ **Apologize** to the neighbors.
- ☐ Return the **borrowed items.**

A List of Major Holidays in North America

Though many of these are obvious, it bears listing. Below are the holidays and other notable dates, listed sequentially, that you **might** need to plan around (or plan for) since your guests might be off from work and traveling:

- **New Year's Day** – January 1
- **Martin Luther King Day** – Third Monday in January
- **Chinese New Year** – Check the calendar.
- **Valentine's Day** – February 14
- **President's Day** – Third Monday in February; a huge ski weekend.
- **Mardi Gras** – 47 days before Easter; check the calendar.
- **Ash Wednesday** – 46 days before Easter; check the calendar.
- **Texas Independence Day** – March 2
- **Saint Patrick's Day** – March 17
- **Daylight Savings Time Begins** (we lose an hour) – First Sunday in April
- **Passover** – Check the calendar.
- **Good Friday** – The Friday before Easter; check the calendar.
- **Easter** – Check the calendar.
- **Patriot's Day** – Third Monday in April – Mass., Maine and Wisconsin
- *Cinco de Mayo* – May 5
- **Mother's Day** – Second Sunday in May
- **Memorial Day Weekend** – Last Monday in May
- **Father's Day** – Third Sunday in June
- **Canada Day** – July 1– Canada
- **July 4th** and the accompanying weekend.
- **Labor Day Weekend** – First Monday in September
- **Rosh Hashanah** – Check the calendar.
- **Yom Kippur** – Check the calendar.
- **Columbus Day** – Second Monday in October
- **Daylight Savings Time Ends** (we gain an hour) – Last Sunday of October
- **Halloween** – October 31
- **Presidential Elections** – First Tuesday in November, every four years.
- **Veterans Day** – November 11
- **Thanksgiving** – Fourth Thursday in November, and the ensuing Friday and weekend, of course.
- **Hanukah** – Early December; check the calendar.
- **Christmas Eve** – December 24
- **Christmas** – December 25
- **Boxing Day** – December 26 – Canada, UK, Australia and New Zealand; not Joe Louis' birth date.
- **Kwanzaa** – December 26 through January 1
- **New Year's Eve** – December 31

BASIC INFORMATION CONCERNING BEEF & PORK

For much of North America, beef and pork contribute to very common entrées, and are often the main protein when entertaining with food. Hamburgers, steaks, the ribs, and many more elaborate dishes derive from these two animals, so it's helpful to understand the basic cuts that you will find available.

Some common tips for preparing both beef and pork:

- Meat should be **fully defrosted before cooking**. If not, the exterior will become overdone before the interior will be able to be cooked properly.
- Raw meat **should not be frozen after it has been thawed** because this increases the risk of food poisoning.
- If using a **marinade, use a non-reactive container** made of either plastic or glass. Metal bowls might react with the acid in the marinade.
- The **marinade should not be reused** in nearly all situations because it might contain bacteria from contact with the raw meat.
- The only instance in which a **marinade can be used again** is **if it is boiled** then used in the sauce or for basting. Even for these purposes it's best to use some of the excess marinade that was not previously used.
- **Meat that has been marinated for a while will take less time to cook** than the same cut that has not been marinated. For example, a twelve hour marinade might shorten cooking time by a third.
- The **outer layer of the cut should be left on during cooking** as it helps to seal in the juices, which keeps the meat tender.
- A **roast should stand for at least ten minutes** before carving so that the juices are absorbed throughout the meat.
- The **meat should be carved across the grain**, which reduces the length of the remaining fibers, and ensures that the slices will be more tender than if cut along the grain.

AN ANNOTATED GUIDE TO BEEF CUTS

Though inspection for safety is mandatory, the grading of the beef is optional. Both are conducted by the USDA. The grading criteria includes the amount of marbling, the age of the animal, and minor factors such as color, texture and firmness. Marbling describes the fat content of the meat, which, in proper proportion, makes the meat more tender and flavorful. The top three levels of beef are Prime, Choice, and Select. Prime is the best quality, the most flavorful and most tender, and accounts for only the top 2% of beef that is subject to grading. Prime is usually found only in expensive steakhouses, though sometimes specialty supermarkets or high-end butchers offer it. Choice grades are the ones most commonly sold at retail, and totals about 45% of all the beef that is graded. Depending on the cut, it will be tender and juicy. Select is the leanest and most inexpensive, but also the least juicy and tender. Incidentally, Prime Rib is a rib roast and does not refer to grading. Certified Angus Beef is a brand of beef, as is Black Angus and Angus. To be eligible for the Certified Angus Beef designation, the quality must achieve the middle of the Choice Grade. If it is the top-quality Prime it will be labeled as such.

To get an understanding of how flavorful or tender a cut of beef will be, it helps to understand where on the animal it comes from. In beef cattle, the most used muscles are in the legs, neck, shoulder, flank and brisket. Cuts from these areas are flavorful, but lean, and require braising, stewing or marinating to prevent the meat from becoming too dry before becoming tender enough to be enjoyable. The less-used muscles are on the back, the ribs, the loins, and the rump. The cuts from these areas are tender, but are less flavorful from the cuts from the other areas. These cuts work best when quickly grilled, fried or roasted so that their juices are preserved, which enhances the taste. Traveling counter-clockwise from the head, the main sections are:

- **Chuck** – This is generally tough and contains plenty of connective tissue, and is usually used for stewing and for ground beef. Slow cooking with moist heat, as in stewing and braising, is preferred for this.
- **Shank** – Flavorful, but tough, and most often sold for stew meat.
- **Brisket** – From the area under the front legs, this is meat layered with fat. Requisite for Texas barbecue, this might be sold in two halves: the "front cut" is more flavorful than the "first cut." Braising, stewing and barbecuing are the best methods for these meats.
- **Plate** or **Skirt** – This meat is tough. The top part is sold as short ribs, the rest is used for fajitas, stewing and ground meat. Skirt steaks have much more fat than flank steaks and so are much juicier. **Fajitas** can be made from both the Inside and Outside Skirt Steak. **Hanger steak** is the thick piece of meat that hangs between the loin and the last rib, and is actually part of the diaphragm.
- **Flank** – The flank steak is boneless and lean, and flavorful. It is often used for **London Broil**. The rest is used as ground meat.
- **Tip** – From the area just before the hind legs, this can be sold as steak or a boneless roast, the tip roast. The rest is used for stews and kabobs.
- **Round** – From the hindshank and ass, this produces round or rump roasts and round steaks. These cuts are generally lean and not tender. Top-round is the most tender cut from this section. The eye-of-the-round is tough and must be braised, if cooked whole. Oven roasting should be

used only for the top quality cuts such as Top Round, which is sometimes used for London Broil.

- **Sirloin** – This tender and flavorful section is used for steaks and roasts, which will be denoted "sirloin" in some form in the grocery or butcher. Frying, grilling, broiling and roasting are best used for cuts from this section.

- **Short Loin** – This is where the best steaks and most tender meat come from. The **T-Bone**, **Porterhouse**, top loin steak (which is called both the **New York Strip** and Kansas City Strip), and **Filet Mignon**. When divided lengthwise, the bottom part is the **tenderloin**. This is the most expensive cut of meat due to its tenderness, though not the most flavorful, which is why it is usually served with a sauce. **Châteaubriand** is from the center, and most tender part, of the tenderloin. For cooking, dry heat methods such as grilling, broiling and roasting are best used. It is especially important not to overcook these meats, as they will lose the tenderness for which you paid so much.

The **supermarket and wholesale club are good places to purchase beef tenderloins**. In a blind tasting test, the respected *Cook's Illustrated* found that tenderloins from these outlets were just as good as those from upscale, mail-order specialty meat purveyors, but at a fraction of the cost. You will typically need to trim a decent amount of fat prior to cooking, if the tenderloin was purchased from the supermarket or wholesale club, though.

- **Rib** – The cuts from the rib are very tender and are a source for some of the best roasts and steak. This provides, most commonly, the short ribs, Rib Roast, and **Rib-Eye** (or *Entrecôte* or Delmonico Steak) and Rib Steak. The short rib is a small piece that has been cut from the main part of a rib. Grilling, broiling and roasting are best employed for meats from this section.

A BRIEF GUIDE TO THE MAGICAL AND WONDERFUL PIG

Though pork is generally white in color and has been marketed as "the other white meat," when cooked it is considered red meat because it contains more of the protein myoglobin than chicken, or fish for that matter. Pork is much leaner than it was years ago, often one-third or one-half as fatty as in the past. So, be careful when following cooking times from those recipes from older cookbooks or that have been handed down several generations.

Pork is not graded in the same way that beef is graded. There are two types of pork: butcher hogs and sows. Butcher hogs are raised specifically for slaughter. These are bred to produce palatable meat. Sows are used to breed more pigs. When the sows are later slaughtered, their meat lacks the taste of the hogs, and therefore the meat is used for processed and cured pork such as sausages and hams. Traveling counter-clockwise from the head, the main sections are:

- **Butt** (or **Boston-Style Shoulder**) – This meat is juicy, tender, and flavorful because of its relatively high amount of fat. The meat cuts include the pork butt roast, pork steak, pork stew meat, pork cube steak, boneless country style ribs, and ground pork. Most of these cuts area benefit from slow cooking methods such as braising. The steaks cut from the shoulder might be somewhat fat-laden, but are tender and flavorful.
- **Picnic Shoulder** – This is the section below the Butt. This is often split into two pieces: shank end and shoulder end. Picnic hams can be purchased as both and roasted. Quite often meat from here is smoked and sold as processed ham.
- **Belly** – The front part of this area accounts for pork spareribs, St. Louis-style ribs and rib tips. The rest of the belly produces bacon and salt pork. Back ribs, or baby back ribs, are from the blade (or shoulder) and center section of the **loin**. Back ribs are often referred to by weight, usually the smaller the better, and more expensive. St. Louis-style ribs are spareribs with the brisket bone trimmed off. Rib tips are the small meaty rib pieces that have been cut from the ribs.
- **Leg** (or **Ham**) – Hams might be purchased fresh, or more commonly are processed into butt ham, shank ham, ham steak, and spiral ham. Fresh hams come from the leg portion and can come either bone-in or boneless.
- **Loin** – For pork, the loin contains the ribs, short loin and sirloin. It is the most important area for fresh pork. The retail cuts include pork chops, rib end chops, sirloin pork roast, boneless pork roast, country style ribs and pork back ribs. Pork chops can come from differing parts of the loin; the most tender are from the center. From the center also come the rib chops and the loin chops, which are similar to T-bone beef steaks. There is also a tenderloin, which makes an excellent dish and which can be a cost-effective and fairly easy piece to cook. The tenderloin lends itself to roasting, braising, pan-frying, broiling and grilling. Other pork roasts include the boneless crown roast, top loin roast, center cut roast, and sirloin roast. Meats from this section are the leanest and can be easily overcooked, which then become dry and not very enjoyable.

Some tips specifically for preparing pork:

- When fully cooked, the **flesh should be at least faintly pink and juicy**.
- **Try hard <u>not</u> to overcook pork**, as it will become tough, dry and less flavorful. The **threat of trinchinosis is eliminated at 137° F** (58.3° C),

though the USDA recommends cooking pork to 160° F (71.2° C) to be certain. If your meat thermometer is calibrated beforehand, you can be more confident cooking to this lower temperature. Cooking to this higher temperature will result in juices that are mostly clear with a slight pink color to them.

- Before roasting pork, it is a good idea to **sear all of the sides** to seal in the juices.

GUIDELINES FOR MAKING A TOAST

Sometimes you are asked to give a toast at a party or a business event. Below are some steps to help you make an original, if not necessarily heartfelt, toast. These guidelines might be more appropriate for a business situation, as a toast with friends will usually be much easier, since you will be more comfortable with your audience, and they will generally be quite forgiving, unless you are very offensive.

- **Keep it short and simple** – No one likes to hear a long-winded speech, which will quickly bore your audience. And, the shorter the speech the less the chance you will embarrass yourself.
- **Mention the past, current, and future** – It is a good idea to mention past successes, the current situation, and future goals.
- **Stay positive** – A vindictive or mean-spirited toast will certainly be a turn-off for some of the guests.
- **Focus on people in general** – Rather than things. And, "we," "us," etc. work well, and are generally better than mentioning specific guests, who might be embarrassed by being the focus of the crowd.
- **Use humor wisely** – You probably believe that you are much funnier than you actually are. You want to avoid offending, insulting or embarrassing your guests and yourself.
- **Make eye contact with nearly every member of the crowd** – This is what you were taught in speech class, and people will pay greater attention if they notice that you might make eye contact with them.

If you know beforehand that you might be asked to make a toast, the most important thing to do is practice the toast before the event with these tips in mind. If the above guidelines prove too much effort, simply say something like, "I'd like to take time to specially thank *so-and-so* for all of their (help / hard work / the great job that they have done / *or some other very brief but pandering crap*). Cheers." Try to make it sound heartfelt, if you can.

A couple of things related to toasting:

- The international sign **announcing a toast** is the **tapping on a glass** with a utensil.
- The **guest of honor**, if there is one, should be the **first** one toasted.
- Again, **you are <u>not</u> as humorous as you think** you are.

It does not have to be hard. Quick and simple. If the toast doesn't result in the amount of laughs you expected or heaps of praise as you had hoped, don't worry. A short bad toast will be quickly forgotten.

KEGS — PURCHASING, TAPPING & POURING

Kegs can be an effective and cost-effective way to provide beer for a fairly large gathering. You might not need this section if you have to worry about hauling a bulky 160 pounds or so up five flights of stairs to a tiny apartment.

SELECTING THE PROPER KEG SIZE

The term keg commonly refers to a **Full Keg**, which is a half-barrel. Domestic beer kegs are typically 15.5 gallons, while the imports' kegs are 13.2 gallons (50 liters). There are also **Half Kegs** (7.9 gallons) and **Pony Kegs** (5 to 5.3 gallons). If you have decided on a keg or kegs for your event, you are probably going to go with the full keg, which is the most cost effective size. It's useful to keep in mind that many interesting imported beers such as the Chimay and Duval are available in North America in the smaller pony keg sizes. These can be fun for special events.

When deciding upon whether or not a keg make sense for your event it is helpful to understand how many people you can expect to satiate with it, and how many six-packs it would replace. The table below provides an estimate on how many people can be adequately served with different sizes of kegs.

Below are some **guidelines for how many beers** you can plan to get out of the different sizes of draft beer assuming **10 ounce pours** and **15% waste** due to foam, spillage, land a lack of patience from your guests at the pump.

- 15.5 gallon keg − 15% waste ≈ **168 cups** ÷ 5 cups each ≈ **34 people**

- 13.2 gallon keg − 15% waste ≈ **144 cups** ÷ 5 cups each ≈ **29 people**

- 7.9 gallon keg − 15% waste ≈ **86 cups** ÷ 5 cups each ≈ **17 people**

- 5.3 gallon keg − 15% waste ≈ **58 cups** ÷ 5 cups each ≈ **11 people**

- 5.0 gallon keg − 15% waste ≈ **54 cups** ÷ 5 cups each ≈ **11 people**

With kegs, you might not only save money in place of purchasing bottled or canned beer, but kegs can be more convenient space-wise as you just need room enough for a large plastic trash where the keg will reside. Having a keg will help free up space in the refrigerator and coolers.

15.5 Gallon Keg   **Six-Pack**

The relationship between the keg and the six-pack is not quite to scale in the graphic above, but hopefully you get the message. Guidelines for equivalency between the other keg sizes and the number of six-packs is shown in the table below.

Let's see if you can follow this.... Below are some **guidelines for how many equivalent bottles** or cans **of beer** you can plan to get out of the different sizes of keg beer. This assumes **15% waste at the keg** and **10 ounce pours** in the 12 ounce cups as above, plus the typical keg dynamics that result in **10% additional thirstiness**. In other words, with bottles or cans there will be less waste, but also less beer consumed.

- 15.5 gallons – 15% waste, but 10% less drank ≈ 126 bottles ≈ **21 six-packs**

- 13.2 gallons – 15% waste, but 10% less drank ≈ 108 bottles ≈ **18 six-packs**

- 7.9 gallons – 15% waste, but 10% less drank ≈ 65 bottles ≈ **11 six-packs**

- 5.3 gallons – 15% waste, but 10% less drank ≈ 44 bottles ≈ **8 six-packs**

- 5.0 gallons – 15% waste, but 10% less drank ≈ 41 bottles ≈ **7 six-packs**

BEFORE THE PARTY

- When purchasing the keg, be sure to get the **air pump** used to pour beer from it, along with a **large plastic trash can** that is used to hold ice around the keg to keep it cold. The former will usually require a deposit.
- The keg should be sold to you cold, and the **keg needs to remain cold**, otherwise there is a good chance that the beer will spoil.

- If possible, **allow the keg to sit** relatively **undisturbed** for a while before tapping, so that the beer can settle. Movement before using will cause more beer to foam when poured.
- Unless you have mostly serious beer drinkers for your keg, it is a good idea to **use 12 ounce cups**, since our experience shows a lot of beer will be wasted with the larger-sized cups due to the excess foam and neglect.
- As is also shown in the previous table, typically, **10% to 15% of beer from the keg will be wasted**. Due to the workings of the air pump and inexperienced beer pourers, this is almost unavoidable.
- But, **people have the tendency to drink more beer with a keg** present than with bottles or cans. This is probably due to the fact that it's easier to lose track on the amount of beers consumed with a keg, as beers are often re-filled before the beer is finished, commonly after just a few sips. Even with 10 ounce pours, people will drink more beer. **10% more beer drank with a keg than from bottles or cans** is probably a good minimum amount.
- If your are using salt to aid the ice in cooling the keg, **do not use too much salt**, which slows the rate that the ice melts, as doing this can freeze the beer lines and damage the keg.
- Due to the interaction with oxygen from the air pump, the **beer in the keg will go bad within twelve to sixteen hours** after being tapped.

DURING THE PARTY

- **Do not over-pump** an air pump as it will result in excess foam. It's easy to be tempted to so, especially with a freshly tapped keg, which pours very slowly.
- In related fashion, **watch for guests who over-pump**. There is at least one at every event with a keg. An air pump simply uses air pressure to force the beer from the keg at a moderate rate. Pumping it more will usually just increase the amount of foam in the beer rather than making it pour more quickly.
- If the beer is foaming a lot when poured, check if the air pump has a **release** so that you can reduce the pressure that is causing the problem.
- You should know how to pour a beer, but in case not, for either beer from a bottle or a keg you should tilt the cup or glass at a **sharp enough angle** to the spout at first **so that the beer falls to the side of the glass** or cup, which reduces the amount of foam. As the beer fills the container adjust it so that it does not spill. Easy enough.
- As beer from a keg is invariably foamy, at least at first, a very good idea is to **pour the beer into pitchers**, and then serve to each person's cup from the pitchers, rather than directly from the keg. Doing this allows the beer

to settle in the larger pitchers, and much less foam is poured into each glass, and much less beer is wasted.

- As a host, you should be aware of the person who stands over the keg pouring his beer until it's nearly **foam-free, wasting** probably a gallon of beer that you paid for in the process. There is always at least one in the crowd.

TAPPING THE KEG

In case you have forgotten from your college days, or relied on the expertise of others, below is an illustrative example of how to tap a keg of beer. It's really not that difficult, if often messy. There will be only three pieces. Along with the **plastic trash can** where the **keg** should reside, the keg should come with a handheld **air-pump**, which is shown in the first image below. A professional hand model was not used for these images, but hopefully these are still helpful.

THE AIR PUMP — TOO OFTEN A SOURCE OF CONSTERNATION

The steps to successfully tap a keg are:

1. **Make sure that the keg is cold** and sitting on ice.

2. **Have a towel handy,** as it's easy to spill some beer during the process. Rather, if you need instructions tapping a keg, you will spill beer.
3. **Clean the bottom of the air pump and** the keg's receptacle (termed a **bunghole**).
4. **Place the air pump into the bunghole** as is shown in the image below.
5. **Turn the air pump clockwise** until it stops, and is firmly in place.
6. **Lock the air pump into place.** This is done by **pulling out the handle** that lies at the side of the pump **then down and locked.** This is shown in the third image, on the next page. This act is the actual tapping, as the lever forces the tap's spout to pierce the seal of the keg, and open the way for the beer to exit the keg. Since the keg is under significant pressure, always **make sure the air pump is properly and firmly affixed, otherwise there will be a mess**.
7. **Try to pour a beer before pumping.** Most likely nothing will come out, but doing this will help you avoid over-pumping at the start.
8. **Pump and test regularly until the beer flows freely,** and without too much foam. If there is an air pressure release, you might need to use this if the beer is too foamy.
9. You should know this, but you and your guests will have to **pump on an intermittent basis** to maintain the proper pressure for pouring the beer. Again, don't go overboard with the pumping.

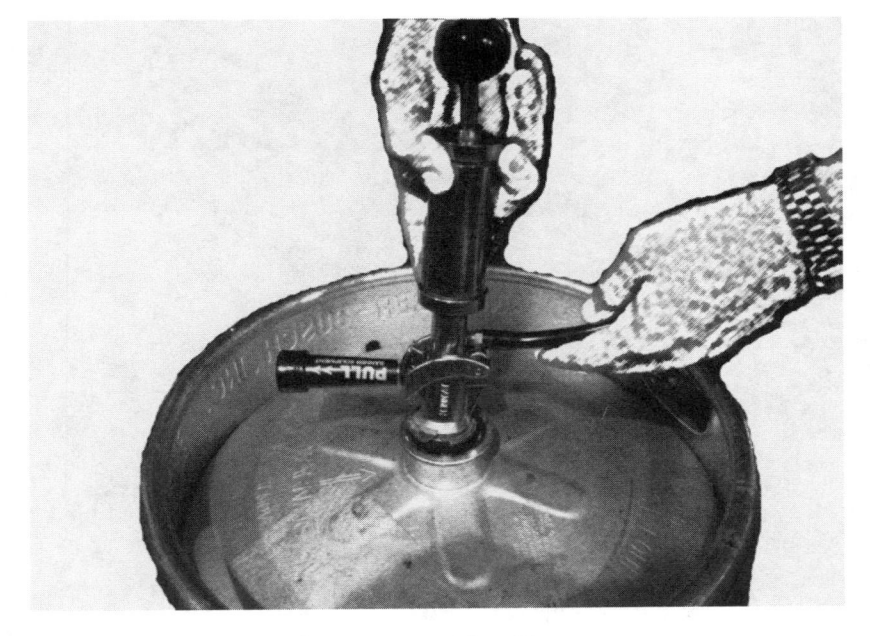

AFFIXING THE AIR PUMP

LOCKING THE AIR PUMP INTO PLACE BY PULLING DOWN THE LEVER

Getting a keg to operate properly shouldn't be that painful or difficult. Even if it is, it should still be worth it.

AFTER THE PARTY

Kegs are much easier to move when empty or nearly so, which should be obvious. If your keg or kegs has not been finished, it's a good idea to pour the rest of the beer out before returning it. This is best done with the air pump and pitcher. Pour the leftover beer down a drain since you probably do not want stale beer on your lawn, nor do your neighbors.

LISTS OF COCKTAIL MIXERS

Below are lists regarding recommended purchases of accompaniments for liquor on three levels of generosity. When the bar is self-service, and you want your guests to have the ability to create drinks with more than two ingredients, the first list below will suit you well. Of course, if you want to satisfy for guests' desire for Margaritas or Bloody Marys, get those mixes.

1) To be able to provide **the necessities** for a cocktail party:

Essential for most events with cocktails:
- Sodas – **Cola, Diet Cola, Sprite** or **Seven-Up**
- Carbonated Mixers – **Club Soda, Tonic Water**
- Non-Carbonated Beverages – **Water, Orange Juice, Cranberry Juice**
- Fresh Fruits – **Limes, Lemons**
- Condiments & Garnishes – **Olives, Maraschino Cherries**
- Drink Mixes – **Sour Mix**

2) For **a more generous bar**, to make a greater variety of cocktails:

When you have a **professional bartender** at your event you might want to have this:
- Sodas – *Cola, Diet Cola, Sprite or Seven-Up*, **Ginger Ale**
- Carbonated Mixers – *Club Soda, Tonic Water*
- Non-Carbonated Beverages – *Water, Orange Juice, Cranberry Juice*, **Grapefruit Juice, Lime Juice, Pineapple Juice, Tomato Juice, Grenadine, Bitters, Milk, Coffee, Cream** or **Half-and-Half**
- Fresh Fruits – *Limes, Lemons*, **Oranges, Green Apples**
- Condiments & Garnishes – *Olives, Maraschino Cherries*, **Pickled Onions, Coarse Salt, Nutmeg, Cinnamon**
- Drink Mixes – *Sour Mix*, **Bloody Mary Mix, Margarita Mix**

3) **To make almost every cocktail** you might want to serve:

If you are want to be able to make **nearly every type of cocktail**, use this list:
- Sodas – *Cola, Diet Cola, Sprite or Seven-Up, Ginger Ale*
- Carbonated Mixers – *Club Soda, Tonic Water*, **Energy drinks**
- Non-Carbonated Beverages – *Water, Orange Juice, Cranberry Juice, Grapefruit Juice, Lime Juice, Pineapple Juice, Tomato Juice, Grenadine, Bitters, Milk, Coffee, Cream or Half-and-Half*
- Fresh Fruits – *Limes, Lemons, Oranges, Green Apples*, **Strawberries, Raspberries, Cucumber**
- Condiments & Garnishes – *Olives, Maraschino Cherries, Pickled Onions, Coarse Salt, Nutmeg, Cinnamon*, **Mint Leaves, Coconut Milk, Peach Nectar, Whipped Cream, Orgeat Syrup**
- Drink Mixes – *Sour Mix, Bloody Mary Mix, Margarita Mix*, **Daiquiri Mix**

CHECKLISTS FOR SUPPLYING DIFFERENT EVENTS

Below are quick reference guides for different types of parties and several popular numbers of guests to entertain. For other sizes, you can do the math to expand or contract. Amounts for items are given when believed to be useful. You will know your crowd, so adjust accordingly.

CHECKLIST FOR A COCKTAIL PARTY FOR 10 PEOPLE FOR 3 HOURS

We assume that you as host are manning the bar, or it will be self-service.

ALCOHOL

LIQUOR
- ☐ **Vodka** (1 - liter bottle)
- ☐ **Gin** (1 - 750 ml bottle)
- ☐ **Bourbon** (1 - 750 ml bottle)
- ☐ **Scotch** (1 - 750 ml bottle)
- ☐ **Light Rum** (1 - 750 ml bottle)
- ☐ **Dry Vermouth** (1 - 375 ml bottle)

BEER & WINE
- ☐ **Micro / Import Beer** (2 - six-packs)
- ☐ **Light Beer** (2 - six-packs)
- ☐ **Red Wine** (2 - 750 ml bottles)
- ☐ **White Wine** (1 - 750 ml bottle)

ACCOMPANIMENTS & SUPPLIES

OTHER BEVERAGES
- ☐ Sodas – **Cola** (2 liters) **Diet Cola** (1 liter), **Sprite** or **Seven-Up** (1 liter)
- ☐ Carbonated Mixers – **Club Soda** (6 - 10 ounce), **Tonic Water** (6 - 10 ounce)
- ☐ Non-Carbonated – **Water**, **Orange Juice** (2 qt.), **Cranberry Juice** (1 qt.)
- ☐ Fruit – **Limes** (6), **Lemons** (3)
- ☐ Condiments & Garnishes – **Olives** (1 jar)

- ☐ **Ice** (2 - 8 pound bags)

FOOD
- ☐ **Appetizers** – Even just cheese and crackers might be sufficient.

SUPPLIES
- ☐ **Cocktail Napkins**
- ☐ **Trash Bags**
- ☐ **Toothpicks** – For the appetizers
- ☐ **Clear plastic cups** – If no glassware

ACCESSORIES

GLASSWARE & BARWARE
- ☐ **Martini Glasses**
- ☐ **Cocktail Glasses**
- ☐ **Martini Shaker**
- ☐ **Wine Glasses**
- ☐ **Beer Glasses**
- ☐ **Wine Opener** (with **Bottle Opener**)

DISHWARE
- ☐ **Appetizer Plates**
- ☐ **Serving Platters** or **Plates**
- ☐ **Forks**
- ☐ **Serving Utensils**

CHECKLIST FOR A COCKTAIL PARTY FOR <u>25</u> PEOPLE FOR 3 HOURS

With this size cocktail party, as above, we are assuming that you as host are manning the bar, or the bar will be self-service. With this size, it will still be very manageable. It makes sense with a larger crowd you will have a wider range of tastes, and so a wider range of libations.

ALCOHOL

LIQUOR
- [ ] **Vodka** (2 - liter bottles)
- [ ] **Gin** (1- 750 ml bottle)
- [ ] **Bourbon** (1 - 750 ml bottle)
- [ ] **Canadian Whisky** (1 - 750 ml bottle)
- [ ] **Scotch** (1 - 750 ml bottle)
- [ ] **Light Rum** (1 - 750 ml bottle)
- [ ] **Dry Vermouth** (1 - 375 ml bottle)

BEER & WINE
- [ ] **Micro / Import Beer** (4 - six-packs)
- [ ] **Light Beer** (4 - six-packs)
- [ ] **Red Wine** (4 - 750 ml bottles)
- [ ] **White Wine** (2 - 750 ml bottles)

ACCOMPANIMENTS & SUPPLIES

OTHER BEVERAGES
- [ ] Sodas – **Cola** (3 liters) **Diet Cola** (2 liters), **Sprite** or **Seven-Up** (1 liter)
- [ ] Carbonated Mixers – **Club Soda** (15 - 10 ounce), **Tonic Water** (15 - 10 ounce)
- [ ] Non-Carbonated Beverages – **Orange Juice** (1 gal.), **Cranberry Juice** (½ gal.)
- [ ] Fruit – **Limes** (15), **Lemons** (8)
- [ ] Condiments & Garnishes – **Olives** (1 jar)
- [ ] Drink Mixes – **Sour Mix** (2 packages)
- [ ] Water – **Small bottles** (36 - 12 ounces) are easy for your guests and inexpensive.

- [ ] **Ice** (4 - 8 pound bags)

FOOD
- [ ] **Appetizers** – Even just cheese and crackers might be sufficient.

SUPPLIES
- [ ] **Cocktail Napkins**
- [ ] **Trash Bags**
- [ ] **Toothpicks** – For the appetizers
- [ ] **Clear plastic cups** – If no glassware

ACCESSORIES

GLASSWARE & BARWARE
- [ ] **Martini Glasses**
- [ ] **Cocktail Glasses**
- [ ] **Martini Shaker**
- [ ] **Ice Buckets & Tongs**
- [ ] **Can Opener**
- [ ] **Wine Glasses**
- [ ] **Beer Glasses**
- [ ] **Wine Opener** (with **Bottle Opener**)
- [ ] **Coolers** (or **Ice Chests**)

DISHWARE
- [ ] **Appetizer Plates**
- [ ] **Serving Platters** or **Plates**
- [ ] **Forks**
- [ ] **Serving Utensils**

CHECKLIST FOR A COCKTAIL PARTY FOR 50 PEOPLE FOR 3 HOURS

With this cocktail party for fifty, we would hope that you have hired a bartender. The range of liquor depends on how generous you want to be. Providing vodka, gin, bourbon and rum will be sufficient for most gatherings.

ALCOHOL

LIQUOR
- ☐ **Vodka** (4 - liter bottles)
- ☐ **Gin** (2- 750 ml bottles)
- ☐ **Bourbon** (2 - 750 ml bottles)
- ☐ **Canadian Whisky** (1 - 750 ml bottle)
- ☐ **Tequila** (1 - 750 ml bottle)
- ☐ **Scotch** (1 - 750 ml bottle)
- ☐ **Light Rum** (1 - 750 ml bottle)
- ☐ **Dry Vermouth** (1 - 750 ml bottle)
- ☐ **Triple Sec** (1 - 750 ml bottle)

BEER & WINE
- ☐ **Micro / Import Beer** (8 - six-packs)
- ☐ **Light Beer** (8 - six-packs)
- ☐ **Red Wine** (8 - 750 ml bottles)
- ☐ **White Wine** (4 - 750 ml bottles)

ACCOMPANIMENTS & SUPPLIES

OTHER BEVERAGES
- ☐ Sodas – **Cola** (6 liters) **Diet Cola** (2 liters), **Sprite** or **Seven-Up** (1 liter)
- ☐ Carbonated Mixers – **Club Soda** (30 - 10 ounce), **Tonic Water** (30 - 10 ounce)
- ☐ Non-Carbonated Beverages – **Orange Juice** (2 gals.), **Cranberry Juice** (1 gal.)
- ☐ Fruit – **Limes** (25), **Lemons** (15)
- ☐ Condiments & Garnishes – **Olives** (1 jar)
- ☐ Drink Mixes – **Sour Mix** (4 packages)
- ☐ Water – **Small bottles** (72 - 12 ounces) are easy for your guests and inexpensive.

- ☐ **Ice** (8 - 8 pound bags)

FOOD
- ☐ **Appetizers** – Even just cheese and crackers might be sufficient.

SUPPLIES
- ☐ **Cocktail Napkins** (500)
- ☐ **Trash Bags**
- ☐ **Plastic Appetizer Plates**
- ☐ **Toothpicks** – For the appetizers
- ☐ **Plastic Cocktail Cups** (400)
- ☐ **Plastic Utensils** (100)

ACCESSORIES

BARWARE
- ☐ **Martini Shaker** (2)
- ☐ **Ice Buckets & Tongs** (2)
- ☐ **Can Opener**
- ☐ **Wine Opener** (with **Bottle Opener** - 2)
- ☐ **Coolers** (or **Ice Chests**)

DISHWARE
- ☐ **Serving Platters** or **Plates**
- ☐ **Serving Utensils**

CHECKLIST FOR A DINNER PARTY FOR **8** PEOPLE

If you feel that linens are important, please use them. Most single guys can get away without owning cloth napkins and tablecloths. Also, we assume that you have the basic utensils to cook each of the dishes for the dinner.

ALCOHOL

LIQUOR
- ☐ **Vodka** (1 - liter bottle)
- ☐ **After Dinner Drink** – Bailey's, cognac, sambuca, etc.
- ☐ **Scotch** (1 - 750 ml bottle)

BEER & WINE
- ☐ **Micro / Import Beer** (1 - six-pack)
- ☐ **Light Beer** (1 - six-pack)
- ☐ **Before Dinner** – Champagne, prosecco, an aperitif, etc.
- ☐ **After Dinner Wine** – Port, Madeira, sherry, etc.
- ☐ **Red Wine** (2 - 750 ml bottles)
- ☐ **White Wine** (1 - 750 ml bottle)

ACCOMPANIMENTS & SUPPLIES

OTHER BEVERAGES
- ☐ Sodas – **Cola** (1 liter) **Diet Cola** (1 liter), **Sprite** or **Seven-Up** (1 liter)
- ☐ **Water**
- ☐ **Ice** (1 - 8 pound bag)

FOOD — Among friends it is not inappropriate to ask that they bring a dish.
- ☐ **Appetizers**
- ☐ **Soup** or **Salad**
- ☐ **Entrée**
- ☐ **Sides**
- ☐ **Dessert**
- ☐ **Cheese**

SUPPLIES
- ☐ **Napkins**
- ☐ **Trash Bags**

ACCESSORIES

GLASSWARE
- ☐ **Wine Glasses**
- ☐ **Beer Glasses**
- ☐ **Cocktail Glasses**
- ☐ **Coffee Cups**
- ☐ **Water Pitcher**
- ☐ **Decanter**

DISHWARE
- ☐ **Appetizer Plates**
- ☐ **Dinner Plates**
- ☐ **Salad Plates**
- ☐ **Soup Bowls**
- ☐ **Dessert Plates**
- ☐ **Serving Platters** or **Plates**
- ☐ **Utensils**
- ☐ **Breadbasket**
- ☐ **Butter Dish**
- ☐ **Cream Pitcher**
- ☐ **Sugar Bowl**
- ☐ **Serving Utensils for each** (3+)

LINENS
- ☐ **Tablecloth**
- ☐ **Napkins**

CHECKLIST FOR A WINE TASTING FOR <u>25</u> PEOPLE

These can be a lot of fun, and done in a variety of ways. As mentioned earlier, it can be quite inexpensive to host if you have your guests each bring a bottle of wine to taste.

ALCOHOL

WINE
☐ **Wine** or **Wines** – For the tasting
☐ **Wine** (3 - 750 ml bottles) – To drink before the tasting; a similar wine to those being tasted, or a light white wine are both recommended for this purpose.

ACCOMPANIMENTS & SUPPLIES

OTHER BEVERAGES
☐ **Water**
☐ **Club Soda** – Actually, to have handy for cleaning a red wine stain.

☐ **Ice** – For this, what is in your freezer is probably sufficient.

FOOD
☐ **Appetizers**
☐ **Cheese**
☐ **Crackers**
☐ **Bread**

SUPPLIES
☐ **Cocktail Napkins** (100)
☐ **Brown Paper Bags** – To obscure the wine bottles during a blind tasting.
☐ **Paper** – For taking notes
☐ **Pens** – For taking notes

ACCESSORIES

GLASSWARE
☐ **Wine Glasses** (30) – It's not a bad idea to have a few extra

DISHWARE
☐ **Appetizer Plates**
☐ **Serving Platters or Plates** – For the appetizers
☐ **Water Pitchers**
☐ **Decanters** – Can be a nice touch

MISCELLANEOUS
☐ **Wine Charms**
☐ **Spit Buckets** – For the wine that is not consumed, if not really for spitting.

CHECKLIST FOR A BEER & WINE PARTY FOR <u>50</u> PEOPLE – 4 HOURS

Skimping on liquor is a good idea when you are hoping to save some money, and it can also help prevent the guests from imbibing too much. Below are some suggestions how to do this.

ALCOHOL

BEER & WINE
☐ **Micro / Import Beer** (6 - six-packs) ☐ **Red Wine** (10 - 750 ml bottles)
☐ **Light Beer** (10 - six-packs) ☐ **White Wine** (4 - 750 ml bottles)

ACCOMPANIMENTS & SUPPLIES

OTHER BEVERAGES
☐ Sodas – **Cola** (3 - six-packs), **Diet Cola** (3 - six-packs), **Sprite** or **Seven-Up** (1 - six-pack)
☐ Non-Carbonated Beverages – **Orange Juice** (1 gal.), **Cranberry Juice** (1 qt.)
☐ Water – **Small bottles** (36 - 12 ounces) are easy for your guests and inexpensive

☐ **Ice** (4 - 8 pound bags)

FOOD
☐ **Appetizers**

SUPPLIES
☐ **Plastic Cups** (200)
☐ **Plastic Plates** (100)
☐ **Cocktail Napkins** (200)
☐ **Trash Bags**
☐ **Toothpicks**

ACCESSORIES

GLASSWARE
☐ **Wine Glasses** (40)

DISHWARE
☐ **Serving Platters** or **Plates** – For the appetizers
☐ **Serving Utensils** – For the appetizers

DEALING WITH HANGOVERS

The best and most sure-fire way to avoid a hangover is to not drink at all. This is a rather drastic measure, of course. If you are going to drink, the best thing to do is to try to not drink too terribly much. You should note the distinction between happily buzzed, and snot-slinging drunk, as it will make a big difference the next morning. As Jack Black replied in *The School of Rock* when asked if being hungover is being drunk, "No, it means that I was drunk yesterday." A hangover is a result of your body and, specifically, your cranial membrane, being dehydrated, but this description doesn't really describe the discomfort.

SOME THINGS TO DO BEFORE THE BINGE, IF POSSIBLE

- Drinking **a glass of milk** with slow the absorption of alcohol into your system and will help protect your stomach from the worst irritants from the various alcoholic beverages you might be consuming.
- Plan to **drink vodka,** as it has fewer impurities than other liquors.
- **Try not to drink coffee**, as it is a diuretic, and will increase the effects of dehydration caused by the conspicuous consumption of alcohol.

SOME THINGS TO DO PRIOR TO GOING TO BED, POST-BINGE

- Since, it is dehydration at work, **plenty of water** or a sports drink like Gatorade before getting to bed is a good way to help prevent, or at least, diminish the often painful effects of a hangover.
- Some kind of **analgesic** like aspirin or ibuprofen can help mitigate the ensuing headache, too. Be careful with these analgesics since these have the potential to cause liver damage when combined with several drinks. Refer to the directions and warning labels before using.

SOME THINGS TO CONSIDER WHILE SUFFERING THE EFFECTS

- **Sleep**. This helps the body recover.
- More **water**.
- More **analgesics**.
- Since an irritated stomach that often accompanies a hangover produces acid, **an antacid might be helpful**. Mineral waters, which are alkaline, and so have similar, if much weaker properties, can also be useful.
- **Vitamin C**. It helps the liver detoxify the blood.
- Sugar, or more specifically fructose, helps the body process alcohol. It also replaces the blood sugar, which might be low the next morning, and might be helping to cause you to feel weak. **Eat something sweet**.

- **Vitamin B** seems to help some people.
- The **hair of the dog**, as this replaces the lost blood sugar and satisfies the body's temporary addiction to alcohol. Can't be recommended for everyone, everyday, though.

Hangovers are never fun, but, unless you have done something truly terrible, be sure never to follow that promise made in the depths of the pain to never drink again. Or, that is our recommendation, at least. You can't keep that vow anyway. Cheers.

WEIGHTS AND MEASURES FOR COOKING & MIXING

US Measurement Equivalents for Volume:

Dash (Pinch)	=	$\frac{1}{16}$ teaspoon		
60 drops	=	1 teaspoon		
1 teaspoon	=	$\frac{1}{3}$ tablespoon		
1 tablespoon	=	3 teaspoons		
2 tablespoons	=	$\frac{1}{8}$ cup	=	1 ounce
3 tablespoons	=	1 jigger	=	1½ ounces
4 tablespoons	=	¼ cup	=	2 ounces
8 tablespoons	=	½ cup	=	4 ounces
16 tablespoons	=	1 cup	=	8 ounces

More US Measurement Equivalents for Volume:

2 cups	=	1 pint	=	16 ounces
1 quart	=	2 pints	=	32 ounces
2 quarts	=	4 pints	=	64 ounces
4 quarts	=	1 gallon	=	128 ounces

Metric Equivalents for Volume:

¼ teaspoon	=	1 ml
1 teaspoon	=	5 ml
1 tablespoon	=	15 ml
1 cup	=	237 ml
1 pint	=	473 ml
1 quart	=	.9463 liter
1.06 quarts	=	1 liter
1 gallon	=	3.785 liters

Metric Equivalents for Weight:

.035 ounce	=	1 gram
1 ounce	=	28.35 grams
4 ounces	=	113 grams
1 pound	=	454 grams
2.2 pounds	=	1 kilogram

Useful Measurements for Butter:

1 tablespoon	=	½ ounce				
2 tablespoons	=	1 ounce	=	¼ stick		
8 tablespoons	=	4 ounces	=	1 stick	=	½ cup

Good to Note – For cheese, 1 cup shredded = ¼ pound = 4 ounces

Mailing Guidelines

Mailing Invitations — USA

In the U.S., check with the United States Postal Service website for the latest rates, www.usps.com. Most letters will qualify for the first First-Class mail rate (37¢ in early 2006), which translates to about three or four pieces of paper within the regular-shaped envelope. Standard rate divisions are: 0 to 1 ounce; 1 to 2 ounces; 2 to 3 ounces; 3 to 4 ounces; 4 to 5 ounces; and 5 to 6 ounces. The difference between each size is the cost of a postcard stamp (23¢ in early 2006, so from 2 to 3 ounces was 60¢ while from 3 to 4 ounces was 83¢). If you don't have a postal scale at home, you will have to obtain the correct postage at a post office.

There is something called the "Non-machinable Surcharge," where an additional charge (which was 12¢ in early 2006) is required for items weighing 1 ounce or less with any of the following criteria:

- **Square** letters.
- The **height exceeds 6⅛ inches**, or **length exceeds 11½ inches**, or **thickness exceeds ¼ inch**.
- It has **clasps, strings, buttons**, or similar closure devices.
- It is **too rigid** or contains items such as pens that cause the thickness of the piece of mail to be **uneven**.
- It has **an address parallel to the shorter dimension** of the piece of mail.

Standard-sized postcard postage is roughly 60% of the cost of the letter rate (23¢ in early 2006). The postcard must meet the following criteria:

- Minimum size – 3½ inches high by 5 inches long by 0.007 inch thick.
- Maximum size – 4¼ inches high by 6 inches long by 0.016 inch thick.

Postcards over the maximum height or length for the card rate are charged regular First Class Mail letter rates; the surcharge for odd-sized letters might apply. Check at a local post office if you have any concerns about your mailings.

Mailing Invitations — Canada

In Canada, for current postal rates, check the Canada Post (or *Postes Canada*) web site, www.canadapost.ca, which proudly proclaims, "Canadians enjoy one of the lowest basic domestic letter rates among industrialized countries."

HANDLING THOSE DISRUPTIVE GUESTS

Relatively small get-togethers are where you might need to employ some skills and authority as host to ensure that one or more disruptive guests do not greatly detract from your event. With larger parties, these usually unintentionally annoying people can be avoided more successfully, or they are often intimidated into acceptable behavior by the greater numbers.

With this chapter, we try to **identify some of the types of potentially disruptive guests** that we have seen over the years, fairly humorously and in our opinionated fashion, without too much offense. **Then we recommend an action on your part to mitigate their deleterious effect** on your party. These people might be friends, or friends of friends (or possibly you, but it's your party), who exhibit this behavior on a regular basis in social situations, or it could be one-off conduct induced by too many party beverages. It's useful to note that a guest's conduct can change over the course of the event, from enjoyable to humorous to annoying. Worse yet, it might pass through several types of bothersome, boorish or disruptive conduct. Some behavior is much worse than others, and should be remembered so that you might not invite these people to future events.

What to do with those disruptive guests? For each of these types of guests, once they become a detriment to the party, **take them aside, mention their offending actions, and ask them to moderate their behavior**. If there is an alternate suggestion, it is listed after **"What else you might try"** following the description.

Attention Whore – This person feels the need to be at or near the center of attention in their immediate circle for most of the event. If the stories are interesting, it can be tolerated for a while. But, invariably, the incessant stories and conversation turns insipid and becomes distracting then annoying, and detracts from the general enjoyment. At the dinner table, when guests cannot flee, this becomes a problem. *What else you might try* – As the host, at the dinner table, you should gently tell that guest that other people should lead the conversation. If this person does not get the hint, change the topic of conversation each time this person begins talking.

Chick Repellant – This is the male friend who is usually too arrogant and otherwise off-putting to keep a woman's attention for any length of time, but is usually well-behaved, and physically attractive and wealthy enough, or a good enough friend, to keep inviting. *What else you might try* – Unless they morph into the Misanthrope or the Social Hand Grenade, this person can be great to have around, as you will seem much more suave, sensitive and interesting by comparison.

The DJ – This is the person who has to play his choice of your CDs, much to your consternation, especially if he plays the music too loudly or happens to find the most inappropriate music from your collection. *What else you might try* – If this might be a problem, only put out those CDs that you want played during your party. Maybe just burn several CDs for the party, and hide the rest of your music. You can also make sure that you have possession of the stereo's remote control and can adjust the volume down at the very least.

Dog Person – This person tends to bring their dog when it is not entirely appropriate, especially when it is an indoors setting, and then usually expect you to find space, water and sometimes even food for their canine compatriots. *What else you might try* – The dog is already at your place and you will have already been asked for water and space for the dog. If the dog becomes a nuisance, mention that subtly to the owner. If the owner still does not get the hint, suggest more directly that they remove the dog.

Dork – This person is socially inept, but not offensive. *What else you might try* – Introduce them to their brethren, which should be seated out of the way of the rest of the guests, "Have you met Mohammed, Sidney, Clayton and Jugdish? Good. You'll have plenty to talk about." Or, send them to the store to get things, maybe even more than once.

The Downer – This is the person that needs to explain their problems or current state of woe to as many people as possible, and becomes antithetical to any kind of celebratory mood. Parties, and most social gatherings, even wakes (especially involving someone of Irish descent), are an escape from the humdrum of everyday life. These people can dampen your party. *What else you might try* – If this person exhibits this behavior consistently, try not to invite them. Otherwise, try to maneuver them into a small space or a corner where they can do much less harm.

Drama Queen – This person, female or male, usually will draw attention to themselves by noticeably complaining about their current pitiable state. The martyr is a role they often try to play. In addition to changing the tenor of your party, they can be generally annoying. *What else you might try* – These are terrible guests, and a significant show of rudeness might be necessary when admonishing them not to exhibit this behavior at your party.

Drunk, Happy – This person becomes obviously drunk during the party while remaining in a good mood. This person can often remain or become an enjoyable guest, as the butt of jokes, or otherwise. *What else you might try* – Make sure this person has a ride home, and encourage him or her to depart under assistance, if possible. Or, conversely you can let him or her "rest" on a sofa or chair somewhat out of the way.

Drunk, Obnoxious – This is a common sight at almost any social event that lasts several hours and the drinks are flowing readily. This person, who may or may not be an ass when sober, becomes one when imbibing past their limit. At this point this person is a drag on the party, or at least his immediate area. This person is one that you will want to watch. They have potential for property damage and carnage, especially if they get behind the wheel. *What else you might try* – Make sure this person has a ride home, and encourage him or her to depart under assistance, if possible. Unfortunately, coffee will only make him more wide awake. Food will help a little, but time is the only cure, which will hopefully be taken away from your event.

Drunk, Sad – This person gets drunk, complains about their lot in life, and then sobs loudly making everyone around uncomfortable at first, then annoyed. *What else you might try* – This person is huge downer for the party, even worse than The Downer. Try to arrange a ride for this person and get them away from your party as quickly as possible. Try not to invite in the future.

Drunk, Sleeping – They get drunk, sit, get comfortable then fall asleep and stay asleep. *What else you might try* – Usually not a problem provided there is a place for them to sleep in peace, if they don't snore too loudly, and have eventual transportation home. It's also a good, if somewhat immature, idea to have markers handy and placed next to Sleeping Beauty. Your other guests can scribble their appreciation or other thoughtful suggestions on this person.

Drunk, Violent – This person gets drunk then belligerent. And, nothing can ruin a party more quickly than a fight. *What else you might try* – Though two of these can be a source of entertainment during your event, provided their belligerence is directed toward each other, it's best to get these people to leave. If that does not work, with another trustworthy guest or two explain that violence will not be tolerated, and possibly escort this person from the party. If all else fails you might want to call the police. You don't want them to drive, so arrange for someone to take them away, if not the police.

Drunk, Vomiting – This person is drunk as hell, and throwing up. *What else you might try* – Before they pass out, ask if this person is a drummer in a rock band. If so, they are probably a goner. Otherwise, have one of their friends take care of them, and try to get them to depart.

Embarrassing Relative – Due to a coincidence in travel schedules, you sometimes have to invite the creepy uncle or the cousin with the Obi Wan Kenobi wristwatch who dispenses wisdom from Yoda, or explains the best way to toss twelve-sided dice. These persons quite often fall into one of the other categories of disruptive guests, but a relative of the host gives them special status among the guests and a certain amount of immunity. *What else you might try* – If possible try to prepare your guests as best as possible, but you still might have to apologize profusely afterwards. Try to maneuver your relative into an out-of-the-way corner or into the shadows, or introduce them to someone who can help mitigate their effect on the rest of the party.

The Ex – If you are both still single and physically attracted to each other and on civil terms, this can be a good opportunity to revisit at least one aspect of your old relationship. Otherwise, this can be a big hassle. *What else you might try* – If the breakup was amicable, or mostly amicable, be the bigger person, smile, make eye contact and try to say "hello." This will save your other guests from potential drama.

The Fighting Couple – Though maybe not as loud, or able to consume as much alcohol or as literate as Richard Burton and Elizabeth Taylor in the film version of Edward Albee's *Who's Afraid of Virginia Woolf*, these people can be annoying to the other guests. *What else you might try* – Interject a joke to demonstrate that people are aware of their "issues" and hopefully snap them back to reality and conviviality.

The Groper – Sometimes a male guest gets too friendly, much to the annoyance of a female guest or several. *What else you might try* – It's a good idea to eject them from the party soon after the infraction, provided he hasn't already been assaulted by the woman's husband or boyfriend.

The Ideologue – This is the person that is always spouting their political, religious or philosophical views, usually very extreme, in purely social situations. *What else you might try* – First, mention out loud that it's not polite or good for parties to talk about politics or religion. Maybe say this with a sly smile, maybe not. If the person continues in obnoxious fashion, mention that statement more directly, and maybe send them to another part of the room or another room to get a drink or food.

Keg Fly – You should remember this character from your college days. This is the person, most often male, who hangs around the keg (or it might be your bar, now), not mixing with many other guests, then usually drinks too much and can become obnoxious to the female guests. This person might also be wasting a lot of your beer. *What else you might try* – Try to get them to mix with the other guests, unless you believe they are mostly harmless, just hanging around the keg or the bar. You might also want to ensure they are not pouring lots of foam (which is beer) away.

Kissing Bandit – This is most often a woman who needs or courts attention and will make out with more than one guy at the party. She is usually drunk and has recently broken up with her boyfriend. *What else you might try* – This person can be fun to have provided the other women (and especially yours) don't find out or get too upset. Otherwise, you might have to ask this woman to leave.

Misanthrope – This is a very negative person that seems to find fault with nearly everything, and can change the mood of your party. In hip-hop parlance this person is a hater. *What else you might try* – Try not to invite this fool. If they find their way onto your guest list and into your party, try to improve their spirits by complimenting them: their outfit, some recent success, etc. You might want to stretch the truth, if necessary. If this does not work, and if their poisonous personality continues, encourage them to leave.

Needy Guest – This is typically a friend or co-worker who unnecessarily demands attention from other guests, and too often you as the host, much to the detriment of your enjoyment and your duties as a host. *What else you might try* – Tell them, in so many words, but maybe somewhat sugar-coated, "Listen, loser, fend for yourself. I have to act as host." Continually excuse yourself from this person, and profess how busy you are tending to the needs of the other guests.

Party Coach – If not the host, this person often acts as the surrogate, and tries to get guests to play games and do things. This is usually a control freak, and can typically only work effectively (and so, annoyingly) in smaller groups.

Party Crasher – Our view is that attractive women never fit into this category, unless it is an ex-girlfriend, of course. *What else you might try* – If the person does not fall into this category, you might want to question them so they become uncomfortable. Try to ensure they don't get near the expensive drinks and the best food. And, you might have to end up asking them to leave, politely, or not.

The Photographer – Though photos from your event are usually a good idea, sometimes it goes too far. This is the person who far too often tries to assemble people together for a photo to the detriment of the flow of the party. *What else you might try* – You might simply announce there is a moratorium on photographs.

PDA Couple – Sometimes a couple engages in public displays of affection (PDA) too readily and inappropriately. It's tough to keep them involved in the conversation if their lips are too often locked together. *What else you might try* – Try to shame them into keeping their physical attraction more private.

The Salesperson – This person, quite often an insurance agent or an independent financial analyst, usually interjects business into a purely social situation when it's not appropriate. This person is busy thrusting business cards on unwilling guests, and trying to network and sell, which can change the tone of your event. *What else you might try* – If this becomes an annoyance, simply ask the offender to stop. Try not to invite this person in the future, if they don't seem to get it.

The Slut – This is typically the woman that not very discreetly hits on married guys. *What else you might try* – Depending on your relationship status and your outlook, this guest could be very welcome.

Social Hand Grenade – The person, usually male, is very adept at saying the wrong thing at the wrong time, usually many times, during the event. This person is an aggressive dork. *What else you might try* – Try to keep this idiot away from your boss, your boss' wife, the girlfriend of the guy on steroids, or anyone that you yourself might have an interest in. If you should happen to overhear or witness this person's moronic banter or behavior, be sure to degrade them swiftly and with fervor, so to shut them up. It might work.

Space Invader – This person ignores the North American rules of interpersonal space to cause discomfort. These are usually harmless, though often annoying.

The Storyteller – This is the person who tries to be the center of attention with their overly long, and at often times, boring story.

The Thing that Wouldn't Leave – This is the person that is seemingly clueless when it comes to understanding that it's time to leave. *What else you might try* – Put them to work at first. If they are still around when you want to retire, tell them to get out. Maybe nicely, maybe not.

Wallflower – This person is usually a good person, as you invited them for a reason, usually since you enjoy their company in some circumstances, but are just shy in the presence of people they do not know. *What else you might try* – Introduce them to others. Help them to their feet like a child taking their first steps. Or, begin the intoxication process and push them into the mix.

Weirdo – This person is a similar to The Dork, but stranger, and usually more off-putting. *What else you might try* – If it's certain in your mind that this person is incapable of mixing well with your other guests that evening, don't waste more of your time with them, ignore them, and hope they will not stay much longer.

SUGGESTED REFERENCE & RESOURCE MATERIALS

COOKBOOKS FOR THE NOVICE AND INTERMEDIATE COOK

Below is a short list of cookbooks that we recommend for use in finding recipes suitable for entertaining. These have a number of fairly easy to prepare, inexpensive, and interesting recipes, many that can be made before your guests arrive. Though these are especially useful for the beginner cook, there are numerous recipes that will make these cookbooks fine resources for cooks of all levels.

- *The Best Recipes* – Cook's Illustrated – There is a good deal of explanation of the recipes, which are generally easy to follow, and recommendations for products based on comparative testing.
- *Food Network Kitchens Cookbook* – Jennifer Darling, Editor
- *How to Cook Everything* – Mark Bittman
- *The Joy of Cooking* – Irma Rombauer, et al. – Many recipes, and also very good explanations about products and techniques. A good general cookbook that has been updated for today's cook and kitchen.
- *The New York Times Cookbook* – Craig Claiborne – A wide range of basic, flavorful and well-worn recipes that are generally easy to prepare.
- *Emeril's Potluck: Comfort Food with a Kicked-Up Attitude* – Emeril Lagasse – There are plenty of good recipes that work well for crowds.
- *How to Grill* – Steven Raichlen – The best resource around for grilling.

BOOKS ABOUT THE BASICS OF WINE

If you desire to learn more about wine, below are some good introductory books. These are just a start. There is a great deal of verbiage dedicated to describing the various types, regions, and history of wines, in addition to the yearly publications dedicated to rating individual wines.

- *French Wine for Dummies* – Mary Ewing-Mulligan & Ed McCarthy
- *Great Wine Made Simple* – Andrea Immer
- *Italian Wine for Dummies* – Mary Ewing-Mulligan & Ed McCarthy
- *Jancis Robinson's Wine Course* – Jancis Robinson
- *Red Wine for Dummies* – Mary Ewing-Mulligan & Ed McCarthy
- *Wall Street Journal Guide to Wine* – Dorothy Gaiter & John Brecher
- *White Wine for Dummies* – Mary Ewing-Mulligan & Ed McCarthy
- *Windows on the World Complete Wine Course: A Lively Guide* – Kevin Zraly
- *Wine for Dummies* – Ed McCarthy, et al.
- *Wine with Food* – Joanna Simon

As you can probably tell, we believe that the *Dummies* books about wine are very informative and are especially accessible for the novice wine drinker.

BOOKS ABOUT LIQUOR AND COCKTAILS

- *The Complete Idiot's Guide to Mixing Drinks* – Alan Alexrod & The Players
- *Michael Jackson's Complete Guide to Single Malt Scotches* – Michael Jackson
- *The Pocket Bartender's Guide* – Michael Jackson
- *The Pocket Idiot's Guide to Bartending* – Alan Alexrod & The Players

BOOKS ABOUT ETIQUETTE

If you are concerned about proper etiquette either for yourself or your spouse, below are some well-regarded references including a couple from that North American doyenne of good manners, Emily Post, well, her descendents, at least.

- *The Amy Vanderbilt Complete Book of Etiquette* – Nancy Tuckerman, & Nancy Dunann
- *Emily Post's Etiquette* – Peggy Post
- *Essential Manners for Men: What to Do, When to Do It, and Why* – Peter Post
- *Emily Post's Entertaining* – Peggy Post – "...advice on a whole range of social gatherings."
- *Town & Country's Social Graces* – Edited by Jim Brosseau

BOOKS CONCERNING EVENT DECORATING

If there is a frustrated interior designer in you, below are some resources that can help add another dimension to your party, if you feel that you might need it.

- *The Art of the Party* – Renny Reynolds, et al. – "...a book filled with elegant imagery and romantic photography..."
- *Entertaining by Martha Stewart* – We have heard that this is good. Really. It launched a billion-dollar empire, after all.
- *Perfect Parties* – Alison Price – Many decorating tips from a professional party planner.
- *Preston Bailey's Design for Entertaining* – Preston Bailey – Design tips for lavish events.

USEFUL WEB SITES FOR REFERENCE & FREE SERVICES

Below are several web sites that provide free useful and reliable information for reference on topics related to entertaining or that can be used for your event.

- www.allrecipes.com – Lots of recipes and other information.
- www.americangreetings.com – Internet invitations
- www.bjcp.org – Strictly for hardcore beer aficionados, this is the site for the Beer Judge Certification Program; plenty of information on beers, rating beers, and tasting sheets
- www.cooksillustrated.com – A useful resource for well-tested recipes, cooking tips and product recommendations
- www.epicurious.com – Recipes and other food information.
- www.evite.com – Internet invitations
- www.foodtv.com – Recipes from the Food Network shows and other good stuff concerning food, wine and drink.
- www.functionjunction.ca – "….free web directory dedicated to informing, entertaining and educating the consumer about event and party planning."
- www.mapquest.com – A very useful resource for a map and directions to your event venue.
- www.realbeer.com – A great resource for beer geeks.
- www.sendomatic.com – Internet invitations
- www.specialeventsite.com – "Locate event and party companies and services in your market area…You can request a quote from any of the companies or click directly through to their websites."
- www.verseit.com – Useful verbiage for invitations.

SOME MUSIC SUGGESTIONS

Music is very personal, and you will have your favorites that should work for you and your guests. If you need any help, we present in this section some fairly well-worn or not so well-worn suggestions suited for different parties or different aspects of the same party. **You certainly do not have to play these albums to have a successful event** or play any music at all for that matter; but these albums can provide some much appreciated ambience. Based on our experience and input from so-called experts, the music recommended below can work for a variety of social situations, even if it's not your favorite music, or ours, for that matter. These can supplement your collection even if **these suggestions are not comprehensive** by any stretch.

Ultra Lounge and **Buddha Bar** compilation CDs are great for parties. And, there are compilations suitable for a variety of occasions from retailers like Pottery Barn, Eddie Bauer and even Brooks Brothers.

DINNER PARTY — CLASSICAL MUSIC IN THE BACKGROUND

Consider some classical CD's that will work for conversation-friendly entertaining, wherein the music itself is part of the background. Classical music that is not overly dramatic can make the setting more soothing and sophisticated. There are a number of options available to you, and some suggestions in a classical vein are:

- **Bach** – *Cello Suites*
- **Beethoven** – *Symphony 3; Symphony 9; Overtures*
- **Chopin** – *Piano Works*
- **Mozart** – *Symphonies 35* through *41*
- **Tchaikovsky** – *Ballet Suites*

DINNER PARTY — JAZZIER THAN ABOVE; STILL IN THE BACKGROUND

If you want something a little jazzier, but still planted in the background, then some more modern suggestions are:

- **Buena Vista Social Club** – *Buena Vista Social Club*
- **John Coltrane** – *My Favorite Things; A Love Supreme*
- **Miles Davis** – *Miles Ahead; Kind of Blue; In a Silent Way; Live at the Plugged Nickel*
- **Stan Getz** – *Focus; Stan Getz Bossa Nova*
- **Andrew Hill** – *Point of Departure*
- **Antonio Carlos Jobim** – *Songbook*

- **Lee Konitz** – *Alone Together*
- **Ottmar Liebert** – *The Hours Between Night and Day*; *The Best Of*
- **Abbey Lincoln** – *You Gotta Pay the Band*
- **Mark Turner** – *Yam-Yam*

Cocktail parties, by their very nature, are swanky and lounge-ish, so consider a musical theme that complements this type of atmosphere. There are two basic types of "lounge" music: the classic singer / standards music in the mode of Frank Sinatra, and the more recent Acid Jazz or Trip Hop. Both types of music are just sultry enough to help later in the evening.

Cocktail Party — Evoking the Rat Pack Era

Some classic Sinatra-esque music consists of:

- **Tony Bennett** – *The Art of Romance*; *I Left My Heart in San Francisco*
- **Sammy Davis, Jr.** – *I've Gotta Be Me*
- **Dean Martin** – *Dino: The Essential Dean Martin*
- **The Rat Pack** – *Boys Night Out*
- **Frank Sinatra** – *Songs for Young Lovers* / *Swing Easy*; *Songs for Swingin' Lovers*; *A Swingin' Affair!*; *Come Fly with Me*
- **Sarah Vaughn** – *Sings George Gershwin*
- **Various Artists** – The *Swingers* Soundtrack

Cocktail Party — Latter-day Lounge

Thumping Acid Jazz or Trip Hop can be heard in almost any upscale lounge these days. This is music that helps to set the mood with a bass that you can feel. Some very good examples include:

- **Dido** – *No Angel*
- **Massive Attack** – *Mezzanine*; *Blue Lines*
- **Moby** – *Play*
- **Morcheeba** – *Charango*
- **Zero 7** – *Simple Things*

Outdoor Event

With an event like this, you would not necessarily want to utilize the above suggestions of classical, jazz, or lounge-oriented music, but would probably want to play more mainstream (or familiar) music that we're sure you have oodles and oodles of. Some useful suggestions include:

- **Robert Cray** – *Strong Persuader; Don't Be Afraid of the Dark*
- **The Dave Matthews Band** – *Crash; Stand Up*
- **REM** – *Reckoning; Out of Time; Automatic for the People*
- **Reverend Horton Heat** – *Holy Roller*
- **The Rolling Stones** – *Let it Bleed; Exile on Main Street; Some Girls*
- **Talking Heads** – *Naked; Stop Making Sense*
- **U2** – *Joshua Tree; Achtung Baby; All That You Can't Leave Behind*
- **Various Artists** – *Garden State* Soundtrack; *Grosse Pointe Blank* Soundtrack

OUTDOOR EVENT — BEACH OR POOL

The proximity of water can change the complexion of the event, and so, the soundtrack of the event. "Beach music" and reggae seems to work well, especially at a beach or a pool.

- **Beach Boys** – *Pet Sounds; The Beach Boys Today!; Sunflower*
- **Jimmy Buffett** – *Songs You Know by Heart; Meet Me in Margaritaville*
- **Dick Dale** – *King of the Surf Guitar: The Best of Dick Dale and His Del-Tones*
- **Bob Marley** – *Greatest Hits at Studio One; Natty Dread; Exodus; Kaya; Uprising*
- **Maxi Priest** – *Maxi Priest; Best of Me*
- **Peter Tosh** – *The Toughest*
- **Various Artists** – *Classic Reggae, Vol. 1; The Harder They Come*

MUSIC FOR MOVING

For parties, for dancing, songs are better to recommend than entire albums. For this reason, **it's an especially good idea to create a mix CD** (with an iPod, MP3, etc.) **for the dance music**. Below are some albums, listed in subsections under various broad themes, which have a number of songs that at least some people like to dance to. At the very least, these might be resources for your mix creations.

DANCING — OLDER, POP, R& B AND SOUL

Some of this might be sugar-coated (or cheesy), but just about all of it has an easy-to-find beat and a usually recognizable sound.

- **Neil Diamond** – *Classics: The Early Years*
- **Aretha Franklin** – *The Very Best of Aretha Franklin, Volume 1*
- **Jackson Five** – *The Ultimate Collection*
- **Tom Jones** – *The Best of Tom Jones*
- **Barry White** – *All-Time Greatest Hits*

- **Various Artists** – *Motown: The Classic Years*

DANCING — 1970s — DISCO

Seemingly regardless of the age, women, especially, love this stuff.

- **Abba** – *The Definitive Collection* – Cheesy, yes, but it works….
- **Chic** – *The Very Best of Chic*
- **Various Artists** – *Pure Disco; Pure Disco Vol. 2; Saturday Night Fever: The Original Movie Soundtrack* – Yes, believe it or not, you will be loved for having this one in your collection as the dancing progresses on late into the night.

> **S**ome songs to determine if certain portions of your crowd are sufficiently plied with alcohol (noticeable by the frenzied response, screams, and bad sing-a-longing) are:
> - **Bay City Rollers** – "Saturday Night"
> - **Cheap Trick** – "I Want You to Want Me"
> - **Neil Diamond** – "Sweet Caroline"
> - **Gloria Gaynor** – "I Will Survive"
> - **Rod Stewart** – "Do You Think I'm Sexy"
> - **Village People** – "Y.M.C.A."
> - Anything from the *Grease* soundtrack

DANCING — 1970s — GIVE UP THE FUNK

These grooves are still making their way onto current airplay via sampling by today's rap and R&B artists.

- **James Brown** – *Funk Power 1970: A Brand New Thang; Foundations of Funk: A Brand New Bag, 1964-1969; Greatest Hits*
- **The Gap Band** – *The Best of the Gap Band*
- **Curtis Mayfield** - *Superfly* Soundtrack
- **The Meters** – *The Very Best of the Meters*
- **Parliament** – *The Very Best of Parliament: Give Up the Funk*
- **Various Artists** – *Millennium Party: Funk; New Millennium Funk Party*

DANCING — 1980s

- **Beastie Boys** – *Paul's Boutique*
- **The Cure** – *Boys Don't Cry; Disintegration*
- **Depeche Mode** – *Catching Up with Depeche Mode; Violator*
- **Erasure** – *Erasure Pop!: The First 20 Hits*
- **New Order** – *Substance*
- **Prince** – *Dirty Mind; 1999; Purple Rain; Sign 'O' the Times*

- **Squeeze** – *Singles 45's and Under*
- **Various Artists** – *Pure 80's; More Pure 80's; Millennium: 80's New Wave Party; New Wave Dance Hits: Just Can't Get Enough, Vol. 5*

DANCING — 1990s & BEYOND

Most musical boundaries have seemingly been explored by the end of the last century. There is still great music being made, but it's maybe less groundbreaking, and so, along more of a continuum. Maybe not, but this thought makes for one less list.

- **Chemical Brothers** – *Exit Planet Dust; Dig Your Own Hole*
- **Deee-Lite** – *World Clique*
- **Dr. Dre** – *The Chronic*
- **Electronic** - *Electronic*
- **Fatboy Slim** – *You've Come a Long Way Baby* – Keep in mind that there are a couple of songs with obvious and potentially offensive language.
- **Fela Kuti** – *The Best of Fela Kuti* – For that danceable African vibe.
- **Moby** – *Play* – This can also work in the background.
- **Outkast** – *Stankonia; Speakerboxxx / The Love Below*
- **Primal Scream** – *Screamadelica*
- **The Prodigy** – *The Fat of the Land*
- **Saint Germain** – *Tourist*
- **Seal** – *Seal 2*
- **Snoop Dogg** – *DoggyStyle*

MISCELLANEOUS

These can aptly fill your airwaves, depending on your tastes.

- **AC/DC** - *Highway to Hell; Back in Black* – Rarely has three chords sounded so fun, even today.
- **B52's** – *The B52's*
- **Elvis Costello** – *My Aim is True; This Year's Model; Armed Forces; Imperial Bedroom* – Great pop-rock for adults that doesn't sound dated at all.
- **Al Green** – *Greatest Hits; Let's Stay Together*
- **Pogues** – *The Best of the Pogues; The Very Best of the Rest of the Pogues; Waiting for Herb* – It's amazing what hard-driving rock with more than a little Irish lilt will do to the pace of alcoholic consumption at your event.
- **SugarHill Gang** – *The Best Of SugarHill Gang: Rapper's Delight* – Still lots of fun. There is "Rapper's Delight," of course, but also some other party-jams that will do the trick.
- **Various Artists** – *Frat Rock: Volumes 1 – 4; Millennium Hip-Hop Party*

TYPES OF GLASSWARE

It's doubtful that you will find all of these glasses shown in this section in any one place, with the exception of an expansive bar in a four-star restaurant. And, to throw a successful party you don't need much in the way of glassware or crystal. Certainly, the more formal the event, the more guests will expect fairly nice drinkware. But, in most situations you can get by with one type of wine glass and any moderately-sized vessel for everything else, plus the disposable plastic cups. The next glassware to have would include champagne flutes, pint glasses for beer (and soft drinks), lowball and Martini glasses.

WINE GLASSES

The list below contains most of the main styles of glasses for wine. The numbers match the images in the graphic on the following page. Unless you are a very serious oenophile, there is really no need to have many of these. Having different glasses for red, white and champagne is usually sufficient.

1. **Bordeaux / Cabernet Sauvignon** – These have a moderately-large bowl that typically holds 12 ounces when filled. As with all wine glasses, except for champagne flutes, this should be filled to only one-third full or halfway. You would never use the full capacity of a wine glass.
2. **Burgundy - Red** – This glass has a more balloon-shaped bowl and larger capacity than the standard red wine glass; it holds about 14 ounces.
3. **Champagne Bowl** – Very recognizable, but generally ineffective since the bubbles dissipate quickly due to the wide surface area, which also greatly increases the chance for spilling.
4. **Champagne Flute** – These are tall and thin to help slow the dissipation of the bubbles, typically 6 or 7 ounces in volume.
5. **Chardonnay** – The white wine glass has been growing, but remains smaller than the red. Newer designs are somewhat under 12 ounces.
6. **Chablis / Sauvignon Blanc** – These two similar glasses are typically thinner than the Chardonnay glasses and smaller at 8 or 9 ounces.
7. **German / Alsace** – Purists from either side of the Rhine might disagree with lumping together German and Alsatian wine glasses, but these and their respective wines are sufficiently similar for the rest of us to do so.
8. **Port** – The traditional port glass holds 6½ ounces. It is shaped like a small version of a red wine glass.
9. **Sherry** – The standard Spanish-style sherry glass (called a *copita*) is relatively thin and holds 6 ounces.

VARIOUS TYPES OF <u>WINE</u> GLASSES

BEER GLASSES

The following list contains the most commonly found glasses, but is not nearly as inclusive as the other lists. There seems to be a glass for each of the 100+ Belgian beers, for example. As with the wine glasses, the numbers match the images in the graphic on the following page.

1. **Beer Mug** – 12 ounces and more; this is the classic from the days well before Archie Bunker employed this glass to great effect.
2. **Chimay** – 0.3 liter (10.1 ounces); these bowl-shaped glasses are widely distributed and complement these heady Belgian Trappist beers. As warned on the label, this beer does taste better in a proper glass.
3. **Goblet** or **Schooner** – 16 ounces and larger.
4. **Imperial Pint** – 20 ounces; the common size of a draft beer in the UK.
5. **Kölsch** – These cylindrical glasses, typically 0.3 liter (10.1 ounces) or 0.4 liter (13.6 ounces), complement the unique, delicate ale of the same name. Both the glasses and beer are found almost solely in Cologne.
6. **Pilsner** – 12 ounces; the long thin glass is designed to highlight the bouquet of aromatic, top-quality pilsners. In Germany, pilsners are served in small, somewhat bowl-shaped glasses with stems. These are 0.3 liter (10.1 ounces) in size, and rare to find outside of Bavaria. The effect of these glasses is lost on very light beers.

7. **Pint** – 16 ounces; probably the most versatile of all glasses, as it looks normal when used for beer, water, soft drinks, juices and big cocktails.
8. **Wheat Beer** – 0.5 liter (16.9 ounces); these tapered glasses amply hold the contents of the standard Bavarian wheat beer bottles and the copious, foamy head.

VARIOUS TYPES OF BEER GLASSES

COCKTAIL GLASSES

You might have a problem if you have all of these glasses....

1. **Brandy Snifter** – 4 to 24 ounces; these balloon-shaped glasses are designed to be filled at about 10-20% capacity; the shape concentrates the aroma of the brandy for the drinker.
2. **Collins** – 10 to 14 ounces; this glass is tall and thin, and typically frosted from its base to just short of its rim, otherwise it is the same as a highball glass. Used mostly for Collins drinks, as the name implies.
3. **Double Old Fashioned** – 7 to 13 ounces or so; also with a bump on its base that differentiates it from the lowball glass.
4. **Eggnog Mug** – 12 ounces; a clear glass mug designed for eggnog.
5. **Highball** – 8 to 12 ounces; this glass is relatively tall and used mostly for simple mixers.
6. **Irish Coffee** – 6 to 10 ounces; this is a stemmed glass often with a handle, which is very useful for hot liquids.

7. **Lowball** – 4 to 9 ounces; this is a short glass used for whiskies on the rocks and Martinis on the rocks; also called a **Rocks** glass.

8. **Martini** – 4 to 10 ounces; this is used for Martinis and any other cocktail that is to be served straight up; it is also referred to as a **Cocktail** glass.

9. **Old Fashioned** – 4 ounces, traditionally; almost identical to the lowball glasses except for a bump on the base of the glass.

10. **Parfait** – 8 to 12 ounces; this contour-shaped glass is used for layered drinks, Hurricanes, and desserts.

11. **Pony** – 1 to 2 ounces; this is almost a shot-sized glass with a stem. A pony has traditionally equated to 1 ounce.

12. **Pousse Café** – 3 to 4 ounces; little or no tapering or flaring of the bowl.

13. **Shot** – 1 to 2 ounces; if 1½ ounces, it is a jigger.

14. **Sour** – 4 to 5 ounce; this is a stemmed glass with a thin bowl to help make the slightly foamy sour drinks more enjoyable.

15. **Margarita** – 8 to 15 ounces; this glass seems to get a lot of use during gatherings.

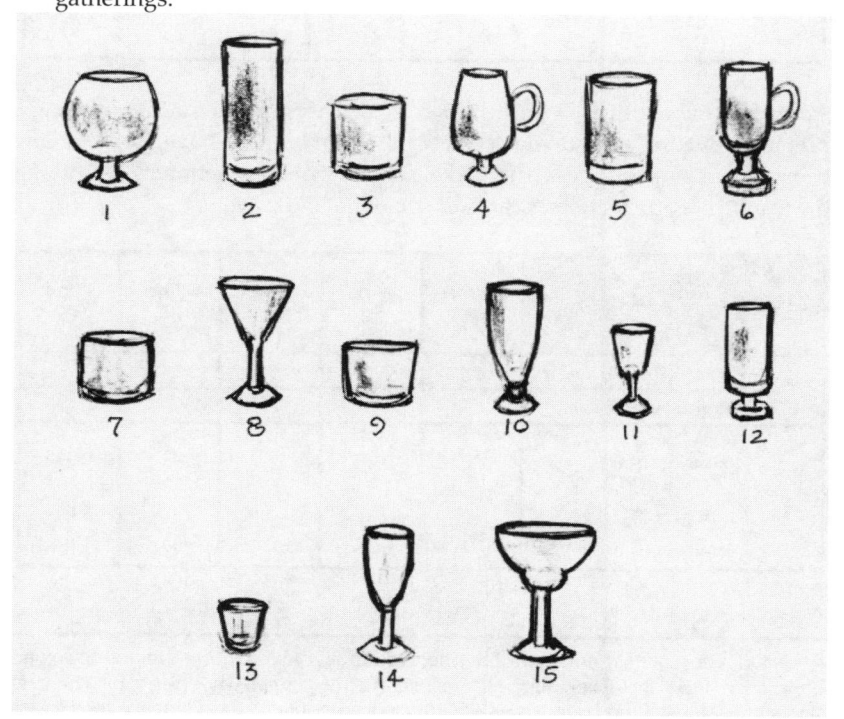

VARIOUS TYPES OF <u>COCKTAIL</u> GLASSES

SAMPLE WINE TASTING TEMPLATES – SIMPLE

This very simple template below can be used for wine and beer tasting events; just adjust and expand the formatting. For this type of tasting, rating wine (or beer) on a 10 point range or a 5 point scale is sufficient. For beer tastings simply change "wine" to "beer," so as not to confuse your guests, which can happen after several rounds.

	Wine #1	Wine #2	Wine #3	Wine #4	Wine #5
Rating (0 – 10)					
Comments					

Adding a row entitled, "Which Wine?" makes this useful for blind tastings. When conducting a blind wine or beer tasting, it helps to have a list of items being tasted so your guests can make a somewhat educated guess. Tallying the results of correct guesses can add some fun to the event.

	Wine #1	Wine #2	Wine #3	Wine #4	Wine #5
Rating (0 – 10)					
Which Wine?					
Comments					

Attention beer geeks, **for serious beer tastings**, you might want to download information from the Beer Judge Certification Program at www.bjcp.org. There is plenty of useful stuff on beers styles and judging beers plus detailed tasting templates.

Sample Wine Tasting Template — Elaborate

This is for the more in-depth or serious tastings. The 20 point scale is more appropriate for this type of tasting. Analyzing individual wines at this level of detail is not recommended casual gatherings. If you use this template, you will certainly want to expand the columns to provide more space for writing.

	Some Useful Descriptive Adjectives	Wine #1	Wine #2	Wine #3	Wine #4	Wine #5
Appearance						
Clarity	Cloudy, Clear, Pure					
Color Depth	Light, Medium, Dark					
Color Intensity	Pale, Moderate, Bright					
Viscosity	Light, Watery, Thick					
Appearance (0 – 5)						
Smell						
General	Neutral, Clean, Attractive, Outstanding, Rank					
Aroma	Fruity, Oaky, Spicy, Floral, Woody, Earthy					
Bouquet	None, Pleasant, Complex, Powerful					
Smell (0 – 5)						
Taste						
Sweetness	Bone dry, Dry, Medium-dry, Medium-sweet, Sweet					
Acidity	Flat, Refreshing, Markedly Acidic, Tart					
Body	Thin, Light, Medium, Full-bodied, Heavy					
Length	Short, Extended, Lingering					
Balance	Low, Good, Very Good, Well, Perfect					
Texture	Creamy, Silky, Elegant					
	What specific flavors do you detect?					
Taste (0 – 10)						
Overall						
Total Rating (0– 20)						

SUGGESTED ON-LINE RESOURCES

You certainly don't need to purchase exotic and expensive ingredients to have a good party. But, if you have trouble finding useful items in nearby stores, below is a list of on-line resources that will help.

Ace Mart – www.acemart.com – Restaurant supplies that can work very well for entertaining at home.

Amazon – www.amazon.com – Of course you can purchase books, music and other items, but it also has an enormous amount of feedback and play-lists from music aficionados who have created best-of play-lists for a great variety of musical tastes.

Arthur Avenue Specialties – www.arthuravespecialties.com – Sicilian and Italian specialties from a well-regarded resource in the Bronx's Little Italy.

Bayou Land Seafood – www.bayoulandseafood.com – Fresh crawfish and Gulf shrimp shipped from Louisiana.

Chef's – www.chefscatalog.com – A great selection of high quality products for the kitchen and also the home bar.

Citarella Fine Foods – www.citarella.com – A wide range of gourmet foods including cheeses, charcuterie, fresh meats, seafood, pastas and other items.

Comeaux – www.comeaux.com – South Louisiana food products including andouille, boudin, tasso, Cajun meat pies and many sausage products.

Cooking.com – www.cooking.com – Offers a wide-ranging assortment of products for cooking and the bar, including all the top brands.

Crate & Barrel – www.crateandbarrel.com – A good source for flatware, cookware and barware.

D'Artagnan – www.dartagnan.com – Highly regarded meats, especially duck, and prepared meat specialties including pâtés, mousses and terrines, smoked meats and other delectables.

Dean & Deluca – www.deandeluca.com – Gourmet food items including charcuterie, cheeses, fresh meats, prepared foods, oils and other high-end food items.

Dinner and a Murder Mystery Games – www.dinnerandamurder.com – A number of murder mystery role-playing games for various sizes are available for purchase and download.

From Italia – www.fromitalia.com – Italian food products from small producers like oils, vinegars, grains and pastas, plus wine.

Great Alaska Seafood – www.great-alaska-seafood.com – An array of excellent Alaskan seafood such as smoked salmon in a variety of types of flavors, lox, fresh salmon, halibut, King Crab and other shellfish.

IKEA – www.ikea.com – Inexpensive and attractive flatware, cooking and serving utensils, and glasses plus other items for entertaining and the house, all sporting clean Scandinavian designs.

iPod + iTunes – www.apple.com/itunes/ – Downloadable music, playlists and other items for your iPod.

Joie de Vivre – www.frenchselections.com – *Foie gras*, pâtés, fresh charcuterie made in the U.S. by traditional methods, and food items from France.

Maine Lobster Direct – www.mainelobsterdirect.com – Fresh Maine lobsters and other New England-favorite seafood shipped to your home.

Mixmag – www.mixmag.net – Download the most current, hot British dance tunes, if you are so inclined.

Molinari Deli – www.molinarideli.com – Maker of Italian-style sausages and a source of cheeses and some Italian-oriented dry goods.

Mozzarella Company – www.mozzarellacompany.com – Acclaimed maker of fresh Italian-style soft cheeses.

MP3.com – www.mp3.com – Lots of downloadable music and links.

Nancy's – www.nancys.com – Frozen food provider of easy-to-use and tasty appetizers such as tartlets, small quiches, crabcakes and spinach puffs.

Paper.com – www.paper.com – Printed invitations and the like.

Party America – www.partyamericastore.com – A resource for a wide range of knickknacks, party favors, decorations, costumes, invitations and other miscellany that you might feel could add to your party.

Penzeys Spices – www.penzeys.com – Spices and seasonings for much of your cooking needs.

Pier One – www.pier1.com – Inexpensive drink-related items such as wine charms and coasters.

Restoration Hardware – www.restorationhardware.com – Has a limited, but very useful array of items for entertaining, specifically appetizer plates, beer accessories, cocktail equipment, and glasses for different types of beverages, alcoholic and otherwise.

Sur La Table – www.surlatable.com – A resource for high quality barware, dinnerware, glassware and other accessories for cooking and entertaining.

Target – www.target.com – Inexpensive products for cooking, dining and entertaining that sounds more sophisticated when pronounced in French [tar-ZHAY].

Tony Chachere's – www.tonychachere.com – Seasonings, mixes, and batters for those authentic south Louisiana flavors.

Vella Cheese Company – www.vellacheese.com – Italian-American and Californian cheeses.

Volpi Foods – www.volpifoods.com – Well regarded St. Louis producer of products made in the Italian tradition including *salame, prosciutto,* and other cured meats.

Williams-Sonoma – www.williams-sonoma.com – High quality items for cooking, serving, dining and drinking plus some food products.

Zabar's – www.zabars.com – Jewish-American food items and cookware from a New York City institution.

Z Gallerie – www.zgallerie.com – Dinnerware, glassware and barware that is a bit funkier and more colorful than most other resources.

Zingerman's – www.zingermans.com – Gourmet items such as oils, vinegars, cheeses and many other high quality foods.

Selected Bibliography

- *A Guide to Pink Elephants – 200 Most Requested Mixed Drinks on Alcohol Resistant Cards, Vol. 2* – Rosen, Richard; Richards Rosen Associates, Inc., New York, New York, 1957
- *All Music Guide to Rock – The Definitive Guide to Rock, Pop, and Soul* – Edited by Bogdanov, Vladimir, and Woodstra, Chris, and Erlewine, Stephen Thomas; Backbeat Books; San Francisco, California, 2002
- *The Complete Bartender* – Feller, Robyn M.; The Berkley Publishing Group, New York, New York, 1990
- *The Dictionary of Italian Food and Drink* – Mariani, John; Broadway Books, New York, New York, 1998
- *Elenora's Kitchen - 125 Fabulous Authentic Italian-American Recipes* – Scarpetta, Elenora Russo; Broadway Books; New York, New York, 2004
- *The Encyclopedia of American Food and Drink* – Mariani, John; Lebhar-Friedman Books, New York, New York, 1999
- *Esquire's Handbook for Hosts: A Time-Honored Guide to the Perfect Party* – Black Dog & Leventhal Publishers, New York, New York, 1949, 1999
- *Food Lover's Companion, Third Edition* – Herbst, Sharon Tyler; Barron's, Hauppauge, New York, 2001
- *Funk & Wagnalls Standard Desk Dictionary* – Landau, Sidney I., Editor in Chief; Funk & Wagnalls, Inc., New York, New York, 1974
- *The Good Cook: Beef & Veal* – Olney, Richard, Chief Series Consultant; Time-Life Books, New York, New York, 1979
- *Great Tastes Made Simple* – Immer, Andrea; Broadway Books, New York, New York, October 2002
- *The Italian-American Cookbook* – Mariani, Galina & John; Harvard Common Press; Boston, Massachusetts, 2000
- *It's All American Food - The Food We Really Eat, the Dishes We Will Always Love* – Rosengarten, David; Little, Brown and Company; New York, New York, 2003
- *Kindred Spirits* – Pacult, F. Paul; Hyperion; New York, New York, 1997
- *Michael Jackson's Beer Companion* – Second Edition – Jackson, Michael; Running Press Book Publishers; Philadelphia, Pennsylvania, 1997
- *Mr. Boston Deluxe Official Bartender's Guide* – Sixty-First Edition – Mr. Boston Distiller; Warner Books; New York, New York, 1979
- *The New Rolling Stone Album Guide – More Than 10,000 of the Best Rock, Pop, Hip-Hop and Soul Records, Revised and Rated* – Fourth Edition; Brackett, Nathan and Hoard, Christian; Fireside; New York, New York; 2004
- *The New York Bartender's Guide* – Berk, Sally Ann, General Editor; Black Dog & Leventhal Publishers; New York, New York, 1997
- *The NPR Curious Listener's Guide to Jazz* – Schoenberg, Leon; Perigee Books; New York, New York; 2002

- *The Penguin Guide to Jazz on CD* – Fifth Edition – Cook, Richard and Morton, Brian; Penguin Books; New York, New York; 2000
- *Pocket Guide to Beer* – Third Edition – Jackson, Michael; Simon & Schuster Inc., New York, New York, 1991
- *The Pocket Bartender's Guide* – Jackson, Michael; Fireside Books; New York, New York, 1987
- *The Pocket Idiot's Guide to Bartending* – Second Edition – Axelrod, Alan and Players, The; Alpha Books, Indianapolis, Indiana; 2003
- *The Signet Book of Cheese* – Quimme, Peter; A Signet Book, New American Library, New York, New York, 1976
- *The Tex-Mex Cookbook* – Walsh, Robb; Broadway Books, New York, New York, 2004
- *The Visual Food Encyclopedia* – Fortin, François, Editorial Director; MacMillian, New York, New York, 1996
- *The Wine Book – The Complete Guide to the World's Wines* – Clarke, Oz; Portland House, New York, New York, 1987
- *Wine with Food* – Simon, Joanna; Simon & Schuster, New York, New York, 1996

About the Authors

MIKE RICCETTI is the author of the successful *Houston Dining on the Cheap* guidebooks, and contributes to several publications concerning food, dining and drinking, plus some less important topics.

MICHAEL WELLS has been in the hospitality business for over twenty years and has managed restaurants, bars, and clubs, and has organized and operated special events in Texas and Hawaii. He is currently the co-owner of the legendary Marfreless bar in Houston.

ACKNOWLEDGEMENTS

Thanks to the following friends and family for their help during the research and writing: Jack Thetford, Gene and Cara Riccetti, Shirl Riccetti, Kathy Haveman, Greg McQueen, Sandy Sweeney, Jay and Shannon Caldwell, David Hinsley, Richard and Chandra Riccetti, Julien DuPont, Hank Fuselier, Dave Feliciano, Dan and Sheila Berggren, Paul and Kristen Heyburn, Kelly Wells, Joe Ann Wells, Shannon Froehlich, Lori Sebastian, Guy Peters, Mike Dalby, Adam Hong, Chad Codrington, Enrico Bracalente, and Chantal Duke.

Index

– Z –